THE
WAYWARD
LAD

The Autobiography of

GRAHAM
BRADLEY

with Steve Taylor

GREENWATER PUBLISHING

A CIP catalogue record for this book is available
from the British Library

ISBN
1 903267 00 5

Printed and bound in Great Britain by the Bath Press Limited

Photography
*Cover and front flap:*Graham Flack
Back cover (Starjestic): Alan Johnson
Back flap: Richard Lappas

To my mother, Sheila.

VI

CONTENTS

IN THE BEGINNING

I have known Graham Bradley for the best part of fifteen years and like many punters I have delighted in him and then despaired of him. But one thing remained constant. I liked him.

So that made it all the more difficult to turn down his approach to write his autobiography. I thought I knew how much work would be involved - I was wrong it was far more - and did not fancy the idea of being pinned down for four months.

More important still, I had read racing biographies before and, with a few exceptions, found them bland, with the subject clearly having no regard for the finished product.

Brad assured me this would not be the case and that he wanted to give people a true insight into his life both in jump racing and out of it. I still would not bite.

But he can be very persuasive and finally I agreed to draft a few chapters just to see what might be achievable. The task was made simpler by the wonderful archive of twenty-three scrapbooks prepared with loving attention by his dad, Norman, who catalogued the bad times along with the good that came in a twenty-three year career. These formed a backbone on which to put significant amounts of flesh.

Brad was as good as his word when it came to giving his time and would take me through any episode required, but there was a problem. No matter how hard I tried to keep him on the given subject when the tape was running, he would go off at tangents as other memories nudged forward. Things were not looking good.

However, shortly after we began he started sending me through scrapbooks in chronological order and leaving notes is small capital letters that explained the story behind the story. It was just what I needed. If he put his thoughts on paper they came through clear and concise with a cutting edge.

Soon I was receiving foolscap sides of notes and anecdotes which were priceless. What I didn't know was that they were conceived at a price. Brad didn't find it easy to put his thoughts on paper and also worked much better at night. That meant he was toiling until sometimes three in the morning and, as a result, rose relatively late. As I was at my desk each day at 8 a.m. this left uncomfortably long parts of the day when we could not communicate, but when we did the enthusiasm of both was infectious.

When a particularly detailed chapter was undertaken he would sit in my kitchen with pencil and sharpener and scribble intently until we got it right.

The original word requirement for the book was 90,000 words but as we warmed to the task it became clear that the story was engrossing, and that target would be passed by a considerable margin. With a relatively high wordage, more and more facts needed to be checked and no matter how apparently trivial the inquiry, Brad always came up for me.

It was also a massive bonus that nearly everyone with whom he had come into contact seemed to like Brad, and that meant I received a positive response when inquiring into specific incidents.

It would be impossible to name all those who helped with the construction of this book although special thanks are due to Monica and Michael Dickinson, David Murray Smith, Jim Old, Richard Guest and Dave Roberts.

Also, Carl Llewellyn, Jamie Osborne, Ronnie Beggan, Graham McCourt, Charlie Brooks, Brian Delaney, Kit Stobbs, Alan Aimes, Dennis and Trevor Davies, Graham Gray. Gordon Nicol of Weatherbys and Michael Caulfield of the Jockeys' Association.

Last but not least: Michelle Morley, Charlie Dawson, Anthony McCoy, Terry Brockley, Steve Youlden, Brian Wright, David Dutton and Michael Condon.

But it was clear to both of us that the first manuscript needed to be read by someone who knew his racing and was enthusiastic and diligent. Above all, he had to be trustworthy. No easy bill to fit but I had no hesitation in asking Graham Cunningham, late of *Timeform*, the *Sporting Life* and now one of the most respected members of the *Racing Post* team. He had a wonderfully safe pair of hands.

Steve Taylor

Lambourn Woodlands,
Autumn, 2000.

GREENWATER'S THANKS TO:

MARTYN CHAPMAN, CHRIS LLOYD, MIKE WILSON, NATALIE TAYLOR,
LORRAINE ROCHE, PETER STOCKMAN, TIM ROBERTS, ADRIAN KNIGHT,
ROBERT SHAW, RICHARD DAWSON, ADRIENNE MAGUIRE,
NICKY GRIMBLY, JONATHON HUDDART, PHILIP HALL,
DAVID C MANASSEH, RICHARD LAPPAS, GRAHAM FLACK AND
ANNE BARCLAY.

FOREWORD
by A.P. McCoy

The following is something that I didn't want to write, and I say that as one of the many, many friends of Graham Bradley. The reason is purely selfish. Like most of his fellow jockeys, I just didn't want him to retire.

I tried hard to talk him out of it and told him with complete honesty that I thought he was riding better for the final five years of his career that he had at any time. I kept telling him that he would be a long time retired and to give himself another couple of years. I really meant it, but I knew, too, that it would allow me to have my greatest friend in racing alongside me when we made those long winter journeys to the races. Also that he would be back in the weighing room to talk with after things had gone wrong in a race.

But his mind was set and I respected him for that, although I knew a chapter of my working life had finished and that the weighing room has lost a little of it's sparkle. I suppose one of the reasons Brad was able to go on so long and even, for a few moments at least, contemplate my pleas, was that his bottle was completely intact. That fearless streak is vital to a jockey and he had it, probably because he selected rides carefully and knew exactly their capabilities. I don't think I've ever met a better judge of a horse than Brad and I believe that he can tell as much from looking at one as he can from riding it - and he can sum up the strengths and weaknesses of riders very quickly, too. But if a young jockey ever came to him for help and advice he would always take time to try and put them right, and if they were very keen he'd invite them to his home and spend hours going through videos to explain how things should and should not be done.

I first met him at the Galway Festival of 1994. I'd ridden only two winners as an apprentice, never set foot out of Ireland and had just been beaten a short head by Richard Dunwoody. Brad was sitting next to Conor O'Dwyer and asked him who the kid was who had just got beat. He then came over to me and said: 'Don't worry son, you'll get the better of him before long.' I didn't know whether to believe him or not but coming from a man who had developed such a strong following in my home country it meant a lot at a moment when my spirits were down after I'd been so narrowly beaten by one of the great jockeys of the last 50 years. When I based myself in England the following year I continued to seek his advice and he was a wise counsellor. One of the biggest problems I had was with my use of the whip. The stewards continually suspended me and it was a very hard time mentally and I was sent to the British Racing School at Newmarket for a corrective course. But, in fact, I learned much more from Brad, who acted like a golf pro and completely dissected my whip action and got it right for me. It was guite funny really, because when I was attending the Britsh Racing School they told me that the jockey best to model myself on was Graham Bradley and given the problems he was having with the stewards in other areas I thought that was a bit contradictory.

As a jockey you had to admire him. He was always cool and carried himself well. I suppose you'd have to say he had class both on and off a horse. I used to watch him on television when I was just a youngster in Ireland and when I saw him ride Morley Street to win at Aintree in 1993 I thought it was absolute perfection.

When I graduated and was riding against him he was always very, very hard to beat. He was top class in a tight finish, strong as well as being extremely stylish, but just as important he was a great tactician and thought carefully how he would approach a race. In my time I've never known anyone combine the two any better but if a young jockey asked him how or why he'd done something, he'd always share his knowledge. Unlike quite a few sportsmen, Brad would willingly give away his trade secrets. he just seemed happy trying to improve the youngsters and would always have a word with the very young lads having their first ride or two and try to calm their nerves. Because of that he became something of a hero to us younger ones. We knew he'd been through some hard times, battled his way back but he'd always done it on his own terms. He was his own man.

But he took his defeats well and I will always remember when we clashed at Punchestown in 1998. Brad was on French Ballerina and I rode His Song, who had been beaten by her at the Cheltenham Festival and new tactics were employed. His Song was a big chasing type and French Ballerina was a typically petite mare and I didn't make her passage that easy. Although there were only four runners in the race, she must have felt like it was twenty four and she knew she'd been in a real barging match on very soft ground, which didn't suit her. He called me everything he could lay his tongue to during the race and as we pulled up, but when we got back into the weighing room he congratulated me on what he considered a good, and perfectly legitimate, piece of raceriding. That's sportmanship of the highest level.

I had the opportunity to see how he handled pressure off the racecourse when I lived with him for three months, when he was under investigation for alleged race fixing. Although he got anxious as time went on he never once wavered because he knew he had done nothing wrong and as such had nothing to fear. And despite all the inevitable upheaval going on, they were still the best digs in town. The difference in my stay and those of a few others was that I said I'd be there for three months and kept to it while some stayed for three years!

Yes, it's true I and the other boys miss him in the weighing room but he's still around if we need a chat or a good night out for that matter.

I know that there is hardly a jockey with a licence who hasn't been waiting for this volume to come out and although the only book most of us read is the form one, we will be making an exception in Brad's case.

So enjoy the journey with him. It has its ups and downs but as I've found out over the years, travelling with him is never dull.

A P McCoy

CHAPTER 1
Never own up

The fantasy of time travel has tantalised us since H. G. Wells first floated the possibility and I doubt there is anyone alive who hasn't mused what they would do given a trip in that mythical machine to stop themselves from making that one mistake which would forever change their life.

I have no doubt that, given the chance, I would go back to Cartmel racecourse on 30 August 1982 and put a hand on the shoulder of the 22-year-old who was about to place a £50 bet on a horse called Cloudwalker and tell him it was the biggest mistake he was ever going to make.

Not that there's anything wrong in having a bet. People do it every day, but when you're a jockey it's *the* crime that cannot be forgiven. When the Jockey Club give you a licence it's there in black and white on page 188 of the 2000 Rule Book: Rule 62 (ii) (b) (1) states that 'It shall be a breach of the Rules of Racing for a jockey during the term of his licence to ... bet or instruct any person to bet on his behalf on horse racing.' Break that rule at your peril.

They say rules are made to be broken and I doubt there's a jockey riding who hasn't indulged in some form of punting over the years, if only for a side bet in the weighing room through boredom. But I don't think there have been many since my mistake who have gone up to a bookmaker on a racecourse and actually had a bet, although before that indiscretion it wasn't quite the same.

As a youngster growing up around the northern tracks I'd often seen jockeys amble out between races, one even had his breeches on, to have a bet on a horse that one of the boys had told him was fancied. Nothing big, just enough to have a night out after work. But they were never caught - and I was.

Still, if you had to find the loveliest spot to shoot yourself in the foot then I managed that alright. Cartmel is one of the most picturesque racecourses in Britain. Nestling in the heart of the Lake District, they usually race there on Bank Holidays and the enormous crowds lead to some of the worst traffic jams you'll ever sit in, but once you park the car, set out a picnic and soak up the country fair atmosphere you're in racing heaven.

I'd been there on Saturday, the first day of the two-day holiday meeting, and had three rides. It was the first of them, Adam Craig in the two mile handicap hurdle, that was going to begin my problems. He started to weaken from the fifth flight, but as we dropped away I could see Tony Charlton on Cloudwalker beginning to fade from two out without looking too worried. I've always considered it a vital part of a jockey's job to know what other horses have done in a race as well as your own, and I came back convinced that Cloudwalker was nailed on to win any moderate hurdle that he was put in. Couple that with the fact he was trained by Mick Lambert, one of the shrewdest trainers around, and owned by respected racing journalist Marten Julian and it didn't take an Einstein to work out that this was a good thing.

I didn't have long to wait before I could see if I was right. He was entered again the day after next, Monday.

Some of the senior riders would stay in the Cartmel area, take in the carnival atmosphere that envelopes the place and hit the pubs.

Sadly I'd got my job to go back to with the Dickinson family who employed me at Harewood in Yorkshire. I was no superstar and being back to ride out on Sunday morning was non-negotiable. There was no exception if it was your weekend to work, and everyone knew their place. It was a yard packed with quality horses and a young team of jockeys bursting to make sure they created the right impression on horseback and off it. The previous season I'd finished second on Bregawn in the Cheltenham Gold Cup and those whose opinions counted reckoned I was going places, but there was still a long road ahead. The last thing I needed was a serious mistake - and yet here I was on the verge of making it.

I was the only one of the Dickinson jockeys riding at Cartmel that fateful Monday and because my single ride of the day, Easy Go for Mick Naughton, was in the last I did my horses in the morning and drove on my own.

A myth has built up over the years concerning my blunder that August day. It's a bit like Humphrey Bogart saying 'Play It Again Sam' in *Casablanca* when, in fact, he never did. I am meant to have gone out in my breeches with a coat over my colours and had the bet, then received an immediate tap on the shoulder. Not true.

When I used to ride at these smaller meetings, I'd always dress in smart casual clothes but on that particular day I was wearing a suit and trilby, a habit I soon got out of. I dropped my gear off in the weighing room and went off to the silver ring in the middle of the course by the swing boats, coconut shy and the funfair, carefully avoiding the big players in Tattersalls. Surely no one would take any notice of a kid having a bet, I was just another punter.

It was only £50 in £10 notes, hardly the crown jewels even allowing for inflation, and the odds of 1-2 would return me a meagre profit of £25. But such is the folly of youth. I thought I was getting something for nothing but in that single, stupid moment I shattered my credibility for a sum that amounted to less than one riding fee.

The race wasn't without its problems but once Cloudwalker

3

came to the front at the fifth the only danger was from him and, despite hanging to the right when Kenny Jones put him under pressure, he won handily enough by two lengths from Miss Mayo and I was off to collect my twenty-five pieces of silver. But I did have one bit of good fortune that fateful day. I walked away without a mark on me after my sole ride slipped up between the last two flights - but the luck soon began to run out.

I slid through the holiday traffic, the two hour journey to Harewood taking 50 minutes longer than usual, and never had another thought about my little walk on the wild side. I'd got away with it. And that's how it looked until a month later when I was coming back from first lot and Michael Dickinson - who ran the yard with his father Tony and mother Monica - pulled me to one side and said that Racecourse Security had arrived and wanted to interview me. There was one man waiting and he sat me down in his car which was parked on the gravel drive just opposite the boss, Tony Dickinson's, house. I hadn't got a clue what he wanted me for.

Later, I came to realise that he was a typical Racecourse Security type, ex-CID. He began by talking about other things, to warm me up, to put me at ease. Then, out of the blue, he slipped in 30 August Cartmel. Even then I still didn't know what he wanted, but he kept probing and finally brought up the name Cloudwalker and hit me with eight words which gave me a hollow feeling in the middle of my chest 'Did you have a bet in the race?'

'No I didn't, definitely not.'

He persisted, 'Well, someone meeting your description was seen in the Silver Ring having a bet.'

'Definitely not me. It must have been my brother Gary. He was with me that day.'

We were about the same height and build so I had to be safe, how could they possibly know?

I kept repeating to myself, 'Keep on denying it and he'll have to go away'. I did, but he didn't. He kept chipping away at me for over

4

an hour, but I wouldn't change my story. Then he began to get serious and told me that the Jockey Club had got signed statements to say that I'd definitely put on the bet and they were going to set up an identity parade.

I now know that they couldn't have done such a thing, but I started to lose my nerve and he knew he'd got me, playing me like a fish on the line, switching from nasty cop to nice cop.

'Listen, if you have had a bet it's only trivial, you'll only get a little fine. The way I see it, you'll be better getting it off your chest. I'll send a report down, get it out of the way and it'll all be low-key, there's no chance of a suspension or anything like that.'

When I heard that I blurted the lot out, telling him it was only £50 and that I'd won £25. He made me sign each page of my confession and went away clutching the damning statement. I may have got it off my conscience, but the trouble was just beginning. That ex-copper had been economical with the truth and I was going to make headlines for the wrong reasons - and not for the last time.

I was riding Bregawn in the Hennessy Gold Cup at Newbury the weekend before I was due at Portman Square for the disciplinary meeting on the Monday and he was the firm ante-post favourite. He'd provided the highlight of my career so far by finishing second to stablemate Silver Buck in the Cheltenham Gold Cup and this was my big chance of a career boost. I'd won the young riders title at the end of the previous season, beating a good friend of mine, David Dutton, by three winners, but I still needed to prove that I could compete with the best on level terms.

That was pressure enough for anyone but when I drove down to Newbury for the first day of the meeting on Friday with Chris Pimlott - another of the Dickinson team of riders - the racing page headlines were about the coming inquiry. There were two problems now, winning the race and what I'd say to the press when I did.

As it turned out, the race was the least of my worries.

Bregawn still had an important role to play in my life and he was magnificent that day. Michael legged me up, having gone through every small detail beforehand. My main job was to get Bregawn jumping, because he could miss one quite badly. But he was excellent in the first half of the race, jumping stride for stride with the exceptional Night Nurse who was giving him just 2lb. We cruised ahead of our stablemates Captain John and Robert Earnshaw two out, and going to the last I knew I had the race in the bag. All I had to do was get over it, but things didn't go to plan and we met it all wrong.

Instead of being positive, I shortened Bregawn's stride and we hit the fence halfway up with a force which almost shot me out of the saddle. All our race winning momentum was lost and Captain John came sailing past and went three lengths clear, but Newbury has a long run-in and I didn't need to press the panic button.

I gave Bregawn precious moments to get balanced and waited a full twenty-five strides before giving him a crack with the whip and the response was immediate. He flew in the final 100 yards, swept past Captain John and won going away by three lengths. I knew this wasn't going to be the last big race we'd be winning.

Michael, who always suffered from pre race nerves, watched the race in solitude from the centre of the course but when he met me on the walk back to the unsaddling enclosure he had a smile on his face that was pure gold. Me? I was ecstatic.

Despite the cloud hanging over me, this was by far my biggest moment, winning one of jumping's classics in my first season as a full jockey, showing confidence in my ability way beyond my years. For an hour the fears and forebodings were swept away by euphoria and I relished the post-race interviews and analysis, pushing the dark spectre of the impending inquiry to the back of my mind.

Sadly, the petty jealousy which haunts all sport was rammed home to me as I got a lift back to Yorkshire with Robert Earnshaw and his wife Denise. 'Ernie' had already made a big impact by winning the previous season's Gold Cup on Silver Buck and I'd leaned over to put my arm around him as we pulled up after the winning line that day in a totally spontaneous gesture. I felt that we'd really achieved something for the Harewood team and I could only have been marginally happier if I'd ridden the winner myself.

Now it was Robert's turn to be magnanimous and, while he wasn't the most outgoing of characters he appeared genuinely pleased for me. But I always thought Denise resented me being at Harewood and thought I was getting rides that should have been her husband's. Robert had also been beaten half a length on the Dickinson's Political Pop in the previous year's Hennessy, when many people thought that a stronger rider might have won, but he was magnificent at getting horses to jump out in the country, so what you lost in his weak finishes you'd gained threefold earlier in the race. I had genuine admiration for his horsemanship and had learned a great deal from him during countless schooling sessions at Harewood.

As we cut our way through the Midlands and headed for Yorkshire I was still keyed up and, like millions of football fans every Saturday night at five o'clock, I was waiting for those stirring trumpets which introduce Sports Report. For once I wasn't even worried about the Leeds United result. All I wanted to hear was the racing section, and then it came. 'The big race at Newbury today, the Hennessy Gold Cup was won by 22-year-old Graham Bradley on Bregawn.' I'd like to know how the rest of the report on my first great moment went, but Denise leaned over from the passenger seat and pushed a tape of ELO into the deck. Maybe we'd have heard a bit more if Captain John had won. I knew exactly what she had done and why she had done it. So did Robert, but he did nothing to correct her. Denise was a hardy, tough little woman who appeared to wear the trousers. If she said 'jump' Robert would ask how high.

Still, there was no point in getting tetchy, so I used my usual escape mechanism and drifted off to sleep.

I was still on a massive high when we got home, so I rounded up my usual team and headed off to the Flying Pizza on the outskirts of Leeds, owned by a good friend of mine, Adriano. Then it was on to the heart of the city and Mr Craig's nightclub for a serious bit of revelry. The long sleep induced by a surfeit of lager meant I didn't see a great deal of Sunday, but the cold light of Monday morning soon came around and brought with it a lonely train journey to London.

In my naive way I didn't think there was any point in taking a solicitor with me to the inquiry at 42 Portman Square. I'd admitted to breaking the rules, and although the papers had speculated that I might be suspended, the friendly Racecourse Security man had told me it was no big deal. I was given a thorough grilling by the Disciplinary Committee and after about an hour I was asked to leave while they deliberated over my sentence.

I didn't know what to expect but I was a very anxious young man as I waited half an hour for the committee to reconvene. I hadn't started smoking then but if I had, I'd have made a big dent in a packet of Silk Cut. I knew the hearing hadn't gone well, but surely I'd only get a small suspension.

I'm good at taking pressure now. God knows I've had plenty of practice - but I was only a kid then and the palms of my hands were nicely moist by the time I was called back in. The retribution was swift.

'Mr Bradley, you have admitted your guilt and therefore your licence to ride has been suspended for two months.'

TWO MONTHS, TWO FUCKING MONTHS!

The words rebounded around my head and I couldn't comprehend it, just could not believe it. All I could think of was that smarmy ex-copper saying it was no big deal and I'd get a little fine. The bastard had played me like a fiddle. This was a smear that would shadow me for the rest of my career. If only I'd had that warning hand on my shoulder on 30 August.

I left Portman Square feeling nothing but contempt for the ruling body of the sport that I had strived to be a part of since I was a child. I had held up my hands and admitted to breaking a rule which I had been led to believe was a minor indiscretion. There was no need to make such an example of me. A stiff fine and a week's suspension would have been plenty. It left a deep wound that never completely healed. I had gone there for a rap over the knuckles and the bastards had cut my hands off.

I hailed a cab for King's Cross and made the lonely journey back to Leeds. I stared blankly out of the windows into the night, praying that no one would recognise me and draw me into conversation. I was Graham Bradley, the banned jockey, and I didn't want anyone to know it.

For the next two months I'd be able to work in the yard, ride horses in work and even take them to the races. But then the knife which had already been thrust in deep would be twisted as I watched someone else win on them.

By the time the train pulled into Leeds I was in a pit of despair and felt guilty about the people I had let down, my family and the Dickinsons', in particular. I never lost faith that I was good enough to bounce back and I did my time quietly. But I'd learned one very expensive and important lesson. Never sign anything. Never own up.

THE WAYWARD LAD

CHAPTER 2
The wall of dreams

Every child has a dream. As they get older it sometimes changes and quite often it simply fades and dies as the reality of life begins to bite in. I was one of the lucky ones because I lived my dream.

That vision of the future never changed. I was always going to be a jockey, preferably on the flat, and it didn't matter what I'd have to sacrifice to get there. Mind you, I didn't start well, weighing in at 9lb 3oz on 8 September 1960, the third child of Norman and Sheila Bradley. It was the first of many encounters with the scales that would become a constant part of my life.

I had preferential treatment from the beginning and, unlike my two sisters Mandy and Jackie and brother Gary, I was born at home in the upstairs bedroom of 38 Second Avenue on a pre-war council estate on the outskirts of Wetherby in West Yorkshire with just Mum and the midwife to give me a round of applause.

But much more important than where I was born is what I was born into, namely an exceptionally warm and loving family. No man can have had a better start to his life and I look back now and know how lucky I was.

The Hallfields Estate, with it's grey brick houses, is

unremarkable and just like many of the housing projects built between the two world wars. And with my dad having started in racing and stayed with it, there was never going to be a surplus of money to move into a more fashionable district. But he put a great amount of work into the place and once the family had left home he bought it from the council and still lives there happily today.

There is no doubt that I was shaped by Dad's passion for racing. I suppose it's a fortunate man who can call his hobby his job, even if it's not a particularly well-paid one, and my earliest memories are of him talking horses over the dinner table. I might not have known what he was talking about, but it all seemed marvellous to me and I couldn't wait to get into it. His enthusiasm also spread to my brother and sisters because we were all mad about horses.

But the love affair with horses had started further back than Dad because his father had worked in the nearby fields behind a rippling team pulling a plough. It didn't take Dad long to follow on. When he was twelve years old he got a Saturday job in the butcher's shop in Wetherby but it was horseflesh that interested Norman and later he joined Tony Doyle who trained just outside the town.

Although he was only 7st, Doyle wouldn't sign him on as an apprentice. People were much smaller then than they are now and the bottom weight in flat handicaps was 7st so a kid needed to weigh just over 6st in order to ride at 6st 7lb to be able to claim the 7lb allowance.

Dad was always going to be too big for the flat so he worked as a lad in the yard and I'm sure that because his hope of being a jockey was crushed so early he subconsciously lived his dream through my success. He was always there for me in his quiet, understated way.

But Dad has always been one of the most conscientious people I know and despite his disappointment he buckled down and developed into a master stableman, a rapidly diminishing breed. And it didn't take him long to begin making an impression. The *Sporting Chronicle*, which ran alongside the *Sporting Life* but was published in Manchester and in consequence had a northern bias, used to give a regular award called 'Guinea For The Lad'. It was the equivalent of today's best-turned-out awards and meant that the lad was given 21 shillings in old money or £1.05. It might not seem much now, but wages in racing have never been high and Norman began to get plenty of these little bonuses. He was impeccable in everything he did and his horses always looked a million dollars.

But memories of the Second World War were fresh and Britain still had an empire to defend. Like every other able-bodied man, Dad was off to do three years' National Service in the RAF from 1950 to 1953 and, when he got on the Leeds to Liverpool express to join up, it was the first time he'd ever been on a train. He didn't learn much about flying either and when he was posted to Germany it was the first time he'd even been abroad. He was never a great traveller and never left England again until he flew to Normandy with me in 1993 when I won on Bokaro at Clairefontaine, near Deauville, for Charlie Brooks. He didn't even have a passport and had to get a temporary one from a post office near Blackbush Airport in Surrey.

After serving King and country Dad went back to Doyle's and was promoted to travelling head lad/box driver, but the yard was going downhill in more ways than one. Most of the boxes had been put up on condition that they were for cattle use only and when the planning authorities found out, Doyle had to move. The string was down to barely fourteen so it was the right time for Dad to be on his way.

He'd also been courting my mum for five years and he says it was love at first sight. He was sixteen when they first met at the local cinema. When the lights went up at the end of the picture he'd been watching he turned round, saw this very attractive young girl, and made up his mind he'd get to know her better.

They were married on 20 February 1954, the year Dad joined Arthur Thompson as travelling head lad/box driver. Thompson, who'd been a tough jockey and won the Grand National for Neville Crump on Sheila's Cottage in 1948 and Teal in 1952, had taken a few falls too many, according to Dad. But he stayed with him for four years until he moved on to fill the same role with Tommy Dent at Rufforth.

It was easy to see why Dad fell for Mum. It wasn't just that she was blonde and very attractive, she also had a wonderful personality, very outgoing and always anxious to help people, something which I'm sure she passed on to her children. When I became a senior rider in the weighing room I'd help any youngster who needed advice - after all, with the scrapes I'd been in, I was in a better position than most to act as counsellor.

Mandy was the first along in 1955. Gary followed two years later, then me with Jackie last in 1963 and although Dad wasn't earning a great wage, nothing was too good for us. Mum had worked first as a clippie on the buses and took jobs at the local chemists, supermarket and as the manageress of the local Wimpy Bar. All the extra cash was to give us treats and although we lived in a council house, the furniture inside was the best she could buy.

We all knew Saturday was treats day and whether she was working or not she'd come home weighed down with bags of goodies. We only had to say we really liked something and she'd go straight out to buy it. Dead soft, but lovely. If Dad wanted his horses turned out the best then Mum wanted the same for his kids. Allens was the best clothes shop in Harrogate, so that's where we were kitted out. But the generosity could backfire on us at Christmas.

She'd buy presents early and hide them away, but if someone came to the house with their kids, mum would break out the goodwill and give them some of our gifts, leaving the Bradley Bunch to stand and watch as our Christmas presents went out the back door! It was the same if she went visiting anyone. She couldn't go empty-handed and always arrived armed with a box of cream cakes from Betty's Bakery round the corner. It's hardly surprising that Dad never had any spare cash.

By the time I was starting to sit up and take some notice at the age of five, Dad had moved as head lad to Jack Hanson, who trained jumpers for himself under permit at Crackhill Farm, Sicklinghall, just outside Wetherby. He had good Flat horses too, but they were handled by specialist trainers like Sam Hall at Middleham. But it was those Flat horses I wanted to get my hands on and there was only one man who could do the job right in my eyes - Lester Keith Piggott.

While other kids were worshipping Moore, Hurst, Peters and the rest of the England World Cup team I was a Piggott man. As far as school at Thorpe Arch Primary was concerned, I was quite good at turning up. And I kept out of too much mischief, getting just the odd smack across the back of my legs from the head mistress, Miss Isam, my first experience of a brush with authority.

Lester just had me in a spell. I idolised him and he was everything that I wanted to be. He was majestic, a genius. He had an aura about him, so cool and unflappable and there were hardly ever any interviews, so he was a bit of a mystery man. But even though I was very young I learned that if you don't think you're the best jockey that ever lived and have massive belief in yourself, you've got no chance of making it. Don't preach about it, just know it and have the mental strength to be your own man.

It wasn't until much later that I understood the punishing regime he'd put himself through to keep his weight down. What I never understood was his ruthless obsession for riding winners that made him go behind other jockeys' backs and phone owners to get on fancied horses. Although I was ambitious, I never had the ruthless streak of Piggott, or of colleagues like John Francome and Richard Dunwoody, for that matter. Still, you can't change the personality you're given.

But at the age of nine I had no conscience and tried to use my limited influence to get Lester the ride on Mr Hanson's best three-year-old, a colt called Sylvalgo.

Dad had taken over the trainer's licence from Mr Hanson and had won a Redcar maiden with Sylvalgo, who was beginning to look a little bit special and was entered for the Dante Stakes at York, one of the major Derby Trials. He was to be ridden by Walter Bentley, who was stable jockey and a very capable northern lightweight able to ride at 7st 6lb. But there was the one-and-only Lester, strong as a lion, a stone heavier which meant no dead weight, and without a ride in the Dante.

I kept on at Dad to get Lester, knowing he admired him nearly as much as I did, and he put the idea to Mr Hanson. But he was very loyal - something I greatly admire now - and said simply, 'Walter Bentley is our jockey and he rides.'

The ground was bottomless, which Sylvalgo loved, and Mum and I screamed him home from the living room at Wetherby and watched him get beaten a head by Activator and Taffy Thomas - another lightweight jockey - with the third horse fifteen lengths away and the subsequent St Leger winner Intermezzo fourth.

Sam Hall, who had trained Sylvalgo as a two-year-old, came up to Mr Hanson after the race, put his arm round his shoulder and said 'You'd have won with Lester on, Jack.'

I was gutted that Dad had missed out so narrowly on winning a principal Derby trial, getting his 10 per cent of the prize money and some priceless publicity. Now, having subsequently suffered the frustration of being 'jocked off' horses in my career, I look back and feel ashamed that I was prepared to see a little man lose out.

However, there was an opportunity for Walter to make good use of his lightweight status because Sylvalgo was entered for the valuable Cecil Frail Handicap at Haydock and was allotted just 7st 10lb. Dad told Mr Hanson he'd win it with his head in his chest but Mr Hanson said it was too near with the Derby only eleven days later. Ever the realist, Dad said, 'He's got no chance in the Derby, it won't be soft enough for him. Lets win the Cecil Frail for £4,000 and have the Derby as a day out.'

Mr Hanson wasn't too pleased and fired back, 'Who the hell are you to tell me my horse hasn't got any chance in the Derby?' To which Dad replied, 'Your bloody trainer!' I think that encounter showed the early signs of strain in their relationship which would cause a split later.

I knew that Lester had revolutionised race-riding by riding shorter than any other jockey, despite being one of the tallest. He understood that balance was all-important, that a horse would carry weight much better when it was distributed over the forequarters, rather than hindering the power produced by the hindquarters, so I set about perfecting my style.

Both my sisters and brother learned to ride, and somewhat surprisingly, it was the youngest, Jackie, who was the best because she was the only one who had no fear. But Dad was adamant that race-riding was not a job for a woman. He never rushed us and I was left to my own devices getting that style right. I knew I'd need the right sort of equipment and even as a youngster I was quite resourceful, buying a length of rope from the local hardware store which I tied into a loop to make stirrups, keeping the rest for reins.

I had a string of three horses, my bed, the back of the sofa and, best of all, the wall outside. God, how I loved that wall. The scuffed grass in front of the houses was the budding footballers' field of dreams. Me? I had the wall of dreams. I would slip the stirrups over that wall, tie the reins to the gatepost and I could be Lester winning on anything, but preferably Nijinsky.

But I was then, as I am to a lesser extent now, shy and easily embarrassed. The puny little lad with sticky out ears would stop the minute anyone came near, but I'd keep my eye on them until they were out of sight and I'd be back in the thick of my own private Derby, making up all the lost ground. And if I needed some opposition there was always Alwyn Suttle, my mate next door, who idolised Geoff Lewis and would take up his position head to head on the opposite wall. But I can safely say that no matter how hard Alwyn rode, Mill Reef never got the better of Nijinsky in countless epic battles.

I'd do the same indoors when it was wet and knew everyone was out. I'd tie the reins to my bed head and be off and so absorbed in a Peter O'Sullevan commentary that I wouldn't hear Mum or Mandy come in until they yelled up the stairs 'Graham, get off that bloody bed.' The Second Avenue stewards had objected!

But I'd added a fourth to my string of horses which put me very close to the real thing - the saddle horse in the tack room at Jack Hanson's stable. I'd go up to the yard with Dad and when everyone was out of sight I'd slip two thick lavenham rugs over the wooden frame so I could use a whip without breaking it. Then I'd tack up and put on a real saddle, tie the reins to the handle of a draw which pulled out from the front of the horse and be at York races in no time. But I wouldn't perform if anyone was there - and quite often there was.

Mr Hanson was a very wealthy and generous man who had made his fortune through the haulage trade and one of the trappings which came with his lifestyle was a butler called Ernest. He looked exactly how butlers should look, tall and skinny with white hair and without a pick of flesh on him. I could never look him in the eye and used to stare at the floor and see these massive feet in immaculately shined black shoes. He never said a word, or smiled, but you could trust him with your life. The only problem for me was that he would come into the tack room in his striped butler's apron to polish the silver once a week and my shyness took over. I'd go off and sulk for an hour and keep a watch out until he'd gone, and the minute he had I'd be straight back and into the action.

All the lads used to watch me without my knowing. Terry Brockley, Jackie Mockrey and David Frost who rode some of the jumpers, would all take a look at me as they walked past the window but I was petrified of anyone seeing me. Then one day Mr Hanson walked in and caught me. I coloured up and thought my ears would explode but he had a kind, appreciative smile on his face and just said, 'Don't stop, carry on to the finish.'

By that stage it was always one of his horses I was riding, Sylvago, Dark Don or Balty Boys, accompanied by a self-hypnotising commentary beating Ard Coal or JFK. Jack listened as I called myself across the line and when I dismounted he just slid up to me, patted me on the shoulder and said 'Well done son, you rode a great race' and then slipped me a tenner, my first-ever present. I felt like a king.

Mr and Mrs Hanson were very kind to all us kids. I used to dream about riding a winner for real in his green and red hooped colours and I got tremendous pleasure when I realised that childhood dream on Mr Hanson's Yahoo at Haydock in December 1986. And I know that it pleased him, too.

Dad knew I fantasised about being a jockey and arranged for a photograph to be taken that I've still got above the fireplace at home. He borrowed some kit off Dennis Ward, who was a genuine lightweight rider, only 7st wet through after a good night out. His boots and breeches fitted me quite well, although the skull cap was like a saucepan and the sleeves of Mr Hanson's colours had to be rolled up three times before I was put on an honest old handicapper called Glenbarry. We even had a number cloth on him and it looked exactly like one of those posed shots that made up the Schweppes racing calendars. I took it very seriously and Mr Hanson took his little mascot into the house to show to all his friends.

Mr Hanson's associates had sent horses to the yard which now contained twenty although I doubt there have been many trainers whose address was a council estate, but 38 Second Avenue was the one in all the Turf directories. I'd started to take an interest in the real horses and while in theory the idea of me becoming a jockey was fine, it wouldn't be quite so easy to put it into practice. I was petrified of bloody horses. I was a timid kid and, looking back, I was frightened of a lot of things then and wouldn't sleep unless the landing light was left on.

The Hanson team was loaded on to horseboxes and driven four miles to gallop at Grange Park, which has a river running by it to the left, and where another trainer, Tommy Shedden, had his yard. I had a morbid fear of that river and always thought Dad was driving the box too near it. Sometimes, I'd literally grab hold of the wheel to try and push the box away from the water.

It wasn't going to be easy making a jockey out of me but Dad had plenty of patience and put me on a grand 15.3 hands pony of Mrs Hanson's named Canasta. He attached me to a lunging rein which allowed me to trot round him in a wide circle with him in complete control, but that still wasn't enough for me. I kept losing my irons and screamed in blind panic, 'Slow down, slow down, you're going too fast.' It was barely a hack canter but I was a nervous wreck. When I look back at my early efforts I still find it hard to comprehend that Lester rode his first winner at just twelve years old.

But Dad knew me better than anyone and was very careful with me, like a young horse that mustn't be rushed. Although, as I got more confident, I kept pestering to do a canter he wouldn't let me and knew that one bad experience would be enough to finish me off. I never did get to ride a canter for Mr Hanson, although I did graduate to riding out with the string on the roads.

But I was conquering my demons and starting to make my own way and joined a local riding school just off the A1 by Wetherby racecourse run by Gordon and Wendy Davies. Even though they weren't relatives I called them Auntie and Uncle. It was here that I met someone who has remained one of my greatest friends and who became a successful, brave but unfortunately brittle jump jockey himself, Steve Youlden.

He went on to ride good horses like Phil The Fluter and Amber Rambler for Harry Wharton, who trained at Wetherby, but when we first met his family had only just moved up from Bristol. I can see him now, a skinny, baby-faced kid with a mop of black hair. He looked just like a little girl from pony club in his velvet cap and cream caldene jodhpurs looking as though they'd been sprayed on to his skinny little legs. His black boots were stuck on the end of his legs with the pull up tabs poking out at the back.

Because of his surname he was nicknamed Yogi, but that all changed a bit later at school when we were picking sides for tennis ball football in the courtyard. A massive kid named David Mobbs who was a foot higher and two stone heavier than the rest of us and didn't have a great memory for names, called out 'We'll have that Boo Boo kid.' That seemed a lot better than Yogi, and I've never called him anything else since.

It was around this time that I first got to ride at a racecourse on the riding school horses, albeit only the car park at Wetherby just over the road. A girl who's remained a good friend ever since, Yvonne Topham, would go with me and Boo Boo and we'd race like madmen with our knees up under our chins.

I was determined to be a jockey and thought it was right to start living the life, just as Lester did, so I began watching my weight, which didn't go down too well with Mum. She'd produce lovely Sunday lunches with the first course a massive Yorkshire pudding filled with gravy and onions, which I loved. But when the roast spuds came out, I'd push them away and tell her I was wasting. I pulled a similar stroke when I stayed with an aunt who gave me cornflakes and I told her I wanted non-fat milk.

But being small had it's downside and being born in September wasn't a big help either. It meant I missed out by a month being in the same class as my mates. I should have started off in the middle grade at Wetherby High when my secondary education began but as there was no room I was pushed into the top stream. I was way out of my depth with those future rocket scientists and in the second year I was dropped back to the middle grade. Thankfully, I never slipped down to the lowest grade, where they thought they'd

21

achieved something if they tied up their shoe laces.

Lack of stature had other disadvantages at a large town school where there was plenty of bullying and fighting and it's something I can't stand to this day. Given the chance I'll always go for the underdog and it's a known fact that I've always preferred to be a lover and not a fighter.

I may have been slightly out of order one day by getting into a space halfway up the dinner queue which Boo Boo had kept for me, but a big lad got hold of me and heaved me out and I ended up getting nothing to eat because the queue was too long. Before the lunch break was up I'd bumped into my brother Gary who soon found the guy who'd thrown me out, grabbed hold of him and hung him on one of the coat pegs. He never hit him, just frightened him to death. He could handle himself, our 'Gaz' and would knock the living daylights out of me if I kept annoying him at home.

My big brother was desperately disappointed not to make it as a jockey but he still got a great deal of pleasure out of my career. He was always there for the big occasions and turned out to be a very handy amateur photographer. You'll see some of his work in this book.

Wetherby High School was one of those schools put up in the mid-1950s. It was pretty uninspiring and it had one major distraction for Boo Boo and me, a large tower block. From the top you could see Wetherby racecourse and that was just too much for us. We'd be off school and away to the track whenever racing was on, bunk in for nothing and get our position on the winning line so we could bet on the horse we thought had won in a tight finish. But it wasn't just the odd bit of truancy that brought me to the attention of the school authorities ...

Boo Boo and I decided to go on a graffiti spree and sprayed the names of some girls we knew all over the school and on some walls around the town. Needless to say, we soon got caught. The school imposed the first of many suspensions that the Jockey Club would add to later and I was banned from attending for two weeks. I was petrified about what would happen when Dad found out and my concern was well founded, because he gave me a good hiding which curbed any artistic tendencies with a spray can that I might have had. Taking pity on me, Dad took me with him to Newmarket the next day and bought me some quality riding gear at Goldings in the High Street, where all the top jockeys shopped. Suddenly, the world seemed a much better place.

But if that two-week suspension gave me a short, sharp shock it was absolutely nothing compared to what was about to hit me.

Despite all the problems that came to me later in my life there was nothing that would ever come within a million miles of devastating me in the way this tragic chapter did. It changed my outlook completely and my approach to life was turned on its head. I became much more appreciative of life and what it had to offer.

Like every boy, my mum was someone very special to me and I know it was the same for Gary, Mandy and Jackie. But when I was nine she became desperately ill and was diagnosed with ovarian cancer.

I had absolutely no idea just how serious such an illness was. All I knew was that she felt very poorly and the doctor was a regular visitor. But he wasn't the strongest of characters and kept prescribing drugs for her because she had a fear of surgery. It wasn't until he was on holiday that his locum called. He needed just one diagnosis to send her straight to hospital for a major operation.

It was savage surgery which took everything away and left mental scars as big as the physical one. Once she returned from hospital she was never the same again and had to undergo radiation treatment which made her whole body ache and meant she couldn't sleep at night. This made her take sleeping tablets.

Many women suffer during their menstrual cycle but for Mum it was now agony. As a result the doctor put her on even stronger medication, and the combination caused massive mood swings. The

23

doctor would prescribe anything she asked for and she became addicted to the powerful painkillers. Dad would go through the house looking for them and flush them down the toilet - the doctor just kept on supplying them.

When these horrible mood swings came, Dad and Mandy did their best to shield Jackie and me and would take us to our neighbours, Mrs and Mrs Handley, but we couldn't miss all the heartache. It was terrible to see this lovely person being torn apart.

But there were still many good times, too.

Although we never stayed away overnight on summer holidays we'd have regular day trips to Sands End near Whitby, which was about an hour and a half from home with Dad driving the Morris Marina.

Mum even took Jackie and me to Blackpool in 1970 for a week. It was the time that my superhorse, Nijinsky, was running in the Champion Stakes. Mick Ferguson, who did Sylvalgo, had worked for Noel Murless. He got a strong tip for their horse, Lorenzaccio, and Mum was ready to put a pound on it. I couldn't see Nijinsky beaten and convinced her to back him instead and, of course, Lorenzaccio won at 12-1. I didn't hear the end of that for months.

But Mum's mental anguish continued and she became more and more dependent on the medication. She was taking so much that she nearly tipped over the edge on three occasions. In the end she had so many toxins in her that she was on a hair trigger and one too many could be fatal.

Then one night in 1974 my world caved in.

I was watching TV downstairs and Dad and Mandy were upstairs with Mum. Dad came down and said, very quietly, 'Your mum's died.' I just went numb and even now I can't remember what I did. I've probably subconsciously blocked it out. All I can remember thinking is that I'd never be able to kiss her and hug her and tell her how much I loved her ever again.

What I can recall is watching television for months after and thinking that nearly every programme had death in it and that that everyone was watching me, which made me feel very embarrassed. I felt I was the only person in the world that such a catastrophe had happened to. The Leeds coroner recorded an open verdict, but there was another problem.

Because I was relatively young at fourteen I wasn't allowed to go to her funeral. Dad and Mandy took the decision that it was kinder to keep Jackie and me away because that's the way younger children were treated then. Not being there to say farewell to my mum has haunted me ever since.

They say that you can remember where you were the day significant things happen in the world, like the assassination of Kennedy and the death of Princess Diana, but no matter how hard I try, I just cannot recall anything about the day of my mum's funeral. I felt I never had the chance to say goodbye. I couldn't comprehend the finality of it and that I'd never see her again. I didn't realise how cruel life could be.

Until I began writing this book, none of my family knew just how much it had affected me and I'm certain that expressing my thoughts has helped exorcise those demons.

Many years later, Mandy was diagnosed with cancer and Dad said to her 'Please be stronger than your mum.'

She was that and so much more. At first it seemed that Mandy was fine when she was given the all clear following a mastectomy, but in the spring of 2000 she was called back and told the cancer had returned. I cannot describe the courage she has shown during her brave fight when her dominant spirit has shone like a star. It was typical that she was as concerned for us as we all were for her. She is a wonderful lady. It makes me feel extremely proud to have her as a sister and at the same time feel so very humble.

With Mum gone it fell to Mandy and Dad to look after Gary, Jackie and me and we were latchkey kids until they got in from work each evening. Even when Mandy got married 18 months later, she still called in every night and came to do the washing at weekends. Mum had made her promise that if anything did happen to her she'd look after us. She didn't let her down.

My best mate Boo Boo went through the same trauma shortly afterwards when his dad, a super fit sportsman who loved cycling, died on his bike on the way to a race. It was something that made our friendship even stronger. But his loss hit me badly because I knew just what he was enduring.

During this awful period things weren't going well between Dad and Mr Hanson, although they were still very kind to us kids. Mr Hanson's daughter, Philipa, was a real star and took us to the City Varieties in Leeds for shows and the cinema when Mum was feeling poorly and Dad was off work with a broken ankle. It was a terrible blow to everyone who knew Philipa when she died from cancer several years later.

But the relationship between Dad and Mr Hanson was breaking down. I think Mr Hanson wanted to take over the training himself and if he'd come right out and said that, Dad would have willingly dropped back to being head lad. But he didn't, and Dad still had 18 months left on his lease at the stables.

Mr Hanson had joined up with Robert Ogden, who is now one of the biggest jump owners in Britain. He had a stud in the same village and they were keen to go into partnership, with Mr Hanson as the trainer.

Little niggles started to creep in, like Dad not being allowed to wash his car in front of the garage any more, as he had done for six years. In addition, Mr Hanson would go out and close the top of the box doors when Dad had gone home, which meant the horses were wringing with sweat the next morning. I hated it because I idolised both Mr and Mrs Hanson and I also thought the world of my Dad, who was a workaholic perfectionist who would have done anything for anyone.

Dad never said much. He just bottled things up like I do, but in the end the Jockey Club had to be brought in and the options were either to pay dad compensation or close the yard down for 18 months. With some reluctance, Mr Hanson paid £1,000. Dad had done himself and the family proud and in his three years with the licence he had turned out sixty-one winners from a yard that had just twenty boxes.

Fortunately, Dad went into partnership with Phil Cockroft in a small racehorse transport business. He also went back to ride out for Tony Doyle, who was still training in Wetherby, and he took me with him. I now got that all-important first canter on a moderate handicapper called Rust Borough.

Any half-decent stableman could have ridden him on a piece of thread and we walked the two miles to Grange Park gallops then set off for a mile canter with Dad setting the pace. It wasn't long before I went sailing by out of control. Then I did the worst thing possible. I pointed the horse at a road with a five-bar fence on the other side, hoping he would stop. Big mistake. I've since learned that the horse has a brain the size of an orange and mine couldn't have been much bigger, either. I couldn't see that there was a strand of barbed wire above the fence and when Dad caught up, Rustborough and I were in an awful mess. I had to walk the poor animal two miles home, dreading meeting anyone because I knew I'd let everybody down.

Luckily, Mr Doyle was a gentleman. In his quiet Irish voice he just said 'One of those things, son. Are you OK?' The wrong words then might have finished me, but he and Dad decided that the best thing to do was give me another chance the next day on a quiet filly doing her third canter. It went much more smoothly and gradually my confidence grew. Fear of the dark evaporated and the landing light no longer burned into the night.

Dad was working hard with the horse transport business and one of their contracts was to pick up the legendary Vincent O'Brien's runners from Leeds-Bradford Airport when they came over for the big northern meetings. We arrived to pick up the 1972 team for the

York August meeting and one of them was Roberto, who'd won the Derby under a wonder ride from Lester. Mr Galbreath's colours were freshly washed and pressed in a cellophane cover in the front of the box with us. I felt like a millionaire just being close to them.

When I watched him inflict the only defeat on Brigadier Gerard in the Benson and Hedges Gold Cup the next afternoon under Braulio Baeza I really thought I was part of the team.

But by the time I was sixteen I wanted to raise my sights and the place for me to emerge on the work riding scene was Tommy Shedden's. He trained sixty horses in Grange Park, including some really good jumpers like Basket, a tearaway two-mile chaser who I'd seen in action many times on my unofficial trips to Wetherby races. Dad knew Jack Auton, his head lad, and they got me a job riding out before school and at weekends, £1 for Saturday, 50p for Sunday. I felt on top of the world when Mrs Shedden used to pay me on Sunday nights. Thought it was the crown jewels.

I soon learned how important a good head lad is and Jack was the first of several great ones I've worked under, including Kit Stobbs with Arthur Stephenson's, Brian Powell at the Dickinsons and Brian Delaney with Charlie Brooks. Jack taught me how to twist hay into a wisp to strap horses muscles, how to make quarter marks on a horse and how to twist and clean the doorway of a box using your pitchfork to leave a neat space to knock out your curry-comb. This left a pile of detritus which the trainer could see when he came round evening stables and he knew you'd done your horse over correctly. The only trouble was if the wind blew it all away. Jack knew all the moves and told me to dampen the floor. In fairness, Dad was the complete stableman, but when you're young you always seem to take more notice of someone outside the family.

It was Jack who usually rode out Basket. To look at he was just like the tearaway two mile chaser Tingle Creek; and just as strong, a big brute of a thing with a mouth like wrought iron. One morning, as the string of twenty were circling and awaiting instructions for the second canter, Jack came out of nowhere on Basket going flat out and completely out of control, see-sawing the reins from side to side. They ran straight through the string sending horses everywhere.

Mr Shedden just stood in the middle of the commotion shaking his head slowly from side to side and watched as Jack did the right thing - unlike me on Rust Borough - and kept Basket going in a big circle - although it took 15 minutes before he could pull him up. Next morning Mr Shedden arrived in the tack room with his trademark dewdrop on the end of his nose and said 'I'll ride Basket today, Jack.' Well, the boys were too shocked to laugh and everyone thought the same, 'Mad old bastard. He'll kill himself.' And he wasn't an awe-inspiring sight either: nearly seventy, six feet tall, hardly a pound over ten stone and riding several holes longer than John Wayne. But as well as having earned tremendous respect, the old boy also had something else because he held Basket and cantered him around the park for a full 20 minutes without breaking sweat. If I hadn't seen it, I would never have believed it.

Despite starting to grow I still wanted to be a flat jockey and it's one of my big regrets that, because I was so single-minded, I never had the slightest interest in going hunting or doing any showjumping. But so that I would get more experience on the flat, Dad split my summer holidays between working for Eric Collingwood at Middleham and Michael Jarvis, who trained a large string at Newmarket and had come up through the ranks himself, looking after the 1966 Derby winner Charlottown as a lad with Gordon Smyth.

Dad knew Michael's head lad John Booth, and he arranged a trip which made a lasting impression on me. I got to ride in a bit of work with Lester and couldn't believe I was doing it and also got to know Michael's stable jockey Bruce Raymond. All the lads loved Brucie. He was a model jockey for anyone to watch and when he retired he became a racing advisor to Sheikh Maktoum Al Maktoum.

Mr Jarvis would have taken me on as an apprentice but by my second trip there in 1976 I was 8st 7lb and Steve Eccles - not to be confused with the jump jockey - got the job. He was quite successful and ended up being champion jockey for a season in Germany, but I knew that flat dream was a non starter. However, it didn't stop me going around to Lester's house and taking a cutting from a bush in his front garden. I took it home with me and planted it, hoping that some of his genius would rub off on me. Sadly, it didn't have a chance, a bit like me becoming a flat jockey.

Towards my seventeenth birthday and still at school, I made my most significant move towards being a jockey and got my first ride in public. Like so many things in my life, it was down to Dad. Steve Nesbitt trained Sweet Slievenamon and had asked Dad to ride her in a mile-and-six amateur race at Redcar. Although he'd always wanted to ride in public he turned it down and put me in for the ride, and providence took over as Jack Hanson ended up drawn next to me! June 18 was my date with destiny and the stalls handlers had a real laugh when I arrived riding as short as Lester Piggott.

Although I'd been to ride her out three times and knew she was useless, it was still a big disappointment when Sweet Slievenamon finished tailed off and I was totally knackered. It crossed my mind that this riding lark might not be all it was cracked up to be. If I'd been able to look up to see who was finishing in front of me I would have seen the subsequently successful Newmarket trainer William Jarvis wandering about in the final furlong before winning on Chance Belle, trained by his father. Jack Hanson was third on the good hurdler Winter Melody and back in fourth was a certain Peter Scudamore on Force Ten. I'd be seeing a lot more of him over the next twenty years.

An inauspicious scholastic career at Wetherby High was coming to a close with just one O level in English language to show for it.

At least that might come in handy for those stewards inquiries!

It was now a question of which jumping yard I should try and get into and Dad was very keen for me to join Fred Winter in Lambourn. He'd always idolised him and, in an ironic twist of fate, I would finish my career at Uplands, though a cruel accident to Mr Winter meant that I wouldn't be working with him.

But Dad gave way to Tommy Shedden and Jack Auton. They said I'd be much better staying in the north and I should go to Arthur Stephenson. Dad finally relented.

I was heartbroken to leave Shedden's and one of the lads who treated me like his own son, the diminutive Peter (Sherlock) Holmes gave me a picture of Mr Shedden's good handicapper Tom Noddy winning with Lester up. I got the great man to sign it and took it with me and taped it above my bed at Crawleas, County Durham. I was now under the care of W.A. Stephenson and my education was starting in earnest.

CHAPTER 3
Who's a pretty boy, then?

Despite the chronic shyness which shadowed me through my early years and into my teens, I had a massive self-belief that has always remained and sustained me throughout my life. But back then it was somewhat misplaced. Quite simply, for a single-minded youth now focused on becoming a jump jockey, I had done frighteningly little schooling over obstacles.

While other kids had been doing pony club and gymkhana, most of my jumping had been either imaginary or leaping small obstacles I'd put up in the copse near home with me doubling as horse and rider.

My time with Shedden, Collingwood and Nesbitt and the trips to Newmarket had been flat orientated, so by the time I was due to leave school at the somewhat advanced age of seventeen, I'd hardly been off the ground.

However my enthusiasm was becoming common knowledge in the local yards and Harry Wharton gave me two rides in amateur flat races: Lord Rochester at Haydock and Burntwood Boy at Leicester. Neither were expected to trouble the judge and duly finished well out the back, but I got a massive buzz arriving at the track knowing

I was part of the action. And that same buzz never left me, right until the day I retired - at least for the major meetings.

It was typical that Harry Wharton gave me a hand. He also made Steve Youlden (Boo Boo) his stable jockey and was one of the first to encourage another young Wetherby lad along the road to jumping stardom, Jamie Osborne. I'd be bumping into him much further down the road when he became one of jump racing's most talented and controversial riders.

Like countless other boys who dream of making it in racing I began to keep a log of all my rides in a thick school ledger which was optimistically large. And with foresight beyond my years I printed on the front in large capitals 'GRAHAM BRADLEY. STRICTLY PRIVATE. KEEP OUT.' I wish certain people had done the same in later years. Happily, the optimism on size wasn't wasted. I kept that record of rides going right to the end and even had to start another one in 1998.

The all-important first jumping ride in public came from the same source as the flat one, Steve Nesbitt, who let me loose on Another Debona in the Cornforth Amateur Riders Novice Hurdle (Division One) at Sedgefield. Having been to Steve's to school him and just about got away with it, I was nicely on edge when I got to the track, which was looking bleak on a chilly 16 November 1977. But schooling pace and racing pace are poles apart. I was little more than a passenger and contributed to the bad mistakes Another Debona made at the fourth and fifth before finishing a weary eighth to Pirate Jack. When I pulled up, the bridle was only over one ear and my complete lack of technique had seen me almost fall off at every hurdle.

I went on to compete in two hunter chases and a point-to-point on Old Tot for Norman Waggott and pulled up Carol H for Norman Birtwistle in another hunter chase. But these were just good schoolmasters who knew a lot more about the game than Mr Graham Bradley (7).

So my flat race poise, as I liked to think of it, wasn't any help to a lad going jumping and my inexperience of getting airborne was a major problem when I went for my first job interview with Jack Berry at Cockerham, just over the county border in Lancashire.

As I was 8st 4lb there was still a glimmer of flat race hope left, so Jack seemed a good bet as he had a mixed team in those days. I was hoping to be apprenticed on the flat, riding some of the horses with higher weights in handicaps and in maidens while also making my way jumping. But these bold plans were built on the theory that I could make a horse jump. A session was arranged for me to school at Cockerham on a lovely July morning and I was sent out with a sound conditional rider of Jack's called John Hansen. Quite simply, I was appalling and suffered the indignity of decking my horse into the bargain. So I scuttled back to Wetherby without hearing another word from a man who has subsequently built up a reputation as a fine trainer of two-year-olds. Jack is also one of the most genuine men who ever held a licence and, despite his success on the flat, he has never forgotten his roots as a journeyman jump jockey. He also does invaluable work for the Injured Jockeys Fund and is hugely respected as a result.

So, the debate about which trainer was going to be the lucky recipient of this true jumping talent continued and the deciding vote against Fred Winter and alongside Tommy and Jack for staying north of the Trent came from Tommy Stack.

Tommy had ridden a couple of winners for Dad but will forever be associated with the Aintree legend Red Rum. He went on to become a classic winning flat trainer based in his native Ireland, winning the 1994 1,000 Guineas at Newmarket with Las Meninas for Robert Sangster. But at this time he was beginning to draw to the end of a long and distinguished career as a jump jockey, riding principally for Arthur Stephenson in County Durham.

Tommy convinced Dad that it was the right move to join W.A. Stephenson and that I'd get a chance if I was good enough. There was no need to write for an interview, a word from Tommy was all that was needed to secure a job at the finishing school of one of the great jumping trainers of the twentieth century. When Arthur Stephenson died aged seventy-two in 1992 he had trained 2,644 jump winners and 344 on the Flat, including the top class sprinter of 1974, Rapid River. Sadly I was never going to feature in his list of winning jockeys.

I had two weeks to wait before the job started and I was so wound up I could hardly get a full night's sleep. This was the big step for me, I wasn't going to be a kid playing at jockeys anymore, I was going to be one.

Dad was away with his horsebox racing, so Gary took me on the 75-minute journey to County Durham and the anticipation was eating away at me. I'd been used to the model yard of Jack Hanson, the old-style precision of Tommy Shedden and the neat professionalism of Michael Jarvis at Newmarket. I didn't know what to expect from one of the true masters of his craft, and I walked into the biggest culture shock of my life.

We arrived after evening stables on a warm summer night and found the hostel which is situated about a mile from the main yard and was a pub in it's former days of glory. Now it was more Munster's Return than Rover's Return. It looked quite sinister despite the late sun and it didn't take the greatest imagination to see what it would be like in the depths of winter.

I was put into a room with two other lads, Trevor Davies and Ian Macafferty, given an iron bedstead, and swiftly decided the best thing to do was keep my head down and say as little as possible. Some of the windows had panes of glass missing, and in the winter it was sleeping bag plus blankets to fend off a light dusting of snow that could cover you if the wind was blowing in the wrong direction. But this was summer, so who cared?

My room-mates gave me the form for the next morning. Down to the big dining room, make up your own flask of tea, put some sandwiches, nearly always cheese, in a Tupperware box and head off up the hill to work. Now, I'd always been taught to be well turned out with jodhpurs and shined boots. In the rush I hadn't taken much notice of my new colleagues as we collected breakfast, but as we made our way to the main yard at Crawleas I felt a little uneasy.

Dad had kitted me out well. In fact, I looked like a model from Goldings of Newmarket in my cavalry twill jods, shiny boots, black puffa jacket plus yellow mittens and whip. But I was on my own. My new workmates had their own uniform and it wasn't like mine. They were in T-shirts, well-worn jeans and wellies. The standard Dunlop variety with a thin sole and worn for all seasons with thick socks turned over at the top to keep out the winter chills.

The best-dressed newcomer in County Durham had another surprise for his new mates and in the style of the senior stablemen in Newmarket and most head lads in big yards, I donned my brown stable smock for mucking out. You've probably seen blokes in hardware shops wearing them with plenty of pens in the top pocket, but the lads of Crawleas had never seen the like.

I thought the smock was sensible, because when you picked up a muck sack and the horse piss came through it and down your back the smell stayed there forever, but there were several whispered glances as I went about mucking out my horses before riding out.

At 7.30 I was back in my puffa and ready for action when I made the acquaintance of William Arthur Stephenson for the first time.

'And who's this little celebrity?' were the first words he ever spoke to me in broad Geordie as I stood before the new boss. He was about five feet nine, very round and looked as friendly as a Cumbrian cliff. At that moment I thought the softest thing on him was his tooth enamel. But he hadn't finished. He then took hold of my ear and pulled me by it, pursing his lips and puffing out a trademark, 'Ooh, ooh, ooh, we've got a pretty boy here.' And from that point on I was always 'pretty boy' to W.A., no matter what. But my education was only in the starting stalls.

The lads thought the boss had probably done a better job than they could have, taking me down the ladder rungs quicker than any snake and the first two lots went by with just a few odd glances that newcomers often get on their first day in a job. But before third lot, W.A. had another surprise. 'Mr Bradley, I've got the right job for you, young man.' He then took me around to some boxes at the rear of the yard. Here I was given a big pot of Stockholm tar, a type of bitumen, with a brush on the end of a long stick. W.A. told me to apply it to the bottom half of the boxes but not before I'd cleaned the crap off the old stuff. In my Goldings rigout I was hardly dressed for the job and I never turned up in those expensive cream jodhpurs again. Myself and a young girl named Lindy, who had also just started, were also given the lowliest job in the yard, collecting 'the heaps' which meant you went round with a barrow and picked up all the mounds of dung and straw left by the lads who had the next worst job, sweeping the yard. Everyone who came had to start with the heaps. You couldn't wait until a new kid arrived and it was passed on because, doing the heaps meant you were last back to the digs and what was left of the hot meal would be fast cooling down. It must have been six bloody months before I got my promotion.

You're a pebble on a rough beach when you first go into a yard. From then on you get rounded off or broken and at this time there were still some pretty barbaric initiation ceremonies which were rife at Crawleas. There were the old favourites, like having your balls smeared with purple antiseptic spray which stayed there for months. Needless to say, that one warranted a few explanations if you were lucky enough to pull one of the many pretty young girls who lived in the area!

There was also a big muck heap in which new lads would be stripped naked and buried up to their necks. And if they were wimp enough to dig themselves out they would then be put a in hay net, winched to the top of the barn and left there all day freezing their tits off!

You could be extra lucky and be upended and have aftershave sprayed up your backside, which must have been excruciating judging by the screams I heard.

Maybe it's because I was so quiet and the boss had got into me early, but for some reason I never had any of that treatment. And although there were a few girls in the yard they were never subjected to that, thank goodness. I suppose the other lads thought it might stop them getting lucky a bit later on. Times change and these practices have largely died out now. It's just as well, otherwise the courts would be filled with people issuing writs.

But I soon found out I was working with a good bunch of blokes and I've stayed friends with many of them ever since. There was my best mate, Graham Gray, who was apprenticed on the flat and was very skinny with a long thin neck, which earned him the name 'Fatneck'. There were plenty more with nicknames that stick in the mind for ever. John Clarke, 'Little Yockle', who was hit by a truck when riding out and lost the sight in one eye; Bobby Beasley, alias 'Weasel', who used to carry his tools and medicines in a big bucket. One time the lads put some bricks in the bottom and he lugged them around for a week before he realised.

Francis McCarthy arrived from Ireland with a suitcase crammed with Elvis Presley LP's and could sing the lot. He was 'Elvis', while Gordon Welsh - who'd ridden winners as an apprentice on the flat in Newmarket and was always twirling his whip, was 'Twiddle.' Gordon went back to Newmarket and worked for Sir Mark Prescott, where he looked after Pasternak, one of the best Flat handicappers of the late nineties.

And there was 'Man's Head', Billy Telford, who was very small and looked as though he had a man's head on a boy's body. He wasn't over blessed with brains, either, and one day W.A. told him to tidy up a horse's mane and tail because someone was coming to look at it. Instead of doing it the right way and pulling the mane with a curry-comb, Billy cut it in a straight line with some scissors which looked awful and completely unnatural.

W.A. was dumbstruck. He huffed, puffed, ran his hand over his head and then shook it from side to side. 'Oh! Man Billy, it's not your fault. It's mine FOR TRUSTING YOU IN THE FIRST PLACE!'

It was excellent psychology and man-management because this way of administering a bollocking made you feel completely worthless. You never made the same mistakes twice.

The most evil-humoured member of the team was Dennis Davies, known to the lads as 'Black Dennis'. In the warm summer months, he'd wipe his wedding tackle on the standpipe in the yard and then laugh as the lads came by to get a drink. He wasn't exactly a bully, but he made the younger lads mind their ways and if they didn't go for a six-pack when he told them to, he'd get them stripped and lock them outside the digs. In a bleak County Durham winter that's no joke.

The former pub that we lived in was run by Mr and Mrs Ronnie Slack with their son, young Ronnie, and it was the stuff of TV sitcoms. Ronnie senior was a sinister-looking bloke. He was small, frail and mean-looking with a metal plate in his head. He walked with a limp and carried a shotgun about which, as you can imagine, didn't endear him to many people. In lots of ways, he bore an uncanny resemblance to Norman Bates in *Psycho*, and most of us were petrified of him.

He laid down strict house rules for the digs, principally: 'Don't come in late, don't come in drunk and strictly no women.'

He must have been an insomniac because he loved to prowl around during the night. He once caught Black Dennis coming in one morning at 4 a.m., well pissed. 'Where have you been, bonny lad?'

'Shaggin' came the snarled reply ... He was never asked again.

Young Ronnie was a few sizes bigger than us younger lads and was a bully, so we kept away from him. But Mrs Slack was generally civil and served up good dinners in the evening, but we had to treat her with caution. She could be very two-faced behind your back.

There were twenty lads living in the pub with a couple of stable girls tucked in on the same floor as the Slacks. There were only two toilets, one for the girls, who had their own shower, and the other for us lads. And if that kind of congestion wasn't enough there was another problem. The four wash basins and two shower cubicles were by the side of the toilet.

It meant that the one thing humans like to do completely undisturbed was impossible. The lock on the lavatory door had been kicked off long before I got there, so you just sat, suffered and hid your modesty behind a paper. There was a sort of gentleman's agreement that you would open the window to let either the stink or condensation out.

Another among our little band was a young lad nicknamed 'Crow' because of his swarthy complexion, black hair and large, hooked nose which looked like a beak. Stable life was cruel in many ways and this lad suffered. He was very quiet, never answered back and if anyone wanted anything done, Crow was the man.

One evening the shower room was heaving and Black Dennis was watching from the throne. Leaning forward with his forearms resting on his knees, he could see Crow and myself putting the finishing touches to our hair, perfectly preened specimens who were certain to pull that night.

Crow only had a towel round him and was bathed in a haze of talc. Taking one last look in the mirror, he splashed on some aftershave and turned to walk out when Blackie wiped his arse and stuck the paper on Crow's back.

The lad never said a word, just kept on going and walked out as though nothing had happened. It was a wicked thing to do but I have to admit Blackie and I nearly wet ourselves laughing. But things like that happened every day at W.A.'s. You just had to like it or lump it.

41

The plate of sandwiches left out for breakfast each morning never changed, cheese and more cheese and you'd eat them in the tack room after first lot at 9 a.m.

There was a black pot bellied stove which heated the place and the paid lads would sit around it while the youngsters did the best they could. Sometimes one of the lads with a car would take a long list to the pie shop in town and if you were a young lad and behaved yourself you might get one brought back. Those hot ham and egg pies were heaven.

Kit Stobbs was head lad and had ridden winners for W.A. when he was younger. He was hard as nails and actually rode a winner at Catterick with a broken pelvis. But he was a great guy to work for and I had immense respect for him. He had his own place tucked away in the corner and he ran the show on a day-to-day basis, but there were times when we had to cheat him, especially if it was raining or snowing in the winter. Kit would sometimes lead the string round the roads and, because he never looked back, one by one we would drop off and nip into a derelict building called the brickworks which still had a roof on it. We'd stand in there on our horses, have a natter and a fag and wait for 9 am to arrive so we could go back to the yard. Kit would have pulled out with a string of twenty and return with three. When he quizzed us youngsters it was always, 'Small boy, where did you get to?' We had to be good with our excuses.

W.A. had so much trust in Kit that he hardly ever went up to the gallops. He knew he'd got a good staff and just asked everyone about their horses when they got back.

The secret to W.A. Stephenson was that he knew how to get the best out of men and beasts. He would go to Doncaster and Ascot sales and buy up all the dodgy ones and then set us to work on them. He would hand you a lunatic and tell you, 'This is your horse, now you go and sort him.' It was like a challenge and you knew that he trusted you and expected you to do it. If you didn't, then you'd let yourself and him down. It was brilliant psychology but he had some of the best lads in the world, partly because they were given the chance to be the best.

He'd run horses that were backward and let them race to fitness, quite often sending a group of twelve to work after racing at courses nearby like Sedgefield, Teesside and Wetherby. He got fined for schooling horses in races when that offence was hardly ever heard of.

But the problem for me was that W.A. never saw me school or ride work. He only ever saw me ride out from the yard and didn't like what he saw. The only time he came on the gallops I got run away with on a lunatic called Supermacado. I rode too short for his liking 'pretty little flat jockey' and it didn't matter what Kit told him, he wouldn't put me up. But that didn't stop him using me at home for a tricky little two-year-old filly called Blushing Chiquita. She was very temperamental and one morning when I got on her she tried to run off. When I grabbed hold of her, she flipped over and I smashed my head against a box wall - no skull caps for riding out or schooling in those days.

I was spark out. I don't know how long for, but the guv'nor told me to go back to the digs and lie down, which was as close as you'd get to an act of compassion from him. By the evening I knew I wasn't right, because my head had swollen to the size of a melon, so I went to see him and knocked on his door. He answered in his braces with his bit of remaining hair slicked over like Bobby Charlton. I always thought he looked a bit like Ronnie Barker playing the caustic shopkeeper in the seminal comedy *Open All Hours* and I got the same kind of unsympathetic response when I told him I still didn't feel right and wanted to go home for a few days.

He had a trademark karate chop which he would feint several times then catch you in the stomach when you'd relaxed your muscles. He delivered it with the withering words, 'Ooh man, you soft beast, what are you wanting to go home for? You needn't ride out, but there's still plenty for you to do, sweep the yard and do the heaps.'

I did get an overnight stay in hospital but that was it, I never went home.

When I did it was usually Dad - or Norm as I'd taken to calling him now - who would call in with his box and pick me up on the way back from any local meetings or the Scottish circuit. Norm's detours off the A1 didn't go down too well with the lads in the box who wanted to get home and it didn't take me long to decide I needed to get mobile.

We were reliant on the senior lads with cars to get us about, either to work in the morning to miss that mile walk, or to get into town to enjoy ourselves. And despite being in an outpost, there was plenty of entertainment in the working men's clubs. You had to be a member with a card but it meant you could sign two girls in. Odd as it sounds now, girls weren't allowed to buy drinks, so they had to ask us to do it for them. There were clubs in every town, Chiltern on Tuesday, Bishop Auckland every Wednesday ... it was never-ending and I seemed to have a different girl in each. Before long I fell in love for the first time with a girl from Crook called Yvonne and my troubles began. Fatneck, who was riding on the Flat and had a car, would drive me over and I'd sit and watch *Dallas* with her mum, dad, gran and brother. Never missed an episode.

Yvonne's mum cooked a lovely tea and made brilliant cakes. She also gave me doorstep sandwiches for work the next day instead of the usual cheesies, which made the other boys jealous. They were lovely people and her dad would drop me back to the digs nearly every night of the week. However, there was an 11.30p.m. curfew which I'd often miss, and sometimes I'd meet Ronnie on the prowl with his shotgun. The Slacks went to W.A. and told him I was a wrong un, and a dirty drunken stop out. They were wrong, but I suppose I hadn't done myself any favours by pinning beer mats on the wall around my bed to wind them up. Soon after, the Slacks kicked me out of the digs and it looked like I was on my way home.

Now, you might have thought I'd be pleased to go, given the spartan regime but the fact is I absolutely loved it there and the lads knew it. A bunch of them went to W.A. and told him that I wasn't a big drinker or a fighter - heaven forbid - and that I was only getting in late because I'd been to see my girlfriend. He was good about it and arranged for me to lodge across the road from the yard with Audrey, who was in the process of splitting up with Billy Redfern, one of Arthur's jockeys. She was an absolute darling and looked after me superbly but it was a purely platonic relationship. The only reason I moved out after six months was because she wanted to get a council house for herself and her four kids and she wouldn't have been able to get one with a lodger in tow. I still send her a Christmas card every year.

I didn't waste much time in learning to drive and, having passed my test first time, I became the proud owner of my first car, a Morris 1000 which the lads rather sarcastically nicknamed Blue Fire Lady. The young bloke who taught me said that I was a natural driver and if I didn't make it as a jockey I should think about becoming an instructor. I should have considered the option because my career was on stop. 'Pretty Boy' was still the only comment W.A. came out with when my name was mentioned for rides, although I had learned plenty about schooling over the Stephenson jumps which were a row of five telegraph poles. One of the older lads, Joe Fluck, a mad Welshman, tried to jump them backwards one day and nearly killed himself. Most of his time was spent cutting W.A.'s hedges in his flat cap and with his dark racing goggles on. When he popped up from behind the privets he looked just like ET and frightened the life out of horses and riders.

Things moved much slower for a young jockey then than they do now, when a bright talent like Richard Johnson can come from being a raw amateur to a top-flight rider in three years. Likewise my young friend A.P. McCoy, who is shredding the record books like no one before him.

When W.A. did decide to let me loose there was never going to be the slightest worry that I'd trouble the judge. I finished tailed off on Mainsforth Hero at Catterick in April 1979 and picked up my first fee of £11.63 after the guv'nor had taken half as was his right. He had another surprise for my second professional ride, Mahalo.

The New Zealand-bred gelding was somewhat surprisingly owned by Ivan Allen, who won the 1984 St Leger with Commanche Run and was also a successful trainer in Singapore, where he survived a murder attempt. He's now one of the leading trainers in Hong Kong, so why he had a yak like this with W.A. is impossible to work out. Added to that, it was a nutcase into the bargain.

Geordie Dun had taken over as W.A.'s first jockey after Tommy Stack's career had been ended by a paddock fall in which in smashed his pelvis at Hexham in September 1977. And Geordie was given a torrid time by Mahalo at the same track, doing a couple of unscheduled laps. Geordie rode him again at Catterick and had to stop the beast by running him into the white boards at the two-mile start. I was given the job of riding the horse at home and soon had him lobbing around with the help of a citation bridle, a brilliant device named after the great American horse who was a very strong puller and for whom it was invented. I'd tamed Mahalo at home so I was given the task in public at Sedgefield and there were no disasters. I was desperate to make a good impression but the horse had no steering and I voiced my concern when W.A. decided to run him at Cartmel, which is a very sharp left-handed track that is constantly on the turn.

Whenever his judgement was questioned, W.A. would puff himself up in frustration and he certainly was now. 'Oh man! You bucket of hens feathers!' As far as he was concerned there was nothing of less use. 'Don't worry, just get him on the inside and the others will carry you round!'

Sure enough, he was right and nothing out of the ordinary happened as we finished a never dangerous seventh to Bannow Breeze, ridden by Tommy Carmody and trained by Tony Dickinson, two men I was going to meet up with in the not-too-distant future.

W.A. was as much a horse trader as a trainer and he would sell anything to anybody: ponies, hunters, cattle, donkeys, the lot. Over the years he'd sold hundreds of horses on, particularly to enthusiastic amateurs like Gay Kindersley, a former trainer himself and living legend of my adoptive home in the Lambourn Valley, also former amateur champions Chris Collins and the Greenall brothers Peter and Johnny. He hardly ever travelled to southern meetings and wasn't even at Cheltenham for his greatest training moment when The Thinker won the 1987 Gold Cup - he was saddling runners at Hexham!

As there were always plenty of horses around the place it's no wonder there were a fair few headbangers among them, but Supermacado was the undisputed champion.

He had earned the *Timeform* double squiggle awarded to complete rogues and pulled like a train with the added attraction of no steering. I rode him around the guv'nor's all weather one day and pulled the biceps in my left arm so badly I was off work for four days. On another occasion he broke free while being lunged and turned arse over tit at a five-bar gate before galloping off down the road. Metal horseshoes and tarmac are not a good combination and he turned over a few times and was cut to shreds when we eventually caught up with him. Jenny, the girl who looked after and worshipped the animal, came hard on our heels, tears streaming down her cheeks and screaming 'Where's my horse, where's my horse?' Enter Trevor Davies, brother of Black Dennis and a man with the same gallows humour. Pointing in different directions he said laconically, 'Well, there's a bit over here ... a bit over there.'

Sadly, by this stage my progress at Crawleas was now minimal and after two further rides on Mahalo and one on the novice hurdler

Churchill Peak I'd earned the grand total of £60.89. When I arrived there were sixteen lads with jockeys licences who were in front of me and in two years I hadn't moved past one of them. It was time to move on.

I was sad to be going, as I'd been with W.A. for the best two years of my life. It had made a man of me and given me a thorough education in the art of survival. I'd grown to love the place and the people. But when I went to his house to break the news I knew that it wouldn't exactly break his heart.

He stood in the doorway of the house, grim-faced with his bottom lip sticking out and the ever-present braces and Brylcreemed 'Bobby Charlton' fold over.

'Guv'nor, I'd like to give you a week's notice ... I've got another job.'

'And where's that?'

'With Tony Dickinson'

He didn't miss a beat and the karate chop to the midriff was only seconds away.

'Ooh! Ooh! Ooh! Man, your mother bred a funny child. I know there might not be much for you here, but there'll be even less for you there.'

Fortunately this was one of the times Arthur got it spectacularly wrong.

CHAPTER 4
Getting promotion

I've always believed in fate. No matter how disappointing, things happen for a reason.

If Norman hadn't split with Jack Hanson I'd probably have stayed with him and ridden their few jumpers. If I'd been lighter, I may have joined Michael Jarvis as a Flat apprentice then got too heavy and become disillusioned with racing. If I hadn't fallen schooling at Jack Berry's I might have joined him and been a middle -of-the-road jump jockey and flat work rider. If Arthur Stephenson had been on the gallops more often he might have seen that I had a good pair of hands and could hold a strong puller. As it was, the only time he did see me I was carted away by that lunatic Supermacado.

If Audrey Redfern hadn't needed a council house I'd have still been in comfortable digs, but with sixteen other lads holding riding licences at Crawleas I might have become disenchanted and taken up that job offer as a driving instructor. If the Dickinsons hadn't moved from Gisburn to Harewood near Wetherby it would never have crossed my mind to try and join them.

'If' is only a small word but destinies are changed by it and Kipling thought it was big enough to deserve a poem. It's very important in my vocabulary.

The idea of joining a top-quality jumping yard close to home was a big attraction for me and I asked Norm to see what he could do. He knew Tony Dickinson casually and approached him about taking me on. The response wasn't good.

'We've got four jockeys in the yard and six youngsters already Norman, and I don't want to take on another, but seeing as it's you, I'll give him a job as a paid lad.'

The Boss - the only name by which anyone, including me, who worked at Harewood referred to Mr Dickinson throughout his life - was always to the point. Norm knew how badly I wanted to join and was aware that once I was in, there was a good chance my ability would be noticed, because the Dickinsons believed in giving youth a chance.

'He'll take it,' said Norm, before pressing on that casual friendship. He's already got a conditional licence, so would it be alright if he kept it and I tried to get him a few rides?'

'Well, seeing as it's you Norm, OK.'

I've always been a Leeds United fan ever since Norm took me to the back of the Kop at Elland Road to see the great team led by the late Billy Bremner. Moving from W.A. to the Dickinsons was like being transferred from Barnsley to Elland Road. Both great clubs, but one with the quality to go to the very top.

However, it had been a long road already for the Dickinsons. The Boss was a good amateur jockey and was champion point-to-point rider in 1954. Monica Dickinson, 'Mrs D' and never anything else, rode in points and was ladies national champion in the show ring at Blackpool in 1950.

The Boss trained under permit and took out a full licence to train at Gisburn in Lancashire in the 1968-69 season and had tremendous success. He had a terrific eye for horses and, whereas W.A. would get the redoubtable Irish dealer Tom Costello to send over a batch of horses unseen, the Boss would go over and hand pick them. It was a real family business. Boss bought them, Mrs D looked after them and fed them, and Michael, who also rode them early on, plotted up where they should run with the military precision of a field marshal.

Michael, or 'Bud' as he was always known in the yard, was exactly the wrong shape for a jockey. Six feet tall and painfully thin to ride at 10st 7lb, he often fell with arms and legs protruding, which meant more than his share of injuries. The one which finally nailed him was at Cartmel in 1978 and left him in intensive care for seven days with liver damage. He retired with 328 winners to his credit, including five at the Cheltenham Festival, a figure he would leave behind when he trained in his own right.

Michael became the linchpin of the training team and was instrumental in the move to a purpose-built yard at Harewood. He never missed a trick and it was due to his inquisitive mind that my chance to join the Poplar House team improved. I hadn't thought much about my two rides on Norman Waggott's Old Tot but Michael had taken note. He'd seen that senior riders like Geordie Dun had fallen on him and that I'd got him round, particularly in the Heart Of All England Hunter Chase at Hexham. In Michael's mind, I had to have some ability.

Michael took over the licence in the 1980 - 81 season, leaving the Boss with a fine career total of 562 winners. But well as The Boss had done, Michael took the Dickinson yard to a whole new level, setting a standard that every jumping trainer strove to match until he moved to train on the Flat in 1984. In his three seasons he sent out 374 winners and, had he stayed with jumping, there's no knowing what he might have achieved.

It was a big wrench leaving County Durham and for all it's rough-and-ready ways there is no doubt it was a winning formula for W.A. Mind you, he hardly sent me on my way with a glowing reference. I still have the half sheet of headed notepaper which states, 'I have had Graham Bradley in my employment for two years and have found him an honest and willing worker.' He obviously didn't see the need to oversell me, but now I was in for the right kind of culture shock.

Poplar House had been erected by local builder Peter Haley and everything was functional. The Boss and Mrs D had a nice, but certainly not extravagant house; Michael lived in a nearby village and the hostel was the big house that had been on the property before building started. I wasn't going to need that apart from for breakfast. I was a 'day boy' and lived at home with Norm and my younger sister Jackie.

There was a main stone yard of forty boxes and a wooden one of twenty around the back, which had been brought from Gisburn. The tackroom had sixty numbered pegs for bridles and at the back was Mrs D's private room where the colours were kept neatly folded in their own pigeon-holes. No one was allowed in there.

I knew I was being pitched into a big pool of riding talent but that self-belief was vital and I knew I'd pull through if I got the chance. It was just as well I had that confidence, because the formidable team of full jockeys was headed by Tommy Carmody, Robert Earnshaw, Kevin Whyte and Chris Pimlott.

The junior riders were a good bunch, too: Chris 'Banner' Bell, who became my best mate on the place, Stephen Burrows, Stephen Hardy and Jonathan Davies. But despite that number it didn't take long to get noticed.

Because there were so many horses to be schooled, the senior riders did all the work over fences and the conditionals would put them over the poles and hurdles - Michael watching everything and missing nothing. There were still plenty of bollockings about riding too short, but they were never bellowed across the schooling ground as some trainers like to do. Michael would take you to one side on the way home and point out exactly what you had done wrong. The criticism was always constructive and he soon realised that I could hold everything and had good hands. By the time I had my first ride over fences later that year I had been able to pick up a tremendous amount from Robert Earnshaw. He was absolutely magic at putting horses over fences, a real joy to watch. Trouble was, he was very weak in a finish, and Michael was quoted as saying that between the pair of us we'd make one good jockey.

That first ride for the Boss came on a horse he owned called Talon at Worcester on 20 February 1980, and once again fate took a hand in my favour. Banner Bell was ahead of me in the order for rides, but although his licence and medical book had been applied for they hadn't come through. Fortunately I already had mine, so I headed south and finished third in a two-and-a-half-mile novice hurdle behind Celtic Rambler, trained by Fred Rimell and ridden by John Burke, who'd won the Cheltenham Gold Cup and Grand National of 1976 on Royal Frolic and Rag Trade. John was drawing to the end of his career and finally overcame a battle with alcohol but still died very young. Incidentally, there was another young 4lb claimer in the race who managed to get his weight under control with a spartan regime and went on to ride Classic winners on the flat, namely Ray Cochrane.

Talon was a massive but slow chestnut gelding who needed plenty of use made of him and we led from the fifth to the sixth before weakening at the last. I went back in the horsebox satisfied that I'd done nothing wrong and, although Tommy Carmody rode him next time, I was given another chance much closer to home when Talon was entered for the Grove Novices Hurdle over two and a half miles at Sedgefield.

The race wasn't until 4.50p.m. Like the rest of the jocks I was paying plenty of attention to the first day of the Cheltenham Festival where the big boys were playing and 90 minutes earlier Sea Pigeon, ridden by Jonjo O'Neill, had got his revenge for defeats by Monksfield the previous two seasons. He'd do it the next year, too, receiving one of the best rides I have ever seen from John Francome. Christ, I envied the artistry of Francome and hungered to get a taste of the Cheltenham Festival. I would get my moment of Champion Hurdle Glory but it was many years away and a lot of work needed to be done. But I would soon be off first base.

Michael had left nothing to chance. He told me I had to make stamina count and we were in front two out. The old horse was very genuine and outstayed Roy Davies on the 5-2 favourite Kilroy Manor by four lengths. Now I was on my way, earning £35.51 and those first newspaper cuttings were pasted into a scrapbook that subsequently stretched to twenty-three volumes, meticulously kept by my dad.

Carmody was on Talon next time out when he won at Sedgefield and there were no moans from me. I was still up there in the clouds having ridden my first winner and I was back on him to make my first trip south to Chepstow in Wales.

The big, galloping track suited him ideally. This time we got the better of John Burke and Fred Rimell, beating their Swashbuckling by two lengths, but the horse had to be brave. We were headed two out but he got back in front at the last to win by two lengths with me asking for everything.

There was one funny moment the day after the race when the report came out in the *Sporting Life*, which enlightened its readers with the news that: 'We are certain to hear more of the 7lb claimer *George* Bradley, who excelled on the winner.' Ever since that day I've been known as George to a large number of my friends in the north. There was one other more accurate hint for the future when Robert Dickinson, a cousin of Michael's who'd come to saddle the horse, said to me in the weighing room, 'The way you rode that horse, Carmody had better look out for his job.'

My celebrations usually took in the same circuit. Drive to the Flying Pizza in Leeds and meet Banner, who'd get a lift over from the hostel, then on to the casino - I'd have a problem in one of them much later - and then drop in to Mr Craig's nightclub. Even at twenty, I had a taste for the better things in life. If it was a general night out and a few lagers with the lads it was usually a pub called The Spacey Houses not far from the yard and run by a bloke named Charlie Gillis. We had some great nights in there, but some terrible mornings after.

The day following Chepstow was also significant because I rode my first winner outside the yard when Mick Easterby gave me the ride on Three Ways at Wetherby. I was full of confidence now and brought him late to win by eight lengths, providing a very special moment with my initial success at my local track.

Mick is still one of the great character's in racing. If James Herriot had ever needed to invent a racehorse trainer for his books, he had a ready-made model in Mick. He's never been one for standing on ceremony no matter who is around and is a master of the one-liner and, when necessary, the putdown.

Ronnie Beggan, one of the Dickinson team of jockeys, was due to ride work for Mick one morning but hadn't left enough time for the hour-and-a-quarter journey from Harewood to Sheriff Hutton. The horses had already pulled out when he drove into the yard and he was profuse in his apologies, 'Sorry I'm late guv'nor but I got lost coming into Sheriff Hutton.'

Spittin' Mick raised his wrist, looked long and hard at his watch then tugged the peak of his cap to a more aggressive angle and said in his broad Yorkshire accent, 'So what did you do then lad, go back to Wetherby and start again?'

Hardly any jump jockeys had agents at this time, but Michael would ring round trainers he knew and get us rides. Likewise, if we were offered any, Michael would go through them and make sure they were alright because he didn't want us riding bad horses. He knew exactly what he was doing because the practice would be invaluable for the time when we were given the chance to partner some of his stars.

That first season at Harewood had gone better than I'd dared hope and I felt confident I was on my way. Fifteen rides had yielded four winners and when the 1980 - 81 season started it would be M.W. Dickinson who held my licence.

It had always been the plan for Michael to take over from the Boss, and with a thoroughness that has been a trademark throughout his career with horses, Michael continued my learning curve. He wasn't happy with my Flat race seat, feeling that I had too tight a hold on a horse's head and was pulling too hard on their mouths when they jumped, restricting their freedom. He took countless videos of schooling sessions which were replayed in the office to the accompaniment of many a good bollocking.

It was the same when a photographer sent in pictures from the racecourse. If he wasn't happy with the way you had hold of the horse's head jumping he was on you in a flash.

Although Tommy Carmody was a terrific jockey with great balance and nerves of steel, the Boss, Mrs D and Michael would get on at him for jabbing a horse's mouth on landing. He was completely different from the more traditional horseman they'd been used to in Michael, whose theory was that you could only make up a head in a finish but could gain ten lengths in a race by fluent jumping.

Tommy was also riding quite a bit for Jimmy FitzGerald and my third winner of the new season was for him on Western Man at Ayr on 21 November. Ironically, it came at the expense of my old mucker 'Fatneck' Graham Gray by a neck.

Jimmy was an absolute gentleman to ride for having been a good jump jockey himself. He was also the man who harnessed the fiery talent of Kieren Fallon when he came from Ireland before moving on to become champion jockey.

The Boss and Michael had a good relationship with Jimmy and they stuck me in for rides with him. The ruddy-faced Irishman, who handled such top-class horses as Forgive 'N Forget, gave me my fourth winner of the season, Dugald at Catterick. And in December he stepped in with my most important winner so far when I rode

Vicomte at the televised Nottingham meeting. I won on him again, but unfortunately it was going to lead to a falling out with Carmody.

Winners on television are essential to get a young jockey noticed and I made full use of my stage. Tommy had come too soon on the horse at Haydock and Vicomte had idled in front before being beaten narrowly. Even at such a young age I relished this kind of challenge and brought Vicomte through late in the Philip Cornes Hurdle Qualifier to collar Alan Brown on the odds-on Pay Related after the last. But Vicomte began to edge to the left and in a matter of strides I had my whip through and into my left hand to straighten him. Not many 7lb claimers would have had the confidence to do that, but I'd been doing it for years on my wall of dreams. Practice makes perfect.

We won again at the Newcastle Christmas meeting, coming late to beat Alan Brown and Bamp, but on my first ride at Newbury he disappointed at 7-4 on when second to Scottish Sound and Mark Floyd in the valuable Ramsbury Handicap Hurdle.

Word soon got back to me that Carmody had gone up to the owner, Trevor Barker, and said that I had been moaning in the yard because I hadn't been given a present. I was absolutely seething, because I'd never asked anyone for a penny piece and had been very grateful to get two televised winning rides on the horse into the bargain. I never said anything about it and bottled it up, as usual, but it gnawed away at me and I knew it wouldn't take much to set me off.

A month or so later we had finished breakfast in the hostel after first lot and started playing pool. It was house rules that the winner stayed on the table but Tommy came up and said 'I'm next'. It was no problem to me who I was playing. But as I bent down to break he said 'I'm breaking' and gave me a very sharp tap on the head with the butt of his cue.

No way am I a fighter, but he'd pulled the pin from the grenade. Completely disregarding that he was considerably older than me and our stable jockey, I went ballistic and a frenzied scuffle ended with him on the floor with my knee on his chest. The other lads pulled me off with me bellowing at him 'Never to mess with me again.' Unfortunately that wasn't the end of it.

I don't know whether Tommy resented us youngsters coming through or not but he was never really one of us and there seemed a bit of 'side' to him. And it didn't take long for the final dust up to arrive.

It was at the Northern Champion Jockeys Dinner at the Scotch Corner Hotel on the A1, a very nice black-tie do. We were getting fairly twisted towards the end of the night and going through the motions of a routine that had everyone sitting on the floor rowing along to a song. Tommy didn't join in but kept flicking beer over us until we finished. Banner Bell retaliated by throwing the remains of a half of lager at him. All square, but not so far as Tommy was concerned ... He came back with a full pint and tipped the lot over Banner, evening suit and all. Well, Banner was my best mate and although he was a big lad he couldn't punch his way out of a wet paper bag. Seeing what Carmody did gave me the red mists. I dragged Tommy outside to the car park and started knocking seven bells of shit out of him. Once again, as in the hostel, it was Chris Pimlott and Kevin Whyte who dragged me off. Fortunately, nothing ever got back to the Dickinsons or, if it did, nothing was ever mentioned to me.

After Tommy returned to Ireland we settled our differences and are on good terms again these days. The whole of racing grieved for him when he tragically lost his young son in an accident.

Although winners are vital it is equally important to have trainers willing to put you up on a regular basis while you are learning your trade, and three who were magnificent to me at this time were Mick Naughton, Alastair Charlton and Andy Scott. Mick is a lovely man who sadly stopped training in Britain just as he said he would if things didn't go right and it didn't pay. My first ride for him was

Tribal Warlord who finished fourth at Hexham on 22 October 1980, and I carried on riding for him when I could until he retired in 1993.

Alastair was very loyal to me and put me on nearly everything he had in the yard. I won four for him that season although one, Marine Cadet, was disqualified after a positive dope test which was traced back to some contaminated horse feed.

This left me in fourth place in the conditional jockeys championship on twenty-three winners behind my stablemate Pimmy on forty-four. Ben de Haan,who went on to win the Grand National on Corbiere in 1983, was second with Brian Reilly, now a Jockey Club starter, third.

I'd also made my first trip to the National meeting, and in the race after Bob Champion and Aldaniti had galloped into racing legend I finished ten lengths second on Ballydonagh in the Page Three Chase for conditional jockeys.

So things were looking up in all directions and by far my biggest payday was not far away. It came at Newcastle in the unlikely surroundings of the members' bar. Alan Jarvis booked me for the first time for two horses, Hill Of Slane and Prince Bai, and they won. Both horses needed to be delivered late and were equally funny, hanging to the left, which brought those hours on the wall back into play. In fact, one journalist wrote of me ' ... switching my whip to the left hand with the adroitness of Scobie Breasley.'

When I joined Mr and Mrs Jarvis in the bar he just turned to his wife and said 'Give the lad a drink' and she pulled out £500 and gave it to me. I'd never seen that kind of money before and was still driving a battered old Morris 1000 that I'd bought for £200. I didn't waste much time in putting a down payment on a blue Ford Escort with white stripes down the side and put the rest away for the rainy day.

That season had gone better than even an optimist like me could have hoped for. Thankfully it was going to get even better - but not before I almost self-destructed.

CHAPTER 5
I am the Walrus

Any secret yearning I had about riding on the Flat had been blown away by a factor that was going to stalk me for the rest of my career. Weight.

Unless you have lived with a constant eye on the scales it is impossible for people to understand how obsessed you become with the spinning dial. It is your own wheel of fortune and if it registers high then you've got problems - and I had them.

My immature attitude to weight is best understood by this example of dedication and weakness. Banner Bell and I used a sauna above a ladies' hairdressers in Harrogate and because we were regulars they would leave the place open late for us. We came out one night after three and a half hours of torture, each losing 6lb of fluid, and found the cars frozen solid. It was only Sedgefield the next day, one of the bleakest outposts in jumping at that time and prone to the frost. It didn't take us five minutes to convince each other that they wouldn't possibly race and we were into the Chinese for chicken fried rice, curry sauce and chips. We washed the calories down with a nice few pints, putting all the weight back on ... with plenty of interest.

Sod's Law intervened, the temperature rose overnight and the course inspection was delayed until an hour before racing. Skipping breakfast was only a token effort to redress the balance of the previous night's excess but there wasn't much else we could do except walk the course with the stewards and try and dissuade them from racing. We had to. We were heavy as lead.

We dug our heels into the ground, shook our heads and kept mumbling 'Can't possibly race, Sir, it's dangerous,' but they didn't pay the slightest attention to two nondescript conditional jockeys. Our hearts sank when the all-clear was announced and, with no sauna at the track, I struggled through on my lightest saddle to do 11st and Banner managed 11st 10lb on one the size of a postage stamp.

At the age of twenty I was on a one-way ticket to obscurity and my body was rebelling from the abuse I had inflicted upon it. The cumulative effect of pee pills and laxatives had taken their toll. So too had the crash dieting that followed binges and endless guilt-ridden hours in scalding hot baths and saunas in an attempt to boil off the excess weight. My metabolism had slowed down to a virtual stop and anything I ate or drank stayed in my body. I filled up like a balloon.

When the season ended I took my first holiday abroad with Banner and had two weeks in Magaluf, cramming in as much debauchery as was humanly possible. I was like the mythical kid in the candy shop and my calorie intake over that fourteen days was obscene for a young man who considered himself a sportsman.

A large breakfast was followed by sunbathing then an early lunch and a few Budweisers before moving back to the beach. On the stroll back to the hotel we'd take in a light snack of burger and chips, and the only calories burned after that came during a shower and shave before dinner. Then it was the nightclubs and eight or nine pints and when the 'munchies' hit us on the way home at 4 a.m. it was time for a bedtime snack of another burger and chips.

After a fortnight of appalling self-indulgence we arrived back at Harewood and I bore a strong resemblance to a beached walrus. I knew the price I had to pay for that two weeks was much too high.

I was just over five feet seven - shorter than Lester Piggott - but when I stepped on to the scales at home without a stitch of clothing I thought someone had been tampering with them for a joke. The needle stopped at a numbing 12st 4lb and my career looked over before it had hardly begun.

Although the holiday had brought my weight worries to a head it was only part of a problem that had been with me all my life. I was not a good eater and was typical of a young jockey in those days who needed to watch his diet. I'd eat hardly anything for three days, but after I'd reached the target weight and ridden I'd be back to the bad old ways. A couple of cans of sugar-laden Coke with some crisps and chocolate on the way home from the races.

I'd be out the same night and have either an Indian, Chinese or a pizza then be back in a downward spiral. I was in a desperate mental state and got depressed because I was heavy. In turn, that would start me bingeing on chocolate. Dieting is a state of mind, but as soon as the phone rang offering a light ride I would automatically feel hungry and head for the fridge and some comfort food.

All the boys at Harewood knew the appalling state I was in and the constant piss-taking forced me into drastic action. I unburdened myself to Michael. He knew more than most about what it was like to deny your body what it craved and had heard of an Irish doctor named Austin Darragh. He'd helped some high-profile Flat jockeys with weight problems and one of the first to consult him was Tony Murray, who continued to ride for many years but tragically took his own life after he retired. I believe he also helped Walter Swinburn in the unequal struggle at an early stage in his career.

I flew into Dublin Airport at 11.15 a.m. and was in the clinic thirty minutes later. After some preliminary tests I went to stay with my aunt, Amy Heaslip. I checked back into the clinic at seven the following morning, gave blood and urine samples and went back to Amy's and returned to the clinic at 11 a.m. Still I hadn't seen Dr Darragh.

The tests started in full at the ungodly hour of 5.45 on Friday morning. Seven blood tests at 30-minute intervals, two urine samples with two hours in between. I was put on a liquid diet of black tea, a bowl of consommé for lunch and dinner and I had to drink as much water as I could. I think I dropped 4lb overnight and saw Dr Darragh for the first time the next morning.

He put me on a treadmill for five minutes and took my pulse, which took nine minutes to return to normal. It takes four and a half for a fit person to do that so here was I, a sportsman who was only half fit. He told me to walk three miles briskly each day, not to sauna or drink alcohol and gave me a book of general exercises to do. He then told me that I was having too much salt, which was making my body retain fluid, and that I was carrying at least 7lb to 10lb that would go within two weeks.

He preached the perils of the diuretics, the pee pills that jockeys thought were heaven-sent but drove you to hell in ever-decreasing circles. You'd start at 11st then have a pill to lose 4lb. After riding you would be so thirsty that you'd drink and drink until you were satisfied and be 11st 1lb, so in the end you just got heavier.

Dr Darragh explained that pee pills force out all the salts from the body along with the vitamins and minerals, which then causes terrible cramps in the calves and toes.

He also told me to roll up my trouser leg and pull down my sock and the indentation it left was a clear sign of how much fluid I was retaining.

I dared not break the iron regime because I knew I'd be a laughing stock back at Harewood if I failed. I didn't smoke at the time, so he put me on some appetite suppressants, which he said would buzz me up but do me no harm, and that I would need them for the amount I was going to eat in the next three weeks.

It was a high-protein diet with a breakfast of one boiled egg or two lean rashers of grilled bacon. Lunch was a single fillet steak or a piece of fish or chicken and dinner was the same, all with black tea. No bread, butter, salt, mayonnaise or mustard. The second week I could add as many green vegetables as I wanted but not root. I had my egg before work, so when the lads where having massive breakfasts of porridge and syrup, then a fry up and toast and marmalade, I'd just sit and read the paper and drink my water.

I stayed off the scales but I could feel myself getting lighter and by the third week I could have the luxury of any vegetables I wanted with my chosen meal. This may sound indulgent, but eating large quantities of food with no condiments whatsoever was a trial, just like munching through dry bread. I wasn't even allowed a solitary tomato or a piece of fruit as dessert because of the natural sugar they contain. I was also drinking literally gallons of water which, combined with the water content of the vegetables, meant I was up three times a night peeing naturally, as opposed to responding to pills.

I stuck with it so religiously that by the time of my twenty first birthday party I had gone from 12st 4lb to 9st 8lb. I phoned Dr Darragh and asked if I could have a glass of champagne. He relented and I realised what I'd been missing.

The weight started to creep back on and I did try to go back to the rigid regime, but it was torture. Life got easier when I lost my claim but in emergencies I'd take chewing gum laxatives before I went to bed. A sickening rumbling stomach would wake me in the morning and the first thing I did was rush to the toilet. Perfecting the timing of intake and the resulting expulsion became a science and when nature called, I had no time to argue the point. Two or three times I got it wrong and took to carrying a spare pair of boxer shorts in the car. In the end I couldn't face the taste of the gum and couldn't put it anywhere near my mouth, let alone chew it. My stomach would turn at the very thought.

However, despite my problems, I never resorted to self-induced vomiting, even after a bingeing session on chocolate when I felt genuinely sick. I first encountered this practice, known as 'flipping', on my trips to America, where it was widespread. When I rode a winner at Monmouth Park, New Jersey, for George Strawbridge, who has owned many good horses in Britain including the top miler Selkirk, I saw some literally sickening sights. Jocks would gorge three hamburgers, two hot dogs, a pint of milk and a can of Coke. They then went straight to a special toilet at the end of the row of eight with an enamel plaque on it saying 'Heavers Only' and brought it all back. Just talking to them they'd tell you they did it all the time. They thought no more of it than having a cigarette.

Over here, I've never known any jump jockeys doing it, although I've heard a couple of the flat boys did indulge.

After I'd moved south I tried another drastic measure, using the car as a sauna, like Lester used to, and I drove five hours to Cartmel with the heat full on and in a sweat suit. I don't possess the greatest endurance for self-denial and kept stopping for drinks, which resulted in a meagre loss of half a pound. When I was in a sauna my pet hate was swilling my mouth with water then having to spit it out and not swallow. That journey was an absolute nightmare and I never did it again.

But jockeys are resourceful individuals and if things were very bad there was one final, desperate throw of the dice; try and beat the clerk of the scales and 'cheat' the weight. I hated doing it but sometimes necessity got the better of integrity. To a jockey, putting up overweight is a public admission of defeat and no avoiding measures were too extreme or inventive.

When it had to be done it was approached with military precision, quite often in collusion with colleagues, it was all out warfare with any guerrilla tactics employed. The weapons were simple and included metal coat hangers, lollipop sticks, thumbs, toes and heels, but those battles with a wily clerk provided hours of laughter on the journey home or when reminiscing later in the pub.

The use of the metal coat hanger was a work of art. It was unwound and slipped through the long tie strip of your cap which reached to the floor. When you were on the scales, and with the extra leverage of the camouflaged wire touching the ground you could lose up to 8lb. To make sure you drew the correct weight when weighing in, your valet had to help by handing you an extra whip before you got to the scales. Once you had placed your skull cap and original whip on the clerk's table, you could then use the other, covered by your tack and number cloth, to use as a lever off the floor.

Lollipop sticks could be used in the same cunning way. They would be taped to the arch of your boot at one end so when lifted it would fall down vertically. A shuffling gait to the scales was needed for this operation and once on the machine, the foot could be left dangling innocently off the platform, three inches off the floor. Only close inspection would reveal the stick, which provided ample leverage to get the right weight.

A well-placed thumb on the scales would gain you a couple of pounds and likewise a casual toe on the floor if the clerk wasn't too observant. A trusted friend could give aid with a heel at certain courses, such as Warwick. If he leant casually over the rail where the saddles are laid ready for collection, an extended heel could fit under the scale platform and a third party with an eye on the dial would whisper instructions 'up' or 'down'.

It was common to weigh out with a small saddle having already had the correct one passed out the changing room window. John Francome once got caught weighing out with no saddle at all but it was like water off a duck's back. As the clerk asked him to lift the large foam pad and number cloth draped over his knee which revealed nothing, Francome just looked up and drawled in a bemused but world-weary tone, 'Fuckin' hell, I've told them valets about that before.'

There were also cheating boots that were made of paper thin leather all round and were impossible to ride in, you might just as well have gone out in your stockinged feet. But a sharp-eye clerk could spot them and when he spoke the dreaded words, 'Are you going to ride in those?' You knew you were in trouble. Some would mark the sole with a chalk mark and check it was there when you came back in so the only option was to cut up a racecard and put it under your arches to stop the stirrup iron cutting in.

Another favourite was to use a false back protector with the protection taken out then replace it with the real thing. I sometimes wonder if the relatives of jump jockeys were ever interned in Colditz!

But it was serious if you were caught weighing in more than the 2lb you were allowed for rain or mud. At best it was a fine, at worst a suspension, and when you were collared it was a major embarrassment.

For me the battle with the scales went on until the end of 1993, when I gave up dieting because I couldn't stand the anguish any longer. Incredibly, I lost weight because my metabolism kicked into gear and my body began functioning normally. Even in the summer break my weight never went above 10st 12lb and, ironically, now that I've stopped riding completely, I'm lighter than during my mid-teens.

CHAPTER 6
I can never thank Michael enough

I went into the 1981-82 season needing only ten winners to lose my 4lb riding allowance and had every reason to be confident of doing it now that I had my weight under some sort of control. And Michael Dickinson had shown his maverick streak once more by deciding to put his faith in the young troupe of riders he had nurtured. I felt as though I could reach out and touch the big time.

As the old season had run to a close, months of speculation on a split with Tommy Carmody ended with the news that he was going home to Ireland. It was no secret that the Dickinsons, and Michael in particular, did not like his ultra short style. In fairness to Tommy, he had dropped his leathers four notches, although it probably still wasn't enough. I'd also taken the hint after too many years of doing it my way and decided to ride longer. But to my posturing eye I wouldn't have looked out of place upsides Clint Eastwood in a spaghetti western whenever I caught my reflection in a window.

Tommy was a great jockey, particularly on the big occasion, and at twenty-four wasn't much older than me. He'd won some of the biggest chases in the calendar, including a hat-trick of King George VI chases on Gay Spartan in 1978 and Silver Buck in 1979 and 1980. He turned down the chance to stay in England with a southern based stable and went back to Ireland, where he was one of the most sought-after jockeys until he retired.

In the yard there was plenty of speculation before the split was made public, and the topic over breakfast was always who we thought would come in. Although we stopped short of making a book on it, Ridley Lamb was hot favourite. He'd ridden winners for the yard and was the horseman type that the Dickinsons and W.A. Stephenson loved. Several years later Ridley, along with another of the Stephenson jockeys, Alan Merrigan, and a young girl were killed in a car accident on the quay at Seahouses, Northumberland. A very good friend of mine, the ex-jockey-turned-valet Steve Charlton, was the only passenger to get out alive.

As we'd virtually made up our collective minds that a 'name' rider was coming in, it was the right kind of surprise when we read the *Sporting Life* story of Tommy's departure which included the statement from Michael, 'Next season I will be using talented young jockeys who already work for me, Robert Earnshaw, Chris Pimlott, Kevin Whyte and Graham Bradley. I will not be appointing anyone in Carmody's place.'

Michael had hardly mentioned it and he just had a knowing smile once he knew we'd seen the story before riding out first lot. It was a time to build dreams.

No one was taking anything for granted, but I'd been given a place on the first-team bus and, although Robert was recognised as first choice, I was clearly a player.

But, as in all things, Michael had thought things through thoroughly. By trusting in youth he knew that he could keep everything in-house, just as he liked it. No detail was too small, no snippet of information unimportant when it came to his horses. Even the water in the yard had to have the right mineral content and could probably have been bottled at source, just like Perrier.

As far as I know, he was the first British trainer to employ interval training, a system Martin Pipe has since used to rewrite virtually every jumping record in the book.

Michael would do it on the all-weather gallop, which was a mile round. He'd canter the horses around one way, pull up and walk them for a couple of minutes, then work them back the other way, gradually increasing the pace. At that time, I honestly think his horses were fitter than anyone's.

Just about the only thing missing at Harewood was a hill that would build stamina. Everything was pan flat, but Michael would overcome that by boxing the horses over to Malton for their final workout where there was a stiff old gallop. He'd also take horses to Wetherby, Doncaster or Catterick racecourses to gallop and school. To avoid the risk of injury but provide experience we schooled them over all bar the last two hurdles. This gave a long, galloping finish to the work and it wasn't particularly hard to spot the future stars, although things didn't always go to plan.

John Sanderson was clerk of the course at Catterick and was concerned about a big galloping session because there wouldn't be any paramedic cover, but Michael charmed his way through the problem and it went ahead.

Graham 'Darkie' Burrows, sadly killed in a motor accident several years later, was working a wooden-headed creature that I looked after named Sensing. After galloping a circuit, Darkie couldn't pull the horse up and he careered through the Tattersalls enclosure, scattering the wooden stools that bookmakers used to gain extra height. What followed was one of the most frightening things I have ever witnessed. At a flat out gallop, Sensing crashed over the metal fence that divides Tattersalls and the members enclosure, turning a complete somersault. Darkie was thrown through the air as though he'd been shot out of a cannon. It would not have been a surprise to find either of them dead but Sensing regained his feet, shook his head and ambled away with hardly a mark on him. And apart from mild concussion, Darkie was alright too. Frightened to call an ambulance because of repercussions from the local health and safety executive, both horse and rider were loaded into a horse box and taken straight home. Both were poorly for a few days but they made a relatively quick and full recovery.

Michael didn't have an open ditch on the schooling ground at Harewood, reasoning that you always had to give horses confidence at home and not frighten them. The fences were unique and divided down the middle, half birch and half in specially made black plastic. I don't know what it was, but if a horse took liberties with the birch, Michael would switch them to the plastic and they would really back off and concentrate.

There's no question that like a football manager with a team, Michael was passionate about his horses and was happier at home with them and being in the office planning their races than going racing. He was quoted at the time saying 'Going racing is a waste of time, I hate it. Once our horses have left for the course my job is done, anyone can put a saddle on them before a race.

'My place is at home. I'll see them go out, watch them work and look around at evening stables. You can't spend too much time with your horses, that's what training is all about, not sitting in the car for hours or drinking in the bar'.

But it wasn't always tranquil when he was at home. He would often watch racing with the lads in the hostel and when one of the good horses got beaten he'd blow his top, take off his shoe and hurl it at the television, before dashing to the pay-phone in the hall and letting rip into the handicapper.

The money he won, and there was a lot of it, all went on the yard and the horses. He drove an old white Mercedes with over 100,000 miles on the clock and even when he went to the hairdressers he would always take the formbook with him. He used to devour the *Sporting Life* and the first thing he'd go to was the results section, where he loved to see the close-up comment 'jumped well' for one of his. It got a bit irritating if you knew one had jumped well for you and didn't get it.

However, there's no escaping the fact that none of us lads who rode for him would have been half the jockeys we eventually became if it hadn't been for Michael's tutelage - but you had to have a hide as tough as a rhino.

That second season with him I rode Badsworth Boy at Ayr and challenged down the outside instead of up the middle of the course, where Michael had insisted I must come because of the better ground. We were beaten a length into third behind Home Ground and he didn't stop bollocking me from the moment I came off the course until I got into the changing room. He stormed off to the car park in a tantrum but cooled down soon after. He then took me out on to the course once more to show me exactly what I had done wrong then watched me ride a treble, two of them for him and one of them, Donjill, got the coveted 'jumped well.'

But that was Michael. He would just lose it and you had to wait ten minutes for the sun to come out again. He definitely got it from his mother because the Boss was always very placid and very rarely raised his voice.

Mrs D had the job of feeding and it wouldn't have mattered if the Queen Mother had come for a look round after the horses had been fed, no one could go near them. She's one of the kindest ladies I've ever met but once she went up you just had to wait for her to come down.

It took me until 27 January to lose my allowance on one of Mick Naughton's horses called Manhattan Island but 28 November 1981 was possibly a more significant date. That was the day at Market Rasen when I made my first public appearance on the horse who was going to carry me into the headlines, Bregawn.

Robert Earnshaw had done a brilliant job schooling the horse before I ever got near him in the Limes Handicap Chase, but it was Bregawn's mind you really had to get to the bottom of. Ride him regularly and you'd get to know how he'd jump and travel and also how he sulked down at the start and wouldn't want to go. Every other day at home he'd plant himself in a ditch or hedge and when he did you couldn't move him with a tractor and tow. The only way was to pull his ears and make a fuss of him and then wait. He was a funny old horse but for all his quirks at the start, he'd give so much at the finish.

There were no worries at Market Rasen. It was a simple hold-up job at the back as he sauntered round with top weight to win by an easy two and a half lengths. But it was only my seventh winner of the season and I didn't see myself with a chance for the young rider's championship. David Dutton - nicknamed 'Donkey' by Alan Brown at Ayr one day as a form of introduction to a girl he was talking to and one of my best friends to this day - was attached to Peter Easterby's yard and looked sure to win it.

Also there didn't seem much chance of getting another ride on Bregawn. He ran four more times before Cheltenham, winning the Peter Marsh Chase at Haydock for Ernie then carrying a 6lb penalty and John Francome in the Great Yorkshire Chase at Doncaster. He then won a handicap chase at Kempton Park for Ernie off 10st 7lb. The ageing but top-class Night Nurse was third trying to give him 20lb, which shows the improvement Bregawn needed to make before getting to Cheltenham.

He failed under a 7lb penalty for Ernie in the Greenall Whitley Chase at Haydock and his chance for the Gold Cup didn't look bright. Not that it affected me. I didn't see any reason why I should ride him, even though Earnshaw would be on the stable first string, the mighty Silver Buck. Happily, Michael had other ideas. He knew just how important it was that the man on board understood Bregawn's quirky ways and, with Ernie spoken for and Francome claimed for the enigmatic Border Incident, he wanted me to take the ride. All he had to do was convince the owner and that wasn't going to be easy.

Martin Kennelly was an Irishman who had firm ideas. He

realised he had a chance in the world's most prestigious steeplechase and wasn't keen on leaving it to a 21-year-old who had never ridden in the race. But Michael stood firm, arguing my case throughout the preceding week and, as usual, got his way. I said at the time that it was the biggest compliment ever paid to me and it was.

But if I felt under pressure, it was nothing compared to what Michael was enduring. Neither Ernie - who was only twenty-two - or myself had any experience of the race. What's more, Silver Buck had hardly had the ideal preparation, having bruised his offhind before Christmas and been in his box for a month after. And although the horse was right back to his best and worked better than the Two-Mile Champion chaser Rathgorman in a gallop before Cheltenham, Michael warned punters two days before that he didn't think Silver Buck would be able to reproduce his best on the heavy ground.

Ever the pessimist, that was something Michael did get wrong. Apart from a mistake at the nineteenth, Silver Buck was always going like a winner, not that I got much of a look at him early, as Bregawn was on a real going day and was up forcing the pace with Tied Cottage. He'd often make at least one serious mistake and it came at the sixteenth, though he never lost much ground and when Silver Buck swept through to lead two out we were there to keep him company.

Silver Buck was a top-quality chaser and we were never going to get to him up the hill, but Bregawn kept going like a hero to finish clear of the rest in second, and as we pulled up alongside all my emotions began to fill me up. Maybe it was relief that I hadn't let anyone down and that I had proved I was good enough when it really mattered.

Whatever it was, I felt as high as if I'd won the race myself and that's no exaggeration. In a totally spontaneous gesture I rode upsides Ernie and put my arm round his shoulder, something picked up by the Press, who reported 'The obvious spirit in the yard was delightfully evident when young Bradley congratulated his colleague after crossing the line.' But Robert wasn't a demonstrative sort of bloke and it wasn't the kind of gesture he'd instigate.

There's no question that the 1982 Cheltenham Festival completely vindicated Michael's decision to let youth have its fling, as all the three Harewood winners were ridden by home boys. Dermot Browne, who would end the season as leading amateur, took the Kim Muir Chase on Political Pop, with Kevin Whyte winning the Two Mile Champion Chase on Rathgorman, a race Michael would go on to win for the next three seasons with Badsworth Boy.

Michael had an amazing capacity for work and must have expended a great amount of nervous energy. He hardly missed a veterinary conference and talked to athletes about their conditioning. He even went to Elland Road to talk with the physio and have a word with the groundsman about grass management.

But now he wanted to see me win the junior riders championship and Dermot take the amateurs title.

At that time, Dermot appeared to have everything, and his slide to disgrace is one of the great lessons for any youngster. He came from one of the best and most hard-working families in Ireland. His father, Liam, had been a decent rider and became one of the best trainers on the Flat, notably through his handling of Dara Monarch who would win the Irish 2,000 Guineas and St James's Palace Stakes at Royal Ascot in 1982.

Dermot came over with a good horse to ride, Ma Maison, and when he walked into the yard for the first time he looked the business. He was driving a top of the range Toyota, wearing a Crombie overcoat and had a gold credit card. To cap it all, he was a dark, good looking kid as well.

Dermot had a very good side to him and would do anything for you but I honestly think he was schizophrenic. He could boil into a seething rage if he thought people were against him or that a girlfriend was playing about. Not that he had any scruples on his own account. I was engaged at the time to the first serious love of my life, Sue Thewenetti, and although the ardour was beginning to cool, Dermot did his best to extinguish the flames by making several plays for her behind my back. I never bothered to find out if he had got up my inside but the relationship with Sue was soon finished.

Dermot is alleged to have done some evil deeds after he left the Dickinson yard. He took part in a BBC documentary that focused on doping in racing and although his face never showed on camera he was subsequently identified as the infamous 'Needleman'. On 27 October 1991 he was warned off for ten years by the Jockey Club for supplying information to a bookmaker and falsifying vaccination records for a horse he then trained, Total Sport. It must have broken the hearts of his parents but nine years earlier his star was bright and Michael set about making him champion amateur.

There were some good amateurs around that year, including Jim Wilson, Paul Webber, and Oliver Sherwood, who all went on to train. There was also young Jimmy Frost, who turned pro and outlasted me, still riding in the year 2000. But it was another budding trainer, Tim Easterby, who was the main obstacle and Dermot needed all the help he could get.

By mid-April I felt I had no chance of catching Donkey Dutton, so when Michael had me down to ride Prince of Padua at Southwell with an outstanding chance I went to his office the day before and told him he might as well put Dermot up. They duly won and my generosity was rewarded with a real purple patch.

I won on My Buck for Michael at Market Rasen and thirteen of my next nineteen rides won. To crown it all, I also won on my last ride of the season, Stop It, at Stratford, and did Donkey by three. He wasn't a happy little camper, but all I can think is that someone must have been looking down on me and it was probably Mum.

The struggle had its lighter moments and it was appropriate that

Andy Scott trained that last winner, the final one of eight he had supplied. Andy ran a timber business alongside training at Alnwick in Northumberland and loved a drink. One night he was blue-lighted by the police and down went the throttle on his Mercedes sports until there was a big enough gap to abandon the car and Andy was away - he knew the area better than the back of his hand. The police came back with tracker dogs and half an hour later Andy calmly walked out of the woods with his hands up shouting, 'I hope you got the driver as well.' He got away with it!

There was also a cheeky twist to winning the title which had Donkey spitting blood when he found out. I rang Wilf Storey for the ride on Little Abbey at Hexham on 31 May and Wilf said 'Sorry, he doesn't run, I've had him turned out in a field for two weeks.'

'Well,' I said, 'you'd better get him in and tidy him up because he's in a walk over tomorrow.' Wilf didn't need telling twice and we trotted over the line 24 hours later.

All the jump jockey's championships were sponsored by the Sportsman Club of London and the riders were invited to a celebration dinner at the club in Tottenham Court Road. I received my award from Jimmy Hill and then proceeded to make the first of many visits to the nightlife of the capital. Thankfully a lot of doormen like to have a fiver on a horse now and then and we had no problem getting into Stringfellows, which was the place to be seen at that time.

That narrow win over Donkey showed just how much I craved success but there were moments over the previous year when I'd been in despair. There would be very dark times in the coming season, too, but fortunately I had the right mentor to support me. I can never thank Michael enough.

CHAPTER 7
Standing in the shadows

On 9 November 1982 the Stewards of the Jockey Club made a public example of me to deter any of my colleagues who might fancy boosting their income illegally.

The two-month suspension for placing £50 on Cloudwalker at Cartmel ten weeks earlier left me reeling. There is never a good time for such a thing to happen but this was the worst, running through the heart of the jumping season when new rides are taken and partnerships cemented for the battles to come. As I arrived back in Wetherby that Monday night, Cheltenham in March seemed a very long way off.

I knew that the racing trade papers would be full of my punishment the following morning and that the racing desks of the national dailies would be giving me full back-page coverage. Considering how much more aggressive sports journalism is now than it was eighteen years ago I can look back and think that I may have got off a little lightly. But I'd also like to think that there was a certain guarded sympathy for the savagery of the sentence.

'Boy Blunder' screamed from the *Daily Star* and 'Bradley pays price for bet' was headlined in the *Mail*.

The *Sporting Life* didn't choose to lead their front page with the story, as they and the *Racing Post* would have certainly done today, choosing instead to publish a twelve paragraph factual report under the headline 'Two-month ban for Bradley.' The last two paragraphs told the story which was unfolding and would shadow me for the following two months. 'Bregawn is earmarked for Haydock on 15 December and the King George VI Chase on Boxing Day'.

'During his suspension Bradley will continue to work for Dickinson and do his two.'

I got mild consolation from the following Friday's *Life*, which carried the headline above the Jack Logan column, written by Sir David Llewellyn. 'Bradley's biggest crime was getting caught,' it read.

He had a point, but likewise, if you do the crime, be prepared to do your time and that's how I had to face the coming eight weeks. There was never any chance of an appeal for leniency and I was lucky to be working in a yard like the Dickinsons. Michael had moulded a fine team spirit. It wasn't quite all for one and one for all - how could it be with so many people anxious to ride the best horses in the yard - but there was a siege mentality which helped me through a rough period.

There would be a few wisecracks from some of the lads but most were sympathetic, well aware that if every jockey who's had a bet at some time owned up to his crime then there wouldn't be enough riders to take part in an average handicap hurdle.

Michael, the Boss and Mrs D were an object lesson in how to handle such a situation and Michael had shown typical solidarity by sending a wonderful written reference to the inquiry. But now it was time to put off thoughts of the racecourse and get back into the swing of regular work in the yard.

I rode out each morning as usual. Then, instead of dashing off to the races after first lot, I would stay on for second lot and possibly a third, but I wasn't given two horses to do over each evening. Instead I did the ones whose lads were away racing and, with the number of horses and winners Michael was sending out, there were always plenty. But while Michael appreciated the extra pair of hands, he knew I'd be far more use to him out in the field.

Michael always said I was easy to teach because I was anxious to learn and when it came to be allotted a job, he had the one for me. Every lad had a bit extra to do at the end of the day, sweep the yard, tidy the tack room, that sort of thing. And Michael found the right position for me.

He had always been up with the latest veterinary developments and continually monitored the blood of each horse. They were usually sent to Newmarket but a new laboratory had opened around the back of Grange Park in Wetherby and it was my job to take the samples there. I'd be off in my smock with a bucket, syringe and a box of needles to take blood samples from all the horses, then I'd shimmy round to the lab on my way home and drop them off.

I was still seeing the horses loaded on to the horsebox in the morning, but it was seeing them come back winners in the evening that gnawed at me in moments of weakness. And moments of weakness are a real problem for a jockey. Ask anyone who has been forced on to the sidelines for any length of time and they will tell you that it's the easiest thing in the world to snack between meals and drink too much. And while I've never been a big eater or drinker, my weight started to yo-yo. I never got to the crazy heights of the previous season because I was petrified of it happening again, but I had to be extremely careful.

The first serious bout of self-pity came soon after my suspension started. It was 15 December and Bregawn was due to make that appearance at Haydock in the Tommy Whittle Chase, which turned out to be a match with Little Owl, the 1981 Cheltenham Gold Cup winner. Bregawn and Robert Earnshaw started 4-11 favourite and I went to listen to the commentary in the local betting shop. But the horse was on one of his funny days and, after continually jumping right around the left-handed track he was easily outpaced. I admit I had mixed feelings about the race. Half of me wanted him to win, while the other, less charitable half was pleased he'd been beaten and that he looked like he missed me.

Christmas was also looming and for once I'd be able to get stuck into a decent lunch with all those calorie-laden extras and not need to worry about an extra three or four pounds creeping on. Christmas Day was always spent with the family in Wetherby, but quite often Christmas night wasn't. When Boxing Day duty called, I often went to the home of Michael Thompson, owner of Bray's Bakeries in Leeds, and used his sauna to melt away the excess.

But weight was the last thing on my mind and instead I was forced to sit out one of Michael Dickinson's most prolific feats of training.

Christmas Monday 1982 goes down as the day Michael sent out twelve winners, but there was a double blow for me. There was a very strong possibility that I would have been given the chance to ride the best chaser I ever sat on, Wayward Lad, in the King George VI Chase at Kempton on Boxing Day. With Robert Earnshaw aboard the even money favourite Silver Buck, I would have been the logical choice. In the event it was the masterly John Francome who brought the seven-year-old through to lead at the last and beat Fifty Dollars More and Richard Linley by two lengths. Silver Buck was a length and half further away, in a brave attempt to complete a hat-trick in the Christmas showpiece.

And what was the previous season's leading junior rider doing while all this success was occurring? Well, in the loosest sense I was involved. The number of runners meant a real shortage of lads. I was sent 'round the corner' to lead up Sooty Whyte on Happy Voyage at Wetherby, and although I made it to the winner's enclosure that Christmas, it never went on to my record - fortunately, neither did six other winners that day! Because I'd had my licence withdrawn, there was nothing to stop me having a bet until I got it back in February. I was well aware just how good the horses were and even helped Michael with their entries.

On that Monday morning I double checked the latest form lines in the *Sporting Life* and set about perming the good things, rounding off with an accumulator on six. I saw the first one connect at Wetherby when Sooty Whyte scored on Delius at 15-8, then Chris Pimlott brought the second home, W Six Times at Market Rasen. After leading Happy Voyage back to his box I just caught the end of Wayward Lad winning the King George at 7-2, and at Wolverhampton five minutes later Dermot Browne completed a treble for Michael with Slieve Bracken at 6-4 having previously won on Brunton Park and Prominent Artist. Just two to go, and my buddy Banner Bell made it five out of five when Londolozi at 5-2 won the Sedgefield handicap hurdle. Now there was just one to go. It was our last runner of the day at Huntingdon, Thornacre in the novice hurdle, due to be ridden by 'outside' jockey Richard Rowe.

The bare result came over with no commentary. It was Thornacre at 2-1 and I'd hit the jackpot. I collected £12,000. All legal and above board with no jockey's licence. It certainly softened the blow to my pride at not riding any of them. But I'd have gladly given it back with interest if I could have ridden Wayward Lad. Money will always be very important but it's never been my god. Whoever said that 'the best things in life are free' was correct. Money can't buy health or love.

And there was one other lad in the yard who had even more reason to enjoy that Christmas. Banner's dad liked a bet and his brave decision to add two more winners to his investment netted £26,000 - no wonder Banner made sure he did the weight at Sedgefield!

When my cash winnings were collected from two local betting shops - there was more to come from Norm's account - it was straight round to the Renault main dealers in Leeds to splurge out on my first new car, a top of the range Fuego 1.6 in black. Banner's dad was generous to him and he chose blue. I must admit we might just have put a few noses out of joint when we cruised into the yard the next day and parked them side by side.

For the record, the other winners Michael trained that day were Marnik, who was ridden by Geordie Dun at Huntingdon. Fearless Imp completed a double for Chris Pimlott and B Jaski at Sedgefield ridden by Jonathan Davies the lad who looked after Bregawn.

There was an unhappy sequel concerning one of the Magnificent twelve, Thornacre. Richard Rowe had told Michael that he thought he was one of the best horses he'd ever sat on. He was a big black brute who looked a chaser but the next year he was bad to school and even Robert Earnshaw couldn't get him over the first fence on his chasing debut at Wetherby.

When Michael came into the breakfast room shortly after to find someone who would ride him next time all the senior boys made their excuses, Pimmy, Sooty and myself. Michael was great like that. If you didn't want to do something you told him straight out, man to man, it was just like talking to one of the other boys.

This unique relationship is best illustrated by an incident when we conditionals were treading back the ground after a schooling session. It was early in the season and a recognised part of your job. When we finished, instead of getting on the tractor and trailer and heading back to find more work in the yard we stripped off our shirts and lay down on the grass sunbathing. Ten minutes later, a long shadow was cast over us. It was Michael. But instead of the bollocking which we deserved and would have got in any other yard, he peeled his shirt off and lay down with us for half an hour, looking up into the sky and talking about the plans he had for us and the horses in the months to come. But that was Bud, just priceless.

When it came to Thornacre there were limits to friendship, but young Patrick Farrell was one of the new boys and anxious to make a good impression. The schooling session which followed created

84

plenty of interest, and unfortunately for Paddy the beast didn't let the senior boys judgement down. Thornacre buried him at the first schooling fence, springing his collarbone. Never volunteer to ride a bad jumper, it's bad enough when you've got to.

There's often a reason why horses jump badly or appear ungenuine and it became apparent in the case of Thornacre. He was diagnosed as a wobbler soon after, which means a horse is suffering from spinal problems.

January dragged by and I couldn't wait to load my tack into the boot of my new car and head for the track. On 5 February my licence came back and I was cleared for action. I'd ridden ten winners before the suspension, but there was plenty of catching up to do. And it was typical of Michael that he had one ready for my first ride back on my home turf at Wetherby.

CHAPTER 8
The famous five

The stigma of the two-month ban still hung over me but the mental armour of invincibility that is part of youth was strapped on tight. I felt I had even more to prove and plenty of lost time to make up for.

As soon as my licence came back I made the short trip to Wetherby. But even my fertile imagination could not have envisaged what lay ahead in the next six weeks, when the pendulum swung majestically my way.

Righthand Man was the chosen one for the Selby Handicap Chase and he was rock solid. Not that he'd started his life at Harewood with much promise. He showed us absolutely nothing early on and in an almost unprecedented move one morning, Michael stuck a pair of blinkers on and told me to get stuck into him. He was slow as a hearse and everyone thought he was next to useless but that morning the blinkers brought out the fire in him and he never wore them again. When he went to the racecourse for the first time at Huntingdon with Ernie on him he bolted up and developed into a very decent novice chaser and top class staying handicapper.

It was a measure of the preparation that Michael put into his novices that Righthand Man had to carry 11st 3lb against seasoned campaigners. He'd won his first novice chase at Sedgefield on 19 October under Robert Earnshaw and then I won the Charlie Hall Pattern Chase on him at Wetherby eleven days later from Galway Blaze, a horse whose career was blighted by injury. His trainer Jimmy FitzGerald produced a great feat in bringing him back to win the Hennessy Gold Cup at Newbury three years later.

The spotlight was beaming on me as BBC viewers saw Righthand Man go off second favourite for the Selby Chase behind Final Argument, who was pulled up by Neale Doughty after being badly hampered four out. Righthand Man, carrying the white, black braces and red cap of Mrs Muriel Haggas, grandmother of Newmarket trainer William Haggas, jumped to the front two fences from home and stayed on to hold Phil The Fluter and Phil Tuck by five lengths.

Although I'd bent the rules I always had the feeling of local loyalty around Wetherby and the warm reception I received on returning to unsaddle gave my confidence for the future a big boost. *Chaseform Notebook* also helped with a nice comment from their senior race reader Alan Amies which included, 'This excellent young rider will not be long regaining his position in the top flight.'

I'd missed Wayward Lad in the King George and also tutored Dermot Browne on how to ride Allten Glazed for Mick Naughton before his win in the £10,000 Mecca Bookmakers Hurdle at Sandown in early December. And just to underline what had gone before me, Righthand Man had sent Michael past the £200,000 mark for prize money that season. My statistics weren't looking bad either at that early stage of my career, having clocked up 400 rides and 76 winners at a strike rate of almost one in five.

It was impossible to see that comeback win getting any sweeter but it did. My best mate from school, Steve Youlden, had followed me into stables a couple of years behind and was battling his way through as a 7lb claimer. Just 30 minutes later he won the novice hurdle on Emandar for Harry Wharton and that was as good as it could get for that day. It would have been too flash to call for champagne in the weighing room, but Saturday night was only hours away and the boys from 'Uncle' Gordon's riding school had come good together. 'Boo Boo' and I thought we'd just about done enough to warrant a tour of the Leeds nightspots to recycle some of their finest lager. We did the job well but it was up at 6.30 for work the next morning. Although I'd ceased to be a regular lad I was still expected to muck out each morning. It's called many things, including character building and keeping heads from swelling, and I was going to keep doing it until the end of that season, no matter what happened.

I'd got back on track at the right time because Cheltenham was only five weeks away and Bregawn had been on the missing list since his blip in the two-runner race with Little Owl at Haydock. It was time for him to tune up and prepare to go one better in the Gold Cup.

Michael chose the Jim Ford Chase at Wincanton, a race the Dickinsons had also used as a Gold Cup warm-up for Gay Spartan in 1979, and it would be a first trip to the track for both horse and rider. Wincanton takes some knowing and is perched on a plateau amid the Somerset hills. On the four-hour journey from Wetherby, I played the race over in my mind and, even though I knew we would start favourite, I was well aware that Bregawn wasn't straightforward and we were up against top quality horses. Brown Chamberlin was one of the previous season's best novice chasers and Combs Ditch had beaten him six lengths on their previous outing. Both had plenty of pace and Wincanton is a track that drains well and even in February can be lightning fast with the emphasis firmly on speed.

Bregawn did it wrong from the start and lost twelve lengths.

Because there was no pace on he'd made up the ground by the fourth and was in front at the tenth and a sitting target. Combs Ditch swept through to head him two out after Brown Chamberlin had dropped away following mistakes, but Bregawn knew how to fight at the end of a race and was only outpaced by half a length close home.

I knew that on the day I hadn't made enough use of his stamina but I'd been worried because of the ground he'd lost at the start. Michael, aware of the problems a jockey faces and also that hindsight is 20-20 vision, decided that Bregawn needed a boost to his confidence before the Gold Cup. He sifted through the Programme Book and came up with the Newent Chase, a limited handicap at Hereford worth £1,800 over three miles one furlong just twelve days before Cheltenham.

Bregawn was in a class of his own, a fact endorsed by no starting price being returned on the eight-runner race, but again he planted himself at the start and Graham Burrows, who travelled Bregawn to the races that day, still had hold of his head when the tape went up. It needed the long tom of the starters assistant to eventually get him going some twenty-five lengths adrift. But he was in a different gear and was in front by the sixth to win by a distance, head in his chest. It was just the psychological thrust he needed and it didn't do me much harm either. We were ready for Cheltenham.

Unless you've been professionally involved in jump racing, it's impossible to explain what the Cheltenham and Aintree Festivals mean to the individual. To use a football analogy, each race is a cup final with the Champion Hurdle, Gold Cup and National as a League title.

Because Michael was exerting an ever-growing influence over the jumping scene, he was the target for everyone, both professionally and in the media. Weeks before the meeting everyone wanted his thoughts on the three days and what his team would be and it soon became clear that he would have five runners in the Gold

Cup.

The question now was who would ride them?

The first two names on the team sheet were Bradley on Bregawn, Earnshaw on Silver Buck. No question. That left Captain John, Wayward Lad and Ashley House and, under normal circumstances, Harewood jockeys would have ridden all three. But while amateur Dermot Browne got lucky by being given the mount on least fancied Ashley House, the mounts on Captain John and Wayward Lad went to 'outside' jockeys David Goulding and Jonjo O'Neill. This left Chris Pimlott and Kevin Whyte out in the cold and it wasn't until many years later that I asked Michael why.

The Boss, still a major influence in the yard, felt that Pimmy had taken rides on too many poor jumpers and wasn't riding as well as in previous seasons. For Kevin it was simply a case of going through a bad patch with just one decent horse to ride, namely the crack two-mile chaser Rathgorman. It was a tough decision but nice guys often finish second.

Michael started preparing the three homeboys on the previous Sunday morning, taking us into the office after breakfast to sort out rides for that week and making a preliminary plan for the Gold Cup. We would open with Delius, unbeaten in three starts, in the Supreme Novices', which began the meeting on Tuesday and would be doubly represented in the Kim Muir Chase for amateur riders with Rednael and Marnik. Browne would be on Delius and Rednael and the top Irish amateur Ted Walsh, now a highly successful trainer and television pundit, would partner Marnik.

Then, as no more than a casual aside, he said that because I hadn't got a ride for the yard on the first day and only had Brunton Park in the Coral Golden Hurdle Final on the Wednesday, I could ride Sabin du Loir, with Pimmy on Lettoch, in the Sun Alliance Novices' Hurdle which starts the second day. Those two rides and Bregawn were going to thrust me to the top of the tree by the end of the week and banish the Cartmel business from most people's minds

91

- apart from a few at Portman Square.

But by the end of the first day Michael was in despair. Delius had started 6-4 favourite and finished fifth, but worse still, lame. Marnik and Rednael went off first and second favourites but fell and were sixth respectively. After such an anticlimax there was no misplaced confidence as we returned to action on the second day.

Sabin du Loir was a typically shrewd buy from France by the Boss. He'd only won in the provinces and when he got him home Michael wondered why he'd bought him. Sabin wasn't the biggest, but the Boss just smiled and told him to 'wait and see'. When he did appear as a four-year-old in February he had grown a bit and never stopped improving, winning three times before he reached Cheltenham, ridden by Dermot, Kevin and myself.

The day before the race the Boss, who owned him, sold Sabin on to Brian Kilpatrick for £20,000 and I don't think an owner ever got better value. Despite having leg problems the gelding went on to become a real chasing favourite, moving to David Murray-Smith and finally to Martin Pipe, where he proved top class up to three miles. Brian, a man who hates to see his horses abused with the whip, continues to keep him as a pet and the only problem the old horse gets now is the occasional touch of sunburn on his nose in summer.

That day at Cheltenham he was dynamite against a mare who would become a Cheltenham legend, the Champion Hurdle and Gold Cup winner Dawn Run. But this was Sabin's day. He just would not accept defeat and he outstayed her up the hill to win by three lengths, with the subsequent 1986 Grand National winner West Tip third and stable first string Lettoch sixth.

It was typical of Michael when he said after the race that the result 'saved me from committing suicide'. But there were much better things around the corner on Thursday.

Jonjo O'Neill, who had a ghost-written column in the *Daily Mirror*, was probably first to acknowledge that training the first five home in the Gold Cup was a possibility when saying, 'Michael Dickinson could fill the first five places in the Gold Cup ... I'm told it's 150-1 about Michael's Famous Five.'

There is no question that the build up to a big meeting was mental torture for Michael. He had dropped a stone in weight from an already lean frame since Christmas and looked gaunt as we met up nearly three hours before the first race. None of the Harewood jockeys had rides before the Gold Cup and Michael took us along with Ginny Leng, the three-day event champion, to walk the course and formulate some sort of plan. Ernie and I had already ridden in the race, so it was as much for Dermot as anyone, and Michael said that ideally he'd like him to make it on Ashley House. He wasted his breath.

I'd ordered a new pair of race-riding boots a year before from the waif-like old Italian Mr Tazali, who used to shuffle round the racecourses. He wasn't cheap but he was without doubt the best when it came to fine leather and boot making.

Never being one for superstitions, the new boots went into action for the first time at 3.32 on 17 March 1983 and they never featured in a more important race.

Although Michael would give plenty of instructions before a race, in the final analysis it was up to you. And with Dermot deciding against making the running, I followed my instincts when Bregawn gave no trouble at the start after being brilliantly led in by Michael's travelling head lad, Graham Rennison. I knew he was going sweetly and took over from the outsider Whiggie Geo at the sixth because I knew we weren't going fast enough. I was travelling too well. Dermot decided to help me along a bit from the twelfth to the sixteenth and it was at the next that Bregawn made his only serious mistake. But he was like a battleship and desperately hard to get the better of when he was firing.

At the top of the hill, where so many hearts have been left speared on the birch, both Captain John and Silver Buck came to apply pressure. Bregawn was equal to it and lengthened again. Unlike Silver Buck, who'd had a knock and missed vital work, he was tuned to perfection. Wayward Lad, who'd also suffered a slight setback, was under maximum pressure, too.

Bregawn bounced over the tricky downhill fence and for the first time I thought it was just possible I might get the big one. Only two to jump and everything to play for, just the last two fences to take.

Make no mistake, running to face two out in the Cheltenham Gold Cup is one of the most daunting feelings in racing. If you are in front then the climb to the finish looks as steep as Everest. If you are five lengths down with your mount plugging on with one gear, then it's never going to be far enough.

I had to ask Bregawn for everything and was very hard on him - these days it would certainly be called excessive use of the whip - but there was only one Gold Cup. Bregawn emptied his pockets for me and battled like a tiger up the hill as the roar of a huge crowd ricocheted off the stands. I sensed something on my inside and immediately switched my whip through to the left - once again I could thank my wall of dreams. There was no way I'd lose this in the stewards room. The main challenger was Captain John, very tired and swaying left and right like a drunk as he chased us home by five lengths with Wayward Lad a length and a half third. Now it was time for Michael to look back and scout for his other troops. Although tired and weakening rapidly to finish tailed off, Silver Buck still held fourth and Ashley House, though out on his feet completed the greatest training feat in jumping history by plodding on to finish twenty-five lengths further back in fifth. The searching gallop that Bregawn had been able to maintain had broken the heart of every other runner. Sadly, in the end it broke his, too.

I firmly believe that he was so brave that day and put in so much effort that he was totally exhausted. It blew his mind and, a bit like a boxer who wins a championship but gets badly beaten doing it,

Bregawn just didn't want to go through that pain barrier again.

People have got short memories and a year later, when he'd lost his enthusiasm, he was likened in the Press to being 'cross as a bag of weasels' and 'as interested as an alcoholic in a lemonade factory'. I know I'll never be able to thank him enough for what he did for me that March afternoon and the first thing I did as we crossed the line was lean up his neck and hug him. It's something I continued to do until I retired. You can't do it without them.

Two other rituals have been constants throughout my career. The night before a big race I'd always ask my mum for a bit of help. And when walking back in after a winner I always thought of Norm at home, painstakingly recording everything on the video and feeling proud of the effort he put into me as a kid.

Both Mum and Dad were with me as I basked in that magnificent glow walking back to the winner's enclosure, moving towards that vast bank of people surrounding it and being swept along by the sea of well-wishers who beat the security cordon each year.

Michael, just eleven years older than me at thirty-three, was wearing a thin smile and admitted he was drained rather than elated and said with typical feeling, 'The last month has been absolute hell, things just got worse and worse the nearer we came to the race. The pressure has been almost unbearable.'

Michael ended up watching the race on TV in the weighing room and 'was just screaming for the boys'. He added, 'I'm fairly hard on myself and very hard on them.' He then gave me a single plaudit that meant a great deal and gave me a large vote of confidence in public 'Graham's a very good judge of pace.' I could live with that.

If I'm really honest, all I wanted to do after I'd weighed in was to milk every possible minute of the adulation, presentations and TV interviews. Instead I had to ride Nicky Tam for Andy Scott in the Ritz Club Chase and I needed that like a bout of toothache. Just to top it off I put up 2lb overweight at 10st 8lb.

After virtually pulling up Nicky Tam on the run-in I still had another great moment to come. A second place on Brunton Park and the win on Sabin du Loir just edged me home in the Ritz Club award for leading rider at the meeting. How lucky was I that the winners were spread around thinly that year? The likes of Jamie Osborne and Tony McCoy have done it with five in recent years and I did it with two and a bit!

As dusk set in over the Cotswolds I stepped up to receive the trophy from Princess Anne and, ever the showman, I'd slipped back to get changed into Bregawn's colours.

I was one of the last to leave Cheltenham that night, going round the owners' boxes just as I had done with Robert Earnshaw the year before. Except this year, I did it on my own.

Back at Harewood the boys were getting ready for a serious party and I finally caught up with them at the Flying Pizza. Although it wasn't quite their style, Mrs D, the Boss and Michael were there and they stuck it out until about 11p.m. They could see my celebrations were taking an inevitable toll and Mrs D knew my form for getting up in the morning better than most. As she turned to leave she caught my eye and fixed me with that all-knowing look: 'Don't be late in the morning Brad.'

'Definitely not Mrs D.'

No sooner had the officers left than the soldiers were on the move to the Spacey Houses where Charlie Gillis would be holding the doors back and risking his licence for 'a late one' that was in a very good cause and would never be seen again. Looking back, I have never seen young men with so much ready money. They had all lumped on at 150-1 for Michael to train the first five home and at 33-1 to handle the first three.

And although we went on until around 3 a.m. there wasn't the slightest chance of me being late in. Yorkshire TV had sent a crew round to film us in the Flying Pizza and they were back to finish the job in the yard next morning. I wasn't going to miss that.

But there was one absentee from the party, a man who'd taught me so much on the schooling ground and done such a good job with Bregawn in his early days.

Robert Earnshaw didn't attend. He said that he didn't feel as though he'd got anything to celebrate.

Strange, considering he'd won the Two-Mile Champion Chase on Badsworth Boy on Wednesday.

There were still a few twists left in the season, not least the surprise I got when my Weatherbys cheque arrived around £2,000 light. It transpired that the winning percentage for jump jockeys in Pattern races had been reduced to 4.48 in line with the Flat. The rule was subsequently reversed and, in any case, Bregawn's owners had promised me a £4,000 present if I won. True to their word, they gave it to me before I left Cheltenham.

I also had my first ride over the Aintree fences in the Topham on Nicky Tam for Andy Scott and Michael provided my first ride round in the Grand National on Political Pop. Although we never really troubled Corbiere and Ben de Haan, we finished an honourable seventh without a serious jumping error.

The last race of the meeting saw me register my first win at Liverpool thanks to the ultra tough Sabin du Loir. Back in his own age group of four-year-olds, the two miles five furlongs of the Fosters Novice Hurdle was made for him and he was never in any danger after leading three out, ending the season unbeaten in five starts.

That victory brought Michael on to 114 winners for the season and equalled the record set by W.A. Stephenson. By the end of the season he'd set a new target of 120, an exceptional total which would stand until Martin Pipe burst upon the scene.

I finished with thirty-four winners, only four less than the previous season, not bad considering I'd been out for two months. It is also interesting to note that £1 placed on every one of my mounts would have yielded a profit of £40. Not that I'd have dared to do such a thing, I'd learned my lesson.

CHAPTER 9
Goodbye to two stars

Those who are closely connected with racing, and jumping in particular, often remark that the game can tame lions. Sadly, I was about to have my tail severely pulled.

With all the impetuosity that comes with youth and inexperience I reckoned I'd got the game sussed. I'd won the Gold Cup and all the right people were taking notice of me. I'd even stopped doing my two horses at the yard and only came in to ride out in the morning, just like the top jocks.

But two massive blows were waiting to hit me. Both could have put my career into rapid reverse from which I would never recover. I was lucky they didn't.

Michael Dickinson was now the professional focus of my life. He stood head and shoulders above his contemporaries and was breaking new boundaries as he rewrote the record books. But most important to me, I was emerging as his chosen one. I may have been professionally arrogant, cocky if you like, but as Michael always said, 'Brad was easy to teach because he wanted to learn.' And I'd learned plenty from Michael. He knew that whatever I did in a race, I'd be doing it for the benefit of the horse and the yard and, although

Robert Earnshaw and I would now be officially sharing the rides, I knew I'd end up as top dog. Then the blow landed.

Michael called all the senior riders and staff into the Harewood office in mid-November to break the news that he was leaving to take the job as private trainer to the biggest Flat owner of that period, Robert Sangster. The pools magnate was playing for massive stakes on the Flat and seemed untouchable. His connection with the legendary Vincent O'Brien at Ballydoyle had yielded Derby winners of the calibre of The Minstrel and Golden Fleece, plus the one that got away, El Gran Senor. Alleged had won the Prix de l'Arc de Triomphe back to back in 1977 and '78 and that fine racemare Detroit, trained by the late Olivier Douieb, went on to provide a third in 1980.

Sangster had bought the historic Manton Estate on the outskirts of Marlborough in Wiltshire and was intent on regaining past glories which had seen Alec Taylor send out a succession of Classic winners from the heart of the Downs earlier in the century.

In Michael he must have seen a reinvention of Vincent O'Brien, who was beginning to wind down after a fabulous career and had been the catalyst for the Sangster success story. O'Brien had earned his stripes in jump racing to the point where he seemed able to perform miracles and Michael in turn had shown that the near impossible was achievable. Plus, there would be the strength of Sangster's Swettenham Stud behind the yard and a long-standing link with Coolmore Stud in Ireland. Nothing would be spared in the rebuilding of the estate to cater for the needs of the late twentieth century and beyond and Michael was to be given free rein.

Despite the lure of Manton I was still amazed when Michael said yes to Sangster's offer and, thinking purely of myself, felt gutted and that the game had finished. I couldn't believe he would leave something like Harewood having poured 100 per cent of his time and energy into the place. I didn't think it could be money, because it just didn't interest Michael. It wasn't until many years later I discovered that money was indeed one of the principal motivations, but typically not for himself.

He told me a story concerning one of the vital backroom boys at Harewood, George Foster, who looked after all the leg problems and went on to train successfully in his own right. Ironically, he returned to Manton in late 1998 as assistant to Peter Chapple-Hyam and when Peter was sacked the following year temporarily took over the licence before John Gosden was installed by Robert Sangster for the start of the 2000 season.

Michael said, 'One of the reasons I moved was the staff. George Foster asked for a Saturday off to go to a wedding in Scotland and when I went into the yard on that Saturday morning he was there. I asked him why he wasn't in Scotland. He told me that the electricity bill had come in and that it was either pay that or go to Scotland but he couldn't do both.

'It brought it home to me that, despite all the success and training 100 winners a season, I couldn't pay these excellent people enough to make a decent living, so when the Manton offer came along I took it.'

Michael would continue at Harewood until the end of the 1983-84 season, when Mrs D would take over the licence. The Boss had suffered an injury when a straw bale fell on him and although a great battler, he would never be quite the same again.

Much as Michael tried to put Manton to the back of his mind and continue to train jumpers for the last time, Manton was a high profile appointment. Inevitably, people were waiting to see how far the boy wonder would rise or fall. It is a matter of racing history that the descent was alarming before Michael resurfaced with Breeders' Cup glory in America.

So what went wrong at Manton?

Michael is certain that he had the wrong ammunition for his guns and said, 'Robert had many of his mares covered by Golden Fleece and Kings Lake, neither of which produced much speed. They were big two-year-olds, many of them immature at 16.1 hands.

'One day a very good lad came up to say that we weren't doing enough with the two-year-olds and I respected his opinion. A few days later another lad who had been with me for a long time and knew what he was talking about said to me that we were doing too much with the two-year-olds.

'And the most worrying thing about the two conversations was that they were both right. I wasn't doing enough to win races with them but in turn I was doing too much for horses that were immature.'

Some things didn't change with Michael. He was adamant that privacy had to be maintained and anyone who worked at Manton had to sign his equivalent of the Official Secrets Act. Even those who came visiting had to sign. He didn't want anything disclosed about methods of training, right down to the vitamin and diet supplements. Because Michael worked so hard to get everything right he was obsessive about secrecy.

He was quite good with the Press, although the time Sir Peter O'Sullevan called and nailed a warning to the Manton mast must have alarmed him. Michael said, 'He had one look around the horses and went straight out and backed Lester Piggott, who'd just started training, to train more winners than me. He could see what I'd got to work with and he won his bet.'

After supervising the lengthy rebuilding programme Michael moved in for one disastrous season in 1986. It yielded only four winners and he was sacked before the following year, no doubt to the satisfaction of a small-minded minority. He was succeeded by Barry Hills, who split with Sangster and built his own complex outside Lambourn following a disagreement. Next to move in was Peter Chapple-Hyam. That young man could not have done better and trained Rodrigo De Triano to win the 1992 Guineas and the Derby with Dr Devious, a horse Sangster had sold on. Despite having his best stock sold from under him to maintain the upkeep of

Manton, Chapple-Hyam continued to send out Group One winners until a poor season in 1999 saw his departure.

Michael had several offers to return to jumping but that was never on the agenda of a man who is exceptionally proud. It was typical of him to plough his own furrow and resurface in America, where he won the Breeders' Cup Mile with Da Hoss in 1996 and brought the gelding back after missing a year through injury to win the same ultra competitive race again in 1998 after just one prep race. The Yanks had already christened Michael 'the mad genius' and the form guide for the Breeders' Cup said tersely, 'The trainer's a god if Da Hoss wins off one prep.'

Wrong, the trainer was Michael Dickinson.

But before Michael left Harewood I was going to be involved in one of the most heartbreaking accidents that happened during all my years in racing, the death of a Dickinson legend.

There were so many fine chasers handled by the Dickinsons that it might seem unfair to single out one, but there is no doubt Silver Buck was special. He'd won successive King George VI chases in 1979 and 1980 and the Cheltenham Gold Cup of 1982. At the age of eleven the glory days were behind him, but despite the heroic efforts of Wayward Lad and Bregawn he was still the apple of the Dickinsons eye. He'd earned £150,000, which, though trivial by Flat standards, was a jumping record.

He was entitled to receive a pampered retirement from his devoted owner Mrs Christine Feather, but a cruel twist was to rob him of this and throw me into despair. Although he was getting on in years, Silver Buck was still a handful both in the yard and on the gallops and only his regular rider Robert Earnshaw or Kevin Whyte rode him out each day. He could be spooked by anything, even a bird flying up from a bush or a piece of paper rustling in the wind. It was probably those nerves which made him the great chaser he was. He was also the strongest horse in the yard and ran away with people right, left and centre.

One morning both his regular riders were away from the yard and I was given the job of riding him out. But there was one fact I wasn't aware of as I took him out of his box, namely that someone had to hold his head while you mounted because he was liable to bolt. Ignorant of this, I just threw my body across the saddle, swung my leg over and we were united in an instant, no worries. And that was my undoing.

We got on really well and did a steady bit of work, cantering a couple of times around the all weather, and he hardly pulled at all.The feeling was that if I got on so well with him, why not let me keep on him. So next morning I did the same thing again, heaved myself into the saddle and everything was grand.

The third morning I was last out in company with Ronnie Beggan, who had come over from Ireland to ride as an amateur and would later make a successful career as a professional. We started with just a walk up the road and a little trot to warm the horses up before coming back to do a canter. As we were coming past the yard it started to rain, so we went in to collect some waterproofs.

Once I'd got them on, I mounted Silver Buck as I had done before, but this time the waterproof fabric made a rasping sound on the saddle which he hadn't expected. He just took off. Running in a blind panic, he went flat out across the yard with me across his back helpless to stop him. I knew that if I jumped off I wouldn't be able to keep my feet and stop him, so I threw my arms around his neck in a vain attempt to put the brakes on. It was useless. He never broke stride until he fly-leapt a four foot wide sand drainage channel, but that hardly checked him and the dull thud as he hit the stable block wall side on was sickening and still haunts me now.

He lay heaving on the concrete path for a couple of minutes and I was beside myself with panic, fearing the worst but not daring to think it might happen. Ronnie went round to the house to find Mrs D and when she came around the corner she had a look on her face that I'd never seen before or since, thank god.

Silver Buck was half up but could barely stand on his back legs, although we eventually got him into the nearest box and I stood there holding him. By now, Mrs D had broken down in tears of anguish and frustration at my stupidity.

I stood in the box with him all alone until the vet came and I'd have done anything to tell him how sorry I was. It was 20 minutes that felt like 20 hours. Periodically, people would put their head over the box door and say nothing. Robert looked over and was in tears. Silver Buck was his pride and joy. They'd supped with the gods together. He was his baby and I'd almost certainly killed him.

Silver Buck was now in a state of shock, shivering but black with sweat and steam coming off him. I prayed like I'd never done before that the vet would be able to save him. Nobody could bring themselves to come and say goodbye to the horse, they were just hoping against hope that he'd be alright. To stand there and wait for the vet was mental torture of the worst kind, far worse than anything I endured much later in my career. I knew it was my fault.

It didn't take the vet long to diagnose a compound fracture of the pelvis and the words no one wanted to hear cut through the air like a scalpel, 'I'm very sorry, there's nothing I can do. I'll have to put him down.'

With that, Mrs D let all her frustration go at me. 'What have you done to my horse? You silly boy, you bloody silly boy.' Quite justifiably a lot worse followed in the heat of the moment.

I didn't know what to do, whether to get into my car and go straight away. But I was down to ride a third lot, so I tacked up and went off up the road.

I hadn't been gone long when the Boss drove upsides me with another lad in the car. He took me off the horse, put the other lad on and drove me back to the yard. That man was absolutely beautiful to me and I'll never forget what he said, 'Brad, I know what horses are like and things like this happen. But Mrs D is going bananas and so is Michael. Neither of them want to see you again. 'I'll slip you into the car park, you just jump into your car and don't come back to the yard until we get in touch with you.'

Although I'd bought my own house I went home to 38 Second Avenue and was inconsolable. I'd gone from Gold Cup hero to pariah in one stupid move. There was nothing Norm or anyone could say to console me and even Banner and some of the boys from the yard were wasting their breath when they rang to cheer me up. I thought I was finished.

Then I got a phone call at six o'clock on the second night, just after the horses had been fed. 'Brad? It's Mrs D here, how are you? Everything all right? Good, well, come back to work and I'll see you in the morning.'

That was the end of it as far as the Dickinsons were concerned and it was never mentioned again. But to this day I still don't like talking about it. I was one of the family and I feel that in a moment of carelessness I let them down badly.

There were some of the right kind of memories, notably riding my one hundredth winner on Golden Fancy for Ian Vickers at Cartmel on 10 July 1984. And riding three winners, two seconds and a third for Michael at Wetherby on Boxing Day topped off by Badsworth Boy in the Castleford Handicap Chase. I also struck up a winning partnership with one of the best novice chasers of the season, Lettoch.

The previous season he'd been Chris Pimlott's ride over hurdles, but Pimmy was falling out of favour and it was my good luck to get Lettoch. Pimmy probably rode too many bad horses outside the yard and this counted against him. He eventually gave up and became a successful agent for, among others, Graham McCourt and myself.

Lettoch took an important early scalp one day at Stratford when starting at 1-2, he beat the subsequent 1985 Cheltenham Gold Cup winner Forgive 'N Forget by a neck.

After getting the better of Noddy's Ryde in the Dipper Novices'

Chase at Newcastle he was cantering when falling two out in the Sun Alliance Chase at Cheltenham and went on to prove he was probably the best novice of that season.

His last run was in handicap company and I unwisely deserted him for Ashley House in the Whitbread Gold Cup at Sandown in April, which he would have won with any luck. Robert Earnshaw rode him and they were badly hampered at the third fence by the fall of Donegal Prince. He still managed to lead three out, but in the finest finish I've ever seen to that race he went under by a short head to the Queen Mother's Special Cargo with Diamond Edge the same distance away in third. But Lettoch paid a high price for his gameness. He was put down shortly after having broken down on both forelegs in the race.

Cheltenham had been a big anticlimax compared to the previous year and Bregawn had run up the white flag in the Gold Cup when only sixth to Burrough Hill Lad. He never won in Britain again and switched to Ireland, where he won a handicap hurdle for Paddy Mullins at Limerick Junction in 1984-85. He ended with the *Timeform* double squiggle for being ungenuine, but I'll never forget what that little bruiser did for me when it mattered.

Sadly, the deterioration of Bregawn mirrored events at Harewood. The old team was beginning to break up with Michael's departure. Mrs D wasn't going to take on any young horses and more worrying still was that severe injury to the Boss caused by that accident with a bale of hay.

In the five years that Mrs D carried on the Boss had severe dips in his health, but he was an extremely resilient man with a great sense of humour. I remember coming back with the string from the gallops and walking past the house one morning during a particularly worrying time concerning his health.

We all looked over when he suddenly appeared between the curtains of his bedroom window and shouted, 'Don't worry boys, I'm still here! I'm not dead yet!' I'll always remember the broad smile on his face that morning. He finally died in 1991 and was, quite simply, one of the best and kindest men I have ever met.

CHAPTER 10
Gentleman Jim

They say that nothing lasts forever and by the start of the 1984-85 season the Harewood team, a dominating force in jump racing for nearly a decade was slowly dismantling.

Michael Dickinson's decision to cut a new path in the mercenary world of Flat racing with Robert Sangster was the start of a gradual but inevitable erosion. Even the greatest football teams are eventually beaten by time.

No doubt if Mrs D had been twenty years younger and the Boss enjoyed better health the ship would have been steadied and strengthened. As it was, despite pronouncements to the contrary, the dominant days of Harewood were effectively over. There would be top quality winners coming out of the yard, but not with such regularity, and the vital infusion of new blood began to stop.

While no one, least of all myself who owed the Dickinsons so much, wanted to jump ship, it is a hard fact of life that you have to look after yourself. If you don't then neither will anyone else.

Kevin Whyte took on the role of assisting Mrs D and still took the occasional ride, although his totals dropped to one and none in the following two seasons before he relinquished his licence.

Chris Pimlott decided against giving full blooded rides to horses that didn't deserve it and, after recording just one winner for the season, he also retired.

Weight was always going to get the better of Banner Bell, who finally gave up the struggle and trained nearby at Castleford. He never handled the quality of horse he'd ridden at Harewood, but if they were good enough they won, and hardly ever unbacked.

Robert Earnshaw accepted an agreement to ride for David Gandolfo in the south whilst maintaining his long link with the Dickinsons and would carry on for another season.

'Rabbit' as he was often called in the yard, had lived on his nerves for quite a while and would get very wound up before he rode. Unable to sleep sometimes before big races, he would retreat to a corner of the weighing room and talk to no one. He certainly wasn't frightened of injury and I just think that the big occasion got to him.

When Robert did hand in his licence he took the same route as several of my former colleagues, including Paul Barton, Phil Tuck and Simon Cowley, who turned from poachers into gamekeepers and joined the Jockey Club police force as stewards secretaries. At least they can understand the problems a rider encounters in the heat of a race. Strange as it may seem, with my wealth of experience both on course and in enquiries, I was never approached to see if I would like to join the club!

Dermot Browne, or 'Murphy' as we called him from the day he joined the yard, accepted a good offer to go to Lambourn as first jockey to Nick Gaselee. It seemed a good move for the talented former amateur champion, joining a yard which housed such good horses as Berlin and Bolands Cross, while still retaining the ride on Mrs D's top class hurdler Browne's Gazette who would whip round at the start of the following season's Champion Hurdle and lose all chance. There have been many aspersions cast over this particular ride, fuelled no doubt by the fact that Browne's Gazette had been heavily backed. But I have to say that Browne's Gazette was very fractious at home and would regularly fly off at right angles.

Dermot's fall from grace was dramatic and full of serious allegations of malpractice in racing of the worst kind. After he was warned off by the Jockey Club for ten years in his absence he was found working at a pony trekking stable in County Clare.

He appeared in a TV programme admitting that he was the infamous 'needleman' who in the late eighties and early nineties was paid £5,000 a time to dope horses at twenty meetings. And during cross examination at the Old Bailey in February 2000, Jamie Osborne said that he had been approached with a bribe of £20,000 by Browne in March 1988 to stop two horses at Cheltenham, Regal Castle in the County Hurdle and Raise An Argument in the Cathcart Chase.

As yet no case has been brought against him. Michael, who observed Dermot at close range for a long time, had a theory that he found it difficult to handle the success which came his way relatively quickly. Although there was an air of sophistication around him when he arrived at Harewood he had seen very little of life and had hardly touched strong drink. It is fair to say that he enjoyed it as much as the rest of us but it probably affected him more. What is unquestionable is that he could be two different people in a very short space of time, one charming and fun, the other raging and dangerous, a real life Jekyll and Hyde.

On a personal level, I never forgave him for trying to seduce my then fiancée Sue Thewenetti with promises of helicopter trips to Ireland and romantic nights in Dublin. I knew they were true because she repeated his every word to me, but I never let him know. I just watched him and made sure I kept my distance.

Ronnie Beggan had developed from an amateur into a stylish professional and also moved south to Lambourn as stable jockey to the mercurial Simon Christian, for whom he won the 1986 Arkle

Chase at Cheltenham. Ronnie also rode with success for Henrietta Knight before retiring to make his way in corporate hospitality. With Ronnie's smooth mastery of the English language, it was the ideal career.

With everyone else making their passage I was left open to offers. One came in from one of the true gentlemen of jump racing, Jim Old, and it was completely out of the blue because I'd never ridden for him before. I took the call at the little house I'd bought at the end of 1982 on a small estate in Wetherby called The Chase. Jim had taken a look at me, liked the way I rode with the best interest of the horse foremost, and offered me the job.

This wasn't going to be an easy decision. Mrs D had intimated that I would be riding the majority of the 50 or so horses she and the Boss would be looking after, and at that stage I didn't want to move away from my roots. Jim was typically understanding and said that he'd take a second retainer on my services for £10,000, plus a travelling allowance and an added percentage for each winner. It was a very neat arrangement and throughout our association Jim was always honourable, with never the slightest sign of the two-faced nature which is the curse of some people in racing. He understood that I wanted to remain based in the north and keep up my contacts, so the only time I was required to school would be when riding for him at a southern meeting nearby, such as Wincanton, Taunton or Chepstow.

Jim had just moved to a purpose-built yard at Dundry just outside Bristol after a successful period training at Ashmore near Salisbury, where he was famed for working his horses around a duck pond. Jim had renovated a magnificent farm house on the estate, but creature comforts were for horses and not humans in his eyes. While I didn't relish the 236 mile journey I knew I was certain of a warm welcome - but that's where the heating stopped. Jim's bedrooms were like iceboxes and I began travelling with my own electric blanket. It was vital for a good night's sleep.

My third ride for Jim that season, Senrab at Hereford on 25 August 1984, was a winner and I finished the season riding ten for him. The best was Mearlin who won the Hoechst Regumate Novices Handicap Hurdle Final for mares run at Newbury in March, but things were not so good the following season.

Jim's yard was badly hit by a virus and his winners dropped from twenty-two to ten with me on just four of them. Jim was now on the ropes. His owners weren't keen on putting up the cash to retain a jockey, so from then on there was no agreement. But we were never far apart and I continued riding for him up to my retirement. Jim moved again, this time to Wroughton, near Marlborough and hard by the Barbury Castle point to point course. He overcame an arson attack on his yard in 1996 and was still going to provide me with one of my biggest successes, albeit by accident.

The more active I became in the south the more trainers used me, forging new links, but it wasn't only the jockeys who had come south from Harewood. Two of the most progressive young horses from the yard, Church Warden and Rhyme 'N' Reason, had been moved by John Moreton, who owned them together with his then partner Juliet Reed. They were now with David Murray Smith, who trained at Frenchman's Yard Stables in Upper Lambourn, built by Duncan Sasse and his father Frank on the proceeds of Rheingold's Arc win in Paris 1973.

The owners were as keen as I was to keep the partnership with the two horses intact and Church Warden won easily on my first ride for Murray Smith in a novice hurdle over two and a half miles at Chepstow in early October. The five-year-old made his next appearance at Wincanton over two miles six, where he started at 2-5 and got beaten by Lonach, and I was the villain of the piece in John Moreton's eyes.

Lonach was a good, relatively unexposed horse trained by Toby Balding who got a flyer out of the gate and was soon twenty lengths clear on a fast track that didn't suit Church Warden. I could never get to Richard Linley and Lonach and they beat us by eight lengths. Moreton was sure I'd stopped Church Warden and wasn't shy of who he told. The Press gave me a hard time but I repeat what I said then, 'We were flat to the boards, he needs three miles, soft ground and a galloping course.' Next time out he went to Cheltenham over three miles one furlong on very soft ground and won doing handsprings by seven lengths. Except I wasn't on him. John Francome took over and in doing so completed the fastest ever fifty winners over jumps.

The fact that Church Warden needed a real test of stamina was well established by the time I was reunited with him in the Stayers Hurdle at the Cheltenham Festival. And although that was an impossible task, he was right up with the leaders and going fairly well when he blundered away his chance at the tenth flight. I also thought it right to confront the owner about his Wincanton allegations, and John and I patched up our differences. I'd be seeing more of Church Warden the following season, and Rhyme 'N' Reason still had a big role to play in the current one in an overseas Grand National. I would also get my hands on the Welsh variety for the first time, but not before I smashed my wrist and didn't know about it for a year.

I fell on Gandouge Lane for Jim at Leicester and, although it was a bit sore, the adrenalin kicked in and I rode Virgin Soldier in the next race. But going back to Wetherby it began to throb and I knew something wasn't right. Sure enough, I was told after an X-ray at the Harrogate General that I'd broken the scaphoid bone in my right wrist. In lay terms this is the central bone coming from the forearm to join with the wrist. It's position between four others makes it difficult to heal because of circulatory problems. The hospital said six weeks and rest. I of course knew better, and was back in two weeks with my wrist braced with a specially made steel and leather support. Although it tended to ache, I thought no more of it until I injured it again a year later, when an x-ray showed it had never healed and was still broken. I didn't argue this time and had a steel pin inserted which is still there to this day.

The cavalier attitude jockeys take to injuries the public perceive as serious should be put into perspective. With most jockeys personal insurance there is a 30 day excess period so, unless you do something very serious like an arm, leg or even worse, you can't claim or your premiums rocket. After three years I didn't bother with personal insurance simply because the odds didn't work out. The premium was around £3,000 a year or £60,000 over a twenty year period-not much more than a week's salary to some footballers. But to get that amount I'd need to be very seriously injured and, although every jockey knows it's out there waiting, it is something you pray won't happen to you. It's certainly the one bet you don't want to be paid out on.

However the cumulative effect of injuries eventually breaks the hardest men. Richard Dunwoody's pain threshold was incredible but a recurrent shoulder injury got him in the end and, after grim warnings from his doctors, he retired in late 1999.

My great friend Boo Boo Youlden suffered more than many jockeys I know. He looked brittle and his bones certainly were. The year after I broke my wrist Boo Boo had a fall at Market Rasen. I picked him up from the ambulance room and all I could see was one arm cradling the other with his coat thrown over his shoulder. I thought I knew a bit about hospitals and accidents, so I said, 'No need to bother going tonight. They'll only tell you it's too swollen to plaster, so you'll have to come back tomorrow morning.' I was basing my assessment on one piddly little scaphoid bone.

He didn't move in the passenger seat, just kept his head bent over and said, 'I think it's a little bit worse than that.' No big fuss, no screaming or swearing and no outward signs of pain. All I wanted to do was get him out for a couple of beers and cheer him up.

He looked awful. We drove straight to Harrogate General, and when they cut his riding glove off, his hand didn't look connected to his arm. It was distorted like the U bend in a pipe and the sight of it made me feel ill. Although he looked like an angel he was a tough devil and came back from that. He had another soft looking fall at Kelso the next season which smashed his shoulder in five places, but that wasn't the one that eventually got him. The final fall was frightening. He was in a novice chase at Sedgefield at the third fence down the back straight, where there was no ambulance track. The horse upsides him chested the fence and did a somersault. As it's rump hit the ground, the hind legs whiplashed. One of the flayling legs caught Boo Boo's left leg just below the knee and both tibia and fibia were smashed. The other jocks heard the crack but hadn't a clue what it was. Steve Youlden had no option but to jump off a horse galloping at 25 miles an hour before he reached the next fence. When the ambulance finally reached him the shattered bones were protruding through the skin of his leg and all he could scream for was morphine. He never lost consciousness and could feel every bump of that rough ride back to the ambulance room.

No man could comprehend the pain he went through and I could have wept when I went to see him in Teesside Hospital. He said to me that he'd never ride again and I couldn't find one single argument against it. I was desperately sorry to see my best mate bow out in such a way after we'd both been fresh-faced kids at the riding school. It was the end of Steve's dream.

Oh yes, a couple of weeks later he received a note from Dr Michael Allen, the Jockey Club Medical Officer, warning him about his conduct on a racecourse towards the St John's Ambulance people.

Such a severe injury puts my damaged wrist in perspective, but it was imperative to me that I got back in time to ride the appropriately named Righthand Man in the Welsh National. I'd ridden him to win his two previous races, staying chases at Cheltenham and Haydock, the latter over four miles, and he was second favourite to lightly weighted stablemate Planetman, ridden by Earnshaw. Mrs D wanted proof that I was right, so Jim gave me a ride on Tinkersfield in a Ludlow hurdle and we came through fine. I went on BBC TV before the race to assure everyone that I was fit enough and the dice rolled my way. That gruelling three miles six furlongs on soft ground in deepest December was food and drink to Righthand Man. Only a seven-year-old, he was always up with the pace and once he led two out nothing was going to pass him. He battled on tenaciously to beat Lucky Vane seven lengths, with Planetman three lengths third after making some bad mistakes.

Although Righthand Man wasn't quick he was extremely genuine, and with any luck, would have given his owner Mrs Muriel Haggas a Cheltenham Gold Cup alongside that won by her daughter Mrs Chris Feather in 1982 with Silver Buck.

He went into the Gold Cup unbeaten in four chases where the accent was on stamina but now he had to produce pace. Good ground wasn't in his favour and he struggled to lie up with the pace set by Drumadowney. We were also hampered by Ballinacurra Lad and Shorty Leech at a crucial part of the race, the fifteenth, where lack of pace made things more difficult and he lost further ground.

When Mark Dwyer came through from the rear on Forgive 'N Forget to lead two out, Righthand Man was struggling and at the last he was all of six lengths down. But that steep hill was made for him. He cut into the lead with every stride yet was still a length and a half behind at the line.

It was a very brave effort and the second time I'd been runner up to Forgive 'N Forget at the Festival, the other being on Brunton Park in the Coral Final of 1983. Righthand Man had one more run that season in the Scottish National at Ayr in April, when he failed by only half a length to beat Androma and Mark Dwyer. But in that race I made one mistake that I've never repeated. I used a new whip and because I wasn't familiar with it, I ended up leaving weal marks on one of the gamest horses I ever rode. I felt ashamed when I saw them.

Although Righthand Man was the nearest I got to the winner's enclosure at Cheltenham that year, I thought I had a real chance of landing the Sun Alliance Chase with Rhyme 'N' Reason, who'd won two of his three chases in the build up and was still improving. In the event, he never jumped with any fluency and finally got rid of me at the seventh. However, the best was yet to come. He was about to make history in the Irish National and ended up completing the Welsh and Aintree National treble, although I would only be involved in the Irish leg.

Murray Smith sent him to Liverpool, where he acted well around the sharp Mildmay Course on the inside of the National circuit. After he had beaten Arctic Beau by a length, the trainer outlined a very ambitious plan, an attempt on the Irish Grand National at Fairyhouse on Easter Monday. This needs to be put in context, as the last English winner of the race had been Don Sancho in 1928 and to cap it all, Rhyme 'N' Reason was only a novice.

Despite a busy season he was still on the upgrade and I flew to Ireland with Murray Smith knowing there was a good chance that my first ride in the country would be a winning one. For the trainer it was a case of returning to his roots. David had been brought up in Ireland and also spent his formative professional years as assistant to Vincent O'Brien during the time of Golden Fleece, Caerleon, Lomond and many other fine horses.

I didn't want to make any mistakes so, as I have always done when confronted with a new course, I walked it. The only problem was that there weren't any size seven wellies around. Just as I'd resigned myself to getting my riding boots soaked, Tommy Kinane, father of multi-flat champion Mick and partner of the legendary Monksfield in his early years, walked into the weighing room.

He had a pair in his car and lent them to me, but he still hadn't finished doing me favours that day.

Just as I was walking back towards the final two fences, Tommy came up to me again. 'Listen to me for a minute,' he said. 'I rode in this race 14 or 15 times and it was always the same with the novice horses, these last two fences find them out when they've really got to race.' He then pointed out how much less the drop was on the outside compared to the middle or inner and added, 'The fences have been rebuilt this year. They are very high and very straight, so my advice to you is come wide when you turn for home. I should have won on Reynards Heir in 1967, but I was badly interfered with over the last two fences by horses coming down or making mistakes and I finished second to Vulpine.'

Tommy had learned his Irish National lessons the hard way and it was very generous of him to help a 'foreigner'. If I had been on the inner when Rhyme 'N' Reason made his only serious mistake at the last, the extra drop would almost certainly have found him out. As it was we had twelve lengths to spare over Seskin Bridge and Martin Lynch. A little bit of history had been made and a love affair started with Ireland that continues to this day.

Although The Irish National was my first win abroad there were new worlds to conquer much further away. I'd been invited to join the British jump jockeys team on a trip to ride against the best in America, Australia and New Zealand and we had a strong team made up of Peter Scudamore, Steve Smith Eccles, Hywel Davies, myself and a very young Richard Dunwoody as reserve.

Alan Lee, then cricket correspondent of *The Times* but who now heads up their racing team, organised the trip with John Doorman and the treatment we received in Maryland was magnificent. We were billeted out with various millionaires and their families. Dunwoody and myself stayed with George and Gretchen Winterstein. The others were placed with Mrs Miles Valentine, whose pink and cherry heart colours were carried by the likes of Whitbread winner Plundering, and Burley Cocks, who did so much to help Bob Champion in his recovery from cancer.

I managed two winners to help beat the Yanks, we lived like kings and were well set up for the next two legs in Australia and New Zealand when we had a five hour stopover in Los Angeles. We took a trip down to Malibu Beach and couldn't believe it. This was before the days of *Baywatch* but that's where they film it now and we got an early preview. Whatever happened in the Antipodes, I was coming back to some of this.

When we got to Melbourne the reception was great with TV cameras at the airport, but the hospitality wasn't quite the same. We were given hostel accommodation that wouldn't have been tolerated in England and, after a swift union meeting, we informed the organisers that this wasn't quite what we were used to and could they please do something about it.

Les Benton, who did so much to bring the Melbourne Cup to world prominence and then transformed the Dubai World Cup, didn't waste any time and we were booked into the five star Southern Palms Hotel, which was good enough for the Beatles when they played Melbourne in the sixties. There was, however, a slight problem for me. Australian weights went down to 9st for jumping and I hadn't been able to do that sort of weight since my days on the wonderwall in Second Avenue. I'd even started smoking to keep my weight down, but after a long season I still had no chance when they generously raised the weights to 10st.

I took over as tour photographer and let young Dunwoody take my place in the team but I still had a pivotal role. It was still a struggle for Hywel to make 10st 5lb, so I had to give a helping hand. When he stepped on the big platform scales at Moonee Valley I placed myself on the opposite side to the clerk of the scales. He was so engrossed in scrutinising the dial that he didn't notice me holding the back of Hywel's breeches to make sure he did the weight. When he came back to weigh in I was ready to oblige again, very discreetly.

By now I'd decided to rest on my American laurels and was out of the running for any rides in New Zealand, where we were due to perform at Tauraunga and Ellerslie. The boys thought they weren't going to be needed either when we arrived at Tauraunga to see the course under five feet of water, reminiscent of Worcester when the river has burst its banks. Despite the locals declaring they'd race the next day, no worries, our team weren't convinced and went into action in various bars. Sure enough, the flood went. They raced the next day and the sauna worked overtime.

We travelled back via Los Angeles and there was no way I wanted just a day's stopover after what I'd seen on the way out. John Doorman managed to change the flights for a week later and, while the married men went back to their nearest and dearest, the singles pair of Bradley and Dunwoody stayed on for a magnificent seven days. There was a strong ex-pat colony in the area to show us the ropes. Boo Boo had taken a summer job riding work for Neil Drysdale and his main ally was Jimmy Duggan, one the nicest scallywags jump racing ever produced.

Jimmy rode a lot of winners, notably on the good hurdler Aonoch in the early eighties. He was also one bloke to whom you didn't say the words, 'I dare you,' especially when he'd had a few beers. Fear wasn't one of Jimmy's best-known qualities, and it is a matter of record that when he took his beloved white Highland terrier Alfie to London they had a dramatic tube ride.

Jimmy walked off the train, having lunched well, and momentarily forgot that Alfie was still on board and the doors had closed by the time he realised his mistake. Jimmy just grabbed hold of the back of the moving car and held on through the tunnel until it reached the next station, where he picked up the puzzled pooch.

We made our base at Besty's Bar on Hermosa Beach run by a great guy, Bobby McAlinden, who played pro soccer for Manchester City amongst others and ran the bar in partnership with

George Best. First day on the beach I saw an absolute stunner on her own. I decided to put my shyness to one side together with my lighter and asked her for a light. 'Can you say that again? I just love your voice.' Evidently, broad Yorkshire was a novelty out there and I never left Linda's side for a week.

She had a flatmate, a photographer, who Duggan kindly offered to make up a foursome with at the local drive-in movie. 'We'll take the one car,' said I, which brought a wry smile from my escort. 'Four don't go in one car to a drive-in,' she responded and I found out why. You park up, attach a sound system to the car aerial and listen to the soundtrack through the radio. Shortly after the titles came up, Linda informed me that the front seats let right down. The film was *Cocoon* and suffice to say I had to wait until it came out on video to see what happened.

CHAPTER 11
The anatomy of a coup

I've always considered myself a fair judge of a horse and since I retired from riding that opinion has been backed by hard cash in the no-holds-barred world occupied by bloodstock agents.

Most people think that it was something I drifted into, but they'd be wrong because I started dealing way back in the mid-eighties. And one of the best deals I ever did was for a horse called Starjestic, who would give a jockey who has since gone on to land the Grand National twice his first winner, and land a massive coup in the process. Three seasons later I was hauled before the stewards accused of jumping off him in a small race at Southwell.

The Starjestic story started with Chris Pimlott and Stuart Isherwood, who were both with me at the Dickinsons and rode for a grand old permit holder who trained near Scarborough called Roy Robinson. He was a bachelor-farmer, getting on a bit and, as with quite a few of that hardy breed, his place wasn't the tidiest. In fact it had to be seen to be believed. He asked me to go up one morning to school a batch of his horses but there wouldn't be any payment. 'Can't afford that,' said the old boy, 'but I'll give you twenty bales of hay.' Well that was handy because Norm now had a livery yard and with hay being about £2.50 a bale I agreed. I asked if I could bring someone with me to help and roped in Boo Boo, who came along in a flatbed truck.

We took the horses to a point to point course near the yard and popped creatures of all shapes and sizes over six fences. The second one I sat on was a seven-year-old novice chase prospect named Starjestic and before I'd jumped anything I leaned over to Boo Boo and said, 'Bloody hell, this feels a real nice horse.' He only jumped six fences but he felt all quality and I fell in love with him. I looked him up in the form book and he hadn't done much after finishing third in a bumper as a young horse. In addition, *Timeform* had him down as a poor jumper with an 'x' alongside a dash that meant he wasn't worth a rating. Despite all this, I had to have him. The trouble was, Roy was a canny old devil and wasn't selling.

After showing nothing when amateur ridden in his first two starts I got on him at Market Rasen where he ran a blinder, finishing a close second and jumping well. His next run at Nottingham was even better and he finished fourth, not beaten far, in a very hot novice chase. I knew he had to be bought.

That Nottingham race was won by Boo Boo on Amber Rambler, who was unbeaten in three subsequent races that season and finished off by beating the subsequent Champion Chase winner Pearlyman at Ayr.

Gringo, a decent horse who had come from Hungary and was trained by Nicky Henderson, was a length second and won his next race by twenty lengths. Just Alick, from Peter Easterby's yard, was third beaten four lengths. He would win three chases that season and, only five lengths back in fourth, was the apparently useless Starjestic. Just to sharpen my interest, he gave me the feeling that he might just have needed the race and would come on again for the run.

Now, if we'd known what the other horses were going to achieve I would have been offering more than £6,000 to Roy even though the horse was rising eight years old, but six grand   still wasn't enough and we had to give him a sweetener. We finally did a deal where the horse continued to run in Roy's name that season and he could keep all the prize money. There was, however, one rather important point. Norm would be conditioning the horse at the livery yard he'd taken just outside Wetherby and Roy could have him back before each race, just to make things legal.

There was a slight blip on his next outing when he ran at Catterick and came down at the third. It was nothing serious, he just over jumped and I knew he was gilt-edged. It was only when I got down to finding a novice handicap chase for him that I realised he was much better than gilt. In fact he was solid gold. I had plenty of time to scan the *Racing Calendar* as racing was off through snow and frost for nearly a month and, when I began comparing weights, I found that the handicapper had discounted the Nottingham run as a fluke.

I settled down with a hot cup of coffee and a packet of Silk Cut and began to piece my way through the fifty-three entries for the Sandall Beat Novices Handicap Chase due to be run over two miles at Doncaster on 24 January. Five of the runners from the Nottingham race were in there, but I couldn't believe just how much the handicapper had underestimated Starjestic.

He was way down the long handicap with the apparent no hopers on 9st 2lb and, as my eyes made their way to the top of the handicap, I could see just what a certainty he was. Amber Rambler, who received 4lb and beat him by ten lengths at Nottingham, had won at Doncaster subsequently and was now set to concede no less than 40lb. Gringo, who beat Starjestic nine lengths at Nottingham, had also gone on to win and now had to concede 39lb. Just Alick had been busier since Nottingham, winning a novice chase then appearing to turn a bit doggy. He had a real mountain to climb as he was rated 42lb superior to our fellow. And as if there was any further need to ice the cake, Bright Sherriff, adrift of our lad six lengths at Nottingham, had gone on to finish third in a novice chase and was now rated 29lb his superior.

It's not often that things like this happen but when they do you've got to maximise them.

I made all the entries I could for Starjestic in two mile novice handicap chases and, after scrutinising them all, the right one surfaced in the Lapley Novices' Handicap Chase at Wolverhampton. It was 14 March 1986, the day after Wayward Lad had gone down by an honourable length to Dawn Run in the Gold Cup. The only problem was that Starjestic had been given a long handicap weight of 8st 13lb. Although the weights did go up 7lb he was still only on 9st 6lb and would have to carry the allotted minimum of 10st. The answer was to find a good 7lb claimer to get his weight down to 9st 7lb. Fortunately, I knew just the kid for the job.

I think I'm a reasonable judge of a jockey and I'd been doing a lot of schooling with a very capable lad at Jim Old's who hadn't ridden a winner but looked the part. His name was Carl Llewellyn. Carl is now famous for his Grand National wins on Party Politics and Earth Summit, but back then he wasn't even a household name in his own household !

I had to put the hard sell on Norm and was, I admit, a bit economical with the truth. 'Who is he and what's he done,' were Norm's questions. I came back full of confidence. 'He's great. Had plenty of experience in point to points and ridden thirty winners - and he'll do the weight no problem.' That was good enough for Norm.

Now, it's a fact that no matter how many winners a jockey rides, the one that always stays with him is the first. And Carl can remember very clearly that particular booking.

He recalls, 'I knew that Brad had to tell a few white lies to get me the ride, but he kept on that I must do the weight because it would look bad if I didn't. He told me not to worry that the horse had fallen because he'd been well schooled over big poles. Nearer the day he said the owner wouldn't be able to get there and it would just be a case of looking after the horse to make sure he got round.

'But when I got to the races he seemed very excited and escorted me everywhere, treated me like a piece of bone china and sorted out a comfortable saddle for me.

'People asked me what I was going to do in the race because the horse had got some form, but I told them that he was having a pop round because the owner couldn't get there.

'When I got into the paddock, Brad was there with Boo Boo and told me that the owner had been able to make it after a dash. Suddenly it was all systems go. I thought "oh shit" and went out to do the best I could.

'Everything went fine and we were cantering when I asked for a big leap four out, where Starjestic put down with me and it was a case of look, no hands. He wasn't brilliant three out, either, but he popped over the last two with me trying to look as stylish as I could on the run-in.'

I'd shouted myself silly from the stands and ran round to meet Carl as he came back to the muddy unsaddling enclosure at the back of the old grandstand. A murky Friday at Wolverhampton in March after the delights of Cheltenham might not be everyone's ideal location, but I wouldn't have swapped it for Malibu Beach.

Carl still remembers his welcome: 'Brad was there with the biggest smile I've ever seen and he gave me a big kiss as soon as my feet hit the grass. 'He kept hugging me all the way back to the weighing room, telling everyone what a great jockey I'd make. I was just a naive kid and didn't understand what was happening. 'He asked me how I was getting back to Jim's and when I said I didn't know he said he'd take me, I think he was schooling the next morning. He did give me a drink as well, which was a bit bigger than a diet coke.'

I gave Carl £200 quid, which looking back was a bit tight, because we'd had it off in style. Starjestic had opened at 9-1, probably nearer 12-1, and had been backed in to 11-2 third favourite.

The new owner was a chap called Tony Nehoria, who made a fortune importing luxury carpets direct from Persia and China straight into peoples homes. He was an absolutely mad gambler known, not surprisingly, as 'Carpets' and he'd told me there would be a £15,000 present for finding him the horse if he won. Carl says I hummed and sang all the way back down the M5 to Bristol. But previously I'd had a bit of explaining to do with Norm, who'd called me quietly to one side after the dust had settled and said, 'That lad's just told me that he's only ridden a few winners in point to points. We're missing about twenty-seven on your figures.'

'Don't worry Norm, he did the job beautifully and he'll be a champion one day,' was my reply. And if Carl Llewellyn hasn't quite achieved that he was my little champion for quite some time. There is just one final twist to that particular tale. The 2-1 favourite that day was Fionnadoir, trained by the legendary Fred Winter, readily held by six lengths in second and ridden by a determined young amateur who was to have a significant part to play in the final quarter of my riding career. His name was Mr C. Brooks. Not for the last time, thanks Charles.

Dunstall Park, Wolverhampton, a stone's throw from Molineux, home of the Wolves football team, had already been kind to me that season. It was the first place that I rode a winner for two of the biggest characters in jump racing, Jenny Pitman and Terry Ramsden. Jenny will go into racing history as the first lady of jump racing and, as trainer of two Cheltenham Gold Cup winners and two Grand National winners, the tag fits her perfectly.

Terry was the essence of Thatcherite Britain in the eighties. A working-class boy who'd made millions gambling on the world financial markets, he was mad keen to play some of it up in the more chancy world of racing. With his long hair and brash style there were plenty of people who wished him to fall and, eventually, they saw it happen.

Jenny has a tongue that could cut hedges and she wasn't shy of using it on anyone who got on the wrong side of her - be they jockey, owner, pressman or fellow trainer. She gave Dean Gallagher such a volley one morning on the Mandown schooling grounds high over Lambourn that he just gave her the reins, told her to do it herself and walked back to the yard and collected his car.

Other trainers were irritated by her strong presence in the media, but from the first day I teamed up with her at Wolverhampton, I never had a cross word with her.

I got to know Jenny and her husband David Stait through Duggie Shaw, who died tragically young with a brain tumour. Duggie was the son of Jim Shaw, who owned several horses with Jenny. I rode the odd one for Jenny when required and whenever I was travelling down from the north to stay with her I'd phone when we were half an hour away and she'd have the tea ready when I arrived. I'd play pool with Dave and we'd talk horses. She loved to talk about the Dickinson stars and could not have been nicer.

Jenny and Dave were well aware that they had potentially a very good horse in Stearsby, owned by Terry, but a terrible jumper. He'd fallen in his three races that season before Dave approached me and said 'Make no mistake Brad, this is a good horse. Will you ride him?'

At the time, he'd been running in a citation bit which was very severe but helped his rider to settle him and drop him out in the rear. I said, 'David, I'll ride him provided you take all that gear off him and let me make the running.'

Dave replied that I'd need something to hold him with and suggested a cross nose band. I agreed as it would help keep the bit straight in Stearsby's mouth. But I still wanted to make the running. No argument from Jenny. I schooled the horse, he was brilliant and we went to Wolverhampton, made all and won easing up by twelve lengths.

We were third to Cross Master in the Sun Alliance at Cheltenham after nearly being brought down in a four-horse pile up and then went to Liverpool for the Whitbread Best Mild Novices Chase. Terry had already won the opening hurdle with I Bin Zaidoon, trained by Jenny and ridden by his number one rider and my great buddy Graham McCourt. By now Terry reportedly had £200,000 going on Stearsby. We were in front from the tenth and although The Langholm Dyer and favourite Strands of Gold were upsides at the last, Stearsby saw them off and beat The Langholm Dyer by a length and a half.

It wasn't until the Scottish National meeting at Ayr two weeks later that I was paid out together with Phil Tuck, who'd finished fourth on Terry's Mr Snugfit in the Grand National. Mick Miller, who was a useful Flat apprentice for Robert Armstrong and worked for Terry, paid me £5,000 in unused £50 notes and I think Phil got the same. And Tony Carroll, who trains now and used to ride work on Terry's horses, also got weighed in as well.

Terry was a lovely man and I feel desperately sorry that his fall was so quick and dramatic. I hope he comes back one day.

CHAPTER 12
Losing the best paid job in racing

I've never been superstitious, unlike many of my former colleagues, but when I travelled to Haydock Park for five rides on Saturday 18 January 1986, I would have done well to heed the names of the two winners I rode.

The first was Sheer Gold, a game mare who slogged through the mud to win the Premier Long Distance Hurdle. It was my first success for Toby Balding. By the start of the following season I would be his principal jockey with one of the most lucrative retainers in jump racing as first jockey to Sir Philip and Lady Harris, who owned her.

However, the second win that afternoon in the Preston Novices Chase was for Mrs D and ominously named A Sure Row. Considering the two years I was about to have with Toby, it was indeed a sign.

Jumping retainers need to be put in perspective with their more lucrative Flat counterparts. In most cases you need to multiply by ten to come to something like a comparison.

Sir Philip Harris was owner of Queensway Carpets and my deal was £10,000 to ride their string, which amounted to only seven. I would also get five per cent of any horses that were bought or sold on their behalf. When you consider some were bought for six figures you can understand just how good that deal was - but it got even better. I would also get double percentage on winners and placed horses, and remember, they wouldn't be hopping round in sellers for £800. Given such a lumpy deal I was hardly going to stop anything - and I didn't. But people have suspicious minds.

There were other benefits from the deal because it allowed Mrs D to have a second claim on me and, after that, I could ride the remainder of Toby Balding's team, which also had plenty of quality.

But as is so often the case in sport it is the most talented players that get you into trouble - and without doubt the star of the Harris string was Kildimo. Together we swept to the heights and also plunged to depths which saw me sacked from the job I coveted.

Kildimo was a useful hurdler but chasing was always going to be his great stage. After winning two handicap hurdles in November 1986, he made his chase debut in a three mile one novice event at Cheltenham. He had plenty to contend with, including Playschool, who would go on to win a Welsh National and, in the view of his trainer David Barons, be got at before an abysmal run in the Cheltenham Gold Cup.

But there were no excuses here and Playschool had no answer when I brought Kildimo through from the rear. I delayed pressing the button until the final 100 yards to win by a cheeky three quarters of a length.

It was same again next time just over a month later at Towcester, when I held him at the rear of the sixteen runner field and had him jumping like a stag. He cruised through to lead two out and won by four lengths, value for more like twenty-four. I won a case of champagne for the ride of the month and everything looked rosy until Ascot six days later. It was 11 February 1987 and the prestigious Reynoldstown Chase.

I dropped Kildimo out in rear as usual because it wasn't an option to have him up with the pace. He had a mouth like wrought iron and once he was fired up it was like pulling against a barn door and getting the same response. But unlike his previous efforts he hardly raised a leg at some of the fences and blundered his way round. His class got him into the action at the twelfth but he weakened at the sixteenth and had no chance when blundering at the next, finishing last of four finishers to Tawridge, beaten nineteen lengths.

Toby came out to meet me at the big iron gates which lead off the course and into the unsaddling enclosure and he was steaming. 'What the fuck was that all about?'

I'm normally very quiet and reserved but this time I wasn't in any mood for appeasement. Looking down at him, I fired back. 'This horse is not fucking right, I don't know why you're bollocking me.'

I went back to weigh in while Toby held court with the assembled Press who were waiting for the fall out. They weren't disappointed.

'I told him that was bloody awful' said Toby. Sure enough, in next morning's papers was the headline 'Bloody Awful Bradley.'

Toby went on to explain his theory. 'He says Kildimo did not jump the first two fences, but having given them fifty yards start what did he expect? It was a quality race and you had to lie handy.'

I countered, 'Kildimo never jumped a fence and kept leaving his back legs behind. The plan was to drop him out and if he'd jumped the earlier fences well, everything would have been fine.' I added that I would not be surprised if he were lame in the morning.

In a show of real petulance concerning the forthcoming Sun Alliance Chase at Cheltenham, which was always Kildimo's target, Toby added, 'Bradley is retained for the horse but I expect he will want to ride either Granville Park or King's College Boy for Mrs Dickinson.'

Nothing was further from my mind. Since I'd joined Toby's team at Weyhill I'd become great friends with two of his conditional riders, Tony Charlton and Richard Guest. Richard, who went on to win the Champion Hurdle for Toby on Beech Road, has developed into one of the most astute horsemen in jump racing and was a sound man even then. When I'd phoned him earlier in the week he told me that Tony had ridden Kildimo work and wasn't happy with him. He had told Toby that the horse had got sore shins when winning at Towcester, but Toby didn't want to know.

Sore shins are best understood in human terms if you imagine trying to run with a blister on your foot. You'd soon stop striding out, and that's what happened to Kildimo. He didn't want to leave the ground because of the pain he would feel on landing and that's why he made mistakes.

There was a picture of Kildimo leaving his legs behind and making an appalling blunder. I'll swear it must have ripped all his back muscles. That area caused him a lot of problems and he always ran with his tail rigid throughout a race, which is very unusual.

The next day's action was up the A1 at Huntingdon, where Robin Goodfellow was running in the Sidney Banks Memorial Novices Hurdle, a good trial for Cheltenham. I used patient tactics on him and he beat some better fancied opponents by a comfortable five lengths.

Toby was magnanimous in victory and after throwing his arm around me and pretending to give me a kiss, said to the assembled Press troupe, 'Graham has half-redeemed himself. The jockey couldn't have done it better today.' He then added that Kildimo was none the worse for his exertions - except for sore shins which had frequently troubled him.

Thanks very much!

Kildimo was given time for his shins to cool down and his next run was the Sun Alliance Chase, the novices Gold Cup and this time it was me who went into the race very much the worse for wear. I'd fallen heavily from Mrs D's Rancho Bernado in a novice chase at Southwell on 27 February and fractured the fibula in my left leg. I said it wasn't broken and, with the aid of some very strong painkillers, I rode two weeks later and was ready for Cheltenham three days after that.

The opening day didn't go well, with Mrs D's Dan The Millar running poorly in the Arkle Chase after looking one of the best two mile novices of the season. He did come back with a good win at Aintree the following month, but my problems came the next day.

I like to enjoy the social scene around Cheltenham but there wasn't much chance of that on Tuesday night as I had to boil myself down to 10st 7lb for Croix de Guerre, owned by my friend Duggie Shaw's father, Jim, and trained by Jenny Pitman, in the Coral Golden Hurdle Final.

There's no such thing as the worst kind of fall. They're all bad, but I don't recommend coming off when you have just hit the front two out in thirty one runner handicap hurdle at Cheltenham, especially if you've got a partially fractured left leg and a touch of the flu.

It was even more annoying and upsetting because I would have dearly loved to have won that valuable race for Jim and Duggie and I was going best of all at the time.

There was never any question of me giving up the ride on Kildimo in the Sun Alliance, which came 35 minutes later, but I looked and felt terrible. Toby amazed me in the parade ring when he told me to ride him exactly how I wanted which I took to be the nearest I'd get to an apology for what he'd said at Ascot. Still, it wouldn't have mattered what he said, I'd have done exactly the same because it was the only way.

Once the tape went up all the aches and pains went as the adrenalin kicked in. Kildimo popped round nicely out the back, five lengths stone cold last for a full circuit and had full tanks when we began to creep closer from the tenth. Once again we waited until two out before getting serious and this was the way Toby liked his horses ridden. Unlike the Dickinsons who liked you up with the pace, Toby would rather you get beat than come too soon.

I didn't want to wait any longer going to the last and kicked past old adversary Playschool before pushing on to beat him seven lengths.

Toby said afterwards, 'He looks awful and shouldn't have ridden, but he's got great faith in the horse.'

Too right. After what had happened at Ascot, if someone else had won the Sun Alliance on him I'd have thrown myself off the top of the stands. I felt vindicated by the result and all the public admonishments hadn't worried me. I wouldn't have ridden Kildimo any other way although, even if I do say so myself, it took balls to do it.

Oh, yes, and I won another case of champagne for best ride of March. I don't know about March, that was one of the best rides I ever gave a horse around Cheltenham in my life. And after finishing with an easy win at Ayr, next year's Gold Cup was not an impossible dream.

Despite our run-ins I liked Toby and loved riding for him. He's a good bloke and excellent value either on the tennis court or at any sport to do with eating or drinking. His wife, Caro, is a genuine sweetheart and I always enjoyed their company on the nights when we had a meal prior to schooling the next morning at Weyhill.

On one occasion Toby was anxious about my bachelor status and asked Caro if there were any suitable daughters amongst the owners. 'I don't think there are,' said Caro. 'Oh, he doesn't want anything special,' said Toby expansively. 'Just needs someone good to jump on his bones.'

Despite late nights, Toby was an habitual early riser, 5.45 being the norm and he took great pleasure in shouting for me at 6.15 even though we didn't pull out until 7.30. I'd leave that challenge until as late as possible, too. But the problems really started when you came back for breakfast and headed for the table. A big open perch on which sat a bloody great parrot had to be negotiated. It didn't like many people but it absolutely detested me and I needed the dexterity of a fly-half to avoid a massive beak which could crack brazil nuts. I never discovered his name but it may well have been Portman Square.

The next season was built around Kildimo's assault on the Gold Cup and started brightly enough when he gave 10lb and a beating to Playschool at Cheltenham. But things got steadily worse and, after starting 2-1 favourite for the Hennessy Gold Cup at Newbury, he was beaten ten and a half lengths into third by Playschool who received just 11lb. He then ran no race in the Welsh National, finishing ninth to the same horse, and clearly something was badly wrong.

I recommended a woman from Yorkshire called Janet Ellis, who had worked wonders using bone manipulation on some of the troublesome Dickinson horses, notably Visconti, who needed a twitch of rope attached to his nose to steady him before a bridle could be put on. Janet gave him one thump behind the ears, his head dropped like a stone, and he was never a problem again. Toby agreed and Sir Philip flew Janet down to look at Kildimo. On examining him she found four old injuries and three new ones, all in his back. She came down twice and put him 100 per cent right, leaving strict instructions that he should only work on level ground and not go around any corners.

His preparation went well. In fact, he was spot on for his next run in the Jim Ford Challenge Cup at Wincanton, where he was up against Desert Orchid who was fresh from finishing third to Charter Party at Sandown when trying to give the subsequent Cheltenham Gold Cup winner 17lb. But Kildimo was right back to his best and, at level weights, easily outpaced the grand grey by a length and a half. It was such an impressive performance that many good judges, including Desert Orchid's trainer David Elsworth, thought the Gold Cup had Kildimo's name on it.

He started equal second favourite at Cheltenham but his injuries began to catch up with him and he wasn't the same horse. I'm not certain Toby stuck to the schedule laid down by Janet Ellis, but either way he never got into the race and finished a disappointing sixth. He ran much better at Liverpool in the Chivas Regal Cup when beaten eight lengths into second by Dessie and looked to hold an outstanding chance in the Whitbread Gold Cup at Sandown, a race which is traditionally the last major chase of the jump season.

I wasn't riding at the two-day Cheltenham fixture three days before the Whitbread, and when Toby asked me to go down to see him I thought it was to talk about arrangements for next season.

He got me outside the weighing room and didn't sugar the pill, 'There's no easy way of saying this, Sir Philip doesn't want you to ride his horses next season. There's nothing I can do about it. He's set in his mind that you're not doing things right and he's lost faith in you.'

I was speechless for about five seconds, unable to comprehend what I was hearing. Realising I'd just lost one of the best paid jobs in jump racing I pleaded with Toby. 'Guv'nor, you can't let him sack me. You know the horse was wrong when he ran in the Gold Cup.' But Toby was adamant, 'Brad, I'm sorry, there's nothing I can do.'

In fact, Richard Guest said later that he was waiting to use the sauna in Toby's house when he inadvertently overheard him talking to Philip Harris about my position. He recalled later, 'It was clear that Harris had a bee in his bonnet about how you rode his horses. 'On a scale of one to ten, Toby defended you about four.' In the end he said, "OK, if that's what you want to believe," and that was that.'

Like many owners, Philip Harris suffered from the blight of friends who always seem to know which jockey is dropping the anchor and for whom. Clearly, someone had put me in the centre of a very unattractive frame.

On reflection, Toby was only beginning a trend that was going to sweep through racing. Owners pay the money and they can have who they like to ride their horses and I suppose that's fair enough. Even Fred Winter had to bow when Sheikh Ali Abu Khamsin said he wanted Richard Linley and not John Francome to ride his horses. The owner nearly always gets the final say in such disputes, although Paul Green came up against old fashioned values when he tried to tell Fulke Walwyn that Peter Scudamore would have to ride an expensive filly he'd put into the yard instead of stable number one Kevin Mooney. The horse had to go, but then Mr Walwyn was the last of a dying breed.

However, I did one very sensible thing when I was sacked that day which any young jockey can learn from. Once again I bit my lip and did my inner suffering in silence. And several years later I was paid back with interest when Toby put me on Morley Street to bring about the downfall of champion hurdler Granville Again in the Martell Hurdle at Liverpool.

Oh yes, and after Kildimo had failed to show anything I was asked to ride him again in 1989. In the event we never managed to get together and he didn't win again until January 1992, when he'd been moved to Sue and Harvey Smith at Bingley in Yorkshire. Ironically, he was ridden by Richard Guest, who had seen Janet Ellis's methods work so well at Fyfield.

CHAPTER 13
The barney with Curley

I had two years on the emotional rollercoaster as stable jockey to Toby Balding. The spell left a lot of memories, but none of them are more vivid than those relating to my bitter confrontation with owner-trainer-gambler Barney Curley in what would become know as 'The Robin Goodfellow Affair'.

Rumour and counter rumour surrounded the case as it continued in the headlines, but because of the closed court policy adopted by the Jockey Club the media were, and still are, reliant on unofficial 'leaks' which do racing much more harm than good. Everyone seemed to have an opinion about the case. Needless to say, many were misguided, so for the first time, I will let you read the transcripts of conversations made and statements sworn by those involved. It provides a startling insight into one of the most malicious and unjustified attacks on my integrity.

Curley is the kind of man you never forget once you've met him. And once you cross him, he never forgets you. The billiard-ball smooth head often covered by a fedora belongs to a single-minded man who is used to getting his own way. His eyes are emotionless and give nothing away. It is a look that could cut steel.

He will battle any system he sees as unjust, be it bookmaker or Jockey Club, and is adept at negotiating his way around rules that might not suit him. Who else would have a national raffle for his country estate in Ireland? He entered the priesthood as a young man and although he left it he can still put the fear of God into some people. And without knowing it, I crossed him at Ascot on 15 November 1986 because he thought I had stopped the novice hurdler Robin Goodfellow.

Not that Barney owned or trained the gelding. He'd simply considered it a good thing and backed it with £8,000 (the figure fluctuated to £12,000) of his own money. But unlike the millions of punters who bite the bullet when they get it wrong, Barney thought he was powerful enough to get his money back and break me in the process.

Toby, who trained Robin Goodfellow for Miss Bridget Swire, is a man whose verbal dexterity is such that he could easily have made a successful career in politics and he wasn't shy of letting his jockeys know if they'd cocked up. After the Kennel Gate Novices Hurdle he was happy - but Barney most certainly wasn't

Robin Goodfellow had shown good form in two runs the previous season, once in a National Hunt Flat Race when second to Riva Rose and then when four and a half lengths third to the very well regarded Tickite Boo at Newbury in November. But he wasn't straightforward to train and a year passed before I rode him to make an impressive seasonal debut at Newbury in the EBF Novice Hurdle Qualifier, beating Puck's Place ridden by Peter Scudamore. I held him up in the rear, let the horse make ground steadily up the long home straight, and he won very easily.

Ten days later at Ascot we lined up for the novice hurdle that was going to result in me receiving an unnerving phone call that would end with Curley being warned off.

I set out to ride Robin Goodfellow much the same as I'd ridden him at Newbury, aiming to settle him and come with a steady run to take the race in the later stages. Unlike his previous race, where he'd been ice cool, Robin Goodfellow was now sweating. This is often a sign that an animal is fretting, but it didn't worry me unduly. I was happy enough turning for home and moved up to track John White on Skygrange - who had won his previous race at Worcester by seven lengths - and I knew I'd got him beaten going to two out. But soon after, Brendan Powell produced Teletrader, who'd won at the previous Ascot meeting by five lengths, with a telling burst and they were away from us. Robin Goodfellow was a beaten horse going to the last and couldn't capitalise when Teletrader veered sharply right before going on to beat us by five lengths.

Sure, I was sorry the horse had been beaten but Toby was philosophical in defeat and knew there would be more races to win. For my side, when you're a jump jockey your thoughts soon turn to the next ride. Mine was Far Bridge for Toby in the Manicou Chase which he won by four lengths, making all and jumping brilliantly.

The day didn't end too well as I had to pull up Toby's Brent Riverside in the last, but as I turned left out of the jockeys' car park and prepared for the three hour drive back to my little place in Wetherby I was satisfied enough with the day's work. I put some Tamla Motown on the tape deck and began to plan my Saturday night out, starting with the Flying Pizza and ending up at Mr Craig's nightclub followed by that oh-so-wonderful lie in on Sunday morning.

But Curley was down a large sum of money, seething and looking for a scapegoat. He soon turned his thoughts to me - and not for the first time. Although I'd never ridden for him, our paths had crossed when I was a youngster with the Dickinsons.

Curley had excellent contacts in the Irish bloodstock world and has a very good eye for a horse. The good natured Tommy Stack, who had the casting vote in me going to Arthur Stephenson, first introduced Curley to the Boss and Mrs D. The meeting resulted in a steady flow of top class horses to the yard.

Us youngsters first got wind of Curley's presence when a permit holder called Bill Tinning, who trained about ten minutes away in Harrogate, brought a hurdler named Western Man to gallop with the Harewood team. Sooty Whyte rode him up behind our good horses, but Banner Bell and I could see that he was alright and had a quiet chuckle when Sooty told everyone that 'He isn't much.' Curley probably owned that one and I would have been surprised if it was Bill Tinning or his wife, in whose name the horse ran, who backed him from 11-1 to 11-4 when Sooty gave him a cool ride to win a selling hurdle at Doncaster in March 1980 on his first appearance in Britain. It was money well spent when he was bought in for 1,700 guineas and he went on to become a prolific winner for Jimmy FitzGerald. The next year I won on him at Ayr.

Curley had been supplying some of the very best chasers that Harewood had seen long before that, but I know there is one he wished he hadn't sent over. This was the appropriately named Buck Me Off, who gave Michael Dickinson his career-ending fall at Cartmel in 1978. There is a touch of irony in the fact that he also sent over Talon, who later became my first winner.

Curley also found some champions, including the legendary Silver Buck, the wayward but brilliant I'm A Driver and Tommy Joe. The arrangement was a simple one. The Dickinsons would pass them on to their best owners, none of whom were interested in gambling, so when the horses were ready to win first time out, Barney would have the market to himself and plunge in.

In his book *'Giving a Little Back'* he states that an eavesdropping telephone operator on the Mullingar exchange was responsible for the opening price of 9-2 when Silver Buck won his first race in an amateur hurdle under Michael's brother-in-law Thomas Tate.

Later on he found 'that the yard's business was becoming common knowledge ... horses were starting 6-4 and 5-4, a complete waste of time.

'There was one man whom I suspected was the principal cause. I used to be continually on to Michael about it but he never made much progress. I went to Michael one day and said, "There's no doubt about it, the rotten apple is Bradley."'

Curley had put two and two together and got three and a half. When a yard was as successful as Harewood, it became impossible to keep the ability of horses secret - just look at the prices of Martin Pipe's runners these days.

Curley underestimated the serious view Michael took of his allegations. In fact, Michael made extensive inquiries to find out where the serious leaks were coming from and employed a private detective. The man scoured the Leeds, Harrogate and York area to find out who was punting what to whom. All he could find was Arnold Wedgwood, who owned a garage in the area, was having £50, sometimes £100 on Dickinson horses, hardly a king's ransom. I owned up straight away, 'Yeah, it's my Uncle Arnold. He looks after my car, does me a good deal and I tell him the odd horse. That was how meticulous Michael was and that was the end of it, although he did find out something else. He told me years later that he understood that Tommy Carmody used to talk to someone in Ireland who might have been a leak. Now, that would have been ironic as it was Curley who influenced the Dickinsons into employing Tommy after Michael finished riding. Perhaps Curley's famed coups had been shot down by friendly fire.

Either way, I was clearly someone Barney Curley didn't trust and, 24 hours after the defeat of Robin Goodfellow, I received a disturbing call from Mrs Dickinson. 'Brad? Mrs D here. I've just had a call from Barney Curley. He's not very happy with you and is saying you stopped Robin Goodfellow at Ascot yesterday. And he says he's going to ring you.'

They don't come any straighter than Monica Dickinson and I was thankful for the warning. I had to wait two more days for my call but this is Mrs D's sworn statement to the Jockey Club Security Department-Investigations concerning that telephone conversation and another:

'At 10.30 am on Sunday , 16th November 1986, I answered the telephone at my home and a man said, 'Is the Boss man in? There's something I want to talk to you both about.' I told him that Tony was out and he then told me he was going to Ireland that afternoon and that his flight was at 1.30 p.m. He asked me to ring him back at his hotel when Tony arrived back and asked me to try and ring before 1 p.m. He gave me his telephone number which I kept.

Although the man did not give his name, I know it was Barney Curley on the phone as I know his voice well. We have bought horses from Barney in the past, but it must be last season that I saw him to speak to. We have not done business with Barney for several years, but would often have a chat with him at race meetings.

At 12.30 p.m. after Tony arrived back I rang the number and spoke to him again. I am not absolutely certain but I'm almost sure I called him Barney when I spoke to him on this occasion. As soon as he knew it was me calling, he said, 'Your jockey stopped that horse in the first race yesterday. I was going to have £20,000 on it, but there were rumours flying about and one bookmaker was backing another horse. I became suspicious so I only had £8,000 on the horse. I have proof that Bradley stopped the horse and that a bookie paid him to do it. I want £15,000 back by Monday, otherwise I'm going to the Jockey Club on Tuesday. I am going to ring Bradley and tell him what I have just told you.'

After telling me about Bradley stopping Toby Balding's horse on Saturday, Curley went on to tell me that Bradley had stopped some of my horses in the past. I just laughed at

146

him, because I just did not believe this. Tony and I have always been completely satisfied with Bradley's riding.

I was rather upset by what I was told by Curley, particularly as I did not believe him and after our conversation, I telephoned Graham Bradley and told him what had been said.

Early during the morning of Wednesday 19th November 1986, Curley again telephoned me and told me he had telephoned Bradley on Tuesday night and said that he had told him that he had proof that he had stopped the horse and what he was going to do to him. I told him he was causing a great deal of bother and that I hoped he knew what he was doing. He then said, 'I don't want any money, I just want the jockey off.'

I do not recall Curley actually stating his name, but I am almost certain I called him Barney once or twice. I recognised his voice as soon as he first spoke to me and I am completely satisfied that the man I spoke to on the three occasions referred to was Barney Curley.

The man seemed quite normal and rational during each conversation. He was certainly not drunk, but in any case, as far as I am aware, Barney does not drink at all.'

I didn't waste any time in contacting my solicitor Guy Faber, who immediately told me to tape any conversation I had with Curley. I also put in a call to Toby Balding, who put me in touch with his solicitor Peter Gorvin. He also said I should tape any conversation and advised me to get in touch with Jockey Club Security.

My call from Curley came in two days later as I was watching television with my mate Graham McCourt. Graham was staying overnight with me before riding the next day at Haydock and

147

witnessed one side of the conversation.

I'd taken the advice to have a tape machine ready and pressed the record button as soon as I heard his distinctive, monotone Irish brogue:

Barney Curley: You rode that horse on Saturday called Robin Goodfellow?

Graham Bradley: Yes.

BC: In the first race?

GB: Yes.

BC: How much did you get for stopping him?

GB:I didn't get anything.

BC: I'd be very careful what I say now.

GB: Yes.

BC: Just think about that ... because I have a bit of a problem.

GB: Go on then.

BC:I would ask you that question again ... you know, and don't dodge the question.

GB: Yes

BC: And I am not a fool, as you know.

GB: Yes.

BC: So do you want me to ask the question again?

GB: Well, look. What makes you think I stopped it?

BC: I'd be very careful of what you say to me, now, because I have a bit of a problem.

GB: Well, go on, tell me what the problem is.

BC: Now, I don't have it because I am going to pass it on to you.

GB: Yes.

BC: You know, it's your livelihood that's at stake.

GB: Yes, that's right ... what are you implying, what do you want?

BC: Well, I'll just tell you the story. As you know, I back horses ... and I back them there myself, mostly on the form book ... I do not recognise the sort of opinions of jockeys because ... I'd be a better judge myself.

GB: Yes.

BC: What's that humming noise?

GB: I don't know, it must be a bit of interference or something.

BC: Right, well I have put a lot of money into this game... and I like the game.

GB: Yes.

BC: Now I never, with all the horses I have had, stopped them to get money off bookmakers. Understand?

GB: Yes, I do.

BC: To make a long story short I had £12,000 on that horse on Saturday ... I was going to have about £24,000 ... the more money I was getting on, the bigger the price I was getting.

GB: Yes.

BC: Well, I'd be a very good judge of racing ... as a matter of fact, I'd be the best judge in England and Ireland of horses running.

GB: Yes. So what are you trying to say - that I actually stopped it and took money off the bookmakers?

BC: That's right.

GB: Yes. Well, look, what is the next step then.

BC: Well, I didn't ring you over the weekend ... and rather than have a hullabaloo or put you in bad form or something, I just waited until now.

GB: What's the next step then?

BC: Well, I just don't know ... you say you didn't stop him?

GB: Definitely not.

BC: Right. OK. Well, you know, I thought I'd ring you up first anyhow.

GB: The ball's in your court now. It's entirely up to you. What do you want to do?

BC: I have a lot of money invested in this game and I love the game ... and it's something I'll have to think about and go to my solicitor or the Jockey Club, or whatever.

GB: Well, what would stop you doing something like that?

BC: Well, if you just tell me what you have to say.

GB: I am telling you that I am totally 100 per cent innocent.

BC: Right. Well, then, Graham, if you are 100 per cent innocent ... you have nothing to fear.

GB: Yes.

BC: I will stake my judgement ... against any man in England.

GB: That is not going to go very far with the Jockey Club, is it, just your opinion? I mean you would be wasting your time ... you are going to need some concrete evidence.

BC: You see, as you know, it is a recognised thing in this game that, you know, people say the horse is not ready or something, give him a quiet run round. The trainer says that and it is a recognised thing in the business.

GB: Yes.

BC: But the other way.

GB: What do you mean, the other way?

BC: Well, it is my opinion that you stopped the horse and drew money.

GB: Yes. You won't have any concrete evidence though, will you? I mean it would be a waste of time going to the Jockey Club unless you knew something.

BC: Well you know, Graham, you were away in America during the summertime, weren't you? ... Well, I had a case against Tattersalls. Now they would be very, very big ... And I didn't move until I thought the time was right and I moved and I won.

GB: Yes.

BC: And everybody said I was mad ... I do not believe in moving except when I can back up my statements.

GB: Yes.

BC: Well, there is no way I am going to blackmail you or something like that ... because I am not that type of person ... but if there is something that I should know, that you want to tell me.

GB: Well, what would I want to tell you?

BC: ... maybe you were feeling sick or maybe you had money problems.

GB: I have certainly not got money problems.

BC: Well, that is right. I hear you have got a new car.

GB: I bought that before Robin Goodfellow, though ... I've been riding professionally now for seven years ... and rode quite a few big winners so surely I can afford to buy myself a car.

BC: You deny completely anything about it.

GB: Yes.

BC: And that's your final word on it?

GB: Yes.

BC: All right. That's OK. I do not know what I am going to do...but I'll certainly have to think about it.

GB: Well, what are you thinking about doing?

BC: I am thinking about going to the Jockey Club.

GB: What good is that going to do you?

BC: I'll be able to sleep in bed at night for starters ... because since I started racing I have run into a good bit of this.

GB: Yes. They are going to laugh at you though, aren't they, if you go down there with no evidence. If it's just your judgement.

BC: I am not a fool you know. That I am not. I'll have evidence ... you know, I am not a fool, no.

GB: Where are you going to get your evidence from, fresh air?

BC: ... I just want to know, have you anything to say, that you might have been sick or something like that...not feeling well. As long as I know that, then bingo.

GB: No. I felt a million dollars. No problems whatsoever.

BC: And that's your final word on the subject?

GB: Yes, it is.

BC: Now, you are sure about this? Look, I have rung you up out of the blue. Maybe you have my conversation on tape. You can play it back.

GB:Mmmm. It definitely is Barney Curley isn't it?

BC: It sure is, Graham.

GB: Yes, that is good. You will let me know what you want to do as soon as you can?

BC: Well, I am not letting you know again, Graham, because I am going to decide what I am going to do, then I am going to do it ... Now have you anything to add? You can think about it there. Are you married?

GB: No.

BC: You live on your own?

GB: Yes.

BC: Right, well you can think about it there ... but I would feel a lot safer if I went to the Jockey Club and discussed this with the Jockey Club.

GB: So you are not going to blackmail me or anything like that?

BC: I certainly am not.

GB: That is fair enough.

BC: Thank God I do not need the money. I just am there to protect racing. That it is not going to go like it did on Saturday, that's all ... I am not going to blackmail you. I have no interest in the world...and you have no fear along those lines.

GB: No.

BC: None whatsoever. I will never ask you about horses, whether they are going to win or lose or ... It is not my scene to ask you to stop horses for me or anything like that.

GB: Yes.

BC: I saw something on Saturday. I thought it was disgraceful and that is it.

GB: Well, you are not a very good judge then, that is all I can say ... in fact, I think you must be fucking blind, to be perfectly honest ... either blind or blind drunk.

BC: Well, I was not blind drunk ... as I have said, I'll back my judgement against anybody watching racing.

GB: Well, you are not a very good judge then, that is all I can say.

BC: Well, I have made a living over the last twenty years backing horses.

GB: Well, I am sick to fucking death of talking to you. You get yourself down to that Jockey Club and you will make a fucking laughing stock of yourself.

BC: OK.

GB: As far as I am concerned you are a fucking big Irish fat cunt and never fucking ring me again, you twat.'

Not the wittiest of finishes, I'll admit, but I was livid that someone like Curley - a licensed trainer - had the gall to think he had the right to make such a phone call. I took the tape to Leicester racecourse and handed it over to a Jockey Club Security man and let the ruling body handle things from there.

The sum Curley staked on the horse tends to change from £8,000 to £12,000, but when he had his bet at Ascot he thought his money would be enough to shorten the horse, instead of which the bookmakers pushed him out from 5-4 to 13-8. Now it is not unknown for bookmakers to have lads in yards who put them wise about the wellbeing or otherwise of horses - how else would they price up a field of unraced two-year-olds or bumper horses?

According to my good friend Richard Guest, who was a conditional jockey with Toby Balding at the time, Robin Goodfellow had knee problems that sometimes made him unsound. I didn't know this, but it wouldn't have been hard for it to work its way back to the betting ring that the horse hadn't worked particularly well.

Two weeks later at Sandown on softer ground than at Ascot, Robin Goodfellow met Skygrange and Teletrader again and was ice cool. He swept through to lead at the last and beat Skygrange by four lengths, a length more than he had when they were second and third to Teletrader at Ascot, only this time Teletrader had an off day and was six lengths back in third. *Timeform Chasers and Hurdlers* for 1986-87 stated, 'The way we read the form book, he (Robin Goodfellow) showed just about the same level of form on his second outing as his third.'

Curley made his complaint to the Jockey Club but I knew they would find nothing wrong. On 19 December, which I took off to do some Christmas shopping, they announced that they had examined Curley's complaint with the help of three professional race readers and were satisfied there was no evidence to support any further inquiry.

My name was cleared but the Jockey Club were not finished with Curley and continued a lengthy inquiry into his phone calls to Mrs Dickinson and to me. On 25 April 1987 he was found guilty under Rule 220 (iii) which governs conduct liable to damage the interests of racing.

Part of the statement from the Jockey Club said, 'The inquiry was held to investigate complaints received concerning threats of a serious nature made by Mr Curley in telephone conversations involving not only Graham Bradley but also another licensed trainer. These events took place before Mr Curley made his own complaint to the Jockey Club.'

Curley, who was training just outside Newmarket, had his licence withdrawn and was banned for two years.

It would be wrong to say I was pleased to see a man's livelihood taken away. Equally, I didn't cry any tears for Curley and felt that this was only one battle and that the war was still to be won.

Sure enough, Curley instituted proceedings to take the Jockey Club to the High Court, but before the case could be heard the Jockey Club granted a re-hearing so that he could be legally represented. And he said, 'The Jockey Club have done more harm to racing in two hours than twenty bent jockeys can do in a lifetime. Not a question was asked by the disciplinary committee and I showed them five videos.

'I felt they were under instruction to have no words with Curley (*sic*). I got to feel they were dealing with a mad Irishman who had done his money at Ascot and was now doing his nut. Well they will find out differently.'

Curley engaged the eminent QC Richard du Cann and, just 101 days after the ban was implemented, a new panel of the Jockey Club Disciplinary Committee consisting of Chairman Christopher Lloyd, Sir Cecil Blacker and Michael Wrigley overturned the previous ruling.

But there was a stinging appendage to the acquittal which said: 'The Committee found that Mr Curley did contact and cause distress to a licensed trainer (Mrs Monica Dickinson) and jockey (Graham Bradley) for the purpose of pursuing a losing bet.

'They consider such conduct to be reprehensible but that, in the particular circumstances it did not amount to a breach of Rule 220 (iii).'

At the time, Curley's retained rider Declan Murphy was serving a suspension for deliberately misleading or endeavouring to mislead the stewards.

I don't know what forced the Jockey Club to backtrack. I had done absolutely nothing wrong and played by the rules. Curley hadn't and received no punishment for dragging racing and myself through the mud in public.

I felt betrayed and had the distinct feeling I had been left holding the shitty end of the stick.

I have no doubt that from the time that the Robin Goodfellow affair began I was a marked man as far as the Jockey Club were concerned. And just to prove it, I was under a three month ban at the time Curley walked.

Although I could never prove it, I had the feeling that I was being tailed by one of the Jockey Club security men during the months following the initial inquiry where I was exonerated. In short, if I hadn't done anything wrong this time, they felt I was sure to do something in the future.

One day at Uttoxeter I came out of the weighing room to go down to the last fence when I saw someone who was beginning to become a regular hanging about the unsaddling area. I thought I'd test him and went to the public toilet. Sure enough, he followed me and came in. He seemed keen to see who I was talking to on the way to the last fence and stood and watched me as I went over the course.

He was a typical ex-CID man failing miserably in his bid to look inconspicuous and he was on my tail back to the weighing room after the race was over. It wasn't something that worried me much, but I should have been much more concerned about a nondescript handicap hurdle at Market Rasen.

The Boomtown Rats hit 'I Don't Like Mondays' would have suited me better had it been re-titled 'I Don't Like Bank Holiday Mondays.' Most jockeys love them because there just aren't enough of us to go round. Even the boys who struggle to make a living get the chance of four or five rides at one of the gaffs which can make the difference between having a summer holiday and not. But my first brush with the Jockey Club had come on such a day at Cartmel back in 1982 and I was going to get the worst suspension of my career when the holiday crowds thronged the Lincolnshire track on Monday 20 April 1987.

Chris Pimlott was now acting as my agent and phoned me late on Sunday night to give me an update for the following day. Pacifiste looked a good thing for Mrs D in the novice chase, there would be two for John Jenkins, and he'd picked up a late spare for the late Ken Bridgwater called Deadly Going which had a chance. Great, four fair rides and a good day's work in prospect.

Deadly Going was first in the Col R. Thompson Memorial Handicap Hurdle over two miles and went off 2-1 second favourite behind Record Harvest at 7-4. Ken's son, Ken junior, told me to have the gelding up with the pace and make the best of my way home from two out.

The horse hadn't got the greatest reputation. He was a bit headstrong and when he stepped at the first and almost fell the jump jockeys autopilot came in. I decided to get him settled and jumping before we did anything else. Orders are orders, but when Plan A doesn't look too good it's advisable to turn to Plan B. The problem was Deadly Going couldn't quicken up when I asked him in the middle of the race, and I admit that I began to lose interest at the same time. In hindsight I should have got stuck into him. It was a mistake which was to give the Jockey Club the perfect stick to beat me with.

Boreham Down, ridden by Geoff Harker, had led from the second and was nearly twenty lengths clear as the field jumped two out. Deadly Going began to pick up, just as the favourite Record Harvest did, but that one was beaten when he fell at the last and Deadly Going ran on to finish ten lengths second with Geoff easing his mount considerably. It would not have mattered one jot what I did on Deadly Going. Even if I'd got off and pushed he wouldn't have beaten the winner.

The stewards called an inquiry. I admitted I hadn't carried out my instructions but told the panel the pace was very quick and my horse had lost his place in the middle of the race. They asked young Ken his view and he said that he was satisfied with my riding. We looked at the film, they asked him again if he was still satisfied, and his answer was an emphatic: 'Yes.'

I added that I thought I'd given him a fairly good ride, which was the only lie I told because I knew that it had been a pretty awful effort. There's no doubt I should have made more of a show, but we all make mistakes. I went out to complete a miserable day when Pacifiste made a bad mistake and unseated me at the fourteenth when travelling strongly with the leaders. Skygrange weakened to finish third in the novice hurdle and Kyoto fell two out in the two mile handicap chase when staying on in second place. But if I thought that was the end of a not-so-perfect day I was badly mistaken.

The stewards called me back after that seventh race and told me they weren't satisfied with my riding. Once again, I was being referred to Portman Square.

I've always had a strong mental approach and wasn't worried when I returned to the detached house I'd bought in Wetherby on the Linton Manor Estate. I hadn't done anything wrong except ride a bad race - and show me a jockey who hasn't done that. I phoned Ken Bridgwater Sr and, although he wasn't pleased I hadn't carried out his orders, he had been in the game long enough to know these things do happen.

Now, given that I had seen the way things work at Portman Square after the Cartmel stupidity all those years previously I should have been more alert. Foolishly, I relied on the belief that I'd done nothing wrong and that innocent people don't get convicted. In short, I let my guard down.

My brother Gary had a good friend called Guy Faber who is a solicitor and dealt with the buying and selling of Gary's houses. He did the same conveyancing work for me and still does. But standing up before the Disciplinary Committee of the Jockey Club is a job for specialist lawyers and Guy wasn't one.

He was very interested in racing and was a part-time racecourse judge for a while and I thought it would be good experience for him to come down to London and represent me at Portman Square. Big mistake. As the inquiry began to warm up on Monday 22 June I realised Guy was out of his depth. He was asking the wrong questions and not putting my case forward with any real force. Mid-way through the hearing I realised I was trying to put a forest fire out with a bucket of water. By the time we were sent out for half an hour while the committee deliberated I was a very anxious man.

I was right to be. When I came back I was told my licence would be suspended until 1 November. It was effectively a three-month ban as we were now in the close season for jumping and the new one opened on 1 August. I was allowed to work in stables and go to the races but there wasn't much immediate chance of that happening because I'd broken my wrist and, while that would take some time to heal, it would be right long before 1 November.

I made noises in the Press suggesting that I would take the Jockey Club to the High Court but that was never an option - I simply didn't have the financial clout of someone like Barney Curley. I'd made the mistake of not taking the right weaponry to Portman Square and paid a heavy penalty. That said, I'm certain the Jockey Club were out to get me and even a tag team of the renowned George Carman and Richard du Cann couldn't have saved me.

Ken Bridgwater, who was an extremely fair-minded man said, 'I feel sorry for the jockey - it is a bit harsh to lose a licence.' But lose it I had. And what of Deadly Going? He ran nine times during the next season and was staying on in second five times. He never won again.

And I still had to had to suffer the indignity of watching Barney Curley have a two-year ban for bringing racing into serious disrepute overturned. Toby Balding was swiftly on the case once that judgement was reversed and sent a letter to the licensing stewards in a plea for fair play. Part of the letter says, 'Bradley has been in the limelight since the emergence of the Barney Curley outbursts over his riding of Robin Goodfellow at Ascot. In this matter, I consider he behaved perfectly properly and responsibly and as you know, subsequent investigations exonerated him completely.

In view of the recent reinstatement of Curley's licence and the form of Deadly Going proving no more or rather less worthwhile than at Market Rasen, I hope that the Stewards will now consider that the sentence imposed on Bradley was too harsh.

There is ample precedent for a review of his case, after which I hope that he will be allowed to reapply for his licence without delay.'

The chances of that were slim to none and I did my time. But I certainly didn't do the crime.

CHAPTER 14
Wonderful Wayward Lad

I've been fortunate to ride some of the best chasers around during my twenty-three years as a jockey and the one who had almost everything was Wayward Lad. He had a very high cruising speed with the ability to quicken off it and inject pace that could settle a race very quickly. He was majestic over a fence.

His sole weakness was the inability to quite stay three and a quarter miles up the Cheltenham hill, which made him one of the best horses never to win the race.

As my career was temporarily sidelined by the stewards with the three-month suspension over Deadly Going, Wayward Lad was about to bow out of the spotlight in the unlikely setting of the Doncaster Sales ring in April 1987.

That this should happen to a fine racehorse who had achieved so much and was now on the run-in to honourable retirement just goes to underline what a perilous path people tread when they enter into racehorse partnerships.

Wayward Lad raced in the maroon and light blue colours of Mrs Shirley Thewlis, who owned 60 per cent of him with farmer Les Abbott owning the remaining 40. And after the old horse had won at Liverpool in April it was generally understood that he would retire to Harewood. It was understood, that is, by everyone except Mr Abbott, who wanted him to go point to pointing.

It may be best to use a football analogy here, because sending Wayward Lad into the pointing field would have been the same as a once great soccer player turning out for an amateur side and watching the young hopefuls kick lumps out of him trying to make a name for themselves.

It was a very acrimonious time and my sympathies were entirely with the retirement plan, but Abbott would not budge, so, as is so often the case, Wayward Lad was sent to the sale ring where he could be bought by whoever wanted him most.

Mrs D is a very formidable lady when roused and she was that and more now. She said, 'The whole situation is awful and Mrs Thewlis is very upset. Wayward Lad went to Mr Abbott's farm a couple of summers ago and didn't come back looking as well as he should have done.

'Mrs Thewlis always said that Michael should have Wayward Lad as a hack when his racing days were over and he should end his days with us. It is very sad that the future of such a great horse who has given so much pleasure to so many people should be resolved in the sale ring.'

But sale ring it was. There was a crush to get a look at the old soldier as he was led round and, although Abbott didn't make a bid, the Irishman Aiden O'Connell was keen to take Wayward Lad to hunt in Limerick and pushed the bidding forward. But the Boss was never going to be denied and when the hammer came down at 42,000 guineas it was one of the most emotional scenes I've ever seen at a sale.

Harry Beeby, the auctioneer, announced, 'Wayward Lad is sold to go back to Harewood - I hope he enjoys his retirement as much as we have enjoyed watching him race.' Mrs D marched into the ring and gave Wayward Lad a handful of his favourite polo mints then threw her arms around the neck that had stretched to victory twenty-eight times in fifty-five starts and amassed earnings of £278,064. She couldn't hold back the tears and said, 'We would have gone higher if we'd had to.'

It was Rusty and Joy Carrier, great friends of the Dickinsons who train in America, who had bankrolled the bid and had told the Boss to buy Wayward Lad no matter how much so that he could travel to the States. The old warrior is still enjoying a happy retirement with them as I write and I know that Michael sees him on a regular basis when he is in the area.

I was moist around the eyes and even such hardened professionals as Jimmy FitzGerald and Mick Naughton were misty-eyed.

And I probably had more reason than most of them to be thankful to the gelding by Royal Highway. Although Robert Earnshaw had ridden him for much of his career, he was winding down as a jockey to try turf farming before eventually joining the Jockey Club. I was given the ride on Wayward Lad and rode him in public for the first time in the Charlie Hall Pattern Chase at Wetherby on 2 November 1985. We came through that readily enough, and although we were going to get each other in trouble during the two seasons we were together the good times won hands down.

The first blip came on our next appearance in the three-runner Edward Hanmer Memorial Handicap Chase at Haydock when he was 4-6 to beat two rivals, the serious one being Forgive 'N Forget and the 6-1 outsider Richdee, whose rider Colin Hawkins was going to be the biggest financial winner on the day.

In a small field with two good horses like Wayward Lad and Forgive 'N Forget the main worry would be lack of pace. Colin was a seasoned pro and knew the score so he came up to me an hour before and said, 'Look, Brad, I'll make it a decent gallop if you give me £300' That sounded good to me, so I went to see Mrs D and she was happy and said she'd sort it out with the owners. But Colin was working on double time and said the same thing to Mark Dwyer, who got the go-ahead from Jimmy FitzGerald to square him up. So Colin got £600 and ended up with second-place money as well. We went to the fifth, the last fence down the back straight and when Richdee dived to his left, Wayward Lad followed him, only worse. He landed in a twenty yard gap in the running rail and collided with it when it started again and unseated me. I was furious but the course layout was to blame because it didn't give the horse a chance to balance himself when he made the deviation. It was changed after that but that didn't help me.

But there was a massive moment waiting for us at Kempton Park on Boxing Day, when Wayward Lad put his doubters in their place and won his third and final King George. It was the sixth time in seven years that the Dickinson family had won the race. The Boss had done it with Gay Spartan and Silver Buck. Michael trained Silver Buck to win it and scored twice with Wayward Lad and now Mrs D had added her name to the list. But it was a cruelly hard race for Wayward Lad and, looking back on it now, I am ashamed at just how hard I was on him. I gave him three turning for home with three to jump and hardly missed him from then on.

He took the lead under strong pressure two out and when Combs Ditch, who had a fine turn of pace, nosed up to challenge at the last he seemed sure to be beaten. But he didn't have that Cheltenham hill to tax his stamina and he pulled everything out for me to win by a neck. Just how fast we were travelling was revealed by time expert Michael Tanner, who told John Oaksey in the *Horse And Hound* that Wayward Lad had produced an abnormal burst of speed from the last fence to the line on soft ground. We went one tenth of a second faster than when Wayward Lad broke the course record in 1983 and nearly a full second faster than Burrough Hill Lad and Combs Ditch the previous year.

There was no question that when roused Wayward Lad was as good as ever but the problem was that he had got very lazy. Mrs D used to ride him all the time and he was her pet. You could have put a child on him he was so quiet, and the older he got the more riding he needed on the racecourse.

Looking back now on his Cheltenham Gold Cup the same season I was brutally hard on him again and I take no pleasure watching the race now. It was undoubtedly the best steeplechase I ever rode in and nine times out of ten Wayward Lad's performance would have been good enough. It was definitely his finest hour at Cheltenham, but in Dawn Run he came up against a great mare at her peak. But without wishing to detract from her length win it was only in the previous couple of seasons that mares had been given a 5lb allowance in the race - it was introduced when she won the Champion Hurdle of 1984 - and any handicapper will tell you that extra burden will make the difference between victory and defeat.

If ever he was going to win a Cheltenham Gold Cup this was his day. I was riding him hard from the top of the hill and he never flinched as he came to head Forgive 'N Forget at the last. Unlike past years he didn't empty quite so early and it was only a magnificent effort by the mare and Jonjo O'Neill that got her home in the shadow of the post. There is no question that had I given a horse that kind of ride during the final five years of my career I'd have been stood down for months - and unlike some other occasions, I'd have fully deserved it.

Those hard races lodged in my subconscious and resulted in two defeats for Wayward Lad that should never have been. The first came on his next outing in the Whitbread Gold Label Cup at Liverpool, where he was up against Dawn Run with two who looked out of their depth, Very Promising and the 40-1 chance Beau Ranger. When Dawn Run fell at the first I thought all my birthdays had come at once and it was just going to be a skip round. But I let him idle and allowed Beau Ranger to get a clear lead. We could never get back to him and were held off by a length and a half.

The other time I should have won on him was the next season in the Sheila's Cottage Handicap Chase at Doncaster. He was really on a going day and went to the front three out, cruising. He was clear at the next and going to the last I let him slow right down to pop it. As a result he lost all his momentum and was headed by the earlier leader Burnt Oak and Simon Sherwood. He couldn't get going again and was beaten a length and a half. I went on TV and made all the excuses I could think of, such as not wanting him to fall, but that was the bravado of youth. I knew I should have won and apologised to the owners and Mrs D afterwards. Typically, they were very good and didn't jock me off him. There are quite a few people that probably would have.

But Wayward Lad was blindingly talented and it was one of my great regrets that I wasn't on him the day he won his last race at Liverpool. After he'd finished an honourable fifth to The Thinker in the 1987 Gold Cup he was most unlikely to run at Liverpool because Mrs D knew he'd had another very hard race. With that in mind, I accepted the ride from Jenny Pitman on Stearsby in the Whitbread Gold Label Cup. By the time Mrs D decided to run Wayward Lad it was impossible to switch mounts, especially as Terry Ramsden had jocked off his retained rider and my best friend in the weighing room at that time, Graham McCourt, so that I could renew my association with Stearsby having won the Welsh National on him in December.

But I ended up doing Graham a favour and stuck him in for one of the most memorable rides he ever had around the Mildmay fences. All I could do was shout encouragement to them both as Stearsby weakened at the fifteenth and Wayward Lad came surging by to collar Simon Legree at the last to win going away by seven lengths for one last hurrah. I'm just sorry I missed it.

CHAPTER 15

The Wetherby Strangler

There is a popular myth that jump jockeys don't cry. Well, I have to tell you that I was in tears during the 1987-88 season and it was nothing to do with losing the retainer from Sir Philip and Lady Harris.

I had already won a Cheltenham Gold Cup and desperately wanted a Grand National to go with it, they are the Premier League title and FA Cup of jump racing. A certain type of horse is needed for Aintree, although with the alteration of the fences it has become less so, and I was certain that Mrs D had the right one for the job in By The Way.

The previous season he looked an outstanding proposition and there was only one problem, albeit a rather significant one. His owner, Mrs Chris Feather, was very much against running any horse in the National, let alone one with the potential of By The Way. She was unmoved by anything Mrs D said, so I took a step which for me was unprecedented and wrote her a letter outlining just why I thought the horse should run in the world's greatest steeplechase. The principal of my argument was that By The Way was such a natural jumper and would have no trouble with the testing fences.

And despite having won the Whitbread Gold Cup two years earlier he was a horse just reaching his full potential at the age of nine, having gone through that season unbeaten in four starts, the last of which was in the Catterick National Trial, where he made all and jumped impeccably to beat Why Forget by eight lengths.

Mrs Feather knew how much it would mean to everyone to win a National - it was the one major chase that the Dickinson family hadn't won - and gave the go-ahead. It didn't take long for the odds to contract and he was soon second favourite behind the previous year's winner West Tip.

The preparation was going so smoothly that I was almost waiting for something to go wrong and the fates didn't let me down. On 29 March I was giving By The Way a sharp bit of work on the Harewood gallops and he faltered with me. I felt him jar as the pain hit him and was out of the saddle and by his head in a matter of strides. The vet took an X-ray which showed a split pastern and that was the end of the National dream for 1987, but this was an injury that would heal and there was always next year.

He was trained specifically for the big race in 1988, with the Boss and Mrs D mindful of his injury, and when By The Way stepped out for the Durham National Handicap Chase at Sedgefield on 9 March he was a solid third favourite for the National with all bookmakers. He was just starting to peak and was running by far his best race of the season. We skipped over the last well clear and set out on the long run-in which is downhill for two furlongs, levels out past the water jump and ends with a slight incline. With half the distance covered disaster hit us. By The Way completely lost his action and gave a sickening lurch before hobbling to a stop. As I slipped off him I knew the National dream had turned into a nightmare once more.

I saw the worst sight a jockey can see. By The Way had broken a leg and all I could do was sit with him as he held his head down to the grass the way all horses do when they are in severe pain. At least you can talk to a human and let them know you're concerned, but with a horse you feel so useless. The vet, who was on hand very swiftly, could see the severity of the injury and was hurrying to put the horse out of his agony. I looked down the course to see Mrs Feather and Mrs D coming towards me, very worried but unaware that the injury was fatal. I put my head into one hand as the other held By The Way's reins and I wept.

The three of us huddled together on the course and cried as the screens went up around By The Way. As we walked away slowly, a single pistol shot resounded behind us. There was no reason to look back. I was in a cloud of despondency when I returned to the weighing room and threw my tack on the table in futile frustration, thinking out loud that it always happens to the good ones. But there was even more misery to come an hour later.

My mind was in turmoil as I took my remaining two rides. The last of them, Bobby Burns trained by Mrs D, started 5-4 favourite for the three-mile novice chase and I hadn't been shy in telling people that I thought he was an absolute certainty. But I made the kind of error which can cause riots and rode a finish a circuit too soon.

As we turned for home for the second time I should have been preparing to go round again, but I completely lost my concentration and was convinced this was the last circuit. Jumping what I thought was the last fence, I came sharply over to the stands rails to avoid the bad bit of ground that may have been the cause of By The Way's demise. I swept past the water jump, and didn't notice that the dolls which cordon it off on the final circuit weren't present. I was determined to make for the smooth strip of ground on the outside that is flattened by the ambulance.

Geoff Harker on the 50-1 outsider Running Shot came with me. Foolishly, we both put our heads down and rode for the line. By the time I looked up and realised there were only two of us that had made this manoeuvre and gone the wrong way it was all too late. We had gone past the dolls that keep you on the right course and were out of the race.

Without over dramatising events, there was uproar. Bobby Burns had been heavily backed with over £11,000 being placed on course, let alone in betting shops, and the scenes worsened to such a degree that I needed a police escort to get back to the weighing room. The stewards showed no mercy. I owned up to making a monumental error and was hit with a £600 fine that would have been a fourteen-day ban if it were to happen now. And what's more, I fully deserved it and said at the time. 'It was a genuine mistake but I deserved some sort of punishment. It's been an awful day.' It's nearly impossible to defend such an unprofessional error, but looking back I was in no fit mental state to ride. I was consumed with grief over By The Way.

And it was even worse for Geoff, who followed me because he thought I knew what I was doing. He'd only picked his mount up as a spare ride after Neale Doughty got off it after feeling unwell and it cost him £600 as well.

This was the second time during the season I'd made a serious mistake with my finishes and one that occurred on 20 January was even more embarrassing.

Graham McCourt had stuck me in for the ride on Trout Angler in the novices handicap chase at Ludlow. He told me it was a good thing and that's exactly how I rode it, with plenty of confidence. We took up the running at the fourth and after a slight mistake at the fifteenth we came clear up the home straight to win by as far as we liked. I looked round three times on the long run-in and was confident I had the race sewn up.

But rather than win twenty lengths and risk a sharp rise in the weights I began to ease down to cut the winning distance as much as I could. I drastically overdid it. Trout Angler had been out in front for a long time and didn't need any encouragement to slow down. In blissful ignorance of two horses fighting out second and third and congratulating myself on a job well done, I got a belated wake-up call as the pair flashed upsides me in the shadow of the winning post.

Neither Clive Cox on Fortascue, John Bryan on Rich Nickel or a blushing Bradley knew which of us had won. I paced the weighing room with a racecard in my hand and an uncomfortable churning in my stomach as I waited for the winning number to be called. In the end there were two, it was a dead heat, but Trout Angler didn't feature in it. We were third and should have won by a minute. My credibility was strung out the length of the Ludlow run-in.

It was a sickener for the trainer Miss Paddy O'Connor, who hadn't had a winner for four years, and she came out with a quote that summed up the situation completely, 'I've just seen hope disappear over the horizon with its arse on fire.' I could do nothing but apologise sincerely for an unprofessional and incompetent piece of jockeyship and held my hands up to the stewards, who fined me £500. Once again, if the same mistake were made now it would be two weeks holiday without question.

But there was at least one man who would have been revelling in my blunders, namely Jeff Jennings, better known as 'Gino', who used to be the boardman in William Hills betting shop in Wetherby. The irony of the Trout Angler debacle is that I'd told my dad, Norm, that 'Gremlin' McCourt said it was a good thing. Dad had actually had a tenner on, which is very rare for him. But much as he liked to see me ride he wouldn't go down to the betting shop, just in case people thought he was punting on my behalf. I remedied that problem when I got him a subscription to the Racing Channel when it began. But his non-appearance in William Hills spared him the rantings of Gino, although they were faithfully reported back to me by two of my good friends, the ex-Leeds players Eddie Gray and Jimmy Lumbsden.

I'll give you a little pen picture of Gino. He's just over 70 now, 5ft 9in and slight with greying ginger hair going bald and a walrus moustache. He walks with his feet at ten to two and wears a blue puffa jacket topped off with a Chicago Bulls baseball cap.

His other job was doing the washing up at the Wetherby Turnpike Hotel, and although he didn't wear glasses he should have done because he had to squint at anything or anyone to make an identification. He had a great line in chat, but only to himself in between races, and although there were plenty of things he hated there were three in particular. Favourites. He would not back favourites, so therefore he didn't like Dickinson horses because they were quite often very short. But top of his list was G.J. Bradley. If a Dickinson horse looked like getting beaten he was off like a dervish screaming at the top of his voice and to no one in particular: 'Tame that Dickinson crab, tame that Dickinson crab.' But more than anything else the one single thing that could send him over the edge and transform him into a frothing maniac was me getting beaten on something he thought should have won.

He'd run the length of the betting shop like some quack doctor working the crowd at a fair: 'Look, look, he's at it again, the Wetherby Strangler's at it again.' And, of course with the help of Messrs Gray and Lumbsden, that particular nickname stuck like glue in certain quarters until I finished riding.

It would certainly have met with the approval of the gentleman who wrote the racing column in *Private Eye* but didn't have the balls to put his name to it and instead signed himself Major Bonkers. He referred to me as 'The Godfather of Yorkshire Racing,' which seemed a bit rich but was enhanced by a brawl over a lovely girl called Sue Bowden, who I was seeing from time to time. I was ordering a drink in the Old Star Inn at Collingingham to celebrate the birthday of one of my longest standing mates, Carl Leafe, who I've know since the days at Second Avenue. Without any warning someone called Ashley Calvert, who was also rather keen on the lovely Sue, tapped me on the shoulder and gave me a whack. Rather than have a ruck in the pub, which was packed, we went outside, where there was a little scuffle before we went our separate ways, my team to the Swan And Talbot, his to the Royal at Boston Spa. Unfortunately, some of my more boisterous mates decided to have another go and burst into the opposition pub. It went off like Saturday night in Dodge City. After leaving pretty quickly I felt very guilty and phoned the next day to pay for any damages. The landlord graciously accepted my apology and a cheque for £700 and sportingly said he wouldn't be pressing charges. The police weren't quite so benevolent and, after an appearance before Wetherby Magistrates on Tuesday morning, both Calvert and myself were fined £100 plus £10 costs and bound over to keep the peace for twelve months. And as for the object of our desire? She told the *Daily Mirror*, 'I have had enough of all men for the moment and I have finished with them both.'

Despite the problem of losing my job with Toby Balding there was at least one new yard I could rely on to give me rides. Norm had decided to make a comeback after sixteen years without a licence and I was delighted. He'd taken a lease on a yard at Ingmanthorpe, not far from home. It didn't take Norm long to get things going and I was able to put some owners his way with plenty of confidence that he knew exactly how to get one right when it really mattered.

Norm quickly got the first winner posted. Considering the touch that had been landed two seasons earlier at Wolverhampton, there couldn't have been a better horse to do it with than Starjestic - nor a more suitable venue than Wetherby. The old horse was ten now and had been with Banner Bell and Lynn Sidall, but he still had a nice turn of pace when it mattered. I was able to wait on him and creep into contention from three out before collaring Trafalgar Blue on the run-in to win by a length.

It was a very emotional moment when I dismounted and I kept thinking about those old chasers Norm had trained for Mr Hanson like Balty Boys and Dark Don. It was typical that Norm told the press that he'd got the best stable jockey in the world. If I'd been a bit quicker I would have countered that I'd had the best and most loyal teacher in the universe.

THE WAYWARD LAD

CHAPTER 16
The man called Uncle

The rumour factory is the biggest industry in British racing. It is working 24 hours a day, 365 days a year, and I have no doubt it has cost me several good retainers and the rides on top class horses. Equally, there is no question that my firm friendship with one man has sent the factory into overtime and soured my professional standing in the eyes of many people, reputedly 'in the know'.

His name is Brian Wright, but in the world of big time gamblers everyone has a nickname. And his is 'Uncle'.

In the cuthroat business of the professional gambler Brian got to the top, graduating from working for street bookmakers in West London to a turnover of hundreds of thousands at Epsom and Royal Ascot.

Like any professional gambler who is being honest he will admit that he has his contacts, and I was one, but the kind of money Brian was having on was always going to make people put two and two together and get six. I make absolutely no apology for my friendship with him. Whenever I have needed wise counsel, both on and off a racecourse it is Brian I have gone to - and he has never let me down.

But when there is a breath of scandal within racing there is only one name that comes up, Brian Wright. Just as the Krays were meant to be behind every protection racket that operated in London during the sixties, his name is first into the frame with Racecourse Security Services whenever there is the first hint of any corruption. He would have needed more tentacles than an octopus to have got his hands into all the scams he is meant to have been involved in.

One mistake he has certainly made is being a success at gambling, because jealousy eats away at many people in racing and Brian has never been shy of using his money for pleasure as well as punting. He's certainly not a 'plastic man'. Everything is cash and it's exaggerating only a bit to say that he always carries a roll of notes with him that would choke a donkey. But despite his high profile punting he is a very understated person. He's a shrewd observer of both people and horses with a mind that's sharp as a tack. During my time riding I found his judgement to be the soundest of anyone I've ever met.

I've known him a long time. We first met at Sandown on 30 November 1984. I came down to ride Rhoecus for Mrs D in the Winter Novices Hurdle and had one ride for Jim Old the next day. Barrie Wright (no relation), who I'd got to know quite well on my few trips south because his brother Tommy was playing for Leeds at the time, introduced us. 'A good mate of mine's got a box here today,' said Bazza. 'You've got to come and meet him, he's a lovely bloke.'

I've always prided myself on being a good judge of character and able to weigh people up in a very short time. After a couple of beers in Brian's box I just knew he was my kind of person. Yes, he had money, but he also had charisma and money can't buy that.

We went for a meal at Blakes Hotel which had one of the best restaurants in London at the time. It would have been easy for Brian to drop me off at a hotel afterwards, but instead he took me home to stay with his family in Twickenham. He married Josie when he was nineteen and his mother-in-law has lived with them ever since,

which must tell you something about his easy-going nature. It was Josie's mum, or 'Gran' as he calls her, who inadvertently gave Brian another nickname. One day she thought it was time he found regular employment and said, 'Brian, I've got you a job - as a milkman.' Brian's mates fell about laughing and although he never took the offer up, the name seemed to stick.

After I'd known him a while I asked him what he did for a living. He looked at me with a smile and replied in his curt, West London accent, 'This an' that.' I never bothered to ask him again. In all the time I've known him we've only ever had one cross word and it ultimately consolidated our friendship. Not too long after we'd met I gave him my view of how a race would go at Ascot and felt that a horse which I was riding wouldn't like the tacky ground. I was wrong and it won.

In those situations he usually says, 'Don't worry mate, I'll wipe my mouth and forget it.' But after we met in the car park that evening he clearly wasn't in the mood to forget anything. In short, he thought I'd turned him over.

The conversation was brief and ended with me telling him to shove his hospitality as far up his arse as he could get it. But in those few seconds he saw in my eyes that he'd really hurt me and that he was wrong. We've never had a cross word in all the years since. When I decided to write this book, I wanted people to know what he's really like, as far as I am concerned, and where he came from and that his friendship is one of my most valued possessions.

Brian's halcyon days on the racecourse were in the boom years of Thatcher's Britain when fortunes were made in the fireball economy and the city and stock market were flying. Racecourses were awash with major players like Terry Ramsden and big punters could get a real bet on.

Those eighties were solid gold, but his story begins over two decades earlier when betting was becoming legal and the game was

wide open for a quick-witted Londoner.

There isn't a trace of the Irish accent that came with him when his family moved over to England in 1958 when Brian was twelve. He didn't do much schooling in his final two years in Ireland and there were precious few ticks in the attendance register in England so he had hardly any formal education. As I've watched him size up situations and make lightning decisions I've often wondered what he might have achieved in the commercial world.

Recalling his early years he says, 'I came over with my mum and dad. We lived in Cricklewood and I'll admit I was a little bit of a tearaway early on until I had my wings clipped with a sharp dose of Borstal, which didn't do me any harm.

'Cricklewood was like the next-door borough, Kilburn, and had a very strong Irish community. There were a lot of navvies working for McAlpines, who were building the new Grandstand at Ascot, and they'd come back to their lodgings and use a pub called The Crown.

'There were very few betting shops then. A lot of business was done by the illegal street bookmakers and I used to act as a runner. The bets were paid out at Starting Price and I soon worked out I was taking more money to the bookie than I was bringing back. I also realised that most of the punters hadn't got a clue, so I began standing some bets myself and built up a nice little pot. I started to form an opinion of my own and I'd go to the races and watch horses run, and you've got to remember that there wasn't much televised racing then and no TV in betting shops. The punters were a lot less informed than they are now - for starters you had different handicappers rating horses in different parts of the country so you could back your opinion against a certain handicapper if you fancied one.

'I'd seen the 1964 Derby and liked the way Indiana stayed on to finish second to Santa Claus. Indiana was owned by Charlie Engelhard, the bloke who Ian Fleming based Goldfinger on, and

went on to win the Great Voltigeur at York, a reliable guide to the Leger. This looked pretty solid form to me but the bookmakers were swayed by reputations, just as they are now. They made 1 Titan, who'd won a handicap with 8st 3lb, the 5-1 co-favourite. But this was more to do with it being ridden by Lester Piggott and trained by Noel Murless than the form book and Indiana was out at 100-7 (14-1). I've always looked for value and I took a view that this was it and stepped in to take £1,000 to £70 five times. Picking up five grand in 1964 was a lot of dough.

'The casinos were also starting to come along but they were a big *no* for anyone who wanted to make a living out of gambling and I did. Casinos were for mugs. The odds and percentages were all against you and when the odds are against you, you don't get involved in betting.

'I liked to watch horses work at Epsom and there were some top trainers there then, people like Walter Nightingall and Ronny Smyth. I used to get a lot of good information.

'Handicaps were my speciality, because you didn't get so many of the big fashionable yards getting involved like they do now. There were specialists at the job but you had to be able to read them - and I did. Ronny Smyth was the man for me. I could read him like a book. I'd watch him get one ready, have a few runs, and when I thought the day was right I'd go to the races and have a good look. If he looked good, too, then I'd have a bet.

'The secret was that he had one particular grey suit that was very smart and he always wore it if he thought he was going to be in the winner's enclosure. It was no good asking him anything. He wouldn't tell you the time.

'One of my best men is Arthur Shaw, who used to play for Arsenal. He's seventy-three now but red hot on the form book. We sorted out two of Ronny's for a big ante-post double in 1973. We had Flash Imp at 28-1 for the Cesarewitch and Only For Jo at 33-1 for the Manchester Handicap at Doncaster. I kept having a few quid

on in bits and pieces and you don't need much at those prices to get a nice few quid. Ronny wore the good suit and they both obliged. It was one of the best touches I've ever had and I won something like £100,000, which was a huge pot then.

'I was a big fan of Nijinsky in 1971 and although he was 11-8 for the Derby there was a bookmaker in Ireland, name of Wilf Todd, who was offering 9-4. The problem was that there was a banking strike in Ireland and all transactions had to be done in cash. Of course, a bit of greed crept in. I sent my whack over and when Nijinsky bolted up I waited for the money to arrive and it never did. When the punters went round the next morning to be paid out there was a sign in his two shop windows simply saying ''Gone fishing''. Wilf was never seen again and was rumoured to have gone to America with his loot. I just had to wipe my mouth and walk away. It wasn't all bad, though, because I'd been backing the horse ante-post in England as well and still came out a good winner.

'I've never owned a horse in my life although plenty of friends of mine have done, like Jim Davidson the comedian who's now on the *Generation Game*. I was introduced to him at Kempton in the early eighties by a racing regular called ''Jimmy The One''. Jim, who is still a great mate to this day, had ten or twelve horses at one time and I used to advise him on different things.

'It was while I was with him looking at his horses down at Trevor Hallett's yard in Cornwall that I first met Barrie. He was riding quite a few of Jim's horses and nearly got into trouble at Ascot in October 1985 on Master Cameron, who was a fine big horse who needed decent going. The ground was very firm and it was only 50-50 that he ran, so we told Barrie to look after him. The trouble was that he looked after him too well, never put him in the race and was lucky not to get a holiday because the horse started 13-8 favourite. But Master Cameron did need heavy ground and he trotted up when he got those conditions at Exeter next time out.

'Lesley Garrett has been a very good friend of mine for years, we

grew up in West London together. The best horse he owned was Romany King and it was me who got him to run the horse in the 1992 National. Romany King was a brilliant jumper and would think he was running loose with only 1lb 3lb on his back. He ran a blinder finishing second to Party Politics. When he was offered over £100,000 for the horse Lesley asked me if he should sell and I told him to "Snap the blokes hand off."

'But racing is all about opinions and I'll back mine against anybody's, although it's not like the eighties when you could get a bet on without any trouble. Two of the biggest single bets I had were on fillies trained by Michael Stoute. Musical Bliss in the 1989 1,000 Guineas took six figures out of the ring. Aliysa, who won the 1989 Oaks then lost the race months later because of a positive test, was another massive winner for me. But I didn't always need the big meetings to make it pay.

'Some of the biggest nights in the eighties were at Windsor. I went there the Monday before Royal Ascot in 1985 and got a very good message for a horse of Willie Musson's in the two-year-old seller called Philosophical. It opened up 14-1, and ended 6-1, and won by four lengths. When I'm holding bookmakers' money I do like to play it up and I really fancied one of Stoute's in the last called Harry's Bar. I was £40,000 up on the night but I never go to the rails and bet myself. My son, Briany, and my son-in-law Paul put the lot on at 7-4. Harry's Bar ended up at 11-10 and won by half a length under an inspired ride from one of the best jockeys we have seen in England over the last 30 years, Walter Swinburn.

'But it wasn't difficult to get those kind of bets on because there was money sloshing about everywhere. That particular night at Windsor, Victor Chandler went on record as saying he fielded a million pounds in his book. But it wasn't just Victor. There were other men you could get on with like Dougie Goldstein and Neville Berry Sr, who'd take bets of £40,000 and wouldn't blink. Then in

the middle nineties it began to get harder and harder to get a bet on.

'Listen, bookmakers are there for one thing and one thing only, to get your money. As soon as they knew you had a brain and you'd got a bit in front of them they wouldn't be long in closing you down. For the last couple of years it was nearly a waste of time. Although I continued to bet, I cut down considerably.

'Then this race-fixing business comes up and mine's the first name that's put in the frame. I couldn't believe what I was meant to have done, and even though I was annoyed, I couldn't help laughing at some of the things that were put in the Press. I had a feeling that Roger Buffham, the head of Jockey Club Security, was feeding them to someone.

'When they pulled the three jockeys in, Jamie Osborne, Dean Gallagher and Leighton Aspell for alleged race-fixing in January 1998, my name was mentioned as well. So, I did the right thing and got on a flight from Spain, went to Charing Cross Police Station, gave a statement and was released without charge after extensive and expensive inquiries. Like the jockeys, I was completely exonerated.

'Then the case of Osborne and the ex-copper Harrington came up at the Old Bailey in January-February 2000, where Harrington tried to get a few quid, saying he was going to square the Old Bill for Osborne and drew 18 months after being found guilty.

'Osborne said under cross-examination that he was offered twenty grand by Dermot Browne to stop Regal Castle and Raise An Argument at Cheltenham in 1988 and didn't take it. But every time the bribe is mentioned it's supposed to be me who instigated it. Absolute bollocks! I had nothing at all to do with it. Just like Victor Chandler, I was never charged with anything when the corruption investigations were going on. But whenever Victor's name came up in court it was always reported that he had been completely exonerated of any wrongdoing. Quite right, too. But with me it's different. Whenever my name crops up it's always with an

additional comment of "well known criminal ..." and never that I'm a serious gambler who has made a lot of money backing my opinion. Don't the police and Jockey Club Security realise that there were quite a few people around who could have put Browne up to something like that. There are plenty of people in racing now who have got a few dark secrets they'd like to keep.

'I think it was Buffham who leaked a story that I'd organised a Golf Tournament for some jockeys in Spain in June 1998. Absolute crap. I've never organised a golf tournament in my life.'

The golfing holiday was all my idea and came about because of a break I'd had in Mijas, Spain, the year before with some of the Irish jockeys including Conor O'Dwyer, John Shortt and Ger Lyons. The place we stayed in was a multi-story flea pit but the golf courses were brilliant, so I decided that I'd do it with the English lads the following year.

The right opportunity arose when I was invited out to the sixtieth birthday party of Vee Shaw - who with her husband Ron has had horses in training with Paul Cole and Charlie Egerton - and I'd ridden quite a few winners in their colours. I was on an all-expenses paid trip, four days and three nights in the five star Byblos Hotel. Ron always stayed there in the Presidential Suite and he also owned the two magnificent golf courses either side of the hotel. He also had terrific connections in the real-estate business out there and organised a four bedroom villa overlooking the courses which worked out cheaper than the previous year's flea pit. Tony McCoy, Carl Llewellyn, Mark Richards and myself were joined by ex-jockeys Boo Boo Youlden and Dave Dutton. Tim Collins, who owned a horse I'd won a lot of races on called Go Universal and the 2000 Cheltenham Gold Cup winner Looks Like Trouble, came with Tom Butterfield, my great mate who owns the legendary Queens Arms at East Garston near Lambourn. We were joined for the social events by Richard Guest, while Richard Dunwoody, who was over

for the Shaw bash, came along for the apres golf. I did the handicapping and loused it up, coming in nearer last than first.

But back in London, the brains of Jockey Club Security, Roger Buffham, was convinced the whole trip had been funded by Brian Wright and, while we were swinging our golf clubs, the police were swinging their axes and knocking down the door of his apartment in Chelsea Harbour. When the police arrested the bloke who was house sitting for Brian he asked them why.

'We'll you're a friend of his,' to which he came back with, 'If you arrested all Brian's friends you'd need fucking Wembley Stadium to fit 'em all in.'

Brian did make the hour journey from his place in Valderrama and he paid for one night. That was it, although it didn't stop Buffham.

When Mark Richards got back and was working at Royal Ascot, Buffham sidled up to him using his best police technique and asked him for names and places. The one name he really wanted was Brian Wright. Was he there? Did he organise it? Did he pay for everything? Mark told him the lot - there was nothing to hide - but all Mr Buffham had to do was check the flights and he would have seen that all the tickets were paid for on each individual's credit card.

All this was filtering through as I stayed on for the second week and the magnificent hospitality of Ron and Vee. Charlie Brooks was there, along with Miriam Francome. In fact, Charlie liked Ron so much that he wouldn't train a horse for him because he didn't want to fall out with him and lose his friendship.

Another member of the party was Henry Ponsonby, a legend in Lambourn and one of the first to make a success of racehorse syndicates. He has them now with Henry Cecil, Paul Cole, Fulke Johnson-Houghton and Mick Channon. He also fancies himself as a member of the paparazzi and had heard that the tabloids would pay £2,000 for a picture of Brian. Not realising that he'd been at one of

the nearby tables the night before, Henry asked me if I could give him the address. I played him like a fiddle: 'I'm not sure Henry, but it's somewhere in the Mijas area.'

Nothing if not resourceful, he went to the local telephone directory and bingo! There was Brian Wright, Mijas. He found a long lens camera from somewhere and all he needed now was a getaway driver and a baseball bat in case the so-called 'Mr Big' got ugly. It was late in the afternoon and cocktails had been liberally taken when he tried to recruit Brooks as the driver, but he hadn't taken into account the hospitality of the Shaws. 'Me? Getaway driver? I can hardly walk, Henry, let alone drive,' said Charles. But the two grand was too much for Henry, so he went off on his own. When he reached the address he found an old man in swimming trunks and flip flops with a hose pipe watering his flowers.

After a while he wondered what Henry was doing, snooping around and snapping pictures. 'Oy! What do you want?'

'Are you Brian Wright?'

'I certainly am, Captain Brian Wright, ex-British Army. What the hell are you taking pictures of me for? I've been retired fifteen years.'

Finding it very funny himself, Henry told the story when he got back and I was straight on the phone to Brian, but he declined my offer to come up with my Olympus Trip, take a snap and split the two grand.

I've had some of the best times of my life with Brian and he's always given me sound advice, one of the best bits being, 'Your mouth is your most dangerous weapon. Don't get involved in gossip and if you're going to say something wrong about someone bite your lip. It does you no favours and it's pointless.'

I've no doubt that Brian's relaxed and friendly way has opened many doors for me that have stayed closed to others, like one of the most exclusive nightclubs in the world, Tramp. You can't become a member unless the owner, Johnny Gold, invites you personally ...

but Brian's known him a long time.

He said, 'John's a superstar, the real king of clubs. He had to see how you acted and behaved in Tramp before he thought of offering membership. After you'd been there with me for a couple of years I asked him if he thought it was time you got a membership. He said he'd have to think about it.'

A couple of weeks later my membership arrived along with a standing order for £200 a year. Priceless!

Brian still dines out on the night he entertained Frank Sinatra. Johnny Gold had forgotten Frank was coming in with some younger members of his family and the manager, Guido, asked Brian to sit with him and keep him company. Brian still says it was one of the best nights of his life. But Brian's friends come from all walks and I've lost count of the nice things he's done, like paying for my schoolmate Carl Leaf's thirtieth birthday party at Tramp. He loves to see people having fun and has always got time for others.

Not many people realise that Tramp once had a real tramp called Michael who used to sit outside. Brian always used to drop him £50 when he was waiting for the car to arrive, but one night he was very quiet and the doorman told Brian that Michael's mother, who was ninety, was very poorly in Ireland. He peeled off a thousand quid, gave it to the doorman and told him to get the old boy fixed up and put him on a plane to Ireland so he could get to see her before it was too late. I thought that just about summed Brian up.

He's got his own table at Tramp, just at the bottom of the stairs where you walk in. It was a prime spot and he was a magnet for whoever came in. One night he took Steve Dyble, who was unbeatable in the stable lads boxing and is known everywhere as 'Yarmouth' or 'Yarni'. Just as they were going to Brian's table they saw it was occupied by Clint Eastwood and Jerry Hall. Brian knew they were only waiting to go in to dinner so he gave Guido a wink and then said, 'Don't worry about them Yarni, we'll soon be sitting

there. Don't bet your money, bet your life. London to a brick.'

Next thing, Guido says, 'Excuse me Mr Eastwood,' and moves them on to the restaurant. Eastwood, knowing what was going on, shook Brian's hand and said, 'Buddy, I don't know who you are but you must be mighty important.' Yarni still doesn't know it was a wind up to this day.

Yarni is the most successful-ever stable lads boxer and won the heavyweight (10st 7lb) title ten times. There was some ferocious betting as well as boxing on that night at the Hilton hotel in early November and under normal circumstances in 1985 Yarni would have been the banker bet of the night and very short odds. But Taffy Salaman, who trains just outside Swindon, had imported a bit of a ringer, a Russian Jew called Oleg Sidenko who was rumoured to have boxed as a pro in Israel. Taffy saw the chance of a coup and it was clear he was going to be a real threat to Yarni who recalls the preliminaries very clearly.

'He knocked two out in the eliminators at the New Astley Club in Newmarket, gave the Russian salute afterwards and looked over at me and signalled "You're next."

'When we got to the ring on finals night it was well into the early hours because being the heavyweight division we were last on. There were buckets of money for this Russian and when he stripped off he looked a million dollars, just like a pro. I just had my old baseball boots on and the tatty old vest that I always wore.

'Brian never doubted me, stayed loyal, laid the Russian and backed me. Mind you, he must have been worried after the first round because I was in big trouble. That Russian knocked the shit out of me, but it got me going and I smothered him, out thought him and got it on points but it was bloody hard. The place went ballistic when the ref lifted my hand.'

There was one bit of bad news, though, 'I'd put some cash with some mates to get the jackpot, which means you've got to name the winners of all the bouts, and when I got out of the ring I thought

"'great, we've had all the others, we've won the jackpot as well.'" It turned out the bastards had put the Russian in instead of me!'

The stable lads boxing was always a terrific night out but if the Jockey Club had imposed the directive they sent around to all trainers and jockeys in 1999 the gist of which was that they should be careful of associating with undesirables, there would hardly have been a licensed person on the premises. I've no doubt that my relationship with Brian prompted the letter to be sent and I can hold my hands up to one stroke I tried to pull on his behalf. However, it didn't come off.

Brian has always been big on the going and the pace in a race, while I've been a great one for walking courses before racing. If the official going was wrong for one he fancied I'd phone him and it would be, 'OK, mate, I'm not on.'

However, there was nothing we could do about the 1987 Cheltenham Gold Cup, but we did try. Brian had gone for a big treble. The first leg was See You Then, who completed a hat-trick in the Champion Hurdle at 11-10 on the opening day. Pearlyman on Wednesday in the Queen Mother Champion Chase kept the ball rolling and over £100,000 was rolling over on to Forgive 'N Forget in the Gold Cup on Thursday.

Everything was right for Forgive 'N Forget. He'd won the race two years before, was third to Dawn Run in 1986, and there was nothing of her class in this field. But the most important factor of all was the ground, which was perfect when racing started but was mugged by a snow storm as we were going to post. The field was recalled from the start and Forgive 'N Forget's chance was evaporating with every flake of snow that fell.

Down in the steamy warmth of the changing room I wasn't thinking about anything in particular, only that I knew my old ally Wayward Lad would struggle to put up any sort of show up the hill as the ground became bottomless. Brian, however, was thinking on his feet and as we were waiting to be called out to the paddock, he

sent Briany and Paul down to see me. The message was short, 'Try and get the race abandoned.'

It made sense if you had that sort of money at stake and, as for Forgive 'N Forget, he might as well not have left Malton for all the chance he'd got. And the same applied to Wayward Lad. In 1978 the Gold Cup had been postponed until the April Meeting when John Francome came back in triumph on Midnight Court after being suspended for passing on information to the flamboyant bookmaker John Banks.

But the information from the local weather centre was just what I didn't want to hear and, as we were getting warmed up back in the changing room, we were told by the stewards that the forecast was for it to brighten up. They were going to wait. Weather forecasters tend to get it right when it doesn't matter and wrong when it does, like in the summer when you've planned a Sunday barbecue and the monsoon season comes early. Sure enough, they got this one right. The weather began to brighten and the snow started to disappear from the tops of the fences, but each flake that melted into the Cheltenham turf and turned it to mud ate away at Forgive 'N Forget's chance. I still hadn't given up and when we got back to the start I had another go at the starter, Keith Brown, 'It's impossible sir, it's still balling in the horses' feet. It'll be dangerous to them and us. We've got to think about safety.' Mark Dwyer had a moan, too, but we didn't have a prayer as the evening sun began to set over Cleeve Hill and when the tapes went up an hour and twenty minutes late, Brian's treble went down. Cybrandian and Chris Grant set a relentless gallop that was never going to suit Wayward Lad or Forgive 'N Forget. It was a tribute to the courage of both horses that they performed so well in the atrocious conditions. They were both still there with a shout going to the last, but the weather was the winner and Brian's treble sunk in the mud as The Thinker gave my old guv'nor Arthur Stephenson his biggest success.

Brian did what he always does, wiped his mouth and walked

away.

However, he has never walked away from his friends when they've needed him and Declan Murphy is living proof of that. When Declan had the fall from Arcot in the Swinton Hurdle at Haydock on 2 May 1994 that left him in a life-threatening coma, his then girlfriend Jo was in Newmarket 140 miles away and couldn't get there quickly because of the bank-holiday traffic. Brian had watched the race on satellite TV in Spain and phoned me to organise a plane to get Jo and Barney Curley to Walton hospital. He picked up the bill and I can pay him no higher compliment than to say his actions were no more than I would have expected.

Brian Wright is no saint - he'd laugh at the very thought - but I know one thing. In all the time I've been associated with him he has never compromised me and I've never had a better friend. I know for a fact he'd say exactly the same about me.

CHAPTER 17
Going South

I was edging towards my twenty eighth birthday as the 1988-89 season started, and although I had suffered some hard knocks I still had the hunger for racing that was bred into me. I wanted the game badly, the question was, did racing want me quite so much?

It was time to make serious decisions and there is no doubt that my self confidence had been knocked by the loss of the Harris retainer and the two bans from the Jockey Club. Even though I could live with the hefty fines for professional incompetence at Sedgefield and Ludlow, they still niggled me by edging into my thoughts when the mind wanders on a long car journey.

Much as I didn't like facing up to it, opportunities in the north were beginning to dry up and, with Mrs D having made it clear this would be her last season, I would have to pull up my roots and move south. But the decision was made much easier for me by the overtures of David Murray Smith, who had provided me with Rhyme 'N' Reason in the 1985 Irish National.

Although we had gone our separate ways and done well individually, David was now looking for a jockey after his talented first-choice rider Paul Croucher had been tragically killed in a car accident in August at Chaddleworth near Lambourn.

It didn't take me long to take up the offer, so I set about getting my finances in order and had no trouble selling my detached house at Oak Ridge. I then began looking for somewhere in the Lambourn area to be handy for Murray Smith and anyone else who wanted to use me. It was at the height of the property boom and I got in touch with my ex-weighing room colleague Paul Barton, who'd moved from the restaurant business into estate agency. Paul didn't go in for many changes when he was riding and stayed with one trainer, David Gandolfo, for most of his career. But he made up for lost time when he packed up and eventually took another turn to become one of the better stewards' secretaries. While with Drewatt Neate estate agents in Wantage he found me the ideal place in Sparsholt. The only problem was that there was no roof on the property and it wouldn't be ready for three months. I had no option but to rent and took a one-bedroom flat in Wantage where, despite having my buddy Carl Leafe keeping me company and sleeping on the sofa, I was very homesick. The accommodation was a nightmare, with paperthin walls which meant I could hear the most intimate movements of my neighbours. On reflection, I should have taken it as an ominous sign, because I was sliding into four dire seasons that would see me seriously contemplate retirement several times.

But for the immediate future things weren't too bad. My first ride of the season was a winner, Lord It Over for John Jenkins at Fontwell. It was the first time I'd ever opened with a winner, so I was entitled to think it a good omen. My first ride for Murray Smith was also a winner and he had some quality animals in his yard in Upper Lambourn, I was feeling just a touch optimistic. But I didn't know that by the end of the season I would have landed a massive coup, once again had my integrity savaged by the Jockey Club, turned down a retainer for one of the richest owners in the country and then found myself jobless once more. Oh yes, and I'd also miss out on riding the most charismatic chaser since Arkle.

If I'd known half of that I probably wouldn't have set foot outside Wetherby, let alone move house, but by New Years' Eve I'd marked up seventeen winners. With five good months ahead I could reckon on pressing for the half century, injuries permitting. By 24 May I'd added just seventeen to the total, although one of them, Border Tinker, was very important financially.

Many people who follow racing are intrigued by the gamble that nets a small fortune but understand very little about it's conception. Most simply think that it is just a matter of covering up the ability of a horse long enough to ensure that the price is right and then press the buttons to collect. That is defintely not the case and, despite the screams of bookmakers when they are stung, there are many more gambles that end in tears rather than cheers. Fortunately the one I am going to take you through succeeded after several false starts.

Brian Wright, as we have established, loves a bet when the odds are right. Together with Roy Adkins, he asked me to buy a horse capable of landing a touch. Roy was someone I didn't know too well and was more a casual acquaintance of Brian. In 1987 he had control of horses which ran under the name of Running Horse Ltd including Olympic Times who was trained by Reg Akehurst and won some decent handicap hurdles. Roy was always affable when we met and it came as a real shock when he was gunned down at the American Hotel in Amsterdam in September 1990 at the age of 42. The rumours were that he was behind the murder of the Great Trainer Robber Charlie Wilson in April that year and this was a revenge killing. Whatever it was, it was certainly something I didn't want to know anything about.

But both Roy and Brian wanted to buy a horse and have it trained by my dad which meant I could keep an eye on it. I thought I'd found the right article when Border Tinker was entered for the Doncaster Sales in June 1987. He was trained by Alastair Charlton, who I'd ridden for in my early days, and was a fine type of horse who had shown form over hurdles but was begging for fences.

The one thing you must do when bidding at a sale is know your limit and stick to it. I reached mine at 24,000 guineas for Border Tinker and he was bought by a young owner-trainer called Harry Bissill for 25,000 guineas. I phoned Brian, said I'd look for something else, and thought no more about the horse.

I'd got to know young Harry well when we were both working on the film *Champions* back in 1982. In fact, he became a bit of a legend at the shoot pontoon card schools, where he'd blow the day's pay - about £300 - for him and his horse Wang The Miller. Unfortunately, he had a bad fall the season he bought Border Tinker and cracked some vertebrae in his back and neck. As a result he was barred from riding by his doctor. He knew I was keen on Border Tinker as underbidder and phoned to say I could buy him for the same price he paid. The deal suited me grand. I still hadn't found the right article for the touch, but Border Tinker was it.

The main factor in our favour was that although he had won a couple of novice hurdles, he was unexposed on two fronts. He'd done his winning over stiff tracks like Hexham and Carlisle over two miles and two miles one furlong and would certainly be better over much further. Also, he had never run over fences and was the right size to make a chaser. There was plenty to work on and Norm began building him up into a fine specimen.

We decided to go straight over fences as he'd schooled well. There was no need to drop the anchor on him, all we did was run him over two miles at Catterick first time out when the track was too quick and he was short of peak fitness. Next time, on 14 December 1987, he went to a more galloping track, Warwick, but again it was two miles and being a big horse he still wasn't spot on. He never got into the race and finished eleventh of thirteen finishers.

We waited until 23 February and moved him up to a three mile novice chase at Sedgefield. The trip was ideal, but we reckoned he needed soft ground and couldn't believe it when the going came up good to firm. Brian is emphatic about getting the right ground, so the horse ran unbacked and finished second at 11-1, running too well.

In his next race, a three mile novice chase at Market Rasen on good to soft, he looked like a steering job. Although the price was a bit short it seemed so easy that the boys had an interest at 15-8 and they looked like collecting until the fourth last. I was tucked in behind the leaders and getting ready to pounce when Border Tinker hit the fence hard and fell. The boys weren't too happy but had been around long enough to know that these things happen, so Norm and I told them they'd have to wait until next year. In fact, it would be ten months before they got their money back, but with a good bit of interest.

Border Tinker had one more run after Market Rasen but had gone over the top and I pulled him up at Southwell on 31 March. After that Norm took him back, turned him out in a field and freshened him up for the new season. We weren't in any rush. Border Tinker made his reappearance on 28 March in a three mile one furlong novice chase at Warwick, looking in need of the run but performing well until weakening after two miles, and I pulled him up for safety's sake before the third last. The main thing was that he'd given me a really good feel. I knew he was back to his best and ready to go in. But most important, since his second placing he'd fallen and been pulled up twice. The handicapper didn't think he was much good, so all I needed to do was find the right race. It appeared almost a month later at Sedgefield on 25 January in the shape of the Downhill Novices' Handicap Chase.

The handicapper had rated Border Tinker only twenty-one - the best chasers in the country were up in the mid-seventies - but he still had top weight of 11st 10lb, which showed how poor the race was. Next was Invisible Thief, trained by Arthur Stephenson and rated fifteen, then Croghan Star of James Dooler's on four followed by Kaim Park of Mary Reveley's rated three. The remaining three

195

runners were all on nought. Thanks to the time he finished second at Sedgefield we knew that Border Tinker handled the track and, although the official going was good to firm, it rode a lot softer. In fact, the only worry I had was what price the boys were going to get to their money when they lumped on. And the only way to ensure the odds were right was to tell absolutely no one.

This was much harder than it would seem as some of my best friends were involved in Norm's yard. There was also the added problem that I was a relatively high profile jockey who would attract interest if I travelled up to Sedgefield from the south. Brian came up with the idea for Barrie Wright to ride Border Tinker. Initially, I had no problem with that because Barrie was a good jockey who didn't make many mistakes. But the day before the race I bottled out, although I couldn't bring myself to tell him. We were in the changing room at Chepstow when I pulled him to one side and gave him my mobile phone. Norm was on the other end and wasn't pulling the punches. 'Barrie, Graham's got to ride that horse, he knows all about him, I'm sorry.' Barrie was stunned as he turned the phone off and looked at me. 'Bazza, you can't ride him, I can't take the risk of anything going wrong.' I knew he'd taken it hard and needed a winner, but that statement tells you everything you ever wanted to know about me as a jockey. I knew how important this was and just how much money would be going on. I also knew the horse inside out and I knew that I had the inner confidence in my own ability. When it really matters and the chips are down I am the coolest bloke you'll find. And for a day like this I wanted all the decisions left in my hands.

Norm and myself were so confident that we told the owners we'd both pack up if the horse didn't win. But it was vital that everyone outside us four, plus Barrie, thought that the horse was only going for a run round to wait for another day. The two lads who worked in the yard, Paul Crooks and Peter Salmon, were very good friends of mine. There was also Boo Boo Youlden and his fiancée, Sally

Hainsworth, in whose name Border Tinker ran. I couldn't tell any of them.

I knew all the horse had to do was jump round, but even down at the start I played the part and told the other lads not to worry about me because my horse broke blood vessels and would need the race. In fairness, Border Tinker was a big horse who always looked as though he was carrying too much condition but that was him. He was fit as a fiddle and well tuned up for the concert. They swallowed it hook, line and sinker.

I jumped Border Tinker off to make all and never saw another horse until I looked round after the third last when we were a distance in front. All I could think of as we turned for home and went to the last was whether the boys had got all their money on and what my present would be when settling day came.

When I pulled up Paul Crooks came out on to the course to collect his horse and I'll never forget the betrayed and disgusted look on his face as he reached for the reins. He thought I'd put him away, and our friendship was a bit special as I'd spent three years sitting next to him at Wetherby High School and was best man at his wedding. He couldn't believe it. But before he gave me a right volley I sorted it out.

'Don't worry Paul, you and Pete will be looked after. There'll be £500 for each of you.'

Well, that did the trick. Paul beamed and said, 'Brad, if you're ever going for a touch again I don't want to know. Just do the same. The most I'd have had on was £20 - and I probably would have told someone.'

Brian and Roy managed to get on £30,000 each at odds of 5-1 down to 7-2 and left the next day for a two-week holiday in the Bahamas. Norm says that whenever Paul and Pete saw a plane while riding out during that fortnight they'd both look at each other and say, 'Hope them two owners get back safely.'

Boo Boo had watched the race with Norm and when I came

cruising clear he said, 'Bloody hell, Norm, he's going very well for a horse that's not off.' Norm replied, 'Not off? It'll win ten minutes.' Boo Boo needn't have worried, they'd backed it for him as well.

He came down to the Snooker Championships at Sheffield where my good friend John Parrott was playing. Brian's son, Briany, gave me my present of £10,000 along with another £4,000 to square up the people we hadn't told. I was glad Boo Boo was with me. I hadn't got enough pockets to put all the money in.

But a banana skin was waiting just around the corner when I fell foul of the stewards at Southwell on 23 March. I was faced with the possibility of being banned for a very long time and it was only the dedication of a photographer that saved me.

Starjestic had developed into a real family favourite since landing the touch that gave Carl Llewellyn his first winner under Rules back in 1986, but when he made a mistake and got rid of me three fences from home in the Lambert Parker and Gaines Handicap Chase he could so easily have finished my career.

Ironically, I nearly didn't ride him because I was very late leaving to get to Southwell after schooling in Lambourn. I even phoned Norm to make sure he had another jockey standing by in case I didn't make it. The ground was heavy, which didn't suit Starjestic, who started 5-4 favourite with Sidvic second best at 7-4 and Comedy Fair the outsider of three at 11-4. I always rode Starjestic to come with a steady run and I had everything in hand when we began to close on Sidvic, who was about five lengths clear with three to jump. But Starjestic made an uncharacteristic mistake. He put his hind legs in the ditch, which made him lurch through the fence and shot me out over his left shoulder.

The stewards called me in and I admit I was a bit relieved to see a familiar face on the panel. It was Harry Bissell who'd sportingly sold me Border Tinker and played cards rather badly. But Harry, who died tragically young in a tractor accident, studiously avoided any eye contact and said nothing. Because Norm had left for home they couldn't interview him and said they'd reconvene the inquiry at the next meeting two days later. It was a long way for me to come considering I didn't have a ride there. By then they'd called in the betting intelligence officer, who said there was £4,200 in the ring for Starjestic but £6,000 for Sidvic and £5,400 for Comedy Fair. The implication was that Starjestic wasn't fancied even though he was favourite.

Despite Norm's statement that the horse had made a mistake the stewards would not exonerate me and referred me on to the Disciplinary Committee at Portman Square. Things were now looking bad, but I remembered that Alan Johnson, a first-class racecourse photographer, had been at that third last fence because it was an open ditch which can produce exciting shots. I phoned and asked if he'd got anything and he said that there was a clear shot of Starjestic with his hind legs in the ditch. He sold the picture to *The Times*, who ran it on Monday 27 March, and offered to give a sworn affidavit to the Jockey Club on what he had seen. This was curtly declined. They were intent on an inquiry. The only trouble was, they couldn't decide when and the stigma had to ride alongside me for an uncomfortably long time.

There was also the question of Starjestic earning his keep, so he ran on his next suitable engagement which, somewhat ironically, was back at Southwell nearly a month later on 24 April. I rode exactly the same race as before in a contest that was much more competitive with thirteen runners. He picked up ground steadily from the eighth to lead at the last and win by three quarters of a length.

With the Jockey Club still waiting to announce an inquiry, some punters took the view that in racing you're guilty until proved innocent and began booing as I returned to the winner's enclosure. That was all I needed after the torment I'd seen Norm go through and the stress it was causing me. I just raised my right arm with one finger pointing skyward, inviting the bastards to swivel on it.

Incredibly, the Jockey Club didn't call the inquiry until 24 May, nearly two months after the incident which allowed rumour and innuendo to breed freely. But I'd learned my lesson during my previous dealings with the Jockey Club. This time I was going to London armed with some serious legal weaponry. I engaged the top criminal defence lawyer in the north of England, Leeds-based Peter McCormick. The Jockey Club were convinced I'd jumped off and wanted rid of me. To this day I firmly believe that without that picture and Peter's help I was looking at a very long warning off that could run into years. Had that happened, my credibility would have been left so low that I would never have ridden again.

People have said to me that with all my appearances at Portman Square I must have got used to it. But I never have. It makes no difference at all that you know you're innocent. The air of uncertainty plus the power they wield makes you get edgy and sweaty and your pulse quickens until it feels like a jackhammer pounding. In the weeks leading up to an inquiry like this there are endless questions from journalists building up the pressure and it never goes away. At the inquiry everything is shown on a massive TV screen that magnifies every twitch that you make. It is just one horrible experience.

The betting intelligence officer appeared to be the principal witness against me and came in with a sheaf of notes to reel off the names of three bookmakers who had laid Starjestic, names I had never heard of. McCormick was on him like a terrier at a rabbit.

The first name was read out again. 'In any way, shape or form can you possibly associate my client with that person?' snapped McCormick.

'No'

Before there was any time for elaboration the exchange was cut dead with a curt 'Thank You!'

The second name was read and the same question put. Again the

200

answer was in the negative, and before the betting intelligence officer had a chance to say another word, came the cutting 'Thank you!'

He completed the *coup de grace* when the final name was read out and then parried with the identical question to the first two.

There was no way I'd ever heard of the names being mentioned, and that final clipped 'Thank you!' finished the Jockey Club attack.

It still took the Disciplinary Committee, chaired by John Sumner, two and a half hours to acquit Norm and myself of any wrongdoing. Once again I hid my true feelings for an authority that seemed focused on dragging me through barbed wire - even though they had clear photographic evidence that the horse had made a mistake.

I said, 'I am very relieved and grateful to my solicitor. Both my father and I are delighted. We had a fair hearing, the Jockey Club is the Jockey Club and they had to inquire into the matter. I was a bit disappointed at the time but accept that not all the evidence was available at Southwell.'

At £300 an hour from the moment he left his office in Leeds to the moment he got back, Peter McCormick didn't come cheap. But he earned every penny that day.

There had been one bright spot in a troublesome season that produced thirty-four winners. Of that relatively meagre total, fifteen had been for David Murray Smith, who was consolidating his position as one of the leading young jump trainers, and I appeared to be an integral part of the team.

David had learned his trade with two masters of the training craft, Dick Hern and Vincent O'Brien. Like them, he was a man of few words. In fact, when we sat over breakfast at Frenchman's Yard in Upper Lambourn he hardly spoke, not just to me but to anyone. He gave the impression of being a very shy man.

But when he was away from the job he was unrecognisable and really good fun. He is no lover of wine or champagne and, while he would drink beer, his beverage of preference was always Gordon's Gin, Schweppes Tonic and lots of ice. He could get through gallons of the stuff. And when he was in full flow was capable of doing anything.

I liked David a lot and like all successful yards he had good and not so good owners. One of the best was Geoff Rowlandson, who is a jeweller and whose black and white diamond colours were carried by some good horses including Rowlandsons Gems and Rowlandsons Jewels. So when I was approached to take the job as first jockey by one of the most influential owners in jump racing, Jersey based multi-millionaire Paul Green I felt obliged to talk to David, even though we had no retaining agreement.

I told him about the offer at the beginning of March. He said that I should do what I thought best but added that he had a full yard and plenty of good young horses coming along.

Paul Green was building a strong team that already included Stepaside Lord, Elementary and Lemhill and would soon add the potentially brilliant Carvill's Hill. But his principal trainer in England was Martin Pipe, and it was impossible to see him jocking off Peter Scudamore for me. After some hard thinking I turned the offer down. It was a mistake.

When David asked me to meet him at York on the last day of the Dante meeting, 18 May, I was anticipating the offer of a retainer for the 1989-90 season. How wrong could I have been?

Almost with an air of embarrassment as we talked in the champagne bar he said, 'I'm afraid a few of the owners don't want you next season and I've got to have a stable jockey who is suitable to everyone.'

I was stunned and I have no doubt that the stigma of the Starjestic affair still being dragged on by the Jockey Club had damaged my credibility.

There were several examples of David's horses running poorly with the blame left at my door only for them to show signs of sickness several days later. One of them, Outside Edge, was 11-8 favourite at Folkestone in February and hardly jumped before I pulled him up. He never ran again that season.

David was also being hit by the recession, which was starting to bite everywhere, and he had been forced to sell his yard to John Moreton before buying it back a few years later. Moreton owned horses in partnership with Juliet Reed including Rhyme 'N' Reason, who had won the 1988 Grand National after being transferred to David Elsworth. Juliet has since become the partner of my friend Carl Leafe and I know that Moreton, who had the exceptional novice chaser Twin Oaks with David before moving him to Gordon Richards, had been no fan of mine ever since our disagreement over Church Warden at Wincanton in 1984.

When we discussed my sacking many years later, David expanded on why he felt he had to finish me. He said, 'Because of the recession I formed a lot of syndicates, nearly all of them with very nice people, but it was very difficult to deal with all the hangers on that came with them. You had ten people being advised by ten others who all seemed to love listening to loose talk on the racecourse and would supply scurrilous theories as to why a horse had been beaten when it simply ran badly.

'It was too much hassle and I just had to let you go.'

That was insult enough but I was shocked when I found out who was replacing me, ... Michael Bowlby. It was just the same when I lost the ride on Kildimo and the job was given to Jimmy Frost. Both are exceptionally nice people and competent jockeys - but I knew I was better than both of them and it cut me deep.

Although I didn't realise it then, the Murray Smith job was going downhill. David would never fully recover from three bad seasons when he was hit by a virus that saw good horses like Aquilifer, Outside Edge and Sabin du Loir moved to Martin Pipe to win top quality races. I liked riding for him. He is a very decent man.

I was left to mull over my next move, but one of my colleagues in the weighing room, Simon Sherwood, had reached his personal crossroads and decided to retire to begin training. This left his brother Oliver short of a stable jockey and he moved in to secure another Wetherby lad, Jamie Osborne, who was maturing into a fine jockey with Nicky Henderson. I said before that I thought I was a good judge of jockeys as well as horses and I had an influence on Jamie's first winner, Fair Bavard at Southwell on 29 March 1986.

Banner Bell and myself had bought her cheaply at the Derby Sale in Ireland the previous year and sold her on to some friends including David Metcalf, for whom I would make a far more significant purchase much later in my career as a bloodstock agent.

She was in training with Harry Wharton in Wetherby with the brief to land a touch. After a few sighters with Boo Boo Youlden on board, Harry had come up with an amateur riders handicap hurdle and was adamant that this kid Osborne should ride. I wasn't happy. I'd never seen him ride and knew that the money was going to be down. But Harry was insistent that if Osborne didn't ride he wouldn't run the horse, so I had to give in.

Jamie remembers me meeting him in the paddock to give him the riding instructions and being a bit concerned that he was riding short. He says I also told him to be very careful not to fall off because there was quite a bit of cash at stake.

I needn't have wasted my breath. Jamie was exceptional and you'd never have known he was riding his first winner. He never once left the inside and those who backed Fair Bavard from 12-1 to 3-1 favourite hardly had a moments worry.

The departure of Simon Sherwood meant that the most coveted ride in jump racing was going spare on Desert Orchid and I had every reason to believe I would get it. I'd been riding regularly for his trainer David Elsworth ever since I'd ridden my first winner for him - Lector at Plumpton in September 1985 - and he was my kind of trainer. He seemed able to get inside a horse and when you came back after riding one of his he would be able to tell you just what you'd been thinking, how the horse had travelled and how the race had ridden. I would put him on a par with Michael Dickinson as one of the two best trainers I've ever ridden for, although like many people who have a touch of genius, he's also got a self destruct button that he can press at any time.

David told me he fancied me for the job and I had two other influential allies in Rodney Boult, David's head lad, and Janice Coyle who looked after the grey. But the one person who mattered was owner Richard Burridge and he could not be swayed. He decided on Richard Dunwoody. I couldn't argue with that one, but it still hit me very hard when David told me of the owner's decision at the Jockeys Awards, the Lesters, in London in April. I felt that the spectre of Portman Square had floored me again. This time I didn't feel like getting up and I said to David, 'I think I'll pack it in.'

Fortunately, I was talking to the right man in Elzie, bless him. He said, 'Don't even think of giving up. You've got a lot to offer and I've got a lot of good horses at my place. I'll give you plenty of rides.'

I knew I could trust him and, having been a jockey once himself, David understood how I was thinking. He was as good as his word, providing me with my best winners of the following season, although the total dropped to thirty.

And there was also a poignant moment when Crusaders Star won the White Swan Handicap Chase at Market Rasen on 29 April. Mrs D had decided to retire at the end of the season and it was the last winner I ever rode for a Dickinson. No jockey ever had a more loyal and trusting family to ride for. They gave me the chance to shine. It was truly the end of an era.

THE WAYWARD LAD

CHAPTER 18
Guinness is good for me

There is a general fallacy that jockeys are inflation proof and aren't affected by the ravages of the economy. They just go out and ride another winner and their troubles are over. If only it were that simple.

No one was safe from the recession that hit in late 1989 and sliced it's way into the early nineties when house repossessions were an uncomfortably common occurence and small businesses were going to the wall daily.

Well, my small business was stretched as tight as a drum and I was given a very unsavoury option to drag it out of trouble. I had begun to take on the guise of a man of property and moved into the new house in Sparsholt, between Lambourn and Wantage, having sold my detached house in Wetherby. Like everyone else at that time, I did well. I'd made £100,000 profit on the house which I then put into a quarter share in a nursing home in Gateshead with three other partners.

With cash that I'd saved, plus a £150,000 mortgage I bought the Sparsholt property and, when it was valued for insurance purposes six months later, it had grown to £245,000. Everything seemed to be coming up roses, but the fertiliser was about to hit the fan in the shape of Black Friday, when the economy shook and every house owner in Britain rattled.

The value of Sparsholt plummeted to £180,000. What's more, the mortgage almost doubled to 14 per cent and on top of that the government brought in new rules concerning nursing homes, which meant I had to borrow more money for my share of the expensive renovations necessary to keep trading.

The only chink of light in my financial nightmare arrived in the shape of Barrie Wright, who came to lodge with me for three weeks and ended up staying three years. It's as well I didn't count on the rent, but his friendship was beyond price.

I had to wait until 11 November before riding my first winner of the season, supplied by David Elsworth and named, somewhat ironically given my track record, Major Inquiry. It came at Cheltenham and, although the next two rides were also winners, I knew things were going to be hard and that the economic climate would make it even tougher. Major Inquiry took my total to four at Ascot on 18 November, but I went a soul-destroying thirty-six rides and six weeks before making the winners' enclosure again. And if one low-life bastard had got his way that wouldn't have happened.

New Year's Eve fell on a Sunday so there was no racing. Barrie was away and I was making some lunch when I answered the phone and someone asked me if I was riding in the first at Cheltenham the next day. Thinking it was a trainer ringing to see if I was available I said that unfortunately I was.

'Yes, I know, you ride Major Inquiry.'

'Well, what did you ask me for?'

'Because there's fifteen grand for you if it gets beaten. On the other hand, it could get a bit messy for you if it wins.'

I kept listening for a while and the caller seemed to know a lot about me and where I lived. Unfortunately there was no such thing as 1471 ringback. In a show of bravado I told him to fuck off and slammed the phone down. But I was worried, very worried.

The phone rang a few minutes later and I half expected it to be one of my more fun loving colleagues phoning to admit it was a joke. Sadly, it wasn't. 'Listen, I'm working for someone who lays very big bets and there will be £15,000 for you before racing tomorrow if you say yes, if not, well ...'

He let the last few letters of the word spin out and I sensed the menace in his voice.

I kept relatively cool and said with a firmish voice but thumping heart, 'Look, I don't know who you are or who's put you up to this but you've got the wrong bloke. Don't call again because I'm phoning Jockey Club Security now.'

In fact, they were the last people I'd be talking to. I had about as much confidence in them as a fox in a dog pound. If I told them and the horse still got beaten I'd be headlines at worst and, at best, another chapter would be added to my dossier. Heads they win, tails I lose.

So I did what I've often done when I've had a problem and need wise counsel. I phoned Brian Wright, always the villain as far as the Jockey Club are concerned but the one man I would have to guard my back.

'Bri, I've just been offered fifteen grand to stop one at Cheltenham tomorrow and the bloke reckons I'm going to get hurt if I don't.'

'Did you recognise his voice?'

'No.'

'Probably a nutter. In any case, no one's going to come near you at a place like Cheltenham and if you see anyone looking a bit dodgy around the house, phone the police straight away. Don't let it worry you, and by the way, will it win?'

'It's got a great chance. He's won over the course and keeps improving. In my book we've only got Stage Player to beat.'

'Thanks very much, don't worry, speak to you soon.'

Somehow I felt better after that. I've talked to Brian about horses I've fancied before and some that I didn't, but it was the sort of thing people are saying on the Racing Channel and Channel Four Racing every day. But the attempted corruption had panicked me. If a rumour like this got out and Major Inquiry did get fairly beaten I would be in trouble, and it couldn't have been for more important connections. David Elsworth was my lifeline back to the top. In addition, my former weighing room colleague Bill Smith, who rode many winners for the Queen Mother, was racing manager to the owner Bill Brown, who was one of the most generous owners a jockey could ride for when he had a winner.

Major Inquiry started 2-1 second favourite for the Steel Plate Trial Hurdle which opened the meeting. Stage Player was just preferred at 15-8 and, although I tried not to show it in the paddock, I was very much on edge having been looking over my shoulder since I got up that morning.

I knew I had to win, and although Major Inquiry was travelling much better than Stage Player when we came to challenge at the last, I left nothing to chance and drove him out for an eight length win. I think David Elsworth asked me why I'd won so far and I made an excuse. I couldn't bear to tell him the anguish I'd gone through. Now all I had to do was wait for another phone call or a knock on the door. For a few days I jumped when either happened late at night, but I never heard another word again. And what's more, I'm certain I did the right thing in keeping quiet about it until now.

The fifteen grand would have come in handy. The nursing home, which was meant to be my pension in later years, haemorrhaged money. I had to reduce my share to a fifth to stay involved, but I did have some good fortune which underlines my slack attitude to money. Several years previously my bank manager in Wetherby had advised me to buy some shares and I'd thought no more about them until now. They were in a safe deposit box in the bank and when I went up to check them I'd got my own little windfall because, while Ernest Saunders and his friends went down in the Guinness share scandal, I'd bought some quite innocently and cashed them in for £20,000, showing a very healthy profit. True, it didn't solve all my problems, but it plugged a hole in the ship until the tide turned.

However, I had one massive bit of luck which could have brought my career to an abrupt end when I unknowingly took the ride on a nut-case called Gospel Rock at Wetherby on 12 January.

Although it was his first ever run there were no danger signs in the booking. He was trained by a sound man in Peter Calver and owned by Jockey Club steward Lord Zetland. He was very keen going to post, so I did the sensible thing and dropped him out stone last, but I was fighting a losing battle and couldn't hold one leg of him, let alone four.

Passing the stands we were twenty lengths clear and out of control and, to make things even worse, the steering went completely turning into the back straight. Instead of going left we carried straight on towards a big privet hedge that was fortified by a chain link fence with three strands of barbed wire along the top.

Hoping he would stop and not being brave enough to bale out I sat tight, but this horse was a real headbanger. He galloped on and demolished the lot, including a concrete post, and we ended up lying on a strip of grass. By a miracle, I didn't have a mark on me and Gospel Rock still had plenty of fight in him. He stood up, shook himself and galloped off over the busy A1 and into Wetherby town centre, where he was finally cornered in the car park of my local, the Swan and Talbot. Talk in the town later was that he'd stopped in at the Royal Oak first but there were no birds in so he moved on!

The racegoers thought they'd seen a ghost when I came out to ride City Entertainer for Charlotte Postlethwaite in the handicap chase half an hour later but there was nothing he could throw at me that would match what I'd just gone through. I took it up after the last to win by half a length.

Geoff Harker rang me shortly after to ask if I thought he should go and school Gospel Rock. I told him that I wouldn't want to be in the same county as him, let alone school him.

David Elsworth had been as good as his word and put me back on Cavvies Clown in the Jim Ford Chase at Wincanton in February. It was the first time I'd been on the horse since we completed a double two years earlier. It was hard on young Ross Arnott, who was now the gelding's regular rider, but Cavvies Clown had become troublesome at the start and with my experience of Bregawn, David and owner Jo Ollivant had given me the ride back. Cavvies Clown reminded me of Bregawn. Even though he wasn't very big he had a great heart which made up for any lack of stature and he was a tremendous jumper.

He was tricky before the Jim Ford, but once he got off he was in a different league and made all to beat Cool Ground twenty-five lengths with my old friend Kildimo a well-beaten second when falling at the last. This race turned out to be my most significant win of the season, although Cavvies Clown could have won the Gold Cup. He was only beaten just under twelve lengths into fourth behind Norton's Coin having given away more than that at the start.

David was never one to get carried away about the ability of a jockey because he had been one himself. As a result, I thought a lot of the quote he made before that Gold Cup when he said, 'I am a great fan of Bradley's. He sits so quiet on horses, has lovely hands and never seems to flap when they get in a bit of a muddle at a fence.' He was right. Seeing a short stride is as important as getting a long one, especially on a novice chaser where balance, timing and soft hands are vital.

With Barrie Wright as a lodger, life was always going to be interesting. Bazza sowed enough wild oats to require a combined harvester and there was one memorable conquest that saw him headline the *Sunday People*.

On one of my visits to Tramp I'd met Pamella Bordes, who was notorious at the time and being called 'The new Christine Keeler.' She was employed as a research assistant to Tory MP David Shaw, while another MP, Henry Bellingham, sponsored her House of Commons Pass. She had a relationship with former *Observer* editor Donald Trelford but the security panic buttons were pressed when it became known she was seeing a cousin of Libyan leader Colonel Gaddaffi in Paris.

Jim Davidson called her Poppadom Pam, because she was hot and spicy and she'd been exposed as a high class hooker charging up to £5,000 a time. One night Bazza and I ended up at Tramp Night Club and she was in there. I did the introductions and gave my man the big build up and before you could say 'they're off' they were. Bazza reckoned the first thing she said was, 'I'm going to fuck you tonight,' and seeing as there was no mention of a five grand downpayment, Bazza was away to her place in Eton Mews. I can't remember how long he stayed, but for a lad who always struggled to do anything below 10st 12lb he was very light for the two weeks he was with her. She even came down to visit him, but she couldn't drive and arrived off the train at Newbury in a full length mink coat which raised a few eyebrows. It could probably have bought the whole train. She'd also had a go at landing the champion Flat jockey Steve Cauthen. He'd made his excuses, as they say, but now she was hooked on Bazza, who could fall in love very easily. Fortunately, he could fall out of it pretty quick too and when she started telling me she was going to be Mrs Wright I thought it seemed all wrong and Bazza agreed. Mind you, he got some terrible stick when the story appeared in print where he was described as 'Her bit of rough,' and how he confided to a close friend, 'She played the man's role and was very dominant ... she was always in the saddle when it came to sex.'

As I said, there was never a dull moment with Bazza. Like me, he was a real party animal, which was just as well because I was landed with an impromptu one at the end of the season.

Some of the thrashes I had in Wetherby were legendary. I always had the fridge full of champagne and beer and it was open house for as long as you liked. Money is obviously important, but to me it's not the be all and end all and I firmly believe it is there to be spent. I often went straight from some of my house parties to work at the Dickinsons and blew away the hangover riding work. Mind you, it was something I found much harder to do as I got older.

As the 1989-90 season finished all us jockeys were looking forward to a bash at Newbury racecourse. Over 300 people had paid £30 a head, but on the day of the party the organiser, Tommy Regan, did a runner with the cash so the show was off. About twenty of my friends were on their way from Wetherby by the time I found out, so I decided to have a barbecue at my place. I don't know how many of the 300 turned up, but the show went on for nearly 24 hours and I was well pleased I didn't have to get up for work after it.

But my thirtieth birthday party at Cloud Nine nightclub in Bradford put that in the shade. The owner was a good friend called Ronnie Hurd and he waived the £600 bill for food when he realised he'd taken £15,000 over the bar.

Black tie was *de rigeur* and 350 guests came from far and wide to have a ball.

CHAPTER 19
Making the right connections

After almost 18 months in the Lambourn area I was feeling a little more comfortable, but I was still missing my old stamping ground in Wetherby and needed only the slightest excuse to drive back for the weekend.

The regular jaunts home meant that Carl Leafe - known as Silas because of his uncanny resemblance to Silas Marner in a current TV production - and myself could team up with our old mates. There was Paul Crooks (Brewis), Mick Makin (Drake), Charlie Dawson (Chuck Mudballs) and, of course, Boo Boo. We'd go out on the town just like the old days and I loved it. Then one night I made my best-ever decision in deciding to take in a place called Josephine's in Harrogate.

It was a cracking club with a Piano bar and restaurant and, after a good meal, we sat around and took in the scenery. It didn't take long before my eye was drawn to two girls sitting at the bar. In my typically shy way I just looked on for a while and then did my usual trick and sidled up to the bar for a bottle of champagne.

Tim Whitaker, whose father Richard trained in Wetherby, asked them if they'd like a drink. They blanked him, so I said, without much chivalry, 'What's wrong with you?' The girl I began talking to was called Andrea. Tim was talking to her friend, whose name was Amanda Wilson, and they were both a bit offish. Although it was Amanda I'd got my eye on I persisted with Andrea and continued, 'What's up with her, why's she miserable?' At this she let it slip that Amanda had split up with her boyfriend. It turned out he was called Billy, a good-looking bastard who was D J at Mr Craig's club. That was all the start I needed.

Craig's was like a second home to me in Leeds and Carl, Boo Boo, Mudballs and the rest of the boys were always in the VIP Lounge. We were well looked after and spent fortunes, but it was a wonderful club. It was eventually sold and the new owners only wanted kids and drinkers and, although I've been back a few times, it is nowhere near the same. But the place was the common ground between Amanda and myself. It got us talking, so I slipped in 'How's Billy?' She looked down her nose at me and said, 'I don't know, ask him the next time you see him.' Anyway, the ice had been broken and she asked me what I did. 'I'm a jockey.' She didn't hide her exasperation. 'Oh no, not another one, I've just finished with a disc jockey.'

I had to think quick. 'No, I'm a jockey that rides horses.' She seemed only marginally more impressed but I carried on and finally conned her phone number. Sadly, that was all the progress I was going to make that night. Mudballs and company were coming on a bit strong to her and Andrea and they couldn't wait to get away. Good judges!

If I thought Amanda was going to be easy to get out again I was mistaken, and whenever I phoned she'd get one of her sisters to put me off. She always seemed to be washing her bloody hair! I even invited her to the Grand National but she blanked that as well. No girl had ever knocked me back so many times before, but eventually my persistence paid off. I'm glad to say it was the shrewdest move

I've made.

When I finally convinced Amanda to move down south with me she proved the best friend and confidante a man could have wished for. She settled into life around the racing crowd, although no one seemed to be able to remember her name. It was during the time that *Blackadder* was on TV and there was an attractive girl in it who was dressed as a man and called 'Bob'. So, when people kept asking Amanda her name she just said 'Bob' and it stuck.

We've been together a long time now, through good and bad times, and I know that I would not have been able to survive without her. She's been my rock.

But there was no denying the fact that I was desperately short of decent rides and without them a jockey can't perform at his peak. Too many bad rides drag you down and it was clear that I needed a good stable to back me.

David Elsworth was terrific and, although I was never retained by him, he inadvertently had a hand in steering me towards the job as stable jockey to Charlie Brooks. It proved a golden spell which would give me the most pride and satisfaction since my days with the Dickinsons.

There was a long courtship before the marriage with a notable tiff that almost scuppered the plan, but 'Elzie' played his part when he reiterated his faith in me by getting me the ride on Desert Orchid in the Tingle Creek Chase at Sandown on 1 December.

Richard Dunwoody had been let off to ride Waterloo Boy and it seemed an impossible task for Dessie to give 16lb to that specialist two miler and upwards of 20lb to the remaining runners. Still, it was a massive public vote of confidence from the trainer and owner Richard Burridge to let me take control of a horse who was the undisputed people's champion.

I'd been down to ride him work at Whitsbury, but I knew he had a mountain to climb at Sandown and, after blazing away in front to the sixth I looked after him from the ninth when he had no chance.

217

Richard chose the right one from the pair. Waterloo Boy started warm favourite at 11-8 but could finish only third, beaten twelve lengths by Young Snugfit and Jamie Osborne with my old partner Sabin du Loir, now with Martin Pipe, two lengths back in second.

The emergence of Pipe was causing Charlie Brooks some anxiety and forcing him to look for a replacement for Peter Scudamore. 'Scu' had been with Charlie's predecessor, the legendary Fred Winter, at Uplands in Upper Lambourn but was becoming increasingly involved with a Pipe team which would go on to put the record books through the shredder.

Charlie felt that he needed his own man and began to take a look at me after he had been talking over his dilemma with John Francome and the much-travelled trainer Rod Simpson. I'd ridden with John and for him when he had a brief flirtation as a trainer and had also ridden for Rod. Both said he should consider me, so he kept his eye on me for a while.

Not that I was having a great season. Of the eleven winners I rode between the start of the season and New Year's Day eight came via the Harewood connection of Richard Beever, who worked there as a lad, Banner Bell and Thomas Tate, who was married to Michael's sister Hazel and provided three winners on the good chaser Ardbrin. But it was 'Elzie' who put me on the winner that would catch Charlie's eye, namely Floyd in the Long Walk Hurdle at Ascot in mid-December.

Charlie was represented by a good staying hurdler, Bokaro, who was going like a winner in front when he fell with Ben de Haan two out. Floyd was one of the gamest staying hurdlers I've ridden and although he might not have beaten Bokaro, he showed great courage to get up on the flat and take Ryde Again by three lengths. He made me look good again later in the season when we dictated the pace to win the prestigious Rendlesham Hurdle at Kempton using front running tactics likened to those employed by Steve Cauthen on the

Flat.

But perhaps more importantly for the future, I'd been given my first ride by Charles Patrick Evelyn Brooks on an uninspiring beast called Bitter Buck at Sandown. Always a man to consider his options, Charlie waited a month and a half before putting me on the same horse at Chepstow, where we were unlucky not to win having swept through to challenge at the last only to crumple on landing.

The partnership was no overnight success. In fact, one afternoon at Ascot in April I had four rides for the stable, pulled up three of them and was unplaced on the other. But two days later the first winner came on Switch in a Plumpton Hurdle. He was owned by the *Daily Mail* diarist Nigel Dempster and there aren't many more enthusiastic owners around. Exceptionally generous in victory, Nigel takes defeats equally well and has a very sound understanding of what can go wrong in a race. He's been a very loyal friend in print and in private over the years we've been associated.

By now Charlie had made up his mind that I was going to be his first choice rider for next season and we were about to hit the jackpot in spades. He was something of a pioneer when it came to running jumpers overseas and, even before Bokaro had run a cracking third to Wonder Man in the Welsh Champion Hurdle at Chepstow on 1 April, the entry had been made for the Corsa Siepi Di Milano at San Siro, Italy, on 13 April. This was the Italian equivalent of the Champion Hurdle and represented a shrewd bit of placing. As Charlie pointed out, 'I don't mind taking on the best Italian hurdlers but I don't want the best British ones joining in as well.' In fact, he'd already placed Bokaro with great effect having won the Queen Mother Supreme Hurdle at Belmont Park, New York, and in his owner, Lady Eileen Joseph, he had a very enthusiastic ally in anything remotely adventurous. Unfortunately, an Italian air traffic controllers' strike stopped her flying in from her home on the Cote d'Azur and it almost scuppered our plans, too. Charlie was anxiously waiting for me at the airport because if I

219

didn't get in he had real problems. It would mean employing a local jockey, which might not have been the best move as the Italian horse of the year Miocamen was raging hot favourite and unbeaten in ten starts. Under those circumstances it would have been hard to know just how forceful a local boy would have been. They definitely looked on us as outsiders.

I did get in the night before but there was no chance of going out. I had to sweat in the bath to do 10st 5lb, but I was up very lively the next morning and we gave Bokaro a sharp sprint on the track just to clear his wind.

As always, I walked the course. Charlie came with me and we decided that as there was no doubt about Bokaro staying two and a half miles, we'd set out to make all, stay out of trouble and not risk getting tightened up by the home team. It went like clockwork. Bokaro jumped fast and clean from the front. Nothing could get near him and he finished full of running, beating the previous year's winner Afkal by twelve lengths with Miocamen ten lengths back in third. The prize money was £41,000 to the winner and, coupled with the money won at Belmont, netted more than if Bokaro had won the Champion Hurdle.

But while Charlie was clever in the ways of the European Programme Book he wasn't nearly cunning enough in the ways of the world. It was at this time that he had begun a relationship with John Francome's wife, Miriam, and she had flown down to Milan for the weekend. John phoned Charlie the morning after the big win: 'Morning, Charlie, well done on winning that race yesterday. One of the papers has just told me they've got a photo of you and Miriam in Milan last night. I'd better speak to her to sort out our story so they don't print it next week.'

Charlie just said, 'OK', and handed the phone over to Miriam, who was lying beside him. Oh dear! If only I could have got to him I would have told him about the same sort of experience I had after taking a girl to spend the night at my place following an evening at

Mr Craig's. The phone rang the next morning and it was someone asking, 'Is my sister there?' I'm not usually quick when I'm woken up but I was soon thinking fast, 'I saw her leaving Mr Craig's with her girlfriends in a taxi. She probably stayed with them or went home.' Now, I'd never heard her talk about a brother, but I did know she had a lunatic boyfriend and, sure enough, it was him checking up. She'd only been gone a few minutes, but it was one of the wisest things I've done and saved a lot of aggravation.

Despite our good start it would be wrong to infer that Charlie didn't have reservations about me or I about him for that matter. When we met to discuss the following season he made it clear that he wanted my services but would not be messed about - Charlie has always been his own man. He was well aware of my reputation because of the high profile clashes with the Jockey Club and had been privately warned against employing me. His mother Caroline had been to lunch with someone connected to Jockey Club Security who said to her, point-blank, 'Oh, I'd tell your son not to employ Graham Bradley.'

Knowing Charlie, that made him even more determined to take me on but he made it very clear what was required. Over a meal at the Queens Arms he said, 'Brad, I'll be employing you, but if you ever let me down you will never ride for me again and what's more, I'll make sure you never ride for anyone else either.' He then said to another mutual friend of ours, 'I've told Brad this will be a very private hiring but a very public firing!'

There was never any chance of that. I said, 'Don't worry Charlie, that's the least of your worries. I would not dream of letting anyone down who has put their trust in me like you have.' In all the time I rode for Charlie I never told him a lie and if I rode a bad race I told him straight away.

It still wasn't all roses though. Charlie had intended to make the offer official at the Perth meeting twelve days after we'd won the Italian Champion Hurdle, but my sleeping sickness almost got me the sack before I started.

I'd gone up to Scotland with Steve Smith Eccles and booked into a lovely little hotel called the Isle of Skye. The plan was to be on the racecourse to school Charlie's three runners at nine the next morning and I put in an alarm call. The trouble was that Smith Eccles and me went out for a meal, then to a club where we got upside down drunk. When the alarm call came the next morning he just picked the receiver up and dropped it, thinking it was someone from the night before trying to be funny.

I woke up at 11.30, looked at Ecc and said, 'Christ! I was meant to be schooling for Charlie at nine and I booked a call.'

He looked at bit sheepish, 'Oh, so that's what it was. I thought it was someone taking the piss from last night.'

Charlie was definitely not amused. He'd gone to the track with three horses to school and no kit of his own, no jodhpurs or boots. So he improvised and wrapped the bandages normally used for a horse's legs and tail around his legs. He must have looked like a First World War soldier wearing puttees, but it stopped his legs getting rubbed raw and he did the schooling himself.

He was still livid, rightly so, when I got to the races, and because the owners weren't there for either Melicus or Espy he didn't bother to come into the paddock and let the travelling head lad give me my instructions. We didn't speak for a few days and he made me sweat for a couple of weeks before he told me I'd defintely got the job. But word had seeped through to the yard that I'd been a naughty boy. Luckily, the right man was there to jump on me from a great height when I was two minutes late on my first morning at Uplands. Step forward Brian Delaney, the head lad.

The horses pulled out at 7.30 a.m. sharp. I rolled up at 7.32 with a cheery, 'morning, Bri.' There was no response.

On the way back to the yard after riding work he pulled his horse alongside and, looking me straight in the eye said, 'Young man, you were late this morning.'

I didn't know what to say because I knew I'd upset someone who wasn't about to be placated. After a few second's pause which heightened the tension he continued in measured tones that did not waver. 'Do you know what time I was up this morning?'

All I could answer was 'No.'

'Five-thirty.'

There was another short pause.

'Do you know what time I get up every morning?'

No time to reply before he answered his own question. 'five-thirty.'

I was metaphorically dangling by the collar with my feet off the ground and there was no change of volume in his voice, which carried the confident tones of someone in complete control.

'If you ever do it again, one of two things is going to happen.' A couple of seconds elapsed. 'Either you'll go, or I'll go and I know which one it will be.'

And just in case there was any wind left in my sails he added, with the air of a schoolmaster who has taken over a troublesome pupil, 'I've heard all about you at Murray Smith's.'

It's true I had been late there a few times but it was clear that this was a man who didn't believe in taking prisoners. When you looked into Brian Delaney's face you saw a countenance etched by thousands of dark, mid-winter mornings and one that had met triumph and disaster on equal footing.

It was hardly the right start to any working relationship but anything further down the line could only be better and I am proud to say that it was the beginning of an admiring friendship which endures to this day. Brian has rightly earned legendary status in Lambourn, having been that rare breed of head lad who can transfer knowledge to others so they can take that same position in other yards. Like Kit Stobbs at Arthur Stephenson's and Brian Powell at the Dickinsons, he was the steel rod which ran through the yard and prevented it bending when the hard times came. When the going got tough, then these men really got going.

So when you get a compliment from someone like Brian it is worth any amount of trophies and I felt tremendous pride when he recalled, 'Charlie was away not long after you joined the yard. I went up to the schooling ground to check how things were going and watched you school a little filly. There wasn't much of her, but the way you put her over those schooling hurdles was the nearest I'd seen since John Francome was up there.'

That's the kind of compliment I cherish from a true master of his craft.

But from the moment I joined the Uplands team I felt I was part of it and it's worth remembering that if my dad had got his way I'd have gone there as a boy and not to Stephenson's.

When I got into the yard each day I felt as though they were my horses and my lads. The horses were always tacked up and led out for me to mount, and the moment we got back to the yard after schooling or working, Brian had someone there to take the horse off me. They spoiled me and I was very grateful, so I would do the very best I could for them, small things like always having a drink with the boys if we were in the same pub. Some jockeys can be aloof, but it wasn't my way. Experience has taught me that you must never forget where you came from.

When you are young things make a greater impression on you and I'd never forgotten the relationship that Bruce Raymond, who was stable jockey to Michael Jarvis in Newmarket, had with the lads. He never forgot how important they were and whenever he cleared out his wardrobe he would bring a pile of top quality clothes for anyone who wanted them. I thought it was a beautiful thing to do. He was simply very kind to them and never forgot to give them a present when he rode one of them a winner. I've got the same nature and decided to follow his example.

I've always been a fanatic with clothes and tried to turn myself

The earliest family connection with horses. My dad's father, Robert, with his team of plough horses

Me at nine months.
Weight problems already

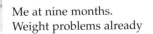

Aged five with my younger sister Jackie.
I was all ears

Mum and Dad in the fifties

My dad, Norman, 19 and as immaculate as ever. Ready to serve King and country

With my older brother Gary (10) and me (7) at Beverley races.
I'd borrowed Dad's binoculars for the day

Done up like a jockey in Jack Hanson's colours on Glenbarry.
I was very young but took this picture very seriously

My imagination ran wild on this one. The saddle horse in Jack Hanson's tack room

One of my first regular rides, aged 12 in 1972 on Tristesse. She wasn't very good but she was quiet

Coming back after that first ride, tired and very much wiser

Looking very confident before my first ride in public on Sweet Slievenamon at Redcar

Getting ready to tar the bottom of the horseboxes at
Crawleas. I learned to dress down to do the job

The hostel at Arthur Stephenson's. Cheese sandwiches the house speciality

Arriving for work at the Dickinson yard at Harewood in the £200 Morris Minor with Steve O'Donoghue hanging out of the window

Eye to eye with Bregawn. A great racehorse and friend

An important win. Taking the Selby Handicap Chase at Wetherby at the expense of Dave (Donkey) Dutton the year I pipped him for the junior riders title

Cantering to post on Bregawn before the 1982 Hennessy Gold Cup. I pushed all the problems to the back of my mind

Left: A spontaneous gesture. Putting my arm around Robert Earnshaw after he had won the 1982 Cheltenham Gold Cup on Silver Buck at the expense of Bregawn

Below: Before that historic Gold Cup of 1983. Holding my niece, Clare, and flanked by my then fiancee, Sue Thewenetti, and sisters Jackie and Mandy

Below: After Bregawn had led home the Famous Five. He's given me everything - and it shows

The only picture of Michael Dickinson's Famous Five after the 1983 Gold Cup. From the left, Wayward Lad (Jonjo O'Neill), Captain John (David Goulding), Silver Buck (Robert Earnshaw), Ashley House (Dermot Browne) and Bregawn

The end to a perfect day.
Just before receiving the trophy for leading rider at the 1983 Cheltenham Festival from Princess Anne

Aintree 1983.
This is exactly the same outfit I wore when placing the bet at Cartmel

A night out with the boys. From left: Banner Bell, Paul Crooks, myself and Steve Youlden

The soccer teams I arranged to play in the benefit match for Sam Berry and Peter Dun at York. Southern team, back row left to right: Richard Linley, Simon McNeill, Graham McCourt, Francis Lee, Dermot Browne, Sir Bobby Charlton. Front row: Mike Summerbee, Jimmy Duggan, Mark Richards and Sam Morshead

North, back row left to right: Alan Brown, Peter Lorimer, Mark Dwyer, David Dutton, Colin Hawkins, Phil Tuck, Steve Charlton. Front: Myself (manager), Bobby Collins, Martin Brennan, Jonjo O'Neill, Martin Pepper and Chris Pimlott

Left: Playing the game with two of my heroes from Leeds United. Peter Lorimer and Eddie Gray

Below: Kildimo in full flight. But look at his tail

Below: Robin Goodfellow beating Skygrange at Sandown. The trouble started when he was beaten

Winning in the colours I'd worn so proudly as a child. Coming back after winning on Yahoo for Jack Hanson at Haydock

Border Tinker lands a rare old touch at Sedgefield

The family at my 30th birthday party.
Norm, Gary, Jackie and Mandy

Two people to whom I owe so much.
The Boss, Tony Dickinson and Mrs D, Monica,
arriving at the 30th birthday party

About to be ejected from Ashley House at The Chair. It took years for me to get it right over the Grand National fences

Shareed wins the Marlborough Cup. I'm glad the top poles had been sawn through

The picture that saved my career. About to be unseated by Starjestic at Southwell

On the floor after Starjestic. The first of many inquiries

Looking thoughtful with Norm as the Southwell stewards debate the Starjestic tumble

Outside the Jockey Club Headquarters after the Starjestic inquiry.
Norm and my legal eagle Peter McCormick.
I had maximum confidence in him

The man called Uncle. Brian Wright

Dinner during the Cheltenham Festival. At the converted barn I always rented, with Nicky Gill and my friend from childhood, Yvonne Topham

Above: Big night out. My table at the Lesters Awards at the Hilton Hotel, London.
Clockwise: Myself, Johan Domija, Jo Wilson, Barrie Wright, Michael Condon, Mike Burke,
Jason Titley, Tom Butterfield, Carolyn Eidesforth, Tim Collins and Amanda Wilson

Below: The intrepid syndicate manager Henry Ponsonby, flanked by Fiona Webber, left, and
Miriam Francome at Vee Shaw's 60th birthday party. Not long before, Henry had gone in
search of a valuable photo

Getting airborne from Black Humour, this time at The Chair in
the Grand National

I'm wide awake and driving for the finish.
Winning the 1996 Champion Hurdle
on Collier Bay

After a day's golf with
Vinnie. The boy certainly
done good!

I'm not looking at the time.
Coming in after winning the 1996 Champion Hurdle
and giving the Vinnie Jones Leeds United salute

On the schooling grounds with Yogi Breisner, the jumping guru

The People's choice. Winning the Martell Aintree Hurdle on Morley Street in 1993.
Richard Dunwoody leads me on Flown and Granville Again, ridden by Peter Scudamore,
is tucked in behind

Celebrating the 1995 Hennessey Cognac Gold Cup win of Couldn't Be Better.
Dean Gallagher and I with the one and only Brian Delaney

The gallant grey Suny Bay beating Barton Bank in the 1997 Hennessey Cognac Gold Cup
at Newbury. It was going to be a long weekend

Celebrating Suny Bay's Hennessy win at the Queen's Arms.
Owner Andrew Cohen, trainer Charlie Brooks and myself holding the cup.
In the background are Bregawn's colours that I wore when we won the
race in 1982

Holding the Hennessy Gold Cup with Dad. We'd been through a lot together

The two most important ladies in my life. Amanda, now my wife, and my wonderful and brave sister, Mandy

Above: I'd do anything for Charlie. Schooling in a Santa Claus suit on Mandown. Brooks used it on the cover of his Christmas cards

Right: In the paddock at Ascot. Charlie has made Lady Lloyd Webber and me smile but Lord Lloyd Webber seems to have missed the punchline

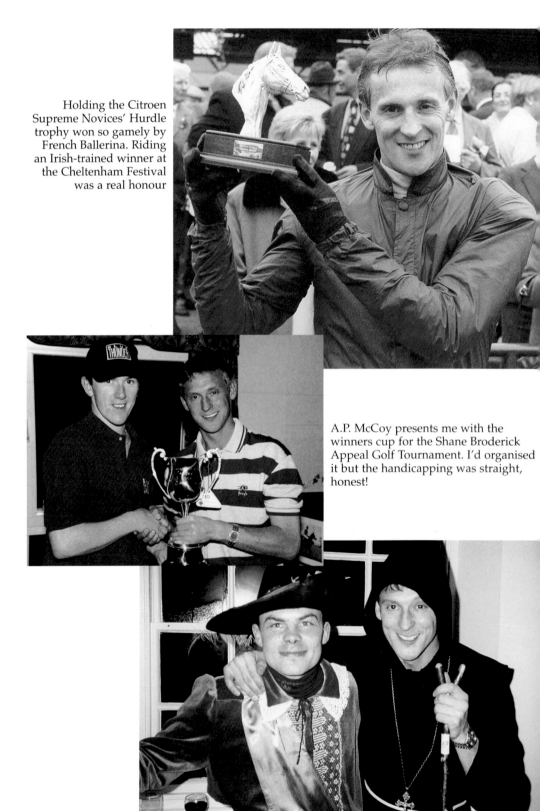

Holding the Citroen Supreme Novices' Hurdle trophy won so gamely by French Ballerina. Riding an Irish-trained winner at the Cheltenham Festival was a real honour

A.P. McCoy presents me with the winners cup for the Shane Broderick Appeal Golf Tournament. I'd organised it but the handicapping was straight, honest!

Fancy dress with one of the nicest men in jump racing. Adrian Maguire

Riding in a sea chase at Bad Harzburg, Germany.
I'm wearing the white cap with bobble

Vicious Circle makes more dreams come true at Ascot with Frankie Dettori

A champion in every sense. Ready
for a big night with 'Wee Anthony'

The best
engagement
I ever made.
My wife Amanda

Above: With the
Anfield Hombres.
Martin Pipe, Steve
McManaman,
Robbie Fowler and
Auetaler

Left: Who'd have
thought we'd have
ended up like this.
With my great ally
Michael Dickinson at
Royal Ascot

I'm back. The first winner after my
release, Brummel at Stratford

He wears it well. Vicious Circle's owner
David Metcalf at the Royal Meeting

Above: One of my biggest fans was there for the last hurrah. With Cathy Baybutt after the final weigh-in

Right: It's all over now. Coming in after the last winner. On The Boil at Haydock. The end of a 23 year journey

Above: The public farewell with the boys at Haydock

Right: The private goodbye at the Queens Arms

Fancy doing this for 70 quid. I did, and I still miss it

out well. I'd get three new suits for the three days of Cheltenham and always had about 30 in my wardrobe. These were supplied by a good mate, Chris Coleman, who is a keen punter and owns the top quality clothes shop, Copperfields, in Moorgate. When I steered Chris the right way it was only a matter of time before I was called for a suit fitting. But I ended up with too many. Luckily, quite a few of the lads were my size and I was pleased to do them a good turn.

The presents for riding them a winner are important, too. Brian says that I was one of the best payers ever to the lads and that no matter what anyone had ever said or written about me, I was very well liked by the staff during my time at Uplands. Well, the same went for me. They were a cracking bunch and just like the Dickinsons, there was a very slow turnover in staff. Once they were on board they tended to stay for a long time.

But when it came to dealing with Charlie, I didn't know what to expect. He'd made a very brave move in buying Uplands from the Winter family at the height of the property boom. Ultimately it would cost him very dear financially and for most of the time I was with him he was under intense pressure. When he'd appointed me he said to some friends that he probably wouldn't like me as a person but that he respected me as a jockey and horseman. He didn't think he'd have much to do with me but everything would be fine as long as I did my job right. I suppose people thought there'd be a culture clash when an Old Etonian met one of Wetherby High's finest but that was never the case. Charlie and I soon became very good friends and the friendship endures just as strongly although we've both retired.

I soon realised that Charlie was a very intelligent young man but was very quiet, like me. He would bottle things up and didn't like confrontations or giving people a bollocking. If it needed to be done, he'd usually leave it to Brian. I got to read him like a book and was well aware of the problems the yard had with viruses and injuries. These would weigh heavily on Charlie and used to send him into a strop. Not an aggressive one, more moody. I got into the habit of saying, 'Morning Charles' If he didn't speak I knew he'd got problems and left him alone until he came around a bit later on. I knew just what he was going though and genuinely felt for him.

It wasn't just Charlie and the staff at Uplands that were so good. They also had some owners who were pure class and there's no doubt that the matriarch figure was Lady Joseph. She was a lady in every sense of the word and adored Charlie. If he came up with a nice horse, she would buy it. When Charlie was crippled financially it seemed very likely that she would buy Uplands from him but there was a problem. I think her family were against it, and she ended up renting the big house from Charlie where the Winters had lived.

Her late husband was Maxwell Joseph who, along with other ventures ran a hotel chain and Lady Joseph knew how to get things right, and completely refurbished at Uplands. She lived in London during the week and Lambourn at the weekend. What's more, she loved to party - and in some style.

She decided on a *blanc et noir* Hallowe'en party, which meant that all guests had to be in black and white and there were enthusiastic discussions on who would come as what. Charlie was first off the blocks. 'I'm going as a ghost,' and Miriam soon had her costume worked out. 'I'm going as a black cat with white whiskers.'

Bob and I weren't going to be outdone and went to an outfitters in Oxford, where she got kitted out as Morticia from the *Addams Family* and I got a Dracula costume. On the night, Mark and Sarah Bradstock, who trained several winners I rode, came to our place to get changed. They'd decided to go as black and white minstrels and weren't sparing the blacking.

Bob looked magnificent with a white face and the eyes picked out black, a long black dress and hair right down to some pointy black shoes. I looked pretty good myself with the wig in a point over my forehead, white face, black eyes and a big black cape with a red collar turned up. It was nicely finished with a set of fangs with fake blood dripping down my chin. With the white shirt and waistcoat I thought I looked a million dollars. When we got to Uplands some of the lads were parking the cars and, although they didn't recognise me, they knew the car and started giggling when they saw me get out. When we went in it was wonderful. There was a reception area for drinks, then you walked through into the dining room where the roof was black with silver stars shining through. There were ice sculptures all around and the wine and champagne were premier cru.

I thought I'd make a big entrance, so I put the cape over my face and walked in doing a big growl like the count does when he's going for a transfusion. The trouble was it was me who ended up transfixed from Transylvania. The room stopped dead. Everyone stared and some actually had their mouths open in astonishment and mine soon dropped with acute embarrassment. *Blanc et noir* meant black-tie and evening dress for the men and elegant cocktail dresses for the ladies. The most daring thing some of the men had done was wear black and white wigs, but we stood out like Rudolph's nose. Or we did until the Bradstocks came tumbling in behind us. When you understand how much care I take with my sartorial turnout you can imagine what was going through my mind and it didn't take Bob long to voice my worst thoughts. Through the corner of her mouth she hissed, 'I'm going to kill you!' It was a scene that Wodehouse could have written for Bertie Wooster, and Charlie had got it wrong, too. He was only wearing a sheet, although I must say Miriam did carry the cat suit off rather well. Fortunately we had one very gracious lady as our hostess and, when Charlie led me up to Lady Joseph, he just cleared his throat and said, 'I do believe this is your jockey.' She was absolutely brilliant. She soon began laughing and just said, 'You look marvellous, go on and have a ball.' It was a beautiful night, excellent wine and gorgeous company. After I'd sampled plenty of the fermented grape I started to enjoy my notoriety and kept going up to the trainers who were there, Nicky

Henderson and John Hills among them, and kept baying for blood. It took quite a while for people to recognise me.

Lady Joseph loved having younger people around and her dinner parties at Uplands were outrageous at times, especially when the two Charlies, Brooks and Egerton, got into their stride. But she just loved it. She was also incredibly brave. All the time that Bob and I knew her she was suffering from cancer, but she always looked so good that we never knew. She must have been in a great deal of pain, but she covered it up with such courage that when she died in November 1994 it came as a great shock. She is missed by everyone lucky enough to have known her.

Although I ended the season with my worst ever total of just twenty-six winners, I was comfortable in the knowledge that Charlie would make me his stable jockey and that things would only get better.

But I had a stark reminder of the good times which had passed when Tony Dickinson died on 25 June 1991. Much as I respected Michael and loved Mrs D, it was the Boss who took me on as kid and gave me a chance twelve years earlier. Looking back, it's surprising that he was called Boss, because there was never anyone who was less bossy. In all the time I knew him he hardly ever raised his voice and when Michael and Mrs D were giving out it was always him who provided sanity to a situation. I'll never forget his kindness to me after I'd caused the death of Silver Buck. And when I rode a finish a circuit too soon on Bobby Burns after the death of By The Way at Sedgefield in 1988 he once again calmed the turbulent waters with the worldly wise words, 'It's happened before and it will happen again.'

I said at the time, 'It was unbelievable that anyone could be so understanding. He was always asking the lads if they were all right, short of money, that sort of thing. He was one of the best men I've ever met and without him I wouldn't be where I am now. I'll miss him greatly.' I still do.

CHAPTER 20
The price of justice

The first winner I rode for Charlie Brooks as his new stable jockey for the 1991-92 season was not one of the stars. But just under four months after winning the Lloyds Of Stafford Novices Chase at Uttoxeter on 19 September, Marouat would hit skid row and the Southwell stewards did their best to pack me along with him.

Marouat was certainly one of the moderate members of Lady Joseph's team and the more he raced after Uttoxeter the worse he got. *Timeform* labelled him as 'Not one to trust', and the four times he raced after winning saw him deteriorate alarmingly. A horse of his calibre was of no interest to Lady Joseph so Charlie decided to run him in a claiming chase in the hope that he would win and entice someone to buy him, problems and all.

He didn't rate high on my list of priorities for the day. I was booked to ride at Wolverhampton only to be switched to Southwell on the morning because the meeting was frozen off. Although he was forecast to start favourite in the racing papers there wasn't a lad in the yard who would put him up to any of his punters as a betting proposition. That, allied to his declining interest in racing and the damning *Timeform* verdict, meant it was no surprise to see him walk in the market from 6-4 to 3-1. In contrast, Martin Pipe's runner Night Vision, who had the next best set of form figures, was backed down from 3-1 to 11-8. When he was running well Marouat was always buzzing from the front and made all, but on this occasion he was reluctant to line up and went with very little enthusiasm. When he dropped himself out from the sixth there was no point in beating him up and risk both of us ending up on the floor, so I pulled him up after the eighth.

After Night Vision won readily by five lengths the stewards decided to hold an inquiry into Marouat, but I didn't see anything to worry about. Yes, I'd been before them with the Starjestic fiasco in 1989 but this was a different set of stewards. However, some things don't change and they were convinced I had not been forceful enough. I kept repeating that Marouat would have gone even slower had I hit him but it was a waste of time.

They called the betting intelligence officer who said he thought the horse should have been favourite. Evidence was also taken from the handicapper, Tony Winlaw, who said the horse should have run perfectly well. The trouble was, no one had told Marouat and, as I was the closest one to him, only I knew just how bad he was going. The stewards went out to deliberate and didn't agree with me.

I was called back in to face the three wise men across the table with my arms behind my back before Mr Readett-Bayley, the chairman, announced, 'Mr Bradley, we find you in breach of Rule 151, because you have not allowed the horse, in our opinion, to run on its merits. We are going to fine you £500.'

All I could say was, Thank you,' but I turned on my heel and left seething. IN THEIR OPINION! Bollocks. What about my opinion? I was riding the horse and now they know better than me - and what's more there was a form book to back me up. Fortunately, in Charlie and Lady Joseph I had tremendous fighters in my corner. Charlie responded by sending a letter to Sir Piers Bengough, who was then chairman of the disciplinary committee, before issuing a stinging statement to the press which read:

'I have written to Sir Piers Bengough inviting him to choose a race to run Marouat in next week in which he can put a jockey of their choice on the horse and we will see what happens then. The whole thing is ludicrous - you need only look at the form book to see this horse has simply lost his form and there is nothing we can do about it.

'We will fight this all the way. This is a slur on me, it is a slur on Brad, and it is a slur on the horse's owner, Lady Joseph. I am really furious about it.

'I watched the race on SIS and you could see that Marouat didn't even want to line up at the start. We can't find anything at all wrong with him - we wouldn't run him if we could - and we have tried everything to rekindle his enthusiasm. But he has lost his form and mentally he doesn't seem to want to know any more. To describe him as unenthusiastic would be diplomatic.

'I am amazed that the stewards think he didn't run on his merits and I take it as a personal insult. They haven't fined me but I feel it is very damaging for me because it casts completely outrageous aspersions on my jockey and I don't like that very much.'

I swiftly lodged an appeal against the £500 fine and set about my attack - I certainly didn't look upon it as a defence - at Portman Square. But once again the quest to clear my name was going to be costly.

It is my experience with horses who turn doggy like Marouat that in nearly every case there is a physical problem which hurts them when they exert. For example, if a horse is stopping quickly it often transpires that he is breaking blood vessels in his lungs. The best way to describe that in human terms is to imagine coming up for air after swimming underwater and then having your head immediately submerged again. You can't breathe.

There was something wrong with Marouat and he was given extensive tests both at the Valley Equine Hospital in Lambourn and the Animal Health Trust in Newmarket. All very expensive but graciously paid for by Lady Joseph. The verdict came back that Marouat did have quite severe damage to his off-hind fetlock and had chronic wearing to his hind toes. It was a condition that rapidly worsened. The unfortunate animal never raced again and was put down to avoid unnecessary suffering.

But there was no doubt in my mind that I was a wanted man and that the Jockey Club wanted to make things as difficult for me as possible. Despite evidence in the form book, it seemed there was one rule for Bradley and one for the others.

The previous season at Wolverhampton Marouat started 11-8 favourite for a novices handicap chase at Wolverhampton. He lost his place at the seventh and pulled up before the eleventh. That day he was ridden by champion jockey Peter Scudamore and there wasn't even an inquiry.

But despite all the evidence in my favour I could not take any chances. I had to engage the best lawyer I could and once again that was Peter McCormick of Leeds. I knew he didn't come cheap but this was a stain that I didn't want on my record and it was going to cost me to get it removed.

Peter's fees for the case would be £2,000. That was way above the legal insurance taken out at the time by the Jockeys' Association, which would provide just £450, but I had to press on. McCormick was extremely thorough in his preparation. We watched the Scrooge Claiming Chase from every available angle, presented the veterinary evidence and discredited the handicappers' evidence that Marouat was entitled to be favourite and should have been giving Noble Vision 10lb instead of 2lb. In fact, on current performance he should have been receiving 5lb from Noble Vision.

Peter made another incisive cut when the stewards' secretary,

William Nunneley, suggested that in one view of the race I was pushing the horse with one hand and pulling it back with the other. When the impossibility of this was pointed out to the panel I thought we'd got a chance, but their faces betrayed nothing.

They sent us out while they deliberated, and not for the first time I wished I'd left a tape recorder to understand what was going through their minds. Would it be a case of, 'We think he might be innocent but let's do him anyway.' I know it seems paranoid but in a civilised society where's the justice in having a closed court? The problem is that when you sign up for your jockeys' licence you agree to abide by the Club rules and they've got you by the short and curlies.

Peter wasn't certain how the verdict would go and that half-hour wait was a nightmare. If it went the wrong way it would be another black mark against me at a time when my career was going forward and looking positive. The last thing I wanted was another 'non-trier' conviction stamped on my record card.

They called us back and very swiftly announced that the Southwell findings had been overturned. Then Nunneley offered a 'No hard feelings', and I didn't really bear any because he was simply doing his job. But in failing to accept my argument he had placed me in a poor light. Without the diligence of Charlie and Lady Joseph and the tenacity of Peter McCormick I could have lost a lot of credence and the cry would have gone up 'Brad's at it again.'

I said, 'Thank you gentlemen,' but felt like saying 'Fuck you.' I came out with the usual platitudes as the press waited, 'Fair hearing, very pleased that common sense has prevailed.' Charlie was delighted and relieved and said, 'I am pleased that the support the owners gave has been justified. They have always had confidence in Brad.'

But the cold hard facts were that clearing my name over an action that should never have been brought cost me £1,500 and a day's loss of earnings for racing at Worcester. Where's the justice in that? One bit of good did come out of it for jockeys in the future in that the premium was upped by the Jockeys' Association to give a larger sum for legal aid.

When Charlie talked about the owners support he was absolutely right. The appeal had been heard on 17 March, nearly two months after the race, but not a single one of the Uplands owners ever questioned me. You can't put a price on such loyalty.

The Marouat episode also meant that I went through the Cheltenham Festival with the shadow cast over me, but I rode my first winner there for five years. And it was a success that exemplified what a grand team Charlie had built at Uplands.

My Young Man was the property of a real sportsman in the late Bill Tulloch. He'd owned top-class chasers for years, including the likes of 1979 Triumph Hurdle winner Pollardstown and Lean Ar Aghaidh, who won the 1987 Whitbread Gold Cup. He also owned the top quality colt and filly Creag-an-Sgor and Mahogany who won the Greenham and Fred Darling Stakes at Newbury in 1984 for Charlie Nelson.

He needed a good chaser and My Young Man had the potential to be just that. The problem was that he was an equine delinquent, so Charlie and I had to set about reforming him. And we did with the help of one of the true horsemasters, Yogi Breisner.

My Young Man had one way of running, flat out with the throttle open. If he met a fence wrong he'd try and go through it and, inevitably, sometimes the fence won. He was a decent novice hurdler when he completed the course but his reputation preceded him for his fencing debut at Newbury. Ben de Haan, who had done all the work on him at home, was injured in a fall the race before, and when Charlie came in looking for a jockey there was a shuffling of feet and dropping of eyes to avoid his gaze. I wasn't on his list at this stage and had a ride in the race anyway. In the end it was Jamie Osborne who took the mount and he never saw another horse as My Young Man made all. After that Newbury win he got rid of Ben at

Kempton then made all under Jamie at Doncaster. He then blundered his chance away in the Arkle at Cheltenham, and by the time I got on him for the big novice chase at Liverpool he had probably gone over the top for the season.

I don't know if Charlie got me to school him early in our first season together to see if my nerve was good but he got his answer anyway. We took him up to school on Mandown and he literally smashed a hole in one of the fences, going flat out. When I returned smiling and said we'd better do it again, Charlie rubbed his chin and said, 'Well, at least I know your bottle's intact.' I never doubted it, but we both knew that My Young Man was showing fences no respect and something had to be done.

We'd seen Yogi Breisner, who was an Olympic three-day eventer for Sweden, working on the schooling ground with Kim Bailey and Oliver Sherwood. Norman Williamson and Jamie Osborne were raving about his methods, so Charlie decided to give him a go. The results were startling. Not only did Yogi sort out My Young Man, he also had a profound effect on me which made the last eight years I was riding the best of my career. I always had the confidence, but he made a crucial difference regarding my technical approach to a fence, just how to present a horse and where. I am certain that the young riders today are more technically aware than I was at the same age. That's not to say they are better jockeys, but they are certainly better prepared because they can continually re-examine their performances.

When we joined the growing band of Yogi's disciples, John Francome was critical on TV and said that if you couldn't get a horse to jump correctly at home you weren't doing your job right. I totally disagreed. Sport is constantly moving forward, driven by experts in various areas. Take golf. Tiger Woods and Colin Montgomerie have specialist coaches and all the top football teams now have fitness trainers for fine tuning and speed work.

There was another fine jumping tutor who operated just outside

Lambourn called Andrew Hoy. He won Olympic three-day event gold medals for Australia and did a magnificent job teaching horses to jump. They included the prolific chase winner Go Universal, who Charlie trained for Tim Collins. Tim's other top-class chaser, Looks Like Trouble, was transformed by Andrew before winning the Cheltenham Gold Cup of 2000. But I found it more difficult to interpret what Andrew wanted. Both Hoy and Breisner were brilliant horsemen, but Andrew wanted you to do it exactly like him and he was just too good to copy. Yogi made it more simple to understand and he was the making of My Young Man.

I couldn't wait for Charlie to get a box full of horses and drive them over to Blewbury. Yogi would make horse and rider concentrate fully. One of his exercises was to take a hurdle out of the ground, place it in front of a fence, and make you jump it going no faster than a trot. It meant the horse had to stand off and pay attention in much the same way as the Dickinsons used the black plastic fences at Harewood.

He would also get you to jump hurdles the wrong way. This can be a dangerous exercise, as the hurdles were rigid and could not fall over, but again it was from no more than a trot. Sometimes you would be placed in front of an open ditch and jump it almost from a standing start. It may sound odd, but both horse and rider were learning all the time and he had a lovely way of telling you if you'd done something wrong without denting your confidence. I used to go up above Lambourn on the schooling ground and loved to work on horses. One was Florid, a decent Flat horse for the late Lord Howard de Walden who wasn't the best jumper. One day I took him over everything in sight, switching from the baby hurdles to open ditches, and by the end of our session he'd jump anything.

But the one thing you couldn't do was take the gas out of My Young Man. He just loved to run and jump and two miles was very near his limit. In his second season over fences he won six of his nine races and, when going for his fifth on the bounce at Haydock, he was up against another fierce front runner in Sure Metal, ridden by Graham McCourt. Down at the start we discussed tactics. 'Well, I'll definitely make it for a mile, mine's a real fruit and nut,' said Graham.

I said, 'Gremlin, there's no way you'll go quicker than this.'

Well, we set off nearly at five furlong pace, and although we were upsides for three fences I'd seen him off by the next and we won by six lengths.

My Young Man went to Cheltenham for the Grand Annual Handicap Chase, where top weight and a notoriously tricky circuit ought to have been enough to find out any front- running two mile chaser. But as I pushed through the crowd from the weighing room to get mounted in the paddock, I was stopped by the legendary Irish trainer Mick O'Toole. 'What'll win this, then, Graham?'

'I will, it's an absolute steering job.' And it was. My Young Man made all and jumped impeccably to give Whatever You Like 24lb and a twelve length beating. It was five years since I'd ridden my last Festival winner on Kildimo in the Sun Alliance Chase and I felt I was truly on the way back.

And so did Barney Curley. Despite the acrimony of the Robin Goodfellow affair he wrote in 'Curley's Comments' on the Oracle text service, 'Race reading is a difficult thing to do well and I suppose that is where I will always have an edge.

'In my opinion, the best jockey performance of the season was the ride that Graham Bradley gave My Young Man at Newbury on Saturday.

'Did you notice how he gave the horse a blow between the third and second last fences? He is probably the best NH jockey in the country at the moment.'

Praise, indeed.

CHAPTER 21
A deadly game

It is uncomfortably easy to become self obsessed in any sport, but racing encourages it. Someone rides a horse that you think you should be on and the first reaction is anger, swiftly followed by a large portion of self pity. It's only natural. Show me a jockey who denies it and I'll show you a liar.

I was feeling a bit sorry for myself as I drove out of Kempton Park the day after Boxing Day 1991. I'd had one ride on the card and Welsh Bard, trained by Charlie Brooks, hadn't done a tap and was always out the back. The previous day I'd been on fire at Wolverhampton. I'd ridden two winners but little did I know that minutes after winning the novice chase on a horse who would carry me to extremes of emotion in the future, Black Humour, a young friend of mine, Philip Barnard, had taken a crashing fall at Wincanton's second last hurdle. It's a particularly bad place because you're racing slightly downhill and Philip hit the ground hard when Sayyure crashed. He was taken unconscious to the neurological unit at Frenchay Hospital, Bristol, but at the time no one outside his family realised how serious the injury was.

As I reached the traffic lights at the roundabout outside the racecourse with my fiancée Bob, I tuned in to the afternoon sports programme to hear news that made the pit of my stomach heave. Philip hadn't regained consciousness and the life support machine had been turned off. Overcome with grief, we pulled the car off the road and cried in each others arms because it all seemed so wickedly unfair.

Philip had been apprenticed to Lester Piggott when he was training on the Flat and, although he was successful, he grew too big and turned to jumping. He was getting good at it, too, and his new boss Tim Thomson Jones was giving him plenty of opportunities. He lodged with a former jump jockey, Mark Floyd, and his wife Jane and was desperately anxious to learn. He'd come round to my place and watch videos and ask endless questions about the different tracks and riding techniques. Other trainers like Martin Pipe were starting to notice him and he had a fine career before him. It was wicked to see him scythed down at the age of twenty-four and there were many tears shed at his funeral in Newmarket. It was typical that the family of such a warm hearted young man should allow his vital organs to be donated to save others.

I became aware very early in my career of the high price some jockeys have to pay and have always thrown my weight behind appeals for the boys who get badly injured. Sam Berry, son of trainer Jack, and Peter Dun, Geordie's brother, both suffered severe head injuries which finished their careers in 1985.

That November I arranged a North v. South jockeys football match at York racecourse. Jonjo O'Neill captained the former and Graham McCourt the latter. But both sides got a bit of help ... Soccer legends Franny Lee, Bobby Charlton and Mike Summerbee turned out for the South and Leeds stalwarts Bobby Collins and Peter Lorimer for the North. I never got to kick a ball as I oversaw the day which ran from 12.30 until 5 p.m. and raised over £5,000 for the two lads. Every one of the jockeys playing knew that it could have so easily been them in the place of Sam and Peter.

I was lucky to get out in one piece with relatively few injuries although, I've fallen, been unseated or brought down about 300 times. The most pain I've ever been in was when I fell on a horse of Toby Balding's called South Parade at Lingfield in December 1988. We were still leading two out when he fell, bringing down Dale McKeown, whose mount, Intuition, landed right on top of me. I felt as though I'd been flattened by a steamroller and my entire ribcage was crushed.

I squealed like a stuck pig but not for long, because I blacked out with the pain and didn't come round until I was back in the ambulance room with blood pouring from my nose. At Redhill Hospital I was X-rayed and told there was nothing wrong apart from several sprung ribs, but I felt terrible. I could hardly breathe, let alone move, so they kept me in overnight. I was out for two weeks and twelve years later my ribs still stick out much further than they should.

I was taught the art of survival by a very astute man in Michael Dickinson. He would often say, 'If you are not happy and feel something is wrong, please, please, stop as soon as you can. Look after the horse and yourself for another day.' It's something I've never forgotten, however bad pulling a horse up early might look to the riders in the stand. The trainers always knew I was doing things for the long term good.

But young jockeys can be put under tremendous pressure to finish, because if they don't, the handicapper will ignore the race when it comes to lowering a horse's mark. As for me, it didn't matter if it was the Gold Cup or a seller, if a horse was in any distress I'd pull up. If you go on when they're feeling something it knocks them back rather than brings them on and when they are out of breath there's no oxygen getting to the muscles. That's when falls happen.

Richard Davis was another young jockey battling his way

towards making a living who paid the ultimate price. Unlike Philip, whose mount had a good safety record, the horse that killed Richard at Southwell in July 1996 was an appalling jumper named Mr Sox. They fell heavily at the first fence leaving Richard with fatal internal injuries. His late removal to hospital was severely criticised in a lengthy report that followed.

His funeral in the Cotswolds was very emotional and afterwards we went for a drink at the house of his parents, John and Ann. We then asked them to come with us to The Plough, a pub near David Nicholson's former yard at Ford which all the jockeys who live in the area use as their local.

We ended up very drunk and someone put on the Fugees recording of the Roberta Flack song 'Killing Me Softly'. Although it may not seem appropriate it was very much the jocks' favourite song at the time. Whenever we were at a party or nightclub we'd all sing along, and on this occasion we formed a circle and sang our hearts out until it finished. Everyone seemed to be coping pretty well, but half an hour later it really began to hit me. I went outside to be by myself, sat in the dark and just cried my eyes out. I thought I was on my own but another jockey, Robert Bellamy, had come out for a walk by himself. He came over, put an arm round me, and we both shed tears. We just realised how awful, sad and final it all was. But in the end we went back in, had a few more drinks and pushed it to the back of our minds. Everything was back to normal the next day. It's not the kind of thing you want to keep coming back.

Jayne Thompson was a very brave girl who was cut down in the full bloom of youth when she fell from Grangehill in a selling hurdle at Sedgefield in May 1986. She was going out with a fellow jockey and friend of mine Geoff Harker, and her father Ron trained near Doncaster. There's no doubt Jayne's heart was fully in raceriding, but I honestly believe that it isn't right for women to ride professional jumping. I know everyone has the right to choose which road they take but it is hard enough for women to make a living on the Flat in places like America and Scandinavia. I realise they are getting more chances in Britain but jumping is different. Their bodies aren't built to cope with serious impact injuries and it's nearly impossible for them to make a decent living riding as they are often obliged to ride bad horses to try and make a name for themselves. If they must compete, then restrict them to hunter chases and point to points. But in my opinion the professional game is too competitive and too risky. And I say that sound in the knowledge that Gee Armytage rode a winner at the Cheltenham Festival and Caroline Beasley won over the Grand National fences on Eliogarty in the 1986 Foxhunters.

I am certain of one thing, when my dad discouraged my younger sister Jackie from going into racing despite her natural ability and lack of fear, he did her a big favour.

One of the bravest ladies I know is Sharron Murgatroyd who lived for horses and racing. On the first day of 1991-92 season, Sharron was riding in the fourth race at Bangor and was tailed off on Independent Air when they turned over at the last and Sharron fell awkwardly. I popped into the ambulance room to see how she was and if she needed a lift anywhere. She was lying flat on the bed but smiled, 'Thanks, Brad, I think I've broken my collarbone or something.' In fact, she'd damaged her neck so badly that she was virtually paralysed from the neck down but, typical of her bravery, she's never stopped raising money for the Injured Jockeys Fund or spinal injury units. She's done parachute jumps and long distance wheelchair pushes and even wrote a thought provoking book called *'Jump Jockeys Don't Cry.'*

I'm afraid they do.

One of the most frightening incidents I've heard of was at Market Rasen in 1988 when Chris Grant fell at the first fence going into the back straight and broke his leg. Martin Brennan came down at the same fence and had the horrible job of trying to console him. It is a harrowing experience when one of your colleagues is writhing in agony and there is nothing you can do. The fence officials put an orange disc marker in the fence to send horses either side of where Chris was lying on the next circuit, while Martin stood in front of him to try and protect him. But he had to jump away at the last minute to save himself and, as Chris was lying there unable to move, one of the horses actually kicked his smashed leg. Martin said it was one of the most sickening things he had ever witnessed. It was like being in front of a firing squad and hoping they were going to miss.

The jockeys went ballistic at the stewards for not dolling off the fence, which would have meant voiding the race and, challenged any one of them to lay on the landing side of a fence with fourteen runners coming over and only an orange marker disc for protection. There weren't any takers and shortly after, with some excellent work from Michael Caulfield of the Jockeys' Association, the rules were amended so that fences could be completely dolled off.

The list of young people who have been maimed or worse pursuing the sport we love is tragically long and will keep growing no matter how many more safety measures are taken. But any step in the right direction is a good one.

Casualties in recent times include Shane Broderick, who was paralysed in Ireland in 1997, and in August 1999 at Perth young Scott Taylor was left with severe head injuries. Every jockey with a licence will rally round to help the cause of a stricken colleague. It's no more than we expect and every one of us knows, 'There but for the grace of God, go I.'

But there have been falls which produce a smile. Graham McCourt came off at Worcester one day and landed head first in some dog shit. Freddie Starr, the comedian who owned Grand National winner Miinnehoma, was standing by the fence and said there wasn't enough money around to get him to do the job.

Graham bumped into him again a few years later in Jenny Pitman's kitchen. He didn't think Freddie would remember him, but he didn't miss a beat and shouted, 'I know you! You're the one with dog shit on his head!' Such is fame.

CHAPTER 22

A stroll down Morley Street

'Which was the best race you ever rode?' It's a simple question and one that I try to answer whenever I'm asked, although the person asking the question usually has his or her own idea before I give my view.

Quite often a jockey will come back after winning an insignificant race at one of the minor tracks in the middle of the week when only the hardened pros are looking on knowing he's achieved a special feat to win on a moderate horse. But in my case it is a matter of record that I rode one of the best, if not *the* best, races of my life when Morley Street won at Aintree in April 1993. Don't just take my word for it. The readers of the *Racing Post* voted his win in the Martell Aintree Hurdle their best ride of the season and I felt it a great honour that so many had taken the time to write in and register their view. There's no doubt it put the seal on a season that saw me re-establish my reputation as a big race rider. And it was even more satisfying as he was trained by the man who had provided me with some top quality horses before we split five years earlier, Toby Balding.

When I was sacked by owner Sir Philip Harris I never fell out with Toby, but I'd hardly ridden for him since and it's worth explaining just how I came to ride a horse who was very much the star of Toby's team at the time. Like so many things in life, it started by doing someone a good turn, one which has been reciprocated many times since by one of the finest horsemen I know, namely Richard Guest.

Guesty was a 7lb claimer when I went to Toby's but even then he was as sharp as a tack and he's never forgotten the day I made myself unavailable so that he could ride a winner. Richard is something of a law unto himself and it was typical of him to throw in his licence a few years back when he thought the stewards were wrong for jumping on him when he looked after a horse in a race. He couldn't beat them and came back to ride with even greater success but that was Guesty. It was a matter of principal and he'd made his point. Back then when he was a kid and I was stable jockey at Toby's there was never any dividing ground as far as I was concerned. We were all together and the same applied to Tony Charlton, who was the other conditional jockey in the yard and went on to become David Elsworth's right-hand man. But Guesty remembers one particular morning at breakfast.

'I asked the boss if I was going anywhere the next day, knowing that a horse I'd previously won on was running. Toby said that Bradley was stable jockey and it was his ride. Fair enough.

'You pulled me to one side and asked if I thought it would win. I said it would if it rained. So you went to the car and phoned Mrs D, to say you'd ride two for her at Wetherby and then told Toby you weren't available. I got the ride back and it duly won, but how many stable jockeys would let you back on a horse that you'd told them would probably win?'

It's a favour Guesty has repaid with interest and he remains one of the most loyal friends I've got. He has the ability to see inside a horse and know what they're thinking but then he's bred for it, being a Guest. There was a time when his family and relations were employed at every level in racing during the seventies and eighties. They used to say you could shout down a mine shaft in Newcastle and a footballer would come up, and by the same token, you only had to call at most yards and there'd be a Guest somewhere.

I'd been to see Richard in hospital in mid-December after he'd smashed his leg in a fall at Wolverhampton and did my best to cheer him up. Shortly after I'd left, Leslie Garrett, who owned Romany King, phoned to see how the patient was. The talk soon got around to the horse, who was quite high profile having finished second to Party Politics in the previous season's Grand National. He was due to run in the SGB Chase at Ascot the following weekend and the conversation moved on to who would ride him. Guesty said, 'Les treated me like a second father. I told him you had just been in to see me and why not let you ride the horse? That was good enough and he insisted on it, even though Toby had someone else in mind.

'The horse might not have been quite so good as he once was. He was beaten a fair way into fourth behind Captain Dibble but you didn't make any excuses. You just said the horse wasn't right and that got you back in with Toby.'

It wasn't that Toby and I had a massive fall out. It was more a case of going our own way and he had done well with Jimmy Frost and Guesty riding most of his horses. He'd trained a Grand National winner, Little Polveir, and two Champion Hurdle winners, Jimmy winning the 1991 race on Morley Street and Guesty piloting Beech Road to a surprise win in 1989.

I've always thought that I could throw a celebration party, but my young friend surpassed my best efforts. Guesty started the party a few hours after the Champion Hurdle at the Gas Club in Cheltenham and kept it going for the next 24 hours. He says it began on the top floor of the club and he kept on moving down and ended up in the basement. He carried on for a few days after that but he said at the time, 'It's cost me five grand but I don't regret one penny.' And looking back on it he reflected, 'I don't think I rode for eleven days after that, but it's the way I was. I think it's a shame that some of the lads who ride today would rather go home and have tea and biscuits with their granny and the form book. I know it's meant to be professional, but it's not the way I was brought up.'

He also had a significant hand in the buying of Morley Street for the late owner Michael Jackson. Michael thought the world of Guesty and the feeling was reciprocated. Whichever yard Richard was based at, he'd always have a horse or two there.

Toby, Richard and Michael went to Charles Radclyffe's establishment in Oxfordshire to try out Morley Street as a young horse and there was a difference of opinion. Guesty recalls, 'I cantered him two furlongs up a bank and said we had to buy him. Toby wasn't keen. He said he didn't think he'd be man enough for fences and he was right, too. But I said to Michael, "Don't worry about that, let's win a Champion Hurdle."'

At the start of the 1992-93 season Jimmy and Toby had split and, although Morley Street had won two Aintree Hurdles for Jimmy, Richard Dunwoody had ridden him to a third victory the previous year and was once again the first choice.

But come Champion Hurdle time Richard had opted for Flown. He had won the previous year's Supreme Novices' Hurdle at the Cheltenham Festival and was 7-2 favourite to follow up in the Champion, but I was delighted to climb aboard Morley Street. I knew he was a true champion but time had made him tricky. However, he still had the full set of gears and I rode him in an amazing bit of work before the Champion. He gave Forest Sun, a very fair horse, three stone and the useful Major Bugler two stone and walked all over them.

We were travelling well enough turning for home in the Champion and I felt there was plenty of horse under me, but Morley Street didn't fancy coming up the hill and trailed in twelfth of the seventeen finishers behind his younger brother Granville Again. Flown finished about eight lengths in front of us but was still well beaten. Even after that defeat I knew there was still fire in Morley Street. More importantly, he'd shown that the extra half mile and level circuit at Liverpool was tailor-made for him.

I went into the meeting with my confidence sky high and it stayed that way after I won the Perrier Jouet Handicap Chase on Black Humour. I'd got him on the floor in the Gold Cup at Cheltenham and knew it had been my fault. He was outclassed, but when he began to lose touch I broke one of my cardinal rules because it was a big race and threw him at his fences. Through no fault of his own, he came down. It was going to be different over the sharp Mildmay Course at Liverpool and, although Charlie was keen to for me to make it, I had different ideas. As I left the paddock to canter on to the course I looked over to him and asked, 'If the pace is too strong, can I drop him in?'

'Do what you like.'

Good old Charlie.

Whether Charlie was quite so relaxed during the first circuit of the three miles one furlong I don't know, but I settled Black Humour some fifty lengths adrift of the front runners and didn't begin to creep forward until the final circuit. But we got there in plenty of time, and with both horse and rider brimming with confidence we took the lead between the last two fences and beat Sikera Spy by a comfortable two lengths. Charlie said with mock horror at the post race interview that I'd been 'Outrageous'.

This was the year of the National that never was following the false start fiasco, but it was also the day Morley Street made history with a fourth win in the valuable hurdle. By this stage he had been landed with the offensive *Timeform* squiggle reserved for untrustworthy horses but despite the presence of Granville Again and Flown I had implicit faith in him. The close-up in the *Sporting Life* said, 'confidently ridden,' and that was just how it felt. Richard Dunwoody set out to dictate from the front and after setting a strong gallop, he slowed approaching four out before trying to catch us out by quickening the pace again at the next.

At the last I was still in third gear, just half a length down knowing I could take Richard when I wanted and thinking a half length win would be nice. I took another tug at Morley Street on the run-in and planned to settle things at the well-trodden path across the course 50 yards from the finish. But Peter Scudamore had switched Granville Again off the fence to challenge on the outside and I just caught a glimpse of him as we neared the path. I shook the reins and said goodbye in a couple of strides as Morley quickened away to beat his sibling by a length and a half. One of the headlines in the papers then next day screamed 'Streetwise!' I suppose you could say that I was. It was the sixth Aintree winner of my career and was enough for me to win a second Ritz Club Trophy as leading rider at the meeting to go with the large Waterford Crystal Bowl I'd won in Bregawn's year at Cheltenham. But the award that was going to mean even more to me was a while in coming.

The competition for the Riding Achievement of the Year at the Lesters night in London was decided by the readers of the *Racing Post*. I had tough opposition from my ultra- stylish colleague Declan Murphy, who went in two handed with exceptional efforts on Fragrant Dawn in the Tripleprint Gold Cup and Bradbury Star in the Mackeson, but Morley Street's devastating Aintree display sealed it. When I went up to receive the award I was travelling rather well when I said that I was very proud of our profession, the resilience we have to show both physically and mentally in all weathers. I finished by saying that I thought all jockeys were bloody heroes and got a standing ovation. I meant every word.

Charlie had been my mainstay and, although we had few strong words, I received the first of only two bollockings I've ever got from him that same season for my riding of Espy at Newbury. He was owned by one of the biggest owners in the yard, David Bott, who had horses with Fred Winter for many years and in whose colours

Charlie won the Foxhunters' at Cheltenham on Observe.

Charlie was emphatic, 'This horse plants himself, don't get left, wake him up.' The worst thing happened. We were left a long way, and although Espy made up some of the ground he was still eight and a half lengths behind Brandeston at the finish. Charlie was fuming, 'What did I goddam tell you? You've made yourself look a prat and people will think you've blocked the horse. It's on television, the owner will have watched it and the Press will be on your back.'

All I could do was own up and apologise, 'Charles, I am very sorry. I was half asleep at the start and should have revved him up.' The episode was closed. And the only other time I got the rough end of Charlie's tongue was on Welsh Bard at Taunton. He was owned by a wonderful old lady who Charlie had also inherited from Fred called Mrs Angela Abacassus and he was probably too good to be running at a track like Taunton. It's very tight and was never a course that I liked much. Neither did Welsh Bard, because he was a bit careful with his jumping. I should have woken him up when we were headed two fences out, but I left it until the run-in and we were beaten by a head. I put my hands up, Charlie swore for a minute, but that was the last time we had a seriously cross word. Not bad in nearly ten years.

I was also starting to get a firm foothold in Ireland. It was a place I would come to look on as my second home and the association certainly prolonged my career by the sheer enjoyment of being there.

The Punchestown Festival, which has gradually grown to rival Cheltenham and Aintree, was just beginning to gather momentum in 1993. And due to Mark Dwyer's bad luck I rode my first winner there when Fissure Seal won the prestigious Heineken Gold Cup Chase. Mark had injured his back the previous Saturday at Market Rasen and we sat next to each other on the flight from Leeds-

Bradford to Dublin. Mark was my kind of jockey, a thinker and very cool. The bigger the occasion the better he was. But he was uncomfortable on the flight and said, 'Brad, I don't think I'm going to be able to ride. I'll see if I can put you in.' He was as good as his word because I'd never spoken to the trainer Harry de Bromhead who was an absolute original. The Irish jocks played the game by telling me that Fissure Seal didn't want to hit the front too soon and, even though I waited until jumping the last, he still idled and we only had a head to spare over Son Of War and young Francis Woods. It was my first winner in Ireland since Rhyme 'N' Reason in the Irish National and it felt just grand to be back.

Twenty-four hours later I made it three when Harry put me on Bishops Hall in the £30,000 J P Harty Memorial Handicap Chase. This one proved much easier, as we challenged at the last and outpaced Second Schedual and Richard Dunwoody by two and a half lengths.

While Bob and I went off to spend the summer in Barbados with the Bradstocks, Charlie was leafing his way through the French Programme Book. By the time I returned and got ready to strip some excess flesh from my bones he'd already plotted our first winner for the season. We'd swopped the customary venue of the Devon coast at Newton Abbot for Clairefontaine, near Deauville, where Charlie had sorted out the right race for the much-travelled Bokaro. Not only did he win that hurdle easily, he won at the track again eleven days later and then went on to make a bit of history.

The French forays suited Lady Joseph well as she could fly up from the South of France and Charlie found a third race for Bokaro, at the considerably more upmarket Auteuil. Charlie was pensive before the race as Bokaro hadn't travelled with his usual ease and had only drunk one bucket of water since the previous day. But Bokaro was rock solid at that time of the season and came to the last flight two lengths clear to beat Alluted eight lengths. The French star Al Capone II was staying on when he fell at the last, but this was

Bokaro's day. In winning he became the first British trained horse to score at the home of French jumping since Mandarin and Fred Winter won the Grand Steeplechase de Paris of 1962 when the bit broke and they had hardly any steering. Our feat didn't quite match those heroics, but we felt we'd done our bit for England and just to complete the job we took several bottles of champagne prisoner.

With eight wins from my first seventeen rides I had made my best ever start to a season, although only two of the victories were in England. Bokaro had provided three in France and there were three in Ireland, all for Tony Mullins and included one of the best novice hurdlers I'd sat on, Padre Mio. The high profile start had a knock on effect and for the first time in quite a while I became a wanted man - this time for the right reasons.

My arrangement with Charlie was on trust and worth more than a cabinet of written contracts, but two offers had come in that I could not refuse. I'd had a couple of rides for Paul Nicholls, who was fast-tracking through the training ranks and was clearly going to do much better in that sphere than as a jockey. His principal owner Paul Barber insisted he employed an experienced stable jockey and, after talking things over with Charlie, I accepted. Paul agreed that if he and Charlie ended with a runner in the same race it would be up to me to choose with no comebacks. Thankfully, there was never a problem.

My strike rate in Ireland had also created the right impression and I took a retainer to ride for Mouse Morris which gave me a firm base to build on over there. I was second choice for the post, but I couldn't complain as the first to knock it back was Ireland's top man Charlie Swan. Mouse had wanted a firm commitment from Charlie to ride his star novice chaser Belvederian. He was reluctant to jeopardise his freelance status, so I stepped in.

Despite the wealth of talent in the Nicholls' yard it was Brooks who provided the first serious home win. Black Humour started the season as he had finished the last with an impressive win in the Charisma Gold Cup at Kempton and would have won the Hennessy Gold Cup at Newbury but for smashing a hole in the cross fence five out. I still don't know how he stood up before going on to finish a close third to Cogent. Meanwhile, Nicholls had a very exciting novice chaser in See More Indians. Like so many of the fine chasers with which Paul has since made his name, he had learned in the point to point field where Barber had a fine nursery for potential champions. He won his debut novice chase at Worcester impressively after making early mistakes and was a young horse going places, but ultimately he would be the cause of my losing the job with Nicholls.

Paul is now a master of his craft and I don't think there is a trainer in England who is better at preparing a chaser. His handling of See More Business to win the 1999 Cheltenham Gold Cup and the preparation of Call Equiname in the Champion Chase and Flagship Uberalles to win the Arkle at the same meeting were object lessons in the art. But at the time I rode for him he was still making his way. He carried his heart very much on his sleeve, so much so that it was often difficult to explain what had happened in a race.

Immediately the lad collected the horse and led me back, Paul was there having run off the stand talking ten to the dozen and quite often saying the first thing that came into his head before his brain was fully in gear. It would have been much better if he'd stood back for five minutes, thought, and then put forward his point. Perhaps we would all have benefited.

See More Indians was without doubt one of the best staying novices in England after he won the Feltham Chase at Kempton on Boxing Day. It was a quality field with both Crystal Spirit and Coulton preferred in the betting, but despite making mistakes which would have cost a lesser horse, See More Indians overcame one final blunder at the last to beat Crystal Spirit two and a half lengths. Paul gave him almost two months off and then pitched him in against some seasoned performers in the Jim Ford Chase at Wincanton, a race I knew all about having won it on horses of the calibre of Cavvies Clown and Kildimo. See More Indians had his job eased when odds-on Second Schedual broke a blood vessel and was virtually pulled up on the run-in, but I still had to be hard on him to beat the favourite's stablemate, Another Coral, by two lengths.

See More Indians was out three weeks later in the Sun Alliance Chase at Cheltenham where he started second favourite to One Man and only half a point ahead of another of my regular rides, Belvederian. Unfortunately, See More Indians ran a very flat race. Although he made some progress from the sixteenth he was well held when he made a mistake three out and I saw no point in hammering him. In hindsight, his hard race at Wincanton may well have left a mark, but Nicholls was annoyed. He said I should have given the horse a few more backhanders and I got the impression that he and the owners were very unhappy.

The writing was on the wall in five feet letters as far as the retainer was concerned and it was virtually over when Richard Dunwoody replaced me in the Future Champions Chase at Ayr in April. When the favourite Baydon Star fell fatally at the thirteenth the way was clear for See More Indians, and he overcame a customary blunder two out to win by nine lengths. I've been jocked off too many times to allow a missed winner to get to me, but when Paul was interviewed after the race and said what a brilliant job Dunwoody had done I was fuming. I broke my golden rule of keeping my mouth shut and called him that night, 'What was so fucking brilliant about that? My granny could have won on him and she's been dead for years.'

It didn't do any good, but it made me feel a lot better, and looking back, it still does.

Although I never lost any sleep over the loss of the ride or the job, my sleeping did put me in an embarrassing position at

255

Worcester towards the end of the season.

I'd gone for a night out in London with Barrie Wright and he'd got tangled up with a very attractive young lady named Angie Lynne, who had made the news for an earlier fling with George Best. She invited us back to her apartment in Knightsbridge and, being a dedicated professional, I decided to get some sleep.

The problem was that there was only one bed. When Barrie and his new friend started fiddling about she decided there was no place for me. I was fired out and on to the floor, which meant that what remained of the night was spent in fitful sleep on the sofa. For obvious reason's, Barrie had got even less sleep than me, but he offered to do the driving next morning even though he was knackered. We arrived a good two hours before the first race and parked right by the last fence opposite the weighing room with the sun beating through the windscreen. Barrie shot straight on to the back seat for some sleep and with an hour to kill I decided to catch up on the lost shuteye before I rode Macedonas for Charlie in the second race, the novice chase.

But as the horses thundered by us in the first I didn't hear a thing. I came round at a quarter to three with Charlie hammering on the window after one of the boys had told him where my car was. I'd only got seconds to get across the course and into the weighing room but by the time I got there Simon McNeill had already weighed out in owner Jim McCarthy's colours. I explained to Charlie what had happened and he took it well. He realised that although I'd obviously had a good night I had at least got to the races in time, shame about over sleeping. There was no real damage done and Simon gave Macedonas a great ride, winning by a cheeky three quarters of a length, which put Charlie in even better humour.

I didn't think the stewards needed the whole truth, so in my haze I began to concoct a story to suit them, something about getting stuck in traffic seemed right. Then a friend from the Press put his head around the door of the jockeys' changing room where I was sitting huddled on the bench getting my tale into an acceptable form.

'I wouldn't do that if I were you Brad. Now the horse has won, Charlie thinks it's very amusing and he's told everyone that you've been asleep in the car.'

All I could to was hold my hands up to the stewards and plead that there had been a precedent when Steve Cauthen, the former Flat champion jockey, had done the same thing at Haydock one day. For once I was shown mercy and they only fined me £100.

I couldn't wait to get away from the course and dashed over to the car. The slumbering Barrie finally stirred as I got in.

'How did it get on?'

'It won.'

'Oh good, well done, lets go and celebrate.'

'Well done! I didn't get there in time to ride it you prat. Let's get out of here.'

CHAPTER 23
Getting lucky in Ireland

For the first time for many years my profile was high for the right reasons on both sides of the Irish Sea. Morley Street had done a magnificent public relations job for me at home and the big chase wins for Harry de Bromhead on Fissure Seal and Bishops Hall had bolstered my reputation in Ireland. I just loved going to the place.

Going up the M4 to Heathrow on Saturday evening after racing in England and catching the flight to Dublin was like going on a mini-holiday. The professionally casual approach that people in Ireland have to racing means that everyone seems to get that bit more fun out of it and I'm sure that it's just like England used to be before the motorways cut down time schedules.

In Britain the racing tribe hardly stay away together for any length of time when it used to be the norm. When the West Country circuit traditionally started the season in August and there was no motorway connection the jockeys would stay down for the whole month, do Newton Abbot and Devon for a few days each week, and enjoy themselves for the rest of the time. When I started riding regularly in the south a group of us including Graham McCourt, Steve Smith Eccles and John Francome would stay at the Palace

Hotel in Babbacombe. It really was like being on holiday.

The younger lads don't seem anxious to do it anymore. Maybe it's the pressures of the game but I think they're missing out. There are exceptions, like the meetings in Scotland and Aintree's National meeting, but even for a close one like Cheltenham I still stay away at the converted barn I've always rented near the course, simply because it makes the three days even more of a special occasion.

In Ireland it is different. Because the road system isn't quite what it could be it makes sense to stay away for meetings together. And the friendships forged sharing a cold bottle of Dom Perignon in a good club or over a brandy in front of a hotel fire in the small hours have become some of my most enduring.

One of my favourite lodgings is the Burlington Hotel in Dublin where I stayed before riding Commercial Artist for Victor Bowens in the £50,000 Ericsson Chase run at Leopardstown on 28 December 1994. My main ride the previous day was Belvederian, who pulled up in the Findus Handicap Chase, but I still had a magnificent night out at one of my favourite haunts, Lillie's Bordello, which is one of the best nightclubs in the world and run by an absolute angel, Valerie Roe. She still looks as gorgeous as the day she won the Miss Ireland title and her sister is married to the Republic of Ireland footballer Niall Quinn. You could bump into anyone at Lillie's, from the U2 singer Bono to Eddie Irvine the Grand Prix driver, but Valerie just made it all happen. She is a terrific organiser.

When I got back to the hotel it had been raining all night and was still hammering down when I woke up at midday. I wasn't feeling my best and fancied turning over for another couple of hours. The ground had been desperate the day before and I couldn't believe they'd race, but then this was Ireland so I phoned to check and, sure enough, it was heavy ground but definitely on.

I gradually came to and watched the first race on TV, in which Dorans Pride handled the ground and Danoli didn't, beating him a distance. I got to the track 45 minutes before my race and didn't think I'd have too much to do apart from survive on Commercial Artist. I'd finished fourth on him in the Mackeson Gold Cup at Cheltenham in November and Mark Dwyer had very sportingly let me get back on him for the Hennessy at Newbury later that month when Charlie withdrew Black Humour on the morning of the race because of the ground.

But realistically, Commercial Artist was only going round for fourth prize of £2,000. The £35,000 first prize looked booked for 'The new Arkle', as Merry Gale had been dubbed. Flashing Steel, owned by Irish Premier Charles Haughey, trained by John Mulhern and ridden by Jamie Osborne, was clear second favourite. Nuaffe was good enough for third and I didn't think we'd got a cat in hell's chance.

Nuaffe went twenty lengths clear and was demolishing fences for fun while Merry Gale sat second, but his jumping was getting worse with each race and he came down at the third. I turned to Osborne, who was upsides me and said, 'That's a touch, James.'

Passing the stands first time, Nuaffe was still well clear and Jamie said, 'Don't you think we should be getting after him?'

'No panic, loads of time yet, James.'

Both our horses were choking their heads off ploughing through the deep mud. Normally we'd have pulled up, but it was a £50,000 race and Nuaffe didn't look like getting round. He began to weaken on the final circuit and, although Flashing Steel was a smart horse, he just couldn't handle the ground.

I took it up on the long run between the last two fences, but Commercial Artist was out on his feet. He slowed to a walk at the last, almost refused, then clambered over to beat Nuaffe thirteen lengths. Flashing Steel walked up the run-in but Jamie dismounted as soon as they'd crossed the line and my old friend Fissure Seal refused after Charlie Swan had remounted following a fall six out.

The ground was unraceable and they'd only have done it in Ireland.

By this stage the performance of Merry Gale was causing Jim Dreaper sleepless nights, as this was the second time he'd fallen at Leopardstown that season. Commercial Artist was also looked on as a dodgy jumper in Ireland, and my performance in getting him round twice in England and winning the Ericsson contributed to Jim and owner Herb Stanley offering me the ride on Merry Gale next time.

As things began to pick up in Ireland it was time to bid farewell to the horse who had helped make my revival possible. Morley Street had failed to settle in retirement and Michael Jackson had put him back into training with Charlie but the horse, who was still only eleven, strained his flexor tendon and was forced to settle for the easy life.

Before starting my association with Merry Gale I notched up a couple of notable firsts, the initial one coming when I rode a winner in the colours of Mr Paul Mellon on Golden Arrow at Cheltenham. I'd always thought he and his colours were something special ever since my neighbour Alwyn Suttle went Mill Reef crazy when we were kids. In fact, I've still got the Mill Reef LP at home, 'Something To Brighten The Morning'.

I also achieved a personal best when I did 10st for the first time since losing my riding allowance when I won on Couldn't Be Better at Cheltenham.

At that time my regular riding weight was around 10st 6lb, so I had to sweat off 8lb to be sure of doing it, but I thought it was worthwhile as the race was the Steve Smith Eccles Handicap Chase and, as he was one of my best mates, I wanted to win it. And having won two races on him earlier in the season I thought Couldn't Be Better was a good thing.

I started reducing the night before and took 3lb off in a hot bath. I did the same thing when I got up in the morning and only had a slice of dry toast and half a cup of black coffee for breakfast before leaving for Cheltenham. I boiled the final 2lb off in the sauna and I can't think of a less appropriately named mount because I couldn't have been worse!

But adrenaline is a very potent drug. During the race I felt absolutely fine, avoiding trouble at the ninth before winning comfortably by twelve lengths from Southolt, ridden by Richard Guest.

Now it was time to address the Merry Gale question, and the decision of the owner to 'jock off' Kevin O'Brien was badly received in Ireland. The respected Irish racing journalist Tony O'Hehir, whose late father Michael was a legend with his masterful commentaries, said, 'Loyalty may be an admirable quality but there has never been an abundance of it in racing and O'Brien is not the first, nor will he be the last, jockey to suffer from the "He who pays the piper, calls the tune" syndrome.'

Now, that is a melody that I have had played to me many, many times. Just as others did when it happened to me I readily accepted the ride - I had to. If an owner isn't happy with a jockey he is always going to get someone else and if I had turned it down, Kevin certainly wasn't going to get the ride back. I did the decent thing and phoned Kevin to tell him I'd accepted and he was a gentleman about it even though he had been hurt. The great Irish trainer Paddy Mullins once said that training a good horse is relatively easy but training the owner of a good horse isn't.

As someone who has been brought up with racing history I was excited about going to Jim Dreaper's yard, and it was a big thrill to see Arkle's old box, which housed the exceptional young jumper Harcon.

But before I sat on Merry Gale in public I insisted on taking Yogi Breisner with me to sort his jumping out. It was the best £300 Herb Stanley spent in his life securing that man's work for the day. In the first couple of minutes in the covered ride, Merry Gale crashed through some show-jumping poles, and owner and trainer must have thought I was barking mad when I began to chuckle. But I knew what Yogi could do and by the end of the session Merry Gale was concentrating and jumping like a puissance horse. The key was his mouth. When it was touched by the rider pulling on the bit his head came up. And when a horse does that he cannot round his shoulders and therefore cannot jump.

Yogi told me to separate my reins, lift my hands six to ten inches off the horse's withers, and support the bit in his mouth very softly but firmly. When I saw a stride going to a fence I would release everything, pushing my hands forward and gripping with my legs. It worked a treat and, although neither owner or trainer said anything after that initial schooling session, I would have been surprised if they weren't impressed by the transformation. I firmly believe that if I'd met Yogi Breisner earlier in my career I could have achieved anything.

When Merry Gale ran, the plan was always to hold him up because he was very strong but Yogi and I convinced Jim that we should let him have a go at his fences. We teamed up first in the Hennessy Cognac Gold Cup at Leopardstown on 5 February 1995 against England's best chaser of the time Jodami. The Cheltenham Gold Cup winner was sent off 13-8 favourite with Merry Gale marginally bigger at 7-4.

At that time in England I had switched from having a northern-based agent in Chris Pimlott to one in the south, Graeme James. Meanwhile, in Ireland my affairs were being well looked after by Michael Condon.

It was Condon who stood in the crowd and heard the response as the once dodgy Merry Gale put in a series of astonishing leaps which brought gasps from the appreciative audience. We were briefly headed by Nuaffe after the second last, but Merry Gale was soon back in front and it was only in the final 200 yards that Jodami caught him before going away to register his third win in the race by three lengths. Mark Dwyer got a seven day ban for excessive use of the whip having hit Jodami twelve times but I had no chance of matching him even if I'd wanted to. Halfway up the run-in I pulled my whip through to my left hand and caught it on my heel. It flew into the air, but I don't think it made one jot of difference. Merry Gale was very tired going to the last and was giving me everything he could. In any case, he'd done everything but win and that great round of jumping made me feel very proud of a job well done.

Jim Dreaper was more than pleased. He said: 'That's the best race Merry Gale has run. Whether he blew up or didn't stay the trip I don't know, but Graham losing his whip may have helped the horse in the long run. I used to think Harcon was the better horse, but after watching Merry Gale perform against Jodami I'm not so sure.'

Yogi was typically low-key and said, 'My interest is not to see my name in print. Where I get my enjoyment is when one gets a team of people together and they all scratch their heads in an attempt to solve a problem. If the outcome works that gives me tremendous satisfaction.'

And I didn't leave without a winner. That quiet genius Aidan O'Brien booked me for what seemed the least fancied of his three runners in the Deloitte And Touche Novices Hurdle, Hotel Minella. I didn't begin to put him in the race until going to the second last and he was full of running when we came to head his stablemates Double Symphony and Trickle Lad at the final flight and was still on the bridle as he crossed the line five and a half lengths in front. Aidan didn't say much, just listened to what I had to say with his head slightly to one side and a thin smile breaking. His horses don't just do his talking, they shout for him.

Things were buzzing along nicely at home and track knowledge gave me a big advantage one afternoon at Fontwell when it was very heavy and I was riding Namaste. I decided to take my wide route and race under the stands rail and then hard under the hedges on the far side of the course. Jockeys are frightened to do it because you seem to be giving so much ground away, but it's like racing on a beach with you on firm sand and those on the inside racing through water. You gain a crucial edge provided you cut over at the bends and save ground. He never came off the bit to win by twelve lengths.

Cheltenham arrived very quickly and, although the highlight appeared to be Merry Gale in the Gold Cup, I had a decent portfolio of rides. Sadly, things didn't get off to a good start with the second of them, Sound Reveille. He had won his four previous chases over decent tracks and had been a good advertisement for the Breisner-Bradley-Brooks team. He started equal third favourite for the Arkle Chase for novices but at the first ditch he made an uncharacteristic blunder, which may have been caused by a shadow. Even though it was only the seventh he had no chance after that and I pulled him up at the ninth.

Charlie met me as I came in off the track with a face like a bulldog chewing a wasp. I was quite chirpy, 'Don't worry, Charles, he's in the Grand Annual on Thursday.' His retort was very un-Brookslike, 'I know, I fucking entered him!' Time to zip the lips, I thought.

Sound Reveille was a bit sore on Wednesday but the chiropractor Tony Gilmore and physio Vicky Marshall had a good look over him and Charlie got me back from my holiday home in the Cotswolds on Thursday morning to give him a school. He was a bit hesitant at first but got better as he warmed up and we went off confident of a good run.

Sound Reveille jumped from fence to fence after leading from the second and battled on like a lion up the hill to beat Auburn Castle a length and a quarter. In doing so he gave me my third Grand Annual. One who wasn't quite so pleased was Oliver Sherwood who had plotted Auburn Castle up for the race and the last horse he expected to see in it was Sound Reveille. Unlucky.

Merry Gale was exhilarating in the Gold Cup. Once again he put in an exhibition round of fast jumping from the front, but the petrol ran out when he was headed by the winner Master Oats two out and he dropped away to be a well-beaten fourth.

After the race, Jim said that he didn't think he'd been firm enough in his instructions and said, 'I told Brad to do his own thing, but Tom Costello, who sold me Merry Gale, always maintained that the horse could not stay three miles in a top-class race when ridden from the front.'

Fair enough, time for a change of plan.

His next run was the Martell Cup Chase at Aintree, where we decided to take our time and it proved the easiest thing in the world to do, because Norman Williamson set a murderous pace on the mare Martomick. With a circuit of the three miles one furlong to go I was still nearly forty lengths behind her, but Merry Gale was going smoothly, jumping well and was superbly balanced. We began to pick up ground steadily through the final mile and a quarter and swept through to collar the mare two out before coming clear to win by fifteen lengths.

But the response I got from Jim wasn't what I'd expected after winning a £31,000 race. In fact, he was strangely quiet and then went on TV and said, 'I wouldn't want Brad riding for me too often, he'd give me a coronary.'

I firmly believe that he thought I had given the horse a bad ride and that I'd fluked a result. Without wishing to sound big headed, I thought it was one of my very best, but then there's no pleasing some people.

I ended up having just one more ride on Merry Gale, in the King George VI Chase when it was transferred to Sandown the following January. Richard Dunwoody rode him in two races before that but opted to ride the eventual winner One Man. Merry Gale never fired and I pulled him up. Shortly after that Mark Dwyer was taken on as regular rider as, apparently, I would not be readily available because of commitments to Charlie Brooks. Bollocks.

I didn't go into the Grand National with any great hopes on Zeta's Lad, although in hindsight I should have done because his last win had come in the Fairlawne Chase at Windsor, where he beat Royal Athlete two and a half lengths giving him 8lb. History now relates that he ended up on the Aintree roll of honour that year in the hands of my good friend Jason Titley.

Since that win, Zeta's Lad had gone backwards and come National Day we didn't get any further than the third - the first ditch - where he made a terrible mistake and got rid of me. Luckily I can't remember a thing about it, although I do have a constant reminder of the fall.

It's a fact that a horse will not step on you if it is physically possible for it not to but in a race like the National they have very little chance to side-step. This time one of the flailing hooves struck me on the left ear and I was out cold for 45 minutes with blood spurting from a cut that needed twenty stitches.

I was detained overnight in Fazakerley Hospital, which meant I missed Titley's celebration party, and even though I was semi-conscious I was gutted. Jason is someone who I've got a tremendous amount of time for both as a man and as a jockey. He has undoubted natural talent and can combine that with a very good brain, hands and horsemanship. In short, he has everything you would look for in a top class rider. And when you've got Titley for a friend you've got one in a million.

It transpired that I'd chipped the hammer and anvil bone in my ear, which is meant to be the hardest one in your body, but I behaved like a typical jockey and convinced myself I would be back for the Irish National nine days later. It wasn't surprising that I didn't make it and as things turned out I wasn't even ready for Punchestown a month later. I had to make do with some commentary work for RTE instead. I still didn't feel right in myself for four months, so I went in for surgery on 14 June at the Acland Hospital, Oxford, to have three small bones rearranged. The operation was supposed to restore the hearing to my left ear, which was now down to 40 per cent. Sadly, it didn't work and my hearing's been getting progressively worse over the years to the point that if there is a lot of background noise I can hear very little on my left side. However, a little deafness is a small price to pay for two decades as a jump jockey, and no matter how acute your hearing is, you certainly won't catch me complaining.

CHAPTER 24
The big sleep

If it were possible to sleep for your country I would have been captain of the international team. I once slept through a massive earthquake in Los Angeles when holidaying with Declan Murphy, but the sleep-in which caused enough rumblings to register high on racing's Richter Scale came in February 1996. It was ultimately responsible for me winning the Champion Hurdle, but it caused me acute embarrassment and looked for a long time like one of the worst own goals of my career.

The ride was up for grabs on the reigning Champion Hurdler Alderbrook, trainer Kim Bailey using the same strategy of just one outing and then straight to Cheltenham which had worked so well a year earlier, though this time there would be one significant change. His stable jockey Norman Williamson was coming back from a broken leg and had damaged his shoulder badly, so Kim approached me to take the ride when Alderbrook made his reappearance in the Levy Board Hurdle at Kempton on 24 February. If all went well I'd also be on him in the big one two and a half weeks later.

When Kim phoned to offer me the ride I thought my birthday had come seven months early.

'You'd better come and have a feel of him on Sunday morning, just get to know him a bit,' said Kim on the previous Thursday. 'We're making quite a show of it. The owner Ernie Pick is coming down and the Press and cameras are going to be there and you can give him a skip up Mandown.'

'Lovely, I'll be there.'

Now there was a slight problem on the horizon. Dean Gallagher's twenty-fifth birthday party at the Foley Lodge Hotel just outside Newbury was organised for the night before and I was very much in two minds about going, being well aware that my sleeping record coupled with a few beers was a recipe for disaster. But Deano's a great mate and I didn't want to let him down.

If Kim had organised the work for the normal time of around 7.30 a.m. I wouldn't have gone to the party. I just would not have been able to trust myself to get up, because I know what I'm like when I get going on a night out. But when Kim said it would be ten o'clock I thought, 'Grand, no worries now.'

Bob wasn't going to the party because she was leaving at 6.30 a.m. for a modelling assignment in Manchester, so I toddled off to Foley Lodge. Aware that Sunday was a big day, I started in the right mode with soft drinks, but as things wore on I got carried away and ended upside down drunk. Lots of fun and frivolity ended with me in the swimming pool and Barrie Wright eventually putting me in a cab at four in the morning. It remains a mystery how the driver got me home because I was sparko on the back seat and my place isn't the easiest to find.

When the cabbie finally woke me up and I got inside the house Bob wasn't very happy, but she made sure the telephone alarm was set for herself at six and before she left she also set the radio alarm at 9.15 a.m. for me. It's brilliant. The alarm goes off, and when the radio starts blaring full blast even I have to get up.

The next thing I know is that I'm being shaken awake at quarter past ten by Aly Branford, a mate from the village who rode a lot of winners for Fulke Walwyn in the seventies.

'Bradders, Bradders, it's quarter past ten. You're late for Alderbrook, for chrissake get up!'

I just opened an eye, looked at the clock and there were four red zeros flashing back at me. We'd had a power cut in the village at nine o'clock in the morning. As a result everything was off - including me from Alderbrook. But this wasn't just another lame excuse from a jockey. It really happened. Michael Caulfield, who runs the Jockeys Association, lives next door and confirmed it. So did Southern Electricity, for all the good it did me.

Bob had been trying to ring me because she knew the state I was in when I came back, but I'd turned off the phone by the bed and couldn't hear it ringing downstairs. When I came to my senses and the realisation of what I'd done hit me I came out in a cold sweat and had a horrible churning feeling in the pit of my stomach. I'm not a panicker or worrier under normal circumstances, but I just couldn't believe what had happened.

I turned to Aly, 'What shall I do, what shall I do, what shall I do?' I sounded like a bloody parrot and felt like one.

'Get down there quick,' was Aly's advice but I said, 'I've got to ring him first,' and stumbled downstairs to get the *Horses In Training* book for Kim's number.

Now, I'd ridden Kim a few decent winners before and always found him a very nice bloke, but he wouldn't have been a real personal friend like Charlie.

I finally got his mobile buzzing.

'Guv'nor, I'm really sorry, I've slept in. The alarm hasn't gone off because there's been a power cut, I'll be there in ten minutes.' It's an excuse he's probably heard a hundred times before but he was incredibly good about it.

'Don't worry, Brad, Jimmy McCarthy was on the gallops schooling for Oliver Sherwood and he's popped the horse for us.

The job's done, get yourself back to bed,' so I did and that was it.

Bob phoned up later and couldn't believe what had happened. I told her, 'There wasn't anything I could do and Kim's been fine about it, but I don't know what the owner will be like.' On her advice I gave Kim a ring that afternoon. I couldn't believe how well he'd taken it, even managing to laugh. But I had been unlucky, because if Jimmy hadn't been there they might have waited for me. However, Ernie Pick, the man who really mattered, wasn't happy and I understood that one thousand per cent. My absence was due largely to bad luck, but all the same it was very unprofessional. Then Kim administered the *coup de grace* that I'd been fearing, 'I'm afraid he doesn't want you. He's going to book somebody else.'

It soon transpired that Richard Dunwoody, who had been linked to Fortune And Fame and Atours, became available to ride the horse at Kempton and Cheltenham. Well, there was nothing I could do to turn the clock back. It had happened, that was it and all I could do was wipe my mouth and walk away. It didn't worry me at all because it had only affected me. I hate making mistakes that cost other people, but I could handle something like this. The worst thing of all was phoning my dad and telling him what had happened, because I knew he'd have been absolutely gutted that I'd missed the chance of winning the Champion Hurdle. He's meticulously logged every race I've won on video and kept scrapbooks with all my winners. I knew full well he would feel this deeply.

I said, 'Norm, it's happened, I was unlucky and there's nothing I can do about it.' That was the end of it.

However, there was one amusing incident that made me smile when I learned about it. That likeable lunatic Jimmy Duggan, a naturally gifted rider who rode good horses for Fred Winter and who'd been away in Los Angeles for three years and had recycled so much beer that he was now tipping the scales at 12st 7lb. He had ridden winners for Kim and was quickly on the phone using his straightest and most plausible voice: 'I hear you're looking for a jockey for Alderbrook. Well, I'm available.

'I've been keeping myself very fit by running to the pub and I've cut right back on the booze as well. I'm actually down to ten pints a night now. But if you want me I'll need a bit of notice, because I'm a bit skint at the moment and can't afford a flight home. I'll have to stow away on a banana boat from San Diego to Liverpool. It should only take me about three weeks.'

Although very amused, Kim declined his kind offer.

I was riding at the Kempton meeting when Alderbrook made his reappearance and I watched on TV in the changing room as he sluiced in by three and a half lengths under Dunwoody. No one said anything to me. All the jockeys knew how I felt, and Alderbrook tightened at the head of the betting for the Champion. But my belief in fate was about to be strengthened again. Jamie Osborne now had the choice of two rides in the Champion. The first was Mysilv, a smashing mare who I'd finished fifth on the previous year. The second was Collier Bay, who I'd ridden to win the Agfa Hurdle at Sandown for my old boss Jim Old in early January at 25-1. He'd improved again and Jamie, Jim's first-choice rider at the time, won the AIG Champion Hurdle on him at Leopardstown two weeks later.

They were both very good horses but Mysilv, who was trained by Charlie Egerton, needed good ground. Conversely, Collier Bay had to have mud - on good ground he'd got no chance. I could ride whichever one Jamie discarded.

On the day before the Champion Hurdle I was playing in an England v. Ireland golf challenge at the Belfry. Jamie had until one o'clock to make up his mind, that was the final declaration time for jockeys. Fortunately, Jim and Charlie are longstanding friends of mine, and both were happy for me to ride Jamie's rejected choice.

It was a lovely day and, with all the facts available, Jamie had to chose Mysilv. It was only 50 - 50 whether Collier Bay would run with the ground the way it was.

But when we came out to play the second round at 1.30 p.m. the rain started and hardly stopped until just before the big race the next day, turning the going from good, fast ground to soft. Clearly, it was good news for Collier Bay, but it all seemed academic because Alderbrook handled all types of ground.

I'd gone straight from the Belfry to my rented converted barn at Toddington, not far from Cheltenham. On the morning of the race I slipped into a hot bath to take off a few precautionary pounds and my mobile went. It was Wally Sturt, owner of Collier Bay and a very staunch supporter of Jim's. I'd always thought very highly of him and the way he stayed loyal to Jim through thick and thin, especially when Jim's horses were riddled with the herpes virus. He was also very generous when you rode him a winner. He asked me how everything was.

'Fine, the rain's come and he's got a chance. We'll give it a go.'

And then out of the blue he hit me with, 'You're not going to stop him, are you?'

I was stunned and bemused at this very strange question. It took me about five seconds to reply and I said, 'Wally, what would I want to stop him for? This is the biggest hurdle race of the season. It's worth 130 grand.'

'Oh, I was just checking to see how you're going to ride him.'

Well, I'd won on Collier Bay at Sandown and at the time I thought I'd made the horse look better than he was. Jamie had chosen to ride Wally's other runner Mole Board that day. The ground was very soft and I came wide once we crossed the Flat course then tight under the privet hedge where the going was much faster. He was a 25-1 rank outsider, but his subsequent win in Ireland showed that he was the best horse in the race and would probably have won whatever I'd done.

I said, 'Wally, I gave him a good ride at Sandown.'

'Well, how are you going to ride him this afternoon?'

'Bounce him out and give nothing away at the start, slot into a nice position and see how it goes.'

'Right,' said Wally, 'There's six thousand quid for you if you win on him.' I was very excited about my prospective little bonus, even if we'd only got a small chance, but I couldn't understand what was going through his mind. Did he honestly think that I wanted to see Alderbrook win?

Everyone, including me, thought Alderbrook was a steering job and couldn't get beat. I focused my thoughts on the race, but I knew I'd have to walk into the weighing room at the meeting I love more than any other knowing everyone would be thinking about me and the opportunity I'd missed.

It got to the stage that I began preparing myself for how I'd cope when Alderbrook won. I planned to congratulate Kim and Richard because I understood the owner's decision. The other jocks were good. They knew what I was going through and left me to deal with it in my own way, quietly and alone.

Both Jamie and I were convinced Alderbrook would win, but you've got to go out thinking positively and I took up my usual position at the start of the two mile hurdle, on the middle to outside. In all the big hurdles at Cheltenham everyone seems to fight for the inside rail, but it's not the shortest way. I've walked the course a hundred times and if you look from the start to the first bend turning away from the stands about four furlongs up the course, you will run in a straight line from the outside. On the inside the course edges ten to fifteen yards to the right after a couple of furlongs and there's always plenty of shouting for room.

The soft ground was perfect for Collier Bay, who had always had trouble with his feet and joints, and when we got level with the stands I began to edge over to my left to slot in and let those in behind have all the trouble of getting tightened up and clipping heels. Everyone says that Cheltenham's a stiff, hard, galloping track but that isn't wholly true because you're nearly always on the turn and there are two downhill runs. It is stiff at the end, so you need a good cruising speed to hold your position early on with class and stamina to see out that final hill. That's what makes Cheltenham the supreme test and a wonderful track. You need the lot.

There are a couple of tricky places. The bend at the top of the hill going to three out in hurdle races is particularly difficult and a lot of races are lost there. One of the best rides I ever saw around there was Charlie Swan on Mucklemeg in the Festival bumper of 1994. He never left the inside and was very brave and bold, basically barging his way through to get the perfect position.

On Collier Bay I was surprised how well I was travelling when we reached that point after Mysilv had given me a good lead at a nice pace. I let him freewheel - you should never push a horse going downhill - and moved upsides Jamie going to the second last. He had a quick look over and knew instinctively that I was going better than him. No matter what Alderbrook did, Jamie knew he'd made the wrong decision and all he could scream at the top of his voice in frustration was, 'Fuck, fuck, fuck, fuck.' Whatever else happened, he knew he'd chosen the wrong one. And to any jockey that hurts badly.

We jumped the second last and then I went for home - I always do when I've got a chance in a big hurdle at Cheltenham. If you can get over to that rail you can often nick a length by staying tight to it. Anyone challenging has to come wide on your right and although I think Collier Bay would have won anyway, I'm sure that move made it certain. Head down and riding flat out, I pinged the last and prayed that nothing would pass us on the run-in. Nothing did, and when I got to the post in front I couldn't believe just how lucky I'd been. But that's fate for you. Sleeping in, the heavens opening and Jamie choosing the wrong one - three chance elements that added up to a fairytale.

Richard pulled up alongside me on Alderbrook and called out, 'Well done, Bradders,' but it wasn't until I was walking back and saw the big TV screen that I realised he was second. When I came back into the winners' enclosure I pushed my right forearm out four or five times in rapid succession. Everyone, including the TV people, thought I was pointing to an imaginary watch but I would never have been so insensitive. In reality it was the Leeds United salute that I did after winning on Morley Street at Liverpool. I've always been good mates with Vinnie Jones, who used to stand in front of the kop at Elland Road and do it when he scored a goal, 'Leeds, Leeds, Leeds.'

I had three rides the next day and a full book on the Thursday. That's when the serious celebrating begins, and I'm happy to report that something I was instrumental in starting a few years previously is now a tradition. With the help of our tea lady Sandra we order champagne into the weighing room and invite a few trainers and people in for a drink after the meeting's over. The bars close half an hour after the last and you can't get away from the place, so why not stay on and have a party? They've got better and better as the years have gone on.

After staggering from the weighing room I popped into the Delabare Hotel for a drink with some good friends of mine from Ireland, Gerry Chalke, John Grace and John English. Ally McCoist and Andy Goram, two Rangers stalwarts, joined a large group for dinner, where I got rid of a large portion of my winning present. When Peter Niven called to pick me up the next morning to go to Fakenham I was still poleaxed. It's a three and a half hour journey to the course in Norfolk and I slept until twenty miles from the track when I woke up and croaked, 'Niv, we've got to stop. I've got to have some black coffee.'

He said, 'You've got 10st 10lb to do.'

'I couldn't care less, I've got to get some liquid and food inside me,' so we pulled into a transport café for three cups of coffee and a bacon sandwich. But I was still in trouble when we got to Fakenham, which has the smallest changing room in the country and you have to step over each others bags to get to your peg. That was too much for me and I fell over twice. I would not have passed a breathalyser before any of my three rides and I have to tell you that it is not very pleasant riding in a maiden chase whilst under the influence. The boys thought it was hilarious, but until I came to write this book, no one ever knew the state I was in except those who were in the weighing room that day. It's like a private club, the inner sanctum, and nobody ever repeats what's been said or done in there. If you did, you'd be blackballed - no one would speak to you. It's like going to school every day but having no lessons to do, it's fun and everyone is so close. You could go on holiday with any single one of them and have a ball and if you're injured, someone will wait to take you home from the hospital, no matter how long it takes. It's something very special and I miss it badly.

Wally Sturt was as good as his word and weighed in with my winning bonus, while I the did the right thing by the lads at Jim's and dropped £500 over to Wroughton so they could have a bit of a party.

I rode Collier Bay in the Champion Hurdle the following year, but the outcome was far from happy. It had been an unbelievably dry winter and he had just one run before the big race, in a hastily added event at Towcester against Relkeel and Escartefigue. I didn't ride him because of a two-day suspension, but Jamie stood in and had to be quite firm to get him home by three quarters of a length from Relkeel.

Although the Cheltenham executive did as much as they could to ease the ground for the Festival conditions were very fast, a fact borne out when Make A Stand clipped 1.1 seconds off the course record. Collier Bay was travelling well enough as we raced up the hill from the start, but he wasn't happy going down to the third and made a bad mistake which jarred his dodgy legs. He was tailed off when I pulled him up before three out.

Collier Bay had started 4-1 second favourite to Jamie's mount Large Action, who was lame when he was pulled up two out and I heard from several friends in Wally's box that Wally had repeatedly called my integrity into question. I fronted him about it shortly after, but he denied it vehemently and asked who had said such scurrilous things. I didn't want to drop anyone in it, although one of them was a respected weighing room colleague, and simply said, 'OK Wally, can I ride him next season?'

'No, no, no. I think he needs a change of hands.'

I think I know what was said in that box at Cheltenham in 1997. Wally was convinced I'd stopped Collier Bay.

While the 1996 Champion Hurdle had gone very much in my favour things hadn't panned out particularly well earlier in the season when I was on the wrong one in the Hennessy Gold Cup at Newbury. And I knew my fate before the race was run.

Charlie had two runners for the race, Black Humour and Couldn't Be Better, and I knew both of them inside out. I'd won the Edward Hanmer Chase at Haydock on Couldn't Be Better on 15 November and was very friendly with his owner, the late Dick Whittle, who lived in East Garston, just outside Lambourn. If the horse hadn't broken blood vessels he would have won a Cheltenham Gold Cup and even as it was he went on to finish third to Imperial Call in the Cheltenham centrepiece later in the season. With 10st 8lb in the Hennessy I thought he was a good thing.

A week before the Hennessy, Charlie put me on the spot and asked me if I would ride Black Humour. He had been bought by Lord Lloyd Webber as a birthday present for Lady Lloyd Webber following the death of his original owner David Bott and they were now the most high-profile owners in the yard. The horse should have won the race two years before when demolishing the fifth last and was a difficult ride who needed a jockey who knew him. He was very straight in his back and had an extremely light mouth.

I wasn't entirely happy: 'Are you insisting I ride him, Charles?'
'Yes.'

'Fair enough, no problem. I'll ride him, but who's going to ride
Couldn't Be Better?'

Dean Gallagher was second jockey at Uplands, but Dick Whittle
wasn't a great fan and was keen for Adrian Maguire to take the ride.
I said to Charlie, 'If it's not Deano, I won't do it. No Deano, no
deal.' It was a big spoof on my part because I would have done
anything for Charlie, but it was very important to me that the ride
stayed in-house. Even though Adrian is a good friend and an
excellent horseman and jockey he wasn't on the team - and Deano
was.

Dick came to the yard and I fought tooth and nail for Deano
because I honestly thought he was as good as anybody in the
country - it's ironic that he ended up with the job that was once
offered to me as first jockey to Paul Green. He was a well-balanced
and stylish flat rider who made the transition to hurdles and fences
through a lot of hard work and dedication. I felt almost sorry for him
that he was only second jockey with his abundance of talent.

Dick listened to everything I'd got to say then just nodded his
head and said, 'OK, it's done.' The only other words he uttered were
to give Deano as much confidence as possible. Charlie, Brian
Delaney, the rest of the lads and myself were very, very, happy.

The next problem we faced was a fixture clash. Newcastle staged
the valuable Fighting Fifth Hurdle on Hennessy day and Padre Mio
- who I had advised Charlie to buy from Tony Mullins for Lady
Joseph - was due to run. He was also now owned by the Lloyd
Webbers and I knew there was only one man for the job - Richard
Guest. Charlie agreed and one phone call was all that was needed to
book him.

There was never much hope of me winning the Hennessy on
Black Humour, but our chance dropped to zero when it came up

very soft. The deep ground was ideal for Couldn't Be Better, though, and Deano gave him the sweetest of rides to bring him home in a canter by fifteen lengths. I know people say that they are 'over the moon' when a mate wins a big one but I can say without fear of contradiction that I genuinely was. If I hadn't won it, at least Charlie and the boys had and I immediately thought of the lads watching the race back in the hostel and Brian looking on from the stands. After pulling up before the second last I trotted home to meet Deano coming in off the track and put my arm around his shoulder in congratulations on a job well done.

Charlie's smile when he met us on the walk back to the unsaddling enclosure was more priceless than the bloody Mona Lisa. We only just made it back to the weighing room in time to scream Guesty home. He gave Padre Mio a peach and beat Chief Minister half a length all out. Although I ended the day without a winner I was sailing six inches off the floor. I was absolutely delighted to have done my bit and seen everyone do well.

We had the mother and father of a party at the Queens Arms that night and everybody went. I've got a wonderful picture of Deano, Brian and myself grinning over the cup. And it was typical that Guesty came down to join in. We carried on during the Sunday lunchtime and must have bored the pants off the other customers as we kept replaying the two videos on the TV in the bar. They got better with each showing.

And Dick Whittle very kindly split Deano's present with me. A lovely bonus from a very nice man.

Not that I hadn't got a very good relationship with the Lloyd Webbers. They had always been very good to me, friendly, supportive and trusting. Although they were good winners, they were also great losers, which is even more important, and they invited Bob and I to many of their parties which were always special. Any time I wanted tickets for a show at the last minute - on Valentines night for example - they never let me down and treated me like one of the family.

I stopped at their house whenever I was riding in Cagnes-sur-Mer and on one occasion I was able to repay their hospitality by overturning a dubious French judgement. I had ridden Lady Lloyd Webber's Garolo to finish a neck second on New Year's Eve 1996 and with racing abandoned in England we had a couple of days on the Cote d'Azur with the Lloyd Webber's racing manager Simon Marsh before Garolo tried to follow up. Once again he ran his heart out in a desperately tight finish, but when the numbers came up on the Pari-Mutuel board we had been placed second. Simon pushed off to catch an early flight back from Nice airport and I was getting ready to jump in the shower when Stuart Cargeeg, a former British jump jockey who was training in the French Provinces, came up to me: 'I'd demand to have a look at the photo finish if I were you.'

'Why?'

'Don't ask questions, just ask to have a look.'

Now was the time I began to wish I'd paid a bit more attention to French lessons at Wetherby High. However, after plenty of gesticulating and talking English with a French accent - somehow you always think they will understand better - I said I wanted to take the photo-finish home for the owner and trainer who weren't present.

The official agreed and I went back to have my shower. About ten minutes after the race there was an announcement that I didn't understand, but when I looked at the TV screen they had reversed first and second. No one apologised, although the chairman of the racecourse said, 'Pardon - it is easy to make a mistake.'

I rang Simon and gave him the good news before he got on the plane, while Stuart quietly informed me that such things had happened before to foreign runners at the Hippodrome Cagnes. English trainers beware. You have been warned.

CHAPTER 25
Man Mood misery

Self-preservation has always been high on my list of priorities, but I would have done myself a big favour and stopped untold aggravation if I hadn't pulled up a horse called Man Mood in a two-runner race at Warwick on 5 November 1996.

The day, like most others, had started early with Tuesday being a work morning at Uplands, and although it is only just over an hour from Sparsholt to the Midlands' course a friend of mine called Paul McCormack drove my car so that Charlie and I could doze.

I woke up as we nosed into the racecourse car park and by coincidence we pulled up alongside Norman Williamson, who looked certain to win the three - runner Oliver Cromwell Handicap Chase in which I was on Man Mood. His mount, Mine's An Ace, was forecast to start a very warm favourite and had much better form than my ride or the other horse in the contest, Drumstick. It was only then that we learned that Venetia Williams, trainer of Mine's An Ace, had pulled him out. Without any evil intent we discussed the probable outcome of the race, something jockeys and trainers do at the races every day of the week, and Norman knew all about Drumstick. He was the last jockey to win on him two seasons

earlier but said that as he'd got older he'd turned doggy and didn't
try very hard. He didn't envy Conor O'Dwyer's job in riding him.

Charlie and I said that Man Mood was also very tricky and had
a wind problem. He choked on the gallops every day he worked and
had gurgled at Leicester the previous year. So despite being three
'experts' we were no nearer finding the winner of the two and a half
mile handicap chase as we walked to the weighing room. I'd got a
busy day, riding in five of the six races, and things got off well when
I won the opener on Chickawicka for Bryn Palling. I was beaten a
neck in the following novice hurdle on Wanstead for John Jenkins
and then won the Earl Of Warwick Handicap Hurdle for Andrew
Streeter on Desert Force. But although Man Mood started odds on
at 4-7 for the next race, I couldn't feel confident about completing
what would have been my second treble of the season. There wasn't
any confidence behind Man Mood in the betting either, as he drifted
from 4-9 to 4-7 while Drumstick hardened from 7-4 to 5-4.

As I had done when riding the horse previously, I let him bowl
along in front because he was always keen and settled better ridden
that way. Everything was fine until turning into the back straight,
where there is a line of five fences, and Man Mood began to falter
before he met the first of them. We got over that, but then he started
to choke and lost his action so, with a big open ditch looming, I
thought, 'Not for you, Bradders, get out of here.' It's something I
have done hundreds of times before and I had no hesitation in
preserving my health and that of the horse by pulling him up as
Conor and Drumstick flew by.

The stewards rightly held an inquiry and heard evidence from
Charlie and myself. I told them the horse had gurgled and lost his
action, while Charlie informed them of the horse's medical history
and said he had only re-entered him for the race because it was re-
opened due to a very small declaration at the overnight declaration
stage. He also explained that Man Mood had been to Bristol
University for a soft palate operation to ease his breathing, but after

working the horse on the treadmill Professor Geoff Lane couldn't find a problem and sent him back. Charlie added that when the horse ran at Worcester previous to the Warwick race he had also gurgled but that he had hoped it was a nervous affliction which might right itself.

With this particular infirmity only one person can tell when a soft palate operation is needed and that is the jockey, because it is not until the horse is put under racing conditions that the palate displaces. This stops oxygen getting to lungs, brain and muscles, which in turn makes the animal falter and lose its action, but after the trauma of racing subsides the palate then rights itself. The racecourse vet, Peter Thorne, explained this to the panel of stewards, who then heard from the betting intelligence officer monitoring transactions in the ring.

He appeared a bit agitated and said one major firm had taken a phone bet of £3,000 for Drumstick but could only get £1,000 on. No big deal there I thought, and it didn't surprise me when the stewards accepted our explanations after they deliberated for a short while. If I thought that was the last I'd heard about Man Mood I was badly mistaken.

Charlie is a very straightforward man with no side and his open views to Man Mood's owner Julian Robbins before the race may not have been the wisest in hindsight. As Robbins stood to win £4,000 in prize money Charlie said he should put £500 on Drumstick to balance the books and make it a no-lose situation. It was poor advice given the subsequent turn of events.

Three days later the Jockey Club Security Division began investigating the betting on the race when their then-spokesman, David Pipe, gave out a cryptic statement, 'Our security department have been having discussions with the Betting Office Licensees Association and is examining betting patterns.' Nothing else was heard until a month later on 4 December, when the *Sun* newspaper broke the news that the Jockey Club were going to reopen the

Warwick inquiry.

It was bad enough that Charlie and I were under the spotlight again, but to read about it in a newspaper before we'd been told anything was outrageous and sadly typical of the leaks springing from the Jockey Club Headquarters at the time. There was a joke going round that I'd made more stops at Portman Square than the 74 bus. It seemed I would be calling again.

The betting movements were totally understandable when you consider the facts. Just like Marouat at Southwell, everyone in the yard knew about Man Mood's problems and any of the lads with punters would have warned them off risking any cash at very short odds on such a dodgy horse. News like that spreads like a bushfire through racing and would have reached the racecourse in plenty of time. But Jockey Club security had the bit between its teeth and were looking everywhere for skulduggery. On 22 November Charlie and I had been asked to hand over printouts of our mobile phone bills for the day of the Warwick race. Both of us refused and on 29 November I received a letter from Mrs A.J. Elsey of the Jockey Club Security department, part of which read:

' .. you will recall that I requested access to the itemised account in respect of your mobile phone.

'You refused this request at the time but I would ask you to reconsider that matter in the interests of demonstrating you simply have nothing to conceal. You will, of course, appreciate the extremely serious nature of this investigation and I am sure you will be most anxious to co-operate in any way.

'In the event that you do decide to change your mind, I would be grateful if you would furnish the itemised print outs for your phone in respect of 4,5 and 6 November 1996.'

This seemed an invasion of privacy so the right person to talk to was my solicitor Peter McCormick, who did such a good job for me in the Starjestic and Marouat cases and had also added Willie

Carson and Jenny Pitman to his list of clients.

I gave him the details and this is part of his response to the demand for the phone accounts:

'We have been contacted by Messrs Bradley and Brooks ... The private itemised accounts of our clients mobile phones are personal documents that contain private and confidential details.

'We cannot advise our clients to allow you access to them because that would simply give you the opportunity to have a 'fishing expedition' and the law of this country is clear that such activities are prohibited.

'Our clients have no wish to be unco-operative, but at the same time your request raises important legal issues which cannot be cast aside.

'Accordingly we confirm that your request for access to the information is denied.'

I never surrendered my accounts, although Charlie was in a different position as he was by now employed by Uplands Bloodstock and the phone was their property. When Andrew Cohen told him to hand over the itemised bill he had no option. It didn't matter because there was nothing to hide, but it was a rather large matter of principle.

Jockey Club Security's hardcore personnel of ex-police were extremely busy around Uplands and interviewed all the stable staff plus Robbins who would give me a massive vote of 'No confidence' while the vigorous inquiries were going on behind closed doors.

Under a headline in the *Racing Post* of late January that read 'Man Mood owner jocks off Bradley,' Julian Robbins declared that he didn't want me on the horse again. Why he felt it necessary to say that in public after the horse had run three times since Warwick without success for other jockeys only he knows. When the horse had run the previous week at Huntingdon under Charlie's assistant and amateur rider Ed James he had started second favourite in a five-runner race and pulled up after weakening rapidly at the eighth.

Raceform noted, 'With his tongue tied down as usual and with first time blinkers, went from coasting to tailing off in a matter of strides. He clearly has big problems.'

For what it's worth, Man Mood also opened up at 6-4 and drifted out to 9-4 before coming in marginally to 85-40. Ed reported to the stewards that Man Mood had gurgled. Evidently Mr Robbins had seen my name alongside Man Mood in some five - day entries and was quoted as saying, 'I was on to the stable straight away and told them again that Bradley was never to ride the horse.' Well, that suited me just fine. If he thought I was pleased to be paired with his horse again he was mistaken. As far as I was concerned, the bloody horse was a disease! In fact, Man Mood didn't run again that season and didn't win another race under Rules in his life, including a few point to points.

Thanks to Mr Robbins, it took until 27 February 1997 for me to receive the news from the Jockey Club that I wanted to hear. A one paragraph letter stated, 'After considering a report from the Security Department covering various issues relating to the running of Man Mood (Fr) in the Oliver Cromwell Handicap Chase at Warwick on November 5 1996, the Stewards of the Jockey Club decided not to hold an inquiry.'

Even though I hadn't done anything wrong, I felt the tension ease as I reread the words. But Man Mood wasn't going to go away.

Fortunately, the rest of the season was moving along nicely and the previous one had ended very sweetly when I rode my first winner in the Queen Mother's colours on Moat Garden, trained by Ian Balding, at a Ludlow night meeting. Not quite Ascot or Sandown, but it meant a lot to me.

Ian, who is Toby Balding's younger brother, also provided a significant winner for me away from the racecourse when I won the Marlborough Cup at Barbury Castle, the only race over timber poles in Britain.

Barbury Castle is set in the heart of the Downs just outside

Marlborough and is the centrepiece of a grand Sunday afternoon out when horse and countryside lovers mingle over car-boot picnics that last long into the afternoon.

I hadn't ridden in the first running a year earlier because I considered it dangerous. The organisers hadn't sawn through the top poles, which meant the horses were jumping unforgiving solid obstacle, just like a brick wall. Although jump jockeys have to be slightly mad to take up the profession, they surely weren't that silly. Espy, who I would have ridden, duly turned a somersault, so I felt completely vindicated. But this year the top poles had been sawn half through which was much safer, and I was one of six professional jockeys to take part, the others being, Brendan Powell, Luke Harvey, Chris Maude, Nicky Dawe and John Ryan.

I was delighted to get the ride on Shareed from Ian, who missed the race as he was saddling Tagula to finish third in the French 2,000 Guineas. First-choice rider was the Swedish three day eventer Dag Albert, who had won a qualifier on the horse the previous month, but he was required in his home country so I was called in. I felt very confident about the versatile 6-4 favourite, who had won on the Flat and over hurdles and fences. He'd schooled well for me the previous week and he hardly put a foot wrong over the seventeen fences, coming home by ten lengths from Brendan on Symbol Of Success. Going over those obstacles was a real throwback to the old days at W.A. Stephenson's where we schooled over telegraph poles. I suppose I must have learned something.

It gave me great satisfaction to accept a different kind of challenge and be equal to it. The lessons I'd learned from Yogi Breisner had given me tremendous confidence to attempt more audacious tasks, and I met another when I began the season early by taking rides in Germany from early June for their leading trainer Uwe Stoltenfub.

Including those three winners at Bad Harzburg I had made a cracking start to 1996-97. From my first twenty-four rides, thirteen were winners and I added another first to my book of unlikely rides when I finished second in a Sea Chase at Hoppegarten. It is a relatively straightforward cross-country race with the bizarre twist that at halfway the horses have to race through a lake. A good swimmer is essential and a change of boots is advised!

I finished off the summer breaking new ground for the third time as part of the winning team for the Silk Cut Challenge at the International Jumping Arena at Hickstead in Sussex. It was run on the first day of the Showjumping Derby Meeting and I partnered the event rider Debbie Edmondson on our joint mount Blossom, who completed the 800 metre course in 82.65 seconds. That little mare Blossom was brilliant. She went long when I asked her, put in a short one when she had to, and while Debbie knew what she was doing, Blossom made me look as though I did, too. We beat some tough opposition because in second place was Josh Gifford's daughter Kristina, who developed into an Olympic-class rider, and her father's stable jockey, my good friend Philip Hide.

Charlie provided my first home win of the season on Country Star at Newton Abbot but two days before I'd had two unplaced rides for Paddy Mullins at Galway. The following day we had a magnificent lunch at Morans On The Weir, one of the best seafood pubs I've ever been to. There was a longest drive competition over a river between thirty Anglo-American-Irish golfers and I won that, too. I was on some kind of high roll and pressed it up by telling them that I was an absolute certainty on Country Star. I am reliably informed that they backed me to a man and cleaned out the local bookmakers as Country Star made all in the two-mile-one furlong handicap hurdle to come home by an unchallenged eleven lengths at 4-5. It was as safe as putting the money in the building society except that you got a better and quicker return.

Although a Suny Bay sickener was waiting around the corner there were some notable examples of loyalty throughout the season which made me feel honoured. Dick Whittle's attitude was exemplary and the Lloyd Webbers were upsides him. When the Cheltenham Festival came along in March rides were looking scarce, but at the first opportunity to use me, the Lloyd Webbers did. Although Jamie Osborne had won the Agfa Hurdle on Double Symphony, who was owned by Anthony Pye-Jeary, whose company does the artwork for Andrew Lloyd Webbers musicals, I was given the ride back in the Cathcart Chase. Unfortunately there was no happy ending as the mare didn't fire and I had to pull her up before the fourth last.

Jamie had also won on Whip Hand for Madeline Lloyd Webber. When he opted to ride eventual winner Shadow Leader in the Supreme Novices Hurdle I was given that ride, too, although his jumping let us down and we didn't feature. He was trained by Jimmy FitzGerald, who I'd ridden for regularly as a kid. Jimmy handled Uncle Ernie for the Lloyd Webbers in the Grand Annual Chase where they also had Garolo trained by Charlie. Garolo was well fancied off 10st. I couldn't dream of doing that weight but with Jimmy's stable jockey Mark Dwyer out injured the ride on Uncle Ernie was going spare. He was a 20-1 chance whose form was going the wrong way, but despite our earlier association, Jimmy wasn't keen to have me on board. Maybe he thought there would be a bit of team riding for the Lloyd Webbers with Garolo in the yellow jersey, but that would have been a complete non-starter with them.

This was one time I would benefit from owner power and racing manager Simon Marsh phoned Jimmy to tell him that I would be on Uncle Ernie. End of story. The horse had never fulfilled the early promise that saw him finish second to Remittance Man in the 1991 Arkle Chase and, although he had more than paid for himself with placed efforts, the win ratio wasn't good and retirement beckoned at the age of twelve. He still had a good cruising speed, though, and I switched him off at the rear until making progress on the outside four out where my young friend A.P. McCoy was making for home on Elzoba. I collared him at the last, and although Uncle Ernie had a reputation for not lasting, he stayed on like a lion for me in what was his final race. He was retired on a high to spend the rest of his days with Jimmy.

It was my fourth win in the race, but if I was pleased then I swear Charlie couldn't have been happier if he'd trained the winner himself. But that was the kind of partnership we had. If it wasn't unique, it was very special.

There was only one race remaining for the meeting, the Vincent O'Brien County Hurdle, where my ride, Lady Daisy for Paddy Mullins, tried to run out at the second last and dropped away to finish twelfth. But there was still the weighing room party after racing to look forward to. Sandy the tea lady ordered in twenty cases of champagne and it didn't take long to demolish all 240 bottles. Quite a bit was drunk by myself and none by the teetotal Tony McCoy. But it is testament to his open-handed nature that he paid for fifteen of the cases to make sure everyone celebrated his magnificent Champion Hurdle - Gold Cup double on Make A Stand and Mr Mulligan.

CHAPTER 26
Suny doesn't shine anymore

Charlie Brooks had been in a financial straitjacket since he bought Uplands from the Winter family for £1.2 million in 1989 and by the summer of 1994 he gratefully clung on to the lifeline thrown to him by Andrew Cohen, who bought the establishment at a price that would have made Charlie's accountant weep.

It meant Charlie would become the salaried trainer of Uplands Bloodstock and although the final decisions would be taken away from him, so too would the worries about paying bills and wages which had continually chipped away at his naturally generous nature.

Andrew was an exceptional businessman who had taken over his father's kitchen goods company, Betterware, and transformed it into a mega company. When it came to racing he didn't know much about me and I didn't have a great deal of knowledge about him. He brought a large batch of horses with him of all shapes and sizes which made the yard numbers look more healthy and the first one to win was an unimposing grey called Suny Bay who would ultimately give me a Hennessy Gold Cup but would so nearly send me in to retirement before it could happen.

When Andrew arrived it was agreed there would be no change to the riding arrangements - there had never been a retainer, only that rock-solid gentleman's agreement between Charlie and me that was better than anything a solicitor could draft. Suny Bay won his first two novice chases in late 1994, but Dean Gallagher rode him both times as they were on a Saturday and on each occasion I was at the principal meeting. On 19 November when he won at Towcester I partnered Couldn't Be Better in the First National Bank Gold Cup at Ascot to finish second to the Lloyd-Webber's Ramylette, trained by Nicky Henderson. On the second, when he won again at Towcester I'd opted for Sandown and won the prestigious Henry VIII Novices Chase on Sound Reveille for Charlie. But if I thought these were errors of judgement they were nothing compared to the one I made when choosing Couldn't Be Better over Suny Bay in the Greenalls Grand National Trial at Haydock Park on 22 February 1997.

I was on Suny Bay when he completed a hat-trick of novice chase wins at Warwick in January 1995 and we may well have won the Reynoldstown Chase at Ascot the following month but for falling when in second place four out. That turned out to be Suny Bay's last run of the season, which meant he missed the Cheltenham Festival and went into the new season still relatively unexposed. He was favourably weighted for his first run out of novice class and was an impressive winner of a handicap chase on his seasonal debut back at Towcester in December.

Charlie decided to go for a big handicap before Suny Bay's handicap mark shot up, so he targeted the Mildmay Cazalet Chase at Sandown. I was at once delighted and dismayed at Suny Bay's weight. 10st 3lb was excellent but it would mean a couple of hot and hungry days for me to do it. Never mind, it would be well worthwhile. But that race, where he started 100-30 favourite, would see him taken out by freakish bad luck and plant the seed in Andrew

Cohen's mind that I was unlucky for him.

We were travelling nicely, tucked in just behind the leaders and moving out towards the back straight on the final circuit when Suny Bay lost his footing and fell. That was bad enough, but as he was struggling to get to his feet his was hit by one of the pursuers - ironically Dean Gallagher on Nevada Gold - and fractured his jaw. It was rotten luck and I should have sensed what lay ahead when neither Andrew nor his party came to see either horse, rider or trainer after the race. They left immediately.

It was over three months before Suny Bay ran again. We bolted up in the Brown Chamberlin Handicap Chase at Newbury and, although there were thoughts of the Irish National, Charlie finished him off for the season. When the horse returned in November I went to Haydock instead to finish second on Couldn't Be Better behind Unguided Missile. Dean Gallagher rode Suny Bay at Kempton, where he weakened quickly after four out having broken a blood vessel. But it was the next time that this pair of good chasers had a fixture clash which would give me the biggest headache.

Their fortunes contrasted dramatically. Couldn't Be Better won the Thyestes Chase at Gowran Park in January, owner Dick Whittle giving me the ride straight back after the Hennessy Gold Cup. Meanwhile, Suny Bay recovered at Uplands with the Grand National as his principal objective, but the right race for both of them was the Haydock National Trial. I had to make a decision.

Not that the pressure was all one way. Charlie was having plenty of problems with Andrew, who had made a massive investment in Uplands, refurbishing the yard, laying down gallops and putting in a swimming pool. He was anxious to see a return on his capital as any successful businessman would. The trouble is that racing, and jumping in particular, is financially very volatile.

There would not have been a better person than Andrew Cohen to work for if things had gone right but the problem was they hadn't, largely due to a virus which had ravaged the yard for two years. He knew very little about horses apart from the basics but had his own strong opinions and Charlie said, 'Brad, it's just like the passengers telling the pilot how to fly the plane.' As far as Charlie was concerned, if Suny Bay didn't win the Haydock race, there would be a new trainer at Uplands.

Charlie explained to me just how hard things were, 'When I go to the races and have a winner, instead of being happy I'm relieved.

'Andrew thinks you are unlucky. Other jockeys are getting on the horses and winning and I've got to let him make the decisions, because if he does and things go wrong then there's no comeback on me. I've got to let him do what he wants because the whole thing is doing my head in.'

Charlie had always fought my corner and when he phoned me one evening I understood him a 100 per cent when he said, 'Bradders, I'm just not enjoying this anymore.' Charlie had steered me off a Hennessy winner in Couldn't Be Better. I also missed an Agfa Hurdle success when he wished me to ride Florid over the eventual winner Double Symphony to placate one of the main owners in the yard, Lord Howard de Walden. But this was down to me. I had to choose between Couldn't Be Better and Suny Bay.

It was easy to understand Andrew's theory on luck. Whenever I couldn't do the weight on one of our runners or chose those at another meeting, someone would get on them and win - usually Jamie Osborne. I knew just how important it was to make the right decision at Haydock and I didn't take it lightly. We worked both horses ten days before the race over a mile and a half up the Farringdon Road gallop and Couldn't Be Better beat Suny Bay out of sight. I fully expected him to win the Greenalls because Suny Bay wouldn't be fit enough.

I rang Michael Dickinson in the States and laid all the facts before him. In my opinion there's never been a better judge of form or circumstances. 'You've got to stick to Couldn't Be Better. He's the best work horse, he's in form and he's well.'

I also asked my dad, who was in the other camp. 'Suny Bay's got Grand National written all over him. Even if you make the wrong choice at Haydock and miss a winner it will only cost you a few quid in the short term. Stick by Andrew Cohen.'

I said, 'Norm, I'm going to stick by my decision which I've based on professional logic. I've got to ride Couldn't Be Better.' It may have been naive of me, but I never once considered that I wouldn't get the ride back on Suny Bay in the National whatever happened at Haydock. Clearly, Norm knew the game better than me.

I was on the wrong one in spades at Haydock. Suny Bay got a peach of a ride from Jamie Osborne whereas Couldn't Be Better dropped away at the fifteenth, broke a blood vessel and finished slightly lame. In contrast to my falling stock, Jamie's had never been higher with Andrew. This was his seventh winner for the yard in eight rides.

But I still couldn't believe it when Charlie dropped the bomb ten days before the National. 'I'm afraid Andrew wants Jamie to stay on Suny Bay at Liverpool, Bradders, I'm sorry but that's it.'

I went through every emotion, devastated, angry, distraught, betrayed and at the end of it, heartbroken. Jamie had done a good public relations job talking to Andrew. Not only could Jamie ride a good race, he could talk one too and I didn't blame him. He was only looking after his own interests and there's only one Grand National each year. But I felt badly let down by Andrew and felt like quitting there and then. I'd thrown my heart and soul into the yard and done anything I was asked, schooling, dieting to do light weights and going to the gaff meetings. I'd done it willingly. I even turned down the chance to ride Veleda for trainer Sue Bramall in the Velka Pardubicka Chase in the Czech Republic. It was the same Sunday as the Uplands Open Day and Andrew was adamant that he wanted me there, talking to the owners and showing off the horses.

I did it, no problem. It was for the good of the team.

All these thoughts went through my mind as I sat on the sofa at home and felt sick thinking about it. At thirty-seven the childhood dream of winning the National was fast turning into a nightmare and I did something I've never done before or since. I phoned an owner up and begged to be let back on a horse.

Andrew was immovable, 'Listen, Brad, you chose the wrong one and Jamie got on with Suny Bay really well. I don't want to split a winning partnership.'

I said, 'Andrew, I've ridden your bumper horses when they've gone straight over fences, ridden your three-year-old hurdlers and done all the schooling. I've never tried to get off one of your horses to go somewhere else, and why should I? I'm your stable jockey.'

I might as well have been talking to the speaking clock. Andrew Cohen's mind was made up.

That was it then, nothing more to be done but to swallow it. And when the story broke in the papers I was muted in my response to the inevitable question. 'I do not want to say too much but obviously I am very disappointed. I really do think that if everything goes his way, Suny Bay has an outstanding chance.'

Thank God I bit my lip.

Kim Bailey dangled the ride on former Cheltenham Gold Cup winner Master Oats, but he didn't run and I took the mount on Lo Stregone for Thomas Tate. Even then there was going to be a nasty twist before we set out for that 1997 Grand National.

The greatest steeplechase in the world has been targeted by extremist groups with monotonous regularity, but this year was different.

I had just one ride before the National on Double Symphony, who was pulled up in the Aintree Hurdle, but six minutes before that at Fazakerley Hospital a message was received using a recognised IRA codeword which claimed a bomb had been planted at the racecourse. Three minutes later a second call was received at the

Police Control Centre at Marsh Lane, Bootle. In the weighing room we were putting the finishing touches to our colours, going through superstitious rituals and secreting any lucky charms in the top of boots. We'd already received the obligatory warning from the chief steward to go steady down to the first - he'd be better off telling greyhounds not to chase rabbits - and what colour flags would be used if they had to stop the race because of animal rights activists. There was also a warning about use of the whip, which would be the last thing on anyone's mind if it came to a tight finish in the world's most famous steeplechase. My valet had just finished tying the orange cap of Lo Stregone when Charles Barnett, the clerk of the course, came in at 3.15 and told us to evacuate the weighing room, grab a coat and go straight to the middle of the course.

Even the jockeys who are riding no hopers get psyched up for the National and stopping the flow of action at this stage is like telling a boxer the fight's off just as he's stepping into the ring. We needed all this like a bloody toothache. The boys took it in different ways, the jokers laughed and the moaners moaned, but we ambled along with the large crowd to where we'd been directed. My optimistic nature made me firmly believe that it was nothing more than a hoax and that it would be sorted out in an hour and we'd be off. Some hope.

None of us had anything apart from the racing gear we stood up in, no money, clothes, credit cards or phones. As the cold began to get to us we were told to move further away, across the course to the other side of the Melling Road, where we stood out like a blind cobbler's thumb in our silks. Everyone seemed to want to talk to us. After a while that got a bit heavy going so Tony McCoy - who had been working for the BBC because of injury - and myself found refuge in an RSPCA caravan, not far from the start. Clare Balding of the BBC joined us and we settled down to a nice cup of tea. Well, isn't that the thing we British do in a crisis?

We were soon very pissed off with events and saw a police car

301

parked in the middle of the course facing the grandstand, so we wandered over to see if we could get an update. The two coppers were from the armed response unit and very genially invited me into the back of the car - the first time such a thing had happened without me wondering if I was going to get done for speeding! It wasn't long before McCoy and my Irish agent Michael Condon were with me and the boys in blue told us that three controlled explosions had been carried out but no bombs found. As we waited for more news the idle chat got around to jobs, and both of them showed us some very formidable firepower that they confidently told us could take someone's head off at a mile. They also said the car we were in had bullet proof glass and was completely reinforced so if there was an explosion right underneath us all it would do was flip us in the air a bit. Brilliant! We had the safest seats in the house.

When the race was finally called off we began to say our goodbyes, but there was one problem. Our terrier, Erik, was still in my car, so the police arranged an escort to the Merc, which already had a sticker on it as having been checked. They had another go with the mirrors scanning the underside before we got Erik out and I managed to get a suit from the boot.

It was time to think quickly and as McCoy still had his mobile phone we got through to the Adelphi Hotel and booked six rooms which we knew we'd have no trouble filling. With no one able to get to the 20,000 cars until Sunday morning, quality sleeping space was going to be at a premium. When we all rolled up to the hotel it was like a bloody fancy dress party with all the jocks in their silks, and one scouser went up to Osborne and said, 'Ere mate, you just come straight from work?'

We bumped into Martine McCutcheon, the former *East Enders* star, who signed some of the boys' colours. Needless to say we all got very pissed in the hotel bar, except McCoy, and two of my great mates who were playing for Liverpool at the time, Robbie Fowler and Steve McManaman, got us four tickets for the game against

Coventry at Anfield on Sunday. Jason Titley, who had won the National for Jenny Pitman on Royal Athlete, was due to ride Nathen Lad for her and asked Robbie to sign the colours. Unfortunately he didn't understand the humour of footballers, and when he looked the next day he found a string of obscenities which he covered with masking tape! Having got a suit I looked almost normal, but hadn't got any shoes so I had to wear my riding boots for two days until we went back on Monday when there was a very free and easy atmosphere. I'd given my valet £800 before racing, and when he gave it back to me it was £600 light. I'd had McCoy as my personal banker, but most of the other boys had left on Saturday afternoon without any cash so the valet shared mine out. I didn't mind a bit and every penny was returned.

A newspaper headline summed it up best. 'When the tension was washed away with smiles,' and there were sixteen jockeys - including me - in the sauna that Monday morning sweating the beer of the previous 36 hours out of the system. The whole country was delighted that terrorism hadn't won and the Grand National was going to be run as a one-off spectacle for free on Monday 7 April 1997 at 5 p.m. Everyone was happy the race was going ahead, everyone that is, except me. I was dreading it.

Lo Stregone didn't have the heart for the Grand National and that year, neither did I. After a mistake at the first his jumping got higher and higher and he was well behind when he made a bad mistake at Bechers second time. I pulled him up before the fourth last and was cantering back between the third and second last, standing up in my irons trying to see the finish. Although my eyesight is much more reliable than my hearing I still couldn't make out what was happening on the run-in except that I could see Suny Bay's white shape very distinctly and there didn't appear to be anything near him. I pulled my goggles down and I'd like to think it was the sharp wind that made my eyes water. I was at the bottom of a pit of despair.

I walked Lo Stregone to the second last, where a fence attendant had a radio pressed to his ear. I asked him what had won and for those few seconds I was like a volcano ready to blow. It was worse than any wait I've had for a photo finish and it seemed like an eternity before he opened his mouth. If the first words he spoke were Suny Bay then I was done with racing forever.

There is nothing more certain than I would have left Aintree that day and never sat on another horse for the rest of my life. If he had said 'Suny Bay' then he might just as well have said, 'Get out of the game, Bradley, you're finished.' I could see Des Lynam interviewing Jamie, Charlie and Andrew while Richard Pitman and Peter Scudamore were giving an expert fence by fence analysis of the race. Sir Peter O'Sullevan's final National commentary would be there to haunt me forever.

'Where the fuck am I going to hide tonight?'

I felt physically sick.

Then he said it, that lovely little scouser said it, 'Lord Gyllene'.

'Are you sure?'

'Yep.'

I sat up in the saddle as though a massive weight had been lifted from my shoulders, which indeed it had. 'Thank the Lord for that.'

I didn't even ask where Suny Bay had finished, I wasn't bothered. He hadn't won, that's all that mattered, he hadn't won.

On reflection, the ground had dried up much more during the 48 hour postponement which certainly detracted from Suny Bay's chance. Strange as it sounds, I may have a splinter group of the IRA to thank for prolonging my career.

Alternately, if a loose horse had carried Lord Gyllene out at the water, which looked very likely for a few strides, I'd now be a 13 stone driving instructor somewhere in America.

I always stop and see my dad on the way back from every National and watch a re-run with him. That night I think he was the only man in England who was happier than me.

Even so, things were going from bad to worse at Uplands and there is no question that Jamie gave Suny Bay a brilliant ride. Andrew Cohen was mad keen to employ Oz.

There was, however, one sporting highlight away from the turf when I featured in the winning team for the Benson and Hedges pro-am at the Oxfordshire. I was a late call to replace Michael Parkinson and played like a dream off eighteen even notching an eagle net albatross at the par five eleventh with two three woods and a 15ft putt. Marc Farry, the French professional, captained our team which was made up of Greg Porter of EMI records and Chris Soden from Carlton TV. In his acceptance speech he said, 'They didn't look like 18-handicap men to me - especially that jockey.'

I'd always been taught to be one step ahead of the handicapper.

THE WAYWARD LAD

CHAPTER 27
Suny side up

Although there had been some quality moments in the 1996-97 season the highlight for me had been the defeat of Suny Bay in the National - and that couldn't be right. I'd ended with thirty-three winners, which was eleven down on the previous year, and on top of that Charlie had told me some bad news:

'Brad, there won't be anything guaranteed from Uplands. Andrew wants to use Jamie Osborne whenever he's available.'

It was time for some serious self-assessment. Should I retire from the game before the game retired me?

I went to the Lesters awards' night in London, certain it would be the last that I would attend as an active jockey. I had become very disillusioned and had lost all heart for the sport. After six years of having the pick of rides at Uplands how could I face going in there knowing that other jockeys would be in front of me? There were very few people I could talk to about the situation, but one of them was Richard Guest, who had been through the mill and come out in one piece. His advice was simple: 'Go on a long holiday, get yourself right in the head then have a re-think.'

It was alright for Guesty. He had the best agent in the business working for him in Dave Roberts, but he deserved it. Before the likes of Adrian Maguire and Norman Williamson had even thought about coming to England, Guesty had been with Dave. Tony McCoy and Richard Johnson were still at school when he joined forces with a man who ranks as the extra special jockeys' agent in jump racing.

When I started out there was no such thing. The Flat boys had employed them for some time, Willie Carson being one of the first, but these days a good agent with the right connections is essential and I wanted to be with Dave Roberts. I'd asked him two years earlier before I joined Graeme James, but he had politely refused and, although Graeme had worked hard for me, it just wasn't happening the way I wanted. His team of jockeys was dwindling and you've got to be with a strong squad where you feed off each other. It might not sound nice but that's how it works.

But that didn't concern me now. I was packing it in and that would be the end of it. Guesty had spoken to Dave about the way I was thinking and I bumped into him shortly after the awards had been made when I was just a little over refreshed. 'David Roberts, you've got to save me, you've got to save me. If you don't take me on I'm going to quit.'

Dave just smiled, 'Don't be silly, you're too good to pack it in.' But it wasn't until we got back to the hotel we were both booked into that he realised I was serious. 'Look, Brad, I'll have a think about it and talk to the lads I'm looking after. If they've got no problems we'll go ahead. There's a few good years in you yet.'

There were no objections from the likes of McCoy, Maguire, Williamson, FitzGerald, Johnson, Dean Gallagher and Andy Thornton, so I was promoted to the premier league for what would be the two most enjoyable seasons in the autumn of my career. Dave Roberts is not only the best agent around, he is an absolute gentleman. During the time I was with him he gave me hope and confidence and we never had a cross word, but he knew how to play me.

'Brad, it looks a bit quiet on Monday and Tuesday and you don't want to be banging around Folkestone and Hereford, but it looks a lot brighter over the weekend.' That suited me fine, but I'd always finish with, 'If there's a winner I'll go.'

I was riding in Ireland one Sunday and he couldn't raise me. Gay Kelleway had phoned for one of the boys to ride one at Taunton on Monday but no one was available. She told Dave it would win, so he said, 'How about using Brad?'

'That's good enough for me,' said Gay. The only problem Dave had was that after tracking me down he had to tell me that I had one ride on Major Change at a track he knew I didn't like. My reply was succinct. 'I'd rather play golf.'

'She says it'll win.'

'I'd better go, then.'

Major Change won the first easily and I was home and able to watch the last two races on the Racing Channel. I had complete faith in whatever Dave told me. It was the ideal partnership and I just wonder what I might have achieved if I'd had him pulling the strings from the start.

Charlie was still doing his best for me at Uplands, although I did think his enthusiasm was misplaced when he asked me to ride Stanmore for Andrew Cohen in novice chases having run only in National Hunt Flat races the previous season. Charlie's reasoning was that the horse was so free on the flat that he wouldn't settle over hurdles and that fences would steady him up. Well, I got him round twice either side of him unseating Simon McNeill, but I looked on it as a serious challenge when Charlie sent him to Cheltenham over two and a half miles. I've always been a good novice chase jockey and as I got older and my nerve stayed firm I got better. The secret is to sit as motionless as possible, stay well balanced and try not to interfere with the horse or get in his way. Just be there with a bit of quiet support when he needs it. That's the theory and it's worked in practice many times, including on Stanmore, who went ahead two out and struggled on well to win by a short head

I also scored an own goal with one of my new 'stablemates' and a good friend, Norman Williamson, at Leicester. The three-runner novice chase had developed into a match between Norman on the 4-11 chance Herbert Lodge and me on Kapco at 11-4. Norman was clear from four out and had the race won when he began to ease down Herbert Lodge on the run-in. When that happens a horse loses all momentum. With 150 yards to go I saw a chance of grabbing victory and threw everything at Kapco before collaring Norman in the final 30 yards to win by two lengths.

The crowd went mad and gave Norman dogs abuse as he came in. I felt very bad, too, but it had happened to me all those years ago on Trout Angler at Ludlow. The last thing on my mind would be trying to get someone in trouble and I was sorry for Norman, who got a fourteen-day suspension. Under normal circumstances, if I was staying on and looked like getting second or third from a rival who was easing his mount I'd give them a call to let them know I was coming and cover themselves. Needless to say, a winner is different.

One of Charlie's old inmates, Senor El Betrutti, had remained one of my regular rides when his owners, Susan and Gerard Nock trained him under permit at their home in Stow-on-the-Wold. Unfortunately when it came to the Murphy's Gold Cup at Cheltenham on 15 November I couldn't do the weight of 10st, so imagine how I felt when I watched on the weighing room TV and saw Jamie Osborne bring the grey home by three lengths from A.P. McCoy on Challenger Du Luc at odds of 33-1. Was this another decent ride that I wouldn't see again? But I was genuinely delighted for Susan and Gerard. They had put a lot of hard work into the horse, who seemed to benefit from being taken away from a big yard, and this was a real triumph for the smaller people. It was precisely the sort of tale which makes jump racing unique. But like any sport it can be cruel, and Jamie was about to find out just how unforgiving jumping can be.

It is the roulette of the game that we pick up winning rides when colleagues are injured and the best example of recent times is Carl Llewellyn, who won two Grand Nationals because of it. He got on Party Politics in 1992 when Andrew Adams was out with a broken arm and in 1998, when Tom Jenks was sidelined, and he took over on Earth Summit. Jamie capitalised on it in the previous year's Hennessy when substituting for Jimmy Frost on Coome Hill, and now the fates were going to ask for payback with interest.

The day after the Murphy's he had persuaded Oliver Sherwood not to run Green Green Desert in the November Novices' Chase and had got off Oliver's Him Of Praise, who won at Towcester, so that he could ride highly-regarded Space Trucker, the 2-1 favourite at Cheltenham. But at the fourth last, Jamie's career was almost ended when he took a crashing fall and in the same instant mine took a swing in the opposite direction. The fall smashed Jamie's left wrist so badly that for many months he had no movement and his career hung in the balance. It wasn't until almost a year later on 31 October that he made an emotional winning return on Coome Hill at Ascot in the race run in memory of his close friend John Durkan, who had tragically lost a brave battle against leukaemia.

But with Jamie out of the way, the dice had rolled in my favour. Three days later at Haydock, Suny Bay was due to make his reappearance in the Edward Hanmer Chase and on Monday morning I got the call I'd been praying for. It was Charlie.

'Right, Bradders. A bit of good news, you ride Suny Bay on Wednesday.'

I was ecstatic, and not for the first time I thanked the Lord that I'd heeded the wise words of Brian Wright, 'Your mouth is your most dangerous weapon.' If I had got into a public slanging match with Andrew Cohen, I doubt I would have been a contender to get the ride back. As it was, Andrew had behaved like a gentleman.

311

Charlie told me that he had never considered that anyone else would ride Suny Bay except me when Jamie wasn't fit. But now the pressure was on.

I usually take pre-race strain in my stride but this was different. I had a point to make to Andrew that I wasn't his jinx jockey. I also had implicit faith in Suny Bay, who was exceptional when fresh, and it didn't take me long to build up plenty of confidence. I sat on him for the first time in eight months on Tuesday morning and he felt wonderful. My mates from Liverpool, Messrs Fowler and McManaman, made the short trip to Haydock and I told them not only to back Suny Bay on the day but to back him ante-post for the Hennessy before the race. Unfortunately, they also spoke to McCoy, who convinced them that Eudipe would win, and they listened to him instead.

During that three miles, Suny Bay gave me a perfect ride round, his only error coming early when he hit the sixth. He jumped like a gazelle and powered clear from three out to beat General Wolfe eleven lengths with the subsequent Cheltenham Gold Cup winner See More Business third. Charlie was saddling runners at Kempton, but Andrew was waiting to receive his star in the unsaddling enclosure and he had every reason to be delighted.

The Hennessy at Newbury was ten days later and now that I had shed the unlucky tag for Andrew I could not have been more confident of taking the race for the first time since I was a kid in 1982. I told everyone that the only way he'd get beaten was if the Russians invaded and booked a table for twelve at the Queens Arms in anticipation of victory.

Although the tension between Charlie and Andrew was growing there was no question that Charlie did a great job with Suny Bay. He virtually trained him from a field where the fresh air helped him avoid any virus and also cleared his lungs to make him less prone to breaking blood vessels. When I went out to the paddock that day I knew I had a horse and a half under me - and just as well.

Suny Bay loved to be in front and was one of the best jumpers I'd ever ridden, but could he make a mistake when he wanted to! Thankfully he chose an early fence - the fourth - to do it this time. He met it wrong, still took off and then bottled it, landing hard on top of the fence. The reins were pulled from my hands, but luckily they got caught on one of his bloody great lugs and I grabbed them before they fell over his head. It was a miracle that we were still together and the blunder must have taken a lot out of him, so I gave him a couple of furlongs to get balanced and back on an even keel. Although he led briefly again at the eighth, his rhythm wasn't right for another mile. Then he eventually pricked his ears forward and when he went on at the cross fence five from home he was running away.

Barton Bank, who had won the 1993 King George and would have won it again the next year but for unseating Adrian Maguire at the last, came to challenge two out but Suny Bay lengthened away to beat him by thirteen lengths looking the class act that he was.

Charlie had watched the race from the inside of the track, just as Michael Dickinson had done fifteen years earlier, and he was wearing a broad but relieved smile when he met me on the course. The stable's three other runners that day had run like drains.

'Well, Charles, it's a good job I didn't fall off or we'd have had an absolute twat of a day.' That was something of an understatement.

It was the last Hennessy that Sir Peter O'Sullevan called for the BBC and it was a pleasure to be on the podium while he presented the cup to Andrew and his wife Wendy. Charlie couldn't stop hugging me. I don't know if he was thinking back to when he talked me off riding the previous year's winner, Couldn't Be Better, but he seemed happier than me and was typically honest when interviewed after the race.

'I thought Brad should have retired at the end of last season but, by God, I was wrong. Last year he would probably have fallen off at the fourth - in fact nine out of ten jockeys would have come off Suny Bay today. Some people were born to be great and he's one of them.' A bit over the top, but very well meant.

We left a trail of empty champagne bottles at various pubs until we got back to the Queens, where my good friend Tom Butterfield had reserved the whole restaurant and put more fizz on ice. And there was another surprise. Bob knew just what this win meant to me and had been on the phone to arrange for all the family to come down from Wetherby. Norm, Mandy, Gary Jackie and my six nieces all came, plus Boo Boo Youlden. They didn't arrive until ten, but things were only starting to warm up. It was also lovely to see most of the lads from Uplands come along, too, including Phil Sharp, who was devoted to Suny Bay and captured the hearts of the nation when he stayed to water and feed the horses during the Aintree bomb scare. My old ally Brian Delaney was there with his wife Jill, and everyone got their hands on the cup and had a drink from it. The party lasted until ten o'clock the next morning, but after doing a lap of honour around the pub I was put to bed at 4 a.m. Unlike Suny Bay, I hadn't got the trip.

When I emerged at midday to pay the bill for dinner and champagne I was too late. Andrew Cohen had paid for the lot, including a hefty bar tab for the regulars. He then took all the family for Sunday lunch at the Hare and Hounds at Lambourn Woodlands, where he and Norm got on famously. If only Norm had been twenty years younger. These were exceptionally kind gestures from a man who was getting the results he richly deserved for ploughing a fortune into Uplands. When things were going well there was no better master than Andrew. If it wasn't for the cursed virus that seemed to hit Lambourn every November, Andrew Cohen would have been the country's leading National Hunt owner, and a star to work for.

But my run of good luck was only just beginning.

Senor El Betrutti now had 11st 3lb in the Tripleprint Gold Cup and with Jamie laid up I was back on him for the return trip to Cheltenham on 13 December. He wasn't a 33-1 shot this time, but his previous big win was looked on as a fluke by bookmakers and punters, who let him start at 9-1 in the nine runner field. Maybe it was the unorthodox preparation that Sue and Gerard gave the grey that put people off, because he was out hunting with the Heythrop the week before. Either way, it definitely suited the Senor who continued to blossom under the individual care and attention. Although he had won over three miles going right-handed, he was very much better over two and a half going anti-clockwise, and that's what he got at Cheltenham. He jumped his way to the front from the third and we never saw another horse, leaving McCoy and Challenger du Luc to follow us home at eight lengths.

But the King George VI Chase at Kempton on Boxing Day brought Andrew, Charlie and myself down to earth with a bump. Although Suny Bay started at 9-4 joint favourite with another grey, One Man, he never fired and was a well-beaten fourth behind See More Business. I was soon squeezing Suny Bay along and trying to persuade him to take hold of the bit, but he was lifeless with no spark. It wasn't the ground and he probably had the virus which really did seem to ravage Uplands each season.

Charlie was desperate to get Suny Bay buzzing again and, ever the individualist, he arranged for a public school over a mile and seven fences at Sandown between the last two races on the Saturday before the Cheltenham Gold Cup. But the horse had suffered a muscle problem and wasn't really fit. What's more, he was galloping with one of the best work horses I'd ridden, Couldn't Be Better, who was partnered by Dean Gallagher.

Deano would have been a stone lighter than me and unbeknown

315

to anyone, I made Charlie put two stone of lead under Couldn't Be Better's saddle. I knew the TV cameras would be on Suny Bay and the Press would be scrutinising him and I didn't want him embarrassed in public. As it was, Couldn't Be Better was still more impressive, so there was no great confidence for Cheltenham, and the Sandown public relations exercise turned out expensive for me. I'd been booked to ride 25-1 shot Mons Warrior for Norman Babbage in the bumper, but I hadn't got time to do both and gave up the ride to Eugene Husband. The stewards fined me £350 for not fulfilling the engagement.

Suny Bay was still short of peak fitness for the Cheltenham Gold Cup and weakened four out to finish a well beaten fifth to Cool Dawn. Even so, he gave me the feeling he was starting to come right, and I made sure I looked after him when he got tired because the Grand National wasn't far away.

With twenty-three years in the saddle behind me I thought I'd done everything on a racecourse that was possible and some that weren't. However, I thank the Lord for giving me one of the most wonderful experiences of my life when I rode Suny Bay in the 1998 Grand National. My record up to that point was uninspiring: in eleven attempts I'd completed only twice. I'd been second over the shorter course for the John Hughes Trophy twice, but the lack of National success left a massive void in my professional life. The 10 minutes 51.5 seconds it took to run the National on 4 April filled that space forever.

It was a shame Andrew wouldn't let me wear the new 'jockey cam' on my helmet so everyone could have taken each exhilarating jump with me, but he thought it was unlucky and there was no way he wanted to tempt fate.

But Suny Bay's National chance was greatly enhanced because I had been kind to him in the Gold Cup. To stress a horse when there's no chance of winning is lunacy. As it was, the consideration put him

316

spot on for Aintree. The only problem we had was that the handicapper had been as impressed as everyone else with his easy win in the Hennessy and his National weight had shot up from 10st 3lb the previous year to 12st. If he'd fallen in the Hennessy then he would probably have won the National but one thing is certain - I wouldn't have been on him. Andrew would have had his unlucky theory completely endorsed.

The build-up to the big race was one of the wettest on record - it was only just raceable - and the mud finished any idea of employing the usual front-running tactics which suited Suny Bay so well. As before every important race I had thought long and hard over my strategy and when I went into the ring I had a firm plan in place.

The year before he'd run a blinder on unsuitable ground to be second, but on that evidence he didn't stay the trip. I approached the cluster of friends and owners, headed by Andrew and Wendy, tipped my cap and was about to give forth chapter and verse on how I was going to change things when Charlie completely stole my moment. Giving a passable impression of a duck - calm on the surface but with his feet going like crazy out of sight - he said in a remarkably assured voice, 'Well, Brad, you must have thought about how you are going to ride him a lot longer than we have. My job's finished now, ride him how you like and don't worry about us, go and do your own thing.'

I could have kissed him.

It was the best decision Charlie and Andrew could have made and it really did give me a lift as I strode over to Suny Bay. As Charlie legged me up I called over my shoulder, 'Don't expect to see me too close on the first circuit, Charles.'

I had a gut feeling that they would go too fast despite the desperate conditions and that very few would finish. I lined up tight on the inner behind the front row and, sure enough, the no-hopers went off at a crazy pace just to get in the shot of the camera car that races on the inside of the track and follows the field down to

Bechers. I was last at the first, where Tony McCoy came down on Challenger du Luc, and I could have easily been brought down by him - perhaps I was lucky for Andrew now.

Suny Bay's stamina was always in the forefront of my thoughts and I never moved off the inner, saving every inch as we reached the Canal Turn first time. With horses falling all around me I kept creeping forward, letting Suny Bay do everything in his own time but mindful he had a massive weight to shoulder. At the Chair in front of the stands we were about ten lengths off the lead and things couldn't have been going better. The leaders kicked again going out for the second circuit while I just sat quiet and let them go. Jumping Bechers second time Earth Summit had moved into third and I was closing on him in fourth. We'd both moved upsides the leader Greenhil Tare Away when he fell at the last ditch four out, and Suny Bay joined Carl Llewellyn and Earth Summit in the air at the third last, both of us going very comfortably. Because of the long run to the second last I had loads of time to look round. I couldn't believe what I saw and turned to Carlos, 'Fuckin' 'ell, hombre we're thirty lengths clear, it's between me and you.'

I don't think he believed me. He wouldn't look round and never said a word, then five strides later he had a peek and saw a previous winner Rough Quest toiling in our wake. We were still locked together crossing the Melling Road, at which point I tried some kidology. 'Steady, hombre, loads of time yet, there's another half mile to go.'

We were still thirty lengths clear going well after the Melling Road. I was praying Suny Bay would outbattle the blinkered Earth Summit if it came down to a fight on the run-in, but I couldn't have been more wrong. The old bastard pinged the second last and when Carlos got stuck into him he went two lengths up. It was game over. Suny Bay battled like a lion yet couldn't give 23lb to a horse who had already won Scottish and Welsh Nationals. Without him in the field we'd have won by a distance from Samlee. As it was we were eleven lengths second best, but I might just as well have won the race the way I was feeling. Going to the second last I really had thought I'd win the world's most famous chase and that feeling made everything that had gone before worthwhile. At the same time I also felt the disappointment of Andrew, Wendy and Charlie, who had seen their grey hero finish second twice on the bounce. And when we came in there was Tom Jenks, Earth Summit's usual rider but ruled out with a broken leg and trying to put a brave face on things. There's no knowing how short-changed he felt.

I firmly believe that in all the thousands of races in which I've been involved this was the best ride I'd ever given a horse. I felt professionally satisfied that I'd turned tactics upside down and so nearly got it right. I'd put my neck on the block because I knew it was the right way to ride him and I'd come away with my head still joined to my body.

Carl was the only other jockey in the field that day to use his brain. Obviously, I regret not having won the race because people only ever remember National winners, but I'll never be the 1998 runner-up. For me and many others Suny Bay put up the best performance over the course since Crisp valiantly filled the same position in 1973 trying to give 23lb to the legendary triple winner Red Rum.

THE WAYWARD LAD

CHAPTER 28
One of the Irish

Since I rode my first winner in Ireland on Rhyme 'N' Reason I always had a feeling of belonging, and the warmth I received every time I went back strengthened the bond. Not that it was a one-way love affair. I managed to do my bit for my Celtic brothers at their spiritual home, the Cheltenham Festival, and joined that rare breed of English jockeys who have ridden an Irish-trained winner at the greatest jumping meeting in the world.

Irish winners at the Festival tend to stay 'in-house' and although they're not averse to using ex-pats like Jonjo O'Neill, Tommy Stack, Ron Barry and latterly Dunwoody, McCoy, Maguire, Williamson and FitzGerald, they very seldom employ us foreigners. There have been exceptions - like the amateurs Gay Kindersley and the Hon. Stephen Stanhope - but the former has Guinness blood coursing through him and there is a good measure of Celt in the latter, who now resides in Ireland.

It is an historical fact that Anglo-Irish relations have been troubled over the years to say the least, and when I was being driven around the meandering roads to countless Irish racecourses, my travelling companions would point an admonishing finger out of the window at a church ruin to remind me of 'Oliver Cromwell's handiwork' as they called it. There's no doubt that they love coming to Cheltenham and make the event what it is, but they are a clan apart and don't readily let outsiders into their fold. So when I secured the ride on that fine mare French Ballerina and kept it to win the 1998 Supreme Novice Hurdles at Cheltenham I felt I had been bestowed with a singular honour.

I first got the ride through the friendship of my Irish agent Michael Condon with Paul Shanahan, who is one of the main men at Coolmore Stud. He put in a good word for me with John Magnier, who ran the mare in the dark blue colours of his wife Sue. Pat Flynn trained her and she had excellent credentials on breeding, being by Istabraq's sire Sadler's Wells out of an Ardross mare who won the German Oaks. She'd also won four listed races on the Flat in Ireland, so there was plenty of class to fall back on.

The first time I rode her was at Leopardstown, when the ground was too soft and she finished a tired third to His Song after making mistakes at the last two flights. She was much straighter for our next appearance at Navan, where I was more worried about her style of running than the heavy ground. She had been very keen and refused to settle in behind at Leopardstown, so I asked Pat if I could try and make all ... 'No problem, do what you like.' Just my kind of instructions. She settled beautifully, jumped like a handicapper to win well, and I felt privileged to keep the ride at Cheltenham even though the main hope of the Irish was His Song, who had already beaten her nine lengths and subsequently finished a length and a half second to the mighty Istabraq in the Irish Champion Hurdle.

But Pat knew what a good horse was having trained the top-quality Montelado to win at two successive festivals, the bumper in 1992 and the Supreme Novices the following year. He was adamant that French Ballerina would be a stone better on good ground, a fact that was confirmed to me by her regular flat rider Kevin Manning, who I'd met when he made a rare visit to Stratford a few days before

Cheltenham.

I was fairly confident she would turn the tables on His Song, but I was unaware she had come into season three days before the race, which luckily didn't affect her. On the big day she looked marvellous. As always before the Festival I left nothing to chance. Not only does the horse have to use everything, so, too, does the jockey. Nerve, brain, experience and confidence are essential for success, and I spent plenty of time going over recordings of races there that my dad had made over the previous twenty years. I formed a picture in my mind of exactly what I was going to do, so when I got into the paddock and John Magnier was looking for a little confidence booster I was very positive.

'Should I back her, Brad?'

'Yes sir, definitely. She's a great each-way bet at 10-1'

In his summing up on Channel 4, John Francome had doubts that she'd stay. I had none. I took up my usual position for hurdle races on the outside to keep her out of trouble and travelled in a straight line to the first bend, where I slotted in behind the leaders and let the others do the shouting. I was very handy going down the back straight after the third and got into the perfect position at the top of the hill, with the leaders and hard on the bridle. I let her freewheel down the hill to the second last, letting everything tighten up in behind. At this point His Song, a big chasing type, was cantering in behind. His super-stylish flat jockey Richard Hughes looked every inch like Lester Piggott with his bum pointing to the sun, but I kept skin-tight on the rail that takes you into the long sweeping bend which sets you up for the last and the moment I squeezed French Ballerina to quicken she unleashed all her Flat pace to go three lengths clear. She was never going to stop going up the hill and, although Hughesie asked His Song for everything, French Ballerina was magnificent that day and beat him by nine lengths.

I have always envied the Irish jockeys for the reception they get when they ride a 'home-trained' winner at the Festival and I still cherish the moment when I walked French Ballerina into the winners' enclosure. It didn't matter that His Song was their banker of the meeting. Win, lose or draw they won't let a betting reversal get in the way of a celebration and the reception they gave us was breathtaking. To this day it remains one of my fondest memories.

John Magnier invited me to the box after racing and kindly gave me a present but Mrs Magnier was even more magnanimous and let a party of us have their house at the K-Club for the Punchestown Festival, which is only five miles away. The group consisted of Nicky Gill, who graduated from a stable lad with Peter Bailey to being one of the most successful builders in the Lambourn area, McCoy, Condon and myself. And never dreaming of taking any liberties with the superb cellar, we went into Naas to stock up on Chardonnay and Budweiser which left the Dom Perignon and premier cru clarets intact.

Not that my house guest McCoy did me any favours when it came to the racecourse. He was on arch-rival His Song in the Country Pride Champion Novices Hurdle on the first day and, with the ground nearly unraceable, it was very much against French Ballerina. With no pace on I doodled away in front making the gallop to suit my mare, but McCoy came upsides going down the back straight and began leaning his strapping horse on to French Ballerina, who wasn't the biggest. They were intimidating tactics - albeit quite legal - and certainly didn't help me. French Ballerina fought like a tigress when she was narrowly headed by His Song three out and just got her head back in front on the run-in, but the spoiling tactics and the ground got to the bottom of her and she was beaten a head in a memorable battle. I called McCoy all the bastards I could think of, but it was a masterful piece of race-riding and illustrates just why he is one of the best I have ever seen.

Unfortunately, French Ballerina never got the chance to produce anything of her calibre at stud. She was fancied to run well in the 1998 Ascot Gold Cup but fractured a hind leg coming out of the stalls and had to be destroyed. I believe she was the one horse that would have given Istabraq a run for his money in the following year's Champion Hurdle. I was proud to be associated with that bonny little mare.

I think that my no-nonsense Yorkshire approach to life stood me in excellent stead with the Irish, and the friendships I made there have been some of my most enduring. Not long after I began my regular visits I was befriended by Conor and Audrey O'Dwyer. They took me to dinner, put me up at their home and went out of their way to make me feel comfortable. I was only too happy to repay the compliment when Conor came over to ride a season for Kim Bailey and he stayed with me until his accommodation was sorted out.

Charlie Swan, who will always be associated with Istabraq as far as the English are concerned, has done much the same job for Irish jockeys that Richard Dunwoody did for the English by combining horsemanship and jockeyship to take riding to a new level of sophistication. Both effectively buried the non-stylist. The legendary owner-gambler J.P. McManus once said that Charlie had 'balls of steel.' Well, he has a good bit more than that including brains, balance and confidence. With due respect to all my former colleagues, I never rode against a better jockey around Cheltenham.

Because of the welcome I always got in Ireland I've always done my bit for the younger Irish lads when they come to England.

Adrian Maguire was one of the first and there's no doubt that his talent is God-given and natural. He has beautiful hands and excellent balance, which gives him a rhythmical strength in a finish. Not long after he became stable jockey to David Nicholson after Dunwoody's switch to Martin Pipe, Adrian was convinced he was being victimised by the Jockey Club for his use of the whip. There was one case in particular that hit him very hard when he was banned for being too harsh on Ramstar in a tight finish with

325

Dunwoody at Warwick in January 1994. The Press went to town and he felt the world was against him. The episode almost broke him. We had some long discussions over his plight and I knew I wasn't wasting my time when I told him quite simply, 'Adrian, you just can't keep breaking the rules. If you drive 100 miles an hour down a motorway every time it suits you, sooner or later you will get nicked. Do it again and you will get banned. And if you carry on speeding they can put you in prison or in the Jockey Club's case, take you out of the game for a very long time.'

He heeded the advice and, make no mistake, there isn't a kinder man or a better horseman than Adrian. He has rebuilt his career after some appalling injuries and is now thriving as stable jockey to Ferdy Murphy's powerful yard near Middleham.

Jason Titley is one of my closest friends and won some of the biggest races in Ireland when he was still a kid. Because of his natural talent, riding came too easily to him. So did other things, including the post-race celebrations. I first saw him at the Listowel Festival of 1993, where he was swinging the trainer of Doran's Pride, Michael Hourigan, around on his shoulders like the blades of a helicopter. Both of them ended up on the floor of the owners' and trainers' bar amid a pile of tables and chairs. Everyone thought it was great entertainment, but it wasn't long before the rides began drying up - and that's what I advised Jason to do! Now, you might think that the pot is calling the kettle burnt-arse here because I've always been top class at celebrating, but I pointed out that there was a time and place for going wild - and one place which certainly was off limits was in front of people who were going to employ you.

Not long after, Jason moved to England to ride for Henrietta Knight and really turned his career around. He picked up the spare ride on Royal Athlete for Jenny Pitman and won the 1995 National and when he returned home to Ireland he was a much more rounded person.

Paul Carberry was another precocious young Irish talent who

used England as a turning point in his career and was a fully paid up lodger at Bradley's Hotel.

Like Richard Hughes, who was his greatest childhood friend, Paul has a legendary jockey for a father in Tommy, who won three Gold Cups and a Grand National before training Bobbyjo to win for Paul at Aintree in 1999. He goes through life without a cloud on his horizon and is another to whom things come very easily. He has John Francome's nonchalance, Mark Dwyer's brain and Piggott's balance.

He also had the constitution of an elephant.

After racing at Leopardstown when we'd both ridden a winner we went into the owners and trainers' bar and downed a couple of large ones, quickly followed by a few more at the Stillorgan Orchard about 15 minutes away. A Chinese in Dublin swilled down by a good few bottles of wine was only a stop-off before we moved on to a great club under the Burlington Hotel called Annabell's where we took in a few more.

Kicked out of there at 2.30 we still hadn't finished and made our way down to Leeson Street and Buck Whaley's, a private club where they only serve champagne and wine just to finish the job off. At six a.m. the music stopped, the lights came up and we had been drinking for twelve solid hours. I staggered to my bed but it was time for Carberry to go to work. Looking unfairly fresh, he jumped into a taxi back to Leopardstown, where he was due to lead Richard Dunwoody and Flashing Steel in a schooling session around the course. Although he was only on a novice, Carberry was never a man for messing around and, after administering two smacks round the arse, he was thirty lengths clear leaving Richard to school Flashing Steel virtually alone. Neither John Mulhern, trainer of Flashing Steel, nor Noel Meade, who handled the novice, were particularly pleased.

They reckon Tommy Carberry was a bit of a lad and there's a saying in racing that 'You can't breed tame ones from wild ones.'

327

Paul was certainly that. Whenever he was asked what he wanted in his vodka the reply never changed, 'More vodka.' Yes, he was Premier League but word began to get around and it wasn't long before the rides began to dwindle. Facing relegation, he came to England as first jockey to the high- flying owner Robert Ogden and it didn't take long for the right kind of doubles and trebles to come Paul's way. Quite simply, people who had never seen him ride couldn't believe what he could do on a horse and, like Jason Titley, his English sabbatical had a sobering effect on him. Paul eventually went back to his old job in Ireland with Noel Meade and swore off the drink. He was still on the water wagon at Cheltenham 2000 and long may it continue.

There is a world of difference between racing in the two countries. Things are more relaxed in Ireland, where there is nowhere near the volume of racing. In England it is quite often six days on the bounce then over to Ireland for Sunday.

Also the dope wagon, as we call the random testing done by the Sports Council, is very high profile in England. The testing is extremely strict. You must strip from the waist to knee to give a urine sample while under constant observation to make certain there's no cheating - talk about bare-arsed cheek! The tolerance level for alcohol is no more than for driving a car and the constant threat of testing makes you very aware of what you can and can't do the night before racing.

Drink, however, has never been a problem for some great Irish jump jockeys including the likes of champions Tommy Stack and Jonjo O'Neill. The newest sensation, A P McCoy, is another teetotaller, but like Tommy and Jonjo he doesn't need the ale to have a good time.

That said, despite being one of the kindest human being's I've ever met, A.P. is a driven man, totally absorbed by his desire to win and be the best. I knew he was something special the first time I saw him. I was sitting alongside Conor O'Dwyer in the weighing room at the Galway Festival in 1994 and watched Richard Dunwoody beat someone, who I didn't recognise, by a short head. Dunwoody, too, was a man possessed when it came to winning and this kid had made him pull out everything from his considerable repertoire. 'Who the hell was that on the second, Conor, he looks a bit useful?'

'He's a 7lb claimer, only a kid who rode a couple of winners for Jim Bolger. They say he's good.' A magnificent understatement.

'Wee Anthony' as he was always called in Ireland, eventually joined my old guv'nor Toby Balding. With both of us being a bit reserved it took me time to get to know him, but when I did I discovered that he had a heart as big as his frame, which is intimidatingly large for a jockey - 5ft 10in. That said, pound for considerable pound I think he is the equal of John Francome. The ride he gave Edredon Bleu in the Queen Mother Champion Chase at Cheltenham 2000 has never been bettered in my opinion. The only question is 'How long will he be around?'

I would love to see him break every record available and set unmatchable targets, but he in turn sets himself impossible standards. Richard Dunwoody was impervious to pain and mastered the painful art of self-denial, but it almost broke him in the middle of the 1990s. He took his foot off the throttle and survived and I've talked long into the night trying to convince A.P. to do the same. They say he's only young and can take it, but in my opinion he puts too much pressure on himself by melting his body down to an unnatural 9st 10lb when it should be nearer 11st 7lb at least. The mental torment will eventually take it's toll. I just hope those who employ him understand what he is putting himself through and realise that the only reason I say this now is because I care about him. He's one of the best friends I've ever had and I want him around for a long time yet.

THE WAYWARD LAD

CHAPTER 29
Brooks bows out

If Suny Bay had cut through the mud and won the Grand National in 1998 Charlie Brooks would probably still be training at Uplands. Victory at Aintree would also have given Andrew Cohen the encouragement he needed to replenish his team with new blood.

Unfortunately, exactly three weeks after that heroic defeat Charlie, too, admitted that he didn't feel he could win and resigned his post as Andrew's employed trainer. It didn't come as a shock.

Despite his public persona of bon viveur there was far more to Charlie. He was a worrier who admitted he was prone to depression and he even went so far as to consult Miriam's father, the Harley Street specialist Andrew Strigner in an attempt to combat the problem. He said, 'I get very depressed and he has put me under hypnosis to instruct my subconscious not to harbour depressed moods. In fact, he has taught me self-hypnosis and I often do it lying down in a darkened room, telling myself to think positively to get me out of any depression.

'People think I'm a laid-back creature but you'll never find anyone as edgy and pessimistic as me.

'You have to be pretty thick skinned to be a devil-may-care type and I'm one of the most thin-skinned people I know.'

Clearly, any confrontations between Charlie and Andrew were going to cut deep and the inevitable breakdown in communication came on Easter Monday, nine days after Aintree. Andrew didn't think Charlie was concentrating his mind on getting Uplands going forward and cited his work for the *Evening Standard* and BBC as distractions. He also laid into him about the virus which was on the horses, adding that when they were fit they had been in the wrong races. Charlie countered by pointing out that Andrew gave him a list of meetings where horses were not to run because he couldn't get there. In the end, the rights and wrongs didn't matter. The party was over.

After Charlie had talked his decision through with Miriam I was the first person he told as we travelled back from Cheltenham.

'I've just had enough, Brad, I don't want to do it any more. I'm really sorry to be leaving you and the rest of the lads in the shit but there's no way I can carry on.

'You don't seem to be very lucky with trainers that you really get on with. Michael Dickinson went off to Manton and now I'm leaving.'

It was typical of Charlie that he was thinking about everyone else, but I understood his problems 100 per cent. There was more to life than working at something you no longer enjoyed. Life is precious, and Charlie still had a lot of living to do.

I said, 'Charles, you don't owe anyone anything. Go out and enjoy yourself - and for goodness sake, don't worry.'

We picked his car up at the Queens Arms and had a drink. And when Charlie walked out of the door, I knew that it was only a matter of time before I'd be looking for something else to do.

Andrew got in touch to say that as far as he was concerned my job was safe for next season and Charlie honoured his contract to the finish. It only left an emotional farewell at the village hall in East Garston where Charlie, Brian Delaney and myself made speeches

332

straight from the heart. We said we'd all miss him desperately and it was the same for Charlie. He'd spent the majority of his working life at Uplands, starting at the bottom and making it to the top where, for me, he always stayed.

Andrew then got me involved in the selection process to find a new trainer and the net was cast far and wide. I phoned quite a few people, including in Ireland, to sound them out and came up with a short-list that I gave to Andrew, who had also advertised the job generating a massive response. The name that came to the top was Peter Scudamore, who had the ideal credentials. Not only had he ridden for Fred and Charlie, he had also played a significant role in transforming Nigel Twiston-Davies into a serious trainer. But Scu turned it down, preferring to marry his media work with his assistant's post with Nigel, so the game was wide open again.

There were five on my list. Ferdy Murphy, Tony Mullins, Pat Murphy, the shrewd Irish amateur rider and trainer Tony Martin who led the way, and last but certainly not least there was Richard Guest. I wanted Guesty to get the job, and if he had then I believe I'd still have been riding into the millennium. Brian liked him, too, and loved his mental approach to training horses. He got down to an interview with Andrew and I begged him to take Guesty on. He'd transformed Harvey and Sue Smith's operation and the improvement he brought in Norman Mason's horses was nothing short of phenomenal, but Richard reckons he didn't quite have the right background to suit Andrew. After winning the First National Bank Gold Cup on Red Marauder at Ascot in November 1998, Andrew generously came up to give his congratulations on a fine piece of training. Knowing he hadn't got the job, Guesty said, 'Thanks, Andrew. Just think what I could have done with all those lovely horses of yours!'

With so much capital involved, the decision could only rest with Andrew and after much sifting he decided to bring Simon Sherwood back into training. 'Sharkey,' who had trained at East Ilsley before relinquishing his licence a year earlier, had the right credentials having trained Cheltenham Festival winners and was the first person to train for the Lloyd Webbers. He came from the right side of the tracks and I'd always got on well with him both when we rode together and while riding winners for him.

In fact, I was enjoying a real Indian Summer to my riding career. At the age of thirty-seven I'd never had so many rides or won so much prize money and I was well-pleased with a final winning total of forty-six. I also won the Benson and Hedges Pro-am golf tournament for the second year running despite having my handicap cut from 18 to 15, this time with Robert Karlsson as the pro. And just to make the day complete I went on to Chepstow and won the last race on the card, a two mile handicap chase on Holly's Pride for Charlie, which made up for missing the awards' ceremony. So, despite Charlie's departure everything seemed to be coming up roses - or was it?

CHAPTER 30
The wrong arm of the law

During the autumn of my career the ladders were more than making up for the snakes of my early years. However, the rough justice I had learned to live with so long ago reared it's ugly head again in January 1998.

Experience had taught me to be wary of the way the Jockey Club policed racing, but this chain of events went far beyond that, so much so that I was left with severe doubts about the law of the land itself.

I was sitting in the office at Uplands at 9 a.m. on Tuesday 27 January having a quick cup of coffee with Charlie Brooks after a schooling session when he told me some news that made me shiver, 'You'll never guess what's happened, Brad. The Serious Crime Squad has been to interview Dean Gallagher.'

I was silent for a few seconds then said, 'Bloody hell, I wonder what that's all about then, Charles?

I then retreated into my own thoughts. What might Deano have done or been involved in? Probably nothing but I was very curious. As the jungle telegraph warmed up more news filtered through. Soon it became clear that two further jockeys had been gathered up in the police swoop, Jamie Osborne and Leighton Aspell. It was getting more unbelievable by the hour.

Charlie and I travelled to Leicester races with the radio tuned in to see when the news broke and how the media would handle it. Charlie phoned Andrew Cohen and opened the conversation by saying, 'Andrew, two of your jockeys have been arrested by the police - guess who.'

Mine was the first name he mentioned but, in fairness to Andrew, it had already crossed my mind on several occasions that with my reputation it was surprising that they hadn't given me a tug as well.

I must admit that with the gallows humour which arrives at times of suffering, Charlie and I began to see a funny side to it. The more we thought, the more it became a complete joke. But when we got to Leicester there was a sombre mood in the weighing room. Rumours of dawn raids and allegations of horse doping and fixed races were surfacing. My demeanour swiftly changed to one of indignation and then complete disbelief that these three men could be linked to a doping racket which allegedly involved two of them riding horses they knew were doped to lose.

Jamie had been on Avanti Express, who was found to have been doped with the drug ACP - a relaxant - after he had been pulled up at Exeter on 7 March 1997. Leighton was the rider of Lively Knight when that one was similarly got at when beaten at odds of 1-7 at Plumpton on 29 March.

Now I know jump jockeys need a streak of lunacy to do the job, but anyone who knowingly sets out to ride a horse that has been given a tranquilliser would need treatment in a mental institution. And my knowledge of the Jockey Club Security department told me that this had a very good chance of developing into a farce which would produce very few laughs but plenty of tears.

For starters none of the three were remotely connected. Leighton was one of the quietest and most sensible lads in the weighing room and lived miles away from the Lambourn area where Jamie and

Deano lived. And as for that pair, while they would pass the time of day, neither moved in the same social circles and if they shared a car journey together it would never have been more than two or three times a season.

No, this was surely a big mistake, but it didn't stop me feeling desperately sorry for the three men involved and their families. How were they feeling when they saw pictures of their loved ones on the front of the racing papers and splashed on the news pages of the tabloids? My family could sympathise with them because they'd been through it. The trouble was that my nearest and dearest would be enduring it again in a year's time - only this time it would be much, much harder.

I admit now that I acted out of character in the aftermath of their arrest and am ashamed to say now that it took me a week to pick up the phone and talk to Oz and Deano. I was frightened in case their phones were bugged, but why should I have been? I had absolutely nothing to hide and they were both very good friends of mine.

As more pieces of the jigsaw became public it became patently clear that if the police and Jockey Club weren't barking up the wrong tree then someone was barking mad. Not even Dick Francis at his most inventive would have had jockeys knowingly riding doped horses. But that didn't stop the Jockey Club making one appalling error of judgement when they withdrew the licences of the three men. It was a move that went dead against the common law of the land that a man is innocent until proven guilty. At a time when they should have been receiving support from their governing body - as footballers were before going on trial for corruption - the Jockey Club kicked their own men when they were down.

The case dragged on. Leighton was eventually cleared in April and Jamie was ruled out of inquiries in October, but Deano was left dangling on bail. And all the time there was a constant drain on his financial and mental resources. At the general meeting of the Jockeys' Association at York that August I told everyone the facts

337

concerning Deano. I informed the large gathering of senior riders how he had been forced to sell his house to meet his legal fees and that something had to be done. The way things were shaping up any one of us could have been put in such an invidious position without a shred of evidence being offered.

I called a meeting at my house in Sparsholt, which happens to be next door to the Jockeys' Association Executive Manager Michael Caulfield. Ten of the top riders attended and Deano came along to explain just how hard things were getting. Among the gathering were Tony McCoy, Mick FitzGerald, Jimmy McCarthy and dear old Richard Guest, who got more irate than the rest of us put together. We all agreed that something should be done when Deano was finally cleared but all those good intentions came to nothing - just like the police inquiries.

The whole sorry business virtually broke Dean Gallagher. There was one occasion when he was on his way to ride four horses at the races and just couldn't face it. He was virtually having a mental breakdown, and it was only the care of his girlfriend, Louise, who took him away to France for a break to get him focused, that helped him through. They have since married and, ironically, France has since seen the reemergence of Dean as a top class jockey in his role as retained rider for multi-millionaire owner Paul Green. But the new lease of life came at a high price both for him and his two colleagues.

Because none of them were charged they could not claim any compensation. All three were left badly out of pocket, but Deano was hit hardest and wasn't discharged until 13 April 1999.

As for Jamie, although blameless of any wrongdoing, he was used by the police to trap a corrupt former detective turned private eye called Robert Harrington, who was found guilty of obtaining money by deception from him at a lengthy Old Bailey trial in January 2000. On 31 March he was sentenced to 18 months imprisonment.

But if I thought the police had overlooked me I was wrong. During 1998 my name had never been seriously linked with the ongoing inquiry except for the odd joke in the weighing room or pub, which I would have expected. But the rumour factory was still active and certain journalists were sowing malicious seeds of doubt about the integrity of particular jockeys. By Christmas the whole sorry affair had found its way off the news pages and, although I secretly thought it was a miracle that I'd never been interviewed I was well aware that if enough mud is thrown then some will stick. With my record, surely I was overdue. I needn't have worried. The boys in blue knew my address.

The phone next to my bed rang at 6.10 a.m. on 8 January 1999. I thought it was Mark Bradstock phoning to make sure I'd be at Letcombe Bassett for schooling at 7.30. Bob was away with her parents in Hull and Mark knew all about my sleeping capabilities. When I picked up the receiver a deep yet pleasant voice said, 'Mr Bradley, it's the Serious Crime Squad here. We're outside your house and have been banging on the door for five minutes but couldn't wake you up. Could you come down and let us in, please?'

In a long history of having to be roused from slumber this was undoubtedly the sharpest wake-up call I've ever had. It was a shock, a massive shock, and I sat on the side of the bed staring into space, at the same time collecting my thoughts with the phone still in my hand. This was no time to panic. Very coolly, I said, 'Hang on a minute while I get some clothes on.' If they'd waited five minutes they could wait five more, so I dived into my Leeds tracksuit and set about hiding a few things. There was a gold Rolex watch worth £14,000 and a cash box with £6,000 inside. Though legally earned, they weren't the sort of thing you want the police discovering, so I hid them in the wash basket, carefully placing some dirty socks and soiled boxer shorts on top of the dirty linen.

I tried to be as calm as possible and ambled down the stairs.

When I opened the door I was faced by two men and a woman and entered into a scene I'd seen hundreds of times on TV. 'Mr Bradley, we are arresting you on suspicion of conspiracy to fix horse races. You don't have to say anything but anything you do may be taken down and used in evidence.' They produced their police I.D. and a search warrant. I didn't see any reason to be uncivil, so invited them into the kitchen and made them a cup of tea. I then took them into my office and informed them that, being a Virgo, I was an extremely tidy and organised person, so everything they would want would be in my four filing cabinets or on my desk. 'It's all there, from A to Z, take what you want.' They would, anyway, so why let them see that they'd annoyed me?

The female PC started rifling the A-B cabinet and thought she'd hit the jackpot early. She triumphantly produced a three-page computer printout featuring a long list of names with amounts of money beside each one. Her eyes glinted like diamonds and I swear she had to cross her legs for fear of wetting herself she was so excited. She held it up to the two men, 'Look at this, look at this!'

I was a bit curious myself and took a peek over her shoulder expecting to see at the very least a string of payments from the team of call girls I was probably running! What I saw made me smile despite the gravity of the situation. 'Oh, that's a list of the donations made on a charity golf day I organised for Shane Broderick, a very young and talented Irish jockey who was paralysed from the neck down in a fall. I've got all the bank books and statements here if you want them, it's called the Shane Broderick Appeal Fund.'

She testily declined my offer but bagged up the list and labelled it. I still wouldn't let them see they'd rattled me but thought, 'You dozy, untrusting cow. If you want to play like that, carry on,' and I just left them to it. But after five minutes I thought to myself, 'Get wise, Bradders, they could be doing anything in there,' so I went back in to keep an eye on them. They bagged and labelled a few things - not as much as I expected - but then there was very little for them to find. I read later that they'd emptied the dustbins of Jamie and Dean and if they did do that to me, I still haven't had the rubbish returned.

I was wandering around in a bit of a daze and asked if I could use the phone, so I called Bob who was great and very calm. I asked her to ring Norm, Mandy, Gary and Jackie and, most important of all my trusty solicitor in Leeds, Peter McCormick. Was I going to need him!

When they'd finished in the office the police asked for my mobile and phone book, which didn't cause me any problem as I'd already got a duplicate one, just in case I ever lost it. They went through every room in the house but surprisingly never opened a drawer or looked under a pillow. When they started poking around the bedroom my heart began racing, a bit like coming under orders for the National, but they never investigated that mucky linen bin. The three coppers were very courteous and after the search said that it was time to go to Charing Cross police station but before we left I grabbed a baseball cap in case of the Press because my hair was in a shocking mess and I never go anywhere without a shower first. I grabbed a scarf and a big thick coat because Deano had told me that it was bloody freezing in those cells.

As soon as the police car pulled away from West Street, Sparsholt, I leaned my head against the window and went to sleep - if they found their way here they could find their own way back without any directions from me. I woke up just as we were passing Buckingham Palace.

They took me in the back way of the police station and asked me to empty my pockets where I had a £50 note for the taxi home - another tip from Deano - and filled in the required forms for the custody sergeant. I had coped quite well with the harrowing situation of watching while my house was invaded, but it wasn't until they put me in that cell and then turned the key that I actually realised how my body was feeling. Bloody awful.

I was pleased I'd brought the coat - it was colder than a witches tit - and although it was the first time I'd seen a cell it was everything I expected and more. Completely functional, no frills, very empty, very plain with a toilet in the corner and a peephole in the door. I curled up on the bed in the foetal position and tried to sleep. The flap over the peephole slid open every 30 minutes but I didn't move. The police were quite pleasant and asked if I wanted tea and toast but I declined and said I'd rather sleep. In the meantime, Peter McCormick had arranged for a London-based solicitor to act for me and when Tamara Cooper arrived two and a half hours later I was mighty relieved to see her. She was a vision. Reassuring, professional and extremely confident, her advice was concise. 'No Comment' to everything until we had found out the precise wording of my charge.

I was waiting in the reception area for half an hour and I looked up on a white notice board and was astonished to see three names in felt pen. Cell 1 Bradley; Cell 2 Brooks; Cell 3 Cochrane. The last named was top Flat jockey Ray Cochrane who won the 1988 Derby on Kahyasi and I just couldn't see how they had put the three of us together. As for Charlie being dishonest, well, it was absolutely laughable. When they had come for him in the dawn raid he was in London and as his partner Miriam Francome said at the time, 'Just about the only thing Charlie's been guilty of in his life is underage drinking.'

When he strolled in with his solicitor I called over, 'Ola (Spanish for hello) Charles, fancy seeing you here.'

'Alright, Bradders?' He smiled, just before his solicitor tugged on his sleeve and whispered something in his ear. Charlie just turned to me and winked. In a strange way it was a bit like those prisoner of war films when the Germans keep bringing in escapees and the banter has to be kept going. When the police asked Charlie to empty his pockets I couldn't resist it. 'You won't find much in there, he never carries any money with him.' They took him off to his cell.

My interview lasted about half an hour and I soon knew what it was all about.

'We have reason to believe you conspired with others to fix the result of a horse race at Warwick on 5 November 1996. What do you have to say about that?'

Quite a lot actually, but 'No comment' would have to suffice.

I thought that Man Mood would never go away. This creaking wreck of a racehorse was coming back to haunt me into retirement.

As I was facing my police inquisitors I was engulfed by the same feeling which used to come over me when appearing before the stewards at Portman Square. The nervous system takes over your body. Despite appearing cool and co-ordinated, your mouth feels like you've just had a local anaesthetic from the dentist, and although your lips and jaw are moving, you can't feel them. Thank god all I was allowed to say was 'No comment.' If it had been any more demanding I simply wouldn't have been able to get it out. No matter how much self-control you have, you can feel your body shivering inside. You then become extremely self-conscious and think that everyone in the room can see you shaking.

'Do you know what choking is?'

'No comment.'

'Do you know what a broken blood vessel is?'

'No comment.'

'Do you know Dean Gallagher?'

'No comment.'

'Do you know Jamie Osborne?'

'No comment.'

They might as well have asked me if my father was called Norman because the answer would have been exactly the same. Tamara Cooper had been explicit. 'You can't answer one question then say no comment to the next. They can't force you to answer anything and you can say absolutely nothing and ignore them completely.

'But they have a list of questions and if you answer any of them, they can ask you a secondary point. These questions will come up time and again at different interviews and if you ever forget what you have said then contradict yourself it may weaken your position.'

It would have simplified the police procedure if I had answered, but my stubborn streak kicked in. Why should I? And while I'm not an educated man I reckon I'm very streetwise, so if I've got a lawyer sitting there advising me, I'd be a fool to ignore them.

There was, however, one question that nearly broke my concentration.

'Do you know anyone called Brian Wright, 'Uncle' or 'The Milkman?''

I couldn't help myself and laughed out loud. I remembered Brian's mother-in-law saying that she'd got him that job as a milkman all those years ago and that he'd now named his villa in Spain 'El Lechero', which is Spanish for 'The Milkman'.

No one else smiled, 'Note for recording, Bradley laughed when asked about Milkman or Uncle.'

They repeated the question.

'No comment.'

I was taken back to the waiting room and Ray Cochrane came in. What the hell did they want him for? I winked at Ray. He did the same and then I was sent back to the cells for an hour.

Ray's case concerned two races, one at Epsom in September 1996 and another at Goodwood in 1998. In the first, a four-runner race, Ray's mount Double Leaf drifted in the market to second favourite and finished second to the favourite, Magellan. At Goodwood his mount Fantastic Light drifted out to 9-4 and finished last. The former rails bookmaker Stephen Little was very unhappy about both races and also cast doubt on the integrity of the Flat v. Jump Jockeys flat race at Chepstow on 10 October 1995, which Declan Murphy won on Jibereen, his comeback ride from injury. It also turned out to be his last and he retired immediately after. In fact, the only dodgy thing about that Chepstow race may have been the draw for mounts, which saw Declan get on a horse that had a very good chance.

After my hour of solitary I was taken out and told by Tamara that I had been bailed until 10 March. I now felt very confused but I was sure of one thing, namely that I didn't fancy doing any interviews for the Press, who were waiting to pounce outside. The police, showing some compassion, let me out the back exit. I swiftly hailed a cab to Paddington and got a fast train to Didcot, where Bob met me on her way back from Hull. Michael Caulfield called round that evening and we talked through the events of the day with all its implications, but as far as I was concerned, life had to go on as normal.

I had two rides at Warwick the next day and at this stage there were no problems coming from the Jockey Club. The public outcry at the unfair removal of the licences of Osborne, Aspell and Gallagher had worked in my favour and a hand-delivered letter from the Jockey Club had been waiting for me at Charing Cross police station stating that I could ride on until further notice. When I walked into the changing room at Warwick all the boys, from the seniors right down to the conditionals, were upbeat and supportive. There was plenty of leg-pulling but it was just what I wanted. I've always had a good relationship with all the valets and Pat Taylor and his son Phil and John Edge were very protective.

Before racing started I was asked to do an interview for the Racing Channel and I readily agreed. The station had always been good to me and I was only too happy to oblige because I didn't have anything to hide.

Deano and myself were riding in the first and the photographers asked us if we'd go out together so they could get a shot. We had no problem with that and walked out to the paddock smiling, although with all the aggravation surrounding us there wasn't a lot to grin about.

I was riding Luke Warm for David Gandolfo, a larger-than-life trainer in every respect with a sense of humour to match his waist measurement. I strode up to him and the owners and said, 'Nice to see a bit of daylight again, I didn't see much of it yesterday. They took me in the dark and let me out in the dark!'

'Gandy' let out a bellow of laughter that engulfed our corner of the paddock. 'Glad to see your experiences haven't dented your sense of humour.'

It hadn't blunted my will to win either, and in a desperate battle to the line we just held off Punters Bar, ridden by my old friend from the north Peter Niven, by a short head.

It was clear that this was going to be a time when friendships were going to be important and even tested, but there was never any doubting the loyalty of Sir Alex Ferguson, the legendary manager of Manchester United. He had joined Charlie as an owner and Simon Sherwood had inherited both Sir Alex and his chaser Yankee Lord. And twelve days after my Warwick success I was in the boss's red and white colours in the Huntingdon winner's enclosure.

Simon, ever the pessimist, told Sir Alex to back his horse each way at 8-1 but to have his win investment on the even money favourite River Bay, which finished second. Fortunately, the footballing knight didn't take the same view as the owner of Man Mood, otherwise I could have found myself asking for my old room back at Charing Cross nick!

It was typical of Sir Alex to do something special for the yard Christmas party and he produced twenty tickets for the Southampton-Manchester United game, which is the nearest the Mancunians come to Lambourn in the Premier League. Unfortunately for Man United fans - though not for us of the Elland Road persuasion - the Red Devils were beaten, but that didn't stop us having a cracking night out after the game. The ever-obliging

Tom Butterfield kept the Queens Arms kitchen open for us until we arrived back at midnight. Sir Alex not only wined and dined well, he also loved getting involved in the gambling games shut the box and liars' dice. Word had got around that he was coming back and there were plenty of people who wanted to talk to him and ask him for an autograph. He made time for everyone, and when he went off to his bed at Charlie's place he had won over a whole new army of supporters.

The next morning he was up early to see me school Yankee Lord with the BBC cameras in action, but I made sure I had my Leeds United hat on over my riding cap just in case Eddie Gray and the boys ever saw the film.

I've become good friends with Sir Alex and thought it a great honour when he agreed to be patron of my benefit year. We still talk racing - only now I can tell him what to back without breaking the rules!

Despite these little oases of distraction I was still tormented by the charge which hung over me and 10 March couldn't come soon enough so that I could get the whole unpleasant business out of my life. By the time I was due to reappear at Charing Cross I had ridden ten winners, but no matter how much I tried to concentrate during a race the terrible stigma of arrest and bail would come back to dog me as soon as I'd unsaddled.

By 10 March the police had not provided any evidence against me, so Peter McCormick said it wasn't worth the expense of him coming down from Leeds. No evidence would mean no charge and the likely outcome was release. The only other option would be re-bail, so Tamara Cooper was left handling my appearance, which was due at 10 a.m. Unfortunately the traffic was bad and I didn't make it until 10.48. To level up the score, the police kept me waiting 40 minutes, but I wasn't worried because I thought my release was a formality. However, as soon as I was interviewed the police told me that I was bailed again to appear on 13 April. Unlucky for some.

Tamara Cooper was surprised and I was very disappointed and depressed. The only possible explanation was that the police were still trying to uncover something they thought would incriminate me.

At 4.30 Deano and Ray arrived and 15 minutes later they were released with all charges dropped. I was genuinely pleased for them both, especially Deano, who had gone through fourteen months of purgatory. But the strain told on him and ultimately he paid a high price. Deeply depressed, he began to drink too much and that piled on the pounds. With his confidence and self esteem at an all time low he began taking cocaine as a crutch. But the crutch became bigger and in April 2000 he failed a random test at Auteuil, Paris and was suspended for six months.

But for the moment, with those two home free, how did that make me look?

No matter how hard I tried to put it to the back of my mind and not worry the saga was starting to rattle my nerves. I became paranoid that I was under surveillance, especially as Deano's car had been fitted with tracking devices by the police. The first one fitted had been dislodged by the rough paths up to the gallops and the same thing had happened when a second was surreptitiously put in place.

I was convinced that my car, too, was bugged in some way and would never talk to anyone on my mobile phone or carry on a conversation in the car with a passenger unless the radio was on to act as a kind of scrambler.

The longer the inquiries went on the more edgy and embarrassed I became, but if I didn't think things could get much worse I was wrong.

I was riding Rightsaidfred in the Irish National at Fairyhouse on 5 April and came down three fences out when all chance of a place had gone. I landed hard on my right shoulder and as I lay on the ground I began to feel sick, a sure sign that something was broken. Unlike some of my colleagues, I've got a very low pain threshold and as I waited for an hour to be moved by ambulance to the local hospital the pain grew progressively worse. Dr Walter Halley and myself were convinced I'd broken my shoulder, even if it was only a hairline fracture. But at Blanchardstown Hospital in Dublin I was given a shot of morphine and had X-rays taken which surprisingly showed nothing broken. I was in too much pain to fly and Jason Titley's girlfriend Leoni Reynolds, daughter of former Irish Prime Minister Albert Reynolds, put me up in her flat in Dublin. Titley repaid me for the nights I'd put him to bed when he lodged with me by very tenderly undressing me and tucking me in.

When it came to flying home the next day, Aer Lingus were as helpful as ever. Their representative at Dublin, Jodi FitzGerald, changed my economy non-refundable ticket up to business class so I could travel back in some comfort. It was just another example of that airline and Jodi in particular going out of their way to help the racing industry. But there was another problem on the horizon - as if I didn't have enough.

Suny Bay was preparing for a third crack at the Grand National and the race was only five days away.

Despite having been beaten in his last two outings - he'd fallen in the Ericsson Chase in December and pulled up in the Gold Cup - the old grey had begun the season brightly with repeat wins at Haydock in the Edward Hanmer and Tommy Whittle Chases. Naturally, I was desperate to be on him for what would turn out to be our last active appearance together in the world's most famous chase. But contingency plans needed to be put in place and, because Andrew Cohen wasn't keen on Deano riding Suny Bay, I got Titley the ride.

When I woke the morning after the fall the shoulder had settled down and I drove straight down from Heathrow to visit my physiotherapist 'Rabbit' Slattery at her surgery in Baydon, just outside Lambourn. Rabbit is the daughter of the remarkable Mary Bromily, who revolutionised sports physiotherapy for jockeys and lectures worldwide on human and animal injuries in sport. Rabbit has learned well from her mother, using her skills to get countless jockeys back in action in half the conventional time. She deduced that I had sprung the joint which joins the collarbone to the shoulder and predicted that with extensive physio twice a day and painkillers I would just about make it in time for Aintree.

Richard Guest had introduced me to Froben, an extremely effective anti-inflammatory drug, and after three 100 mg tablets taken four hours before racing on Friday I could have swung on a trapeze by the time I was due to be tested by the course doctor before riding Door To Door in the three-mile novice hurdle. In order to pass the doctor and prove my fitness I did five press-ups for him in front of the BBC cameras - that's as many as I could have usually done with two good shoulders.

Unfortunately, Suny Bay was not the force of old. When I'd schooled him at home before the big race he'd tried to refuse, which was most unlike him, and I reckoned he now needed blinkers to sharpen him up. But they weren't applied and the old horse didn't do a tap in trailing round to finish thirteenth. Still, you couldn't begrudge him getting a bit fed up with the game. He'd been doing it a long time and owed no one anything. I knew just how he felt.

With everything piling on top of me I seriously began to contemplate retirement at the end of the season. I was still enjoying the Ascots, Aintrees and Cheltenhams but traipsing to the gaffs on Monday, Tuesday and Wednesday was a different story. I'd spent twenty-three years trying to prove myself and I'd had enough. And if it hadn't been for the urge to remove the slur of the arrest, I probably would have quit there and then.

But one major incident might have changed my whole outlook and seen me ride on into my forties. I knew my bottle was still firmly intact and I was riding as well as ever when one morning, three weeks before Cheltenham, a good friend of mine, Tim Collins, rang and asked if I would like to ride his smart novice chaser Looks Like Trouble in the Sun Alliance Chase. I'd ridden a lot of winners for Tim on a bonny little horse called Go Universal and finished second on him in the Tripleprint Gold Cup at Cheltenham and the John Hughes Chase over the Grand National circuit in 1996. Tim is an extremely affable and generous man with whom I'd had countless rounds of golf, dinners and piss-ups. I'd even been on holiday with him - all at his expense.

If the ground was good and Looks Like Trouble ran then I said I'd love to be on him. Andrew Hoy had worked wonders with the horse's jumping and it was Tim's dream to have a Festival winner. He said he'd get back to me and I was surprised when nothing happened, because I thought I would have had a call from his trainer Noel Chance to come and school the horse.

I rang my agent Dave Roberts and told him the situation, and he replied that as far as he knew either Norman Williamson (who was committed to Nick Dundee) or Paul Carberry were going to ride the horse. I phoned Noel straight away and asked him what was going on. He said it was the first time he'd heard my name mentioned but if Tim wanted me that was fine. They were meeting in the morning and he would let me know. I phoned Dave the following lunchtime only to be told that Paul had been booked. I called Noel, who said he wanted someone he knew and rode for him regularly. A little agitated by now, I reminded him that Paul had been back riding in Ireland for the last year. Still no joy. Noel wasn't having me at any price. So I rang Tim. 'I thought you booked me for your horse at Cheltenham?'

'Brad, you misunderstood. I asked you whether you would like to ride him, not would you ride him.'

It was my mistake. I misjudged the strength of a friendship. But Looks Like Trouble won the Sun Alliance following the career-ending fall of Nick Dundee and went on to win the 2000 Cheltenham Gold Cup. I was genuinely delighted for Tim and was one of the first to congratulate him, but a year earlier with all the turmoil, I could have really done with his backing.

13 April arrived with Charlie now back in the country having been away in South Africa when he was due to answer bail in March.

The police had still produced no evidence and, with my solicitor Peter McCormick already engaged in a trial, he sent colleague Rob Rode down from Leeds to represent me. With no evidence and no charge they couldn't possibly bail me again, so surely I had to be released.

Not that the police hadn't been very busy with their inquiries. One of the detective constables on the case had given his number to two third parties telling them to persuade me it would be a good idea to ring him for a chat. The first to be approached - and for the life of me I can't think why - was the Malton trainer Nigel Tinkler. The other was Charlie's former assistant Ed James, who was now training in his own right.

There was another approach to a bookmaker at Warwick who is related through marriage to a jump jockey. When he said he couldn't help the police with their inquiries he was told, 'Well, you know the race was bent, don't you?'

As snippets like this began filtering back I could have been forgiven for getting paranoid and I was still apprehensive as I made the journey up the M4. My good friend Nicky Gill, who I had ridden several winners for on his grand old hurdler Montagnard, was doing the driving. Nicky, who once looked after that good horse Canasta Lad when he was a stable lad with Peter Bailey, has never lost his love of racing even though he has amassed considerable wealth through his building business. He always stays with me at the converted barn I rent for Cheltenham, and the year after I won the

Champion Hurdle on Collier Bay we were walking past one of the art stalls which had an oil painting of the victory. It was a striking work if a bit pricey at £2,800. Half an hour after the last race on Thursday we all went to the weighing room for the usual party, but there was no sign of Gilly until he walked in 20 minutes later with a large brown paper parcel under his arm which he shoved into my chest, 'There you go, present for you.' I knew what it was before I opened it and broke down straight away. It was the painting of Collier Bay. The qualities of some people in this game are unbelievable.

Gilly and my ever-loyal fiancée Bob completed the somewhat subdued party cutting its way through the London traffic and they dropped me off with just a short walk to the police station before making their way to Langan's Brassiere for lunch.

I was concerned that I hadn't got Peter McCormick in my corner because I have absolute faith in him, whereas I had never met Rob Rode before. He was considerably younger than Peter, but after a 15-minute chat we were ready for the interview. It didn't start well.

It was the same small room and Rob moved his chair about two feet to the left so that he had room to cross his legs. The police didn't like this at all and accused him of manoeuvring into a position where he could see their notes. It knocked me off balance mentally and when the 'Record' button was pressed on the tape I felt as though lockjaw had set in. Rob requested any evidence and if they could produce none then said he had told me to make no comment. They had none.

It was the same stupid, stupid questions again and I did as I'd been instructed, 'No comment, no comment.' The policemen began to get verbally aggressive and if I'd had a million pounds I'd have willingly paid it to have Peter McCormick sitting next to me.

Every other question seemed to concern Brian Wright, and then the golfing holiday in Spain cropped up. There was absolutely nothing in it but the stock reply came out. 'No comment.'

The interview was terminated and they said they were going to talk with the office of the director of public prosecutions. They were away no longer than ten minutes before returning to immediately read out a charge:

'Graham John Bradley, you are charged that on or before the 5 November 1996 within the jurisdiction of the Central Criminal Court you did conspire with others to win for yourself or others from bookmakers sums of money through wagering on the event of a horserace at Warwick on November 5 1996, by fraud or other unlawful devices in that together you agreed that Man Mood, ridden by you, would not win the said race. You have been charged under section 1 (1) of the Criminal Law act of 1977.'

I felt as though they were talking about someone else and in some bizarre way that I was just an observer. Rob Rode was visibly shaken and in a few seconds the seriousness of the situation hit me. 'Charged, me? They've got to be fucking mad.' As all the possible repercussions came in thought-waves thumping at the back of my forehead. 'There's not one shred of evidence because there is none to get, yet the bastards have still charged me. How's my dad going to feel when he starts reading all this in the papers?'

Then the fickle nature of British justice began to seep into my mind and I became annoyed and bolshie. 'What a bloody waste of time, more travelling into London, more solicitors, more expense. Fuck me! What if it gets to a trial? It'll clean me out.'

After I'd inwardly calmed myself down I convinced myself that it could never get to trial but that didn't stop the dehumanising process. Now they wanted fingerprints, DNA samples and a mugshot for the files. I had each finger and thumb rolled into black ink and then on to white paper as I'd seen happen in countless films when the criminal breaks down: 'It's a fair cop, guv.' Well, bollocks, there was nothing fair about this.

I had a choice with the DNA sample, either hair follicle or saliva.

I told them 'Leave the bonce alone, I've not got much left as it is,' so they rolled a cotton bud around my mouth for ages and then sealed it in a bottle. They said that if I was cleared I could personally come back to the station and watch it all destroyed. Fat chance of that. Once I was out of this place, they'd never get me back.

Charlie had been and gone very quickly with no charge brought and I was very, very pleased for him. All the same, he had suffered for no reason. He had lost his regular slot on Radio Five Live and was left holding a five-figure legal bill that was non-contestable because, like Dean Gallagher, he hadn't been charged. But most damaging of all was the harm done to his reputation and Charlie was the last person in the world who deserved that. It should never have happened and I hope someone in Jockey Club Security suffers serious pangs of guilt at regular intervals.

I'd arrived at 11.25 a.m., five minutes early and three hours later I was let out of the back door, jumped into a cab, rang Bob and Gilly with the bad news and then joined them at Langan's. I didn't feel like any of the bubbly that Gilly had put on ice and only managed to eat a starter. I had to apologise to the manager for my mobile phone going off continually and I couldn't wait to get home.

I did all my important calls during the hour and a half trip home and, when I finally crossed the front door at 8.30, I put the answer phone on and went straight to bed. I was drained, embarrassed and couldn't face speaking to anyone.

I was due at Bow Street Magistrates Court the next day. Once again I couldn't have Peter McCormick to lean on as he was still otherwise engaged, but I wanted a good man at my side. Michael Caulfield, whose late father was High Court Judge Sir Bernard Caulfield, secured Stephen Clayton who, despite being in his early fifties, was professionally described as a junior barrister.

Michael, Bob and I got the train from Didcot and took a cab to Bow Street and when we told the driver our destination he replied, 'Oh, it'll be busy round there today. That crooked jockey's up and there will be loads of Press and cameras.' He was right.

I arrived at 9.30 a.m., half an hour early, and had a preliminary chat with Mr Clayton, who was very decent. As we were talking we were gradually joined by five other men with their briefs: Adam Hodgson, Glen Gill, John Matthews, Jason Moore and Ray Butler were due to be committed for trial, charged with doping Lively Knight and Avanti Express. I had never seen or spoken to or knew any of them. You come across thousands of people in racing and from all walks of life, but I'd never been near any of them.

At 10.30 a.m. I was called through to Court No.1. Michael and Bob came with me and we sat on a bench and heard the end of the previous case where a massive bloke had been tried and found guilty of terrorising a girl in her car. He had put his fist through the window and threatened her. The judge handed down a six-week custodial sentence and as he was led down to the cells his girlfriend passed him his washbag. He must have known what was coming.

I was called to the dock, which had room for about ten and over the years had held some of the most notorious gangs in criminal history. I shuffled nervously to the far corner and put both hands on the rail which runs along the front. The barristers benches were packed with briefs and I thought, 'Great, I'm first in. They can get me out of the way before they deal with the other five.'

Then, one by one, their names were called and they came to stand beside me. My heart started to quicken and I wanted to shout out, 'What the fuck's going on? Why am I in here with these boys? I've got nothing to do with their case. I've never seen them before in my life, let alone met them!'

I looked across at my brief with my forehead creased to convey my concern, but he was engrossed in some papers. The court was now deadly silent and I would have felt conspicuous if I'd so much as cleared my throat.

Clifford Allison, the prosecutor, stood up. He was a big man, running to fat, with grey wavy hair somewhat dishevelled and with glasses. Despite a good suit he wasn't a winner in the sartorial stakes and he reminded me of a rather larger version of Rumpole Of The Bailey, which until now was my sole reference for this sort of thing.

As he began addressing the court I could hardly hear what he was saying because his voice was so low, but the gist of his speech was that I was in some way linked to the other five. I picked up phrases like 'Crimes of a serious nature, forensic evidence, witness, passports withheld' and there was even mention of 'sleeping with the fishes!' I was stunned that my brief hadn't been on his feet shouting an objection. McCormick would have been up and down like a jack-in-the-box.

The prosecutor continued, saying that investigations were still in progress and it was unclear whether the six would be tried together or I'd have a separate trial.

This was doing my head in. 'Separate trial, you morons!' I inwardly screamed, 'I've done nothing wrong. All I've done is pull up a horse that was distressed and, what's more, the fucking yak has done the same bloody thing since.'

I thought about the miscarriages of justice in the past, including Timothy Evans and Derek Bentley, who were hanged and then pardoned decades later. I was beginning to have my doubts about British justice.

Despite the prosecutor's best efforts, bail was granted at £15,000 and I was told to reappear eight weeks later on 9 June. I had to surrender my passport and pay the money, but most of my disposable income was tied up, so I phoned a long-standing friend of mine, David Metcalf, who immediately posted bail. David and I would be linking in much happier circumstances later in the year.

When we regrouped outside the court I was too shocked to get stuck into Mr Clayton and, in any case, what went on in court could have been par for the course for all I knew.

Bob and Michael left with me and I stopped for photographs - there didn't seem any point in an undignified chase down the street like some pop star on a marijuana charge. I still felt I had nothing to fear so I faced the Press and answered the questions. I told them I was looking forward to my ride at Cheltenham the next day, Country Star, then got in a cab and headed for Paddington.

I was lucky that Tony McCoy was staying with us while his new house was being finished. 'Wee Anthony', or 'The Child' as Bob calls him, has a wonderfully dry sense of humour and he was just what I needed. He kept me smiling until I went to bed and was loyalty personified the next day, but then that's exactly what I'd have expected. He drove Bob and me to Cheltenham and made sure he was by my side when I walked in past the barrage of photographers, but it was a relief to get to the weighing room.

I felt safe in there and everyone was on top form, desperately keen to show their support to keep my spirits up. When it was time to go out for the two-mile handicap chase the boys lined up to make a path for me into the parade ring. Charlie and his mother Caroline, who owned Country Star in partnership with Mrs Stella Towler, were waiting with Ed James, who trained the horse. It was grand to see Charlie and for a few minutes it was just like old times. Country Star had been given to Charlie's mum by his former owner Fahd Salman when the horse broke down, and when I mounted him and trotted round the paddock, there was a warm ripple of applause from the crowd. It was a touching response, especially as I didn't know if it was the last time I'd hear it.

Country Star had a good chance and went off 5-2 favourite. I took him ahead four fences out and he was going well enough for me to think we'd win when he shattered a hind leg before the next fence and I swiftly pulled him up. He was put down within minutes and Sarah, the girl who looked after him, was inconsolable. What could have been a fairytale had turned into a nightmare.

After I got changed I went round all the valets and gave them a hug. I was saying goodbye because in my heart of hearts I thought I'd had my final ride. On previous form I couldn't see the Jockey

Club letting me keep my licence. What's more, the trial could be two years away and by then I'd be finished. I was inwardly seething but there was diddly-squat I could do about it. I would go to the Jockey Club the next day and fight for my livelihood. Fortunately, in a tremendous show of solidarity Peter McCormick cut short his holiday in Spain to be with me. His wife is due my sincere thanks for being so understanding.

We met in the Churchill Hotel for breakfast, but even that great statesman was beaten on occasions and despite the most brilliant oration and argument, Peter never really stood a chance of saving my licence. The hearing was moved above the disciplinary and licensing stewards to the Stewards of the Jockey Club themselves, represented by Chairman Gurney Sheppard, David Oldrey and Michael Wyatt. After they handed down their decision the only right of appeal was in the High Court.

Public and Press response had been positively in my favour, but that counted for nothing at Portman Square and after a 45-minute hearing and 90 minutes of deliberation, my licence was suspended. In a prepared statement, Senior Steward Christopher Spence said, 'The Stewards have not made a judgement on whether or not Graham Bradley is guilty of the charge laid against him but have decided that, in view of the nature and the gravity of the charge, it is inappropriate for a licensed jockey to continue race-riding. It is the Jockey Club's responsibility to preserve the integrity of racing.'

McCormick countered expressing, 'grave concern and astonishment' and argued that the Jockey Club 'had effectively bypassed our justice system and acted as judge and jury.'

Peter did a magnificent job for me but thought that the decision had been made the day before. In short, nothing he or I could have said would have made the slightest difference to the outcome. The Jockey Club tried to sugar the pill by awarding me a payment of £29,000 a year, which would have been the same amount I would have received had I been injured. And in many ways I was injured, because my pride had been knocked and my spirit had taken a severe battering. But at least the money would cover the £2,000 a month that went out in bills.

Up until now I had put on a positive face in public and in order to keep that up I needed an hour to compose myself and settle my emotions before I faced the media. I phoned Dave Roberts and told him I wouldn't be riding tomorrow and then called my dad.

Now composed, I went outside and stated the facts which were that I was very disappointed and that surely each and every one of us is innocent until proven guilty. I reiterated that I had done absolutely nothing wrong and that I was going to fight to the end to clear my name. I thanked my family, friends and Michael Caulfield for their invaluable support and even the Press because, with a few exceptions, they had been very fair to me. I met my sister Mandy and Bob in the Churchill Hotel, where I did a telephone interview for the Racing Channel. After I'd put the phone down I felt exhausted but there was still some very serious thinking to do.

CHAPTER 31
Wandering in the wilderness

As I walked back past the Churchill Hotel and saw my reflection in the darkened glass façade a terrible feeling of finality hit me. I cherished being a jockey and a sportsman and I'd been lucky to earn a living doing something I loved. It had opened doors that would otherwise have been closed and I'd met fascinating people from all walks of life. Most important of all, I'd earned the respect of my peers, which is a jewel beyond price.

I owed racing a lifetime, it owed me nothing. I wasn't a jockey any more and I probably never would be again. I felt like an outcast walking in the wilderness.

But I quickly learned I wasn't alone and was bolstered by a groundswell of support within racing led by 'Wee Anthony', who said, 'I'm gutted. I've been living with Brad for three or four weeks and I know what he's been going through. Anyone who knows Graham Bradley will agree he's a perfect gentleman and if this Jockey Club decision finishes his riding career it will be one of the worst things to happen to racing for a long time.'

Tony continued to show tremendous solidarity above and beyond the call of duty. He refused to move out of the house during the upheaval in case it was seen as a negative response or that he was in some way deserting a lost cause. No doubt there were plenty of people whispering in his ear that he was doing himself no favours by publicly linking himself to me. They might as well have shouted at the moon. McCoy stayed loyal.

Richard Dunwoody said, 'We are all, very, very disappointed and we will do everything in our power to get his licence back. I am very aggrieved at what has happened to Brad.'

Trainer Di Haine made a pointed protest when she withdrew Gemstone - a horse I was due to ride for her at Stratford the day after my licence was taken - and there was support from Michael Dickinson, who phoned from the States as soon as he heard what had happened.

'Listen, Brad, I'm there for you. Whatever it takes I will do it. I'll fly over the best vet in the world, who will explain absolutely everything so that any jury will be able to understand why you pulled that horse up.' To know that Michael was pulling on the team lifted my spirits considerably.

But in the cold light of the following day I had to regroup and take stock of what was becoming an increasingly desperate situation. The road ahead was going to be hard and I didn't know how long, but there was one thing I did know. It was going to be very expensive and that put the fear of god into me. Not only could my career be finished, I could end up potless into the bargain.

As I sat in my study and read through the legal bills one very sad fact emerged. I simply could not afford to retain Peter McCormick over what could be a very long period. Peter was the best, but he charged like a wounded bull, and even though he had been incredibly understanding to me, I would have to let him go. His bill to represent me on my last appearance was frightening, but in a show of great friendship he cut it in half and it was covered by the Jockeys' Association legal insurance. However, Peter required a £5,000 retainer up front to represent me for the rest of the case and that told me he was now out of my league. I felt as though I'd lost a limb when I told him my decision, but he understood a 100 per cent and I go on record as saying he was the most brilliant solicitor I ever engaged.

But the stories I had heard about costs incurred by footballers Bruce Grobbelaar, Hans Segers and John Fashanu in the recent soccer bribes case had me running scared. Even though they were acquitted they were left with bills running into half a million I couldn't face that prospect.

Like most people, I didn't understand the complicated legal system of awards and costs until I was embroiled in it. George Carman QC's reputation and record means he would be the first name on many people's list of barristers, but there is a limit on the amount that can be awarded out of public funds. Any charges above that must be met by the individual and, as in most walks of life, the top tradesmen don't come cheap.

Clearly, I had to find legal representation from somewhere. The phone was going non-stop with well-meaning advice and several legal firms with horseracing experience offered their services for whatever costs were awarded - if any.

I was moving in ever-decreasing circles and becoming more confused by the day. Having naive faith in the British justice system and knowing I had nothing to hide, I seriously considered defending myself. But that would have been stupid. If it came to the Cheltenham Gold Cup, did I want A.P. McCoy to ride my horse or an amateur? End of argument.

I knew that deciding who would defend me would be the hardest and most important decision I would make in my life. With that in mind I spoke to someone who had gained unwanted but valuable experience in the ways of the Law, Jamie Osborne. He unhesitatingly recommended Steven J Barker of Barker and Gillette, New Cavendish Street, London, and I was extremely happy with that appointment. Steven was brilliant and very organised. He was also young, which made it easy to talk with him and explain how I felt. Another plus point was that since defending Jamie until all charges were dropped he had amassed a very good working knowledge of racing which would be priceless. He also didn't require a retainer, wouldn't bill me every month, and would keep costs to the bare minimum. This man was a saint.

Then on April 20 1999 a hurricane blew in that was about to uproot everything.

My mobile phone rang on the coffee table in the lounge and I went out to the garden to get a better signal. Sparsholt is in a fold of the downs and reception is always bad, but there was no mistaking the brusque London accent at the other end.

In very firm words of minimum syllables, Brian Wright said, 'Get Bob's phone and go to where there's a good signal - I'll phone you back.'

I'd become paranoid about using the analogue phone line at home and also the public box at the end of the road. My fear was that both had been bugged, so I made all confidential calls from either of our mobiles.

I leapt into the Merc and went to the top of the Faringdon Road which overlooks Wantage and Lambourn. I turned the engine off and sat at the end of the gallops used by Nicky Henderson and Barry Hills. I waited with five bars of maximum power showing on the mobile display and, after ten minutes, it buzzed into life. It was Uncle and he was on fire.

'What the hell are you fucking about at? Those bastards want your head on a spike, you're the scapegoat. The police, Jockey Club and Buffham all need you to go down to save their fucking arses.

'They'll do anything to get a conviction and you need the best brief there is.'

Talk about going weak at the knees. I'd had some bollockings from trainers in my time and the police had been verbally hard, but it was nothing like this. One of my greatest and most trusted friends whose opinion I truly respected was verbally laying into me with his size nine boots. In all the time I'd known him I had never heard him so angry.

'But Bri, it's going to cost me a fucking arm and a leg.'

'Never mind the money, I'll see to that. You need a top criminal defence lawyer and I know the top man. Take this number down and get on to him as quick as you fucking well like - but move!'

I knew that when I punched in the number of Law Mooney Solicitors I would be raising a few eyebrows. They were already representing one of the alleged dopers, and my family and friends would be appalled that I was apparently on the same legal team. But Brian was my man. I trusted him so implicitly that it didn't matter what anyone else thought. Sure enough, Bob wasn't happy and neither was Norm. 'It doesn't sound very good to me,' was his taciturn summary.

Piers Pottinger of Bell Pottinger (Mayfair) wasn't ecstatic either. I'd known him for many years and had ridden winners for him when he had horses in training with Mark and Sara Bradstock. He is a lovely man who was handling all my press and PR for absolutely nothing. Piers has the best connections and is the right man to have in your corner when there's a big fight in the media.

But I wasn't for moving. I arrived at the Smithfield Street offices of Law Mooney the next day where I met Paul Rexstrew. And after a two-hour briefing I walked out of that office with a spring in my step that had been missing for months.

Firstly, he said there was no need to worry about money, which was a cracking start, and he also told me not to worry about feeling compromised by association. It was a partner in his office who was acting for one of the alleged dopers and it was quite a common occurrence for members of the same legal practice to be involved in the same cases but on different sides. Paul then had a meeting with Piers, which put his mind at rest, and various strategies were devised concerning the media.

The only man who seemed to have a problem now was Mr Clifford Allison of the Crown Prosecution London Branch 1 A, who wrote to me saying that there was considerable interest in my case from four different law companies. Messrs Chalk Smith Brooks (Stephen Clayton), Messrs McCormicks (Peter McCormick), Barker Gillette (Steven Barker) and Law Mooney were all asking for committal papers and requesting standard advance disclosure on my behalf.

He said that he was a bit confused by the situation. Well, if he was confused, how did he think I felt?

I replied, giving Paul Rexstrew power of attorney and then made my apologies to the other parties who were extremely understanding, being well aware of the strain I was under.

The committal papers arrived in two boxes over 1,500 sheets of paper and, with Bob driving, I used the journey to and from Wetherby for a family visit to wade my way through them.

God knows how many trees gave up their lives to produce all the paper, but only three sheets related to me and they contained a statement from Mr Julian Robbins, owner of Man Mood saying that he wasn't happy with the ride I gave his horse at Warwick.

Coming from a man who, in my opinion, wouldn't know a horse if it farted in his face, I was amazed to see this was the sum total of evidence against me. Rexstrew was incredulous and told me that, in his opinion, the CPS had taken a liberty and that I should never have been subjected to such torment. His only explanation was that they had nothing at the moment and were looking for something to come up.

A man can only be charged with concrete evidence and Rexstrew felt that if I had the resources I should be able to sue the police.

Later I was shown a statement from a man who used the unoriginal alias of 'John Smith' making some wild allegations that were complete bollocks.

I'd have liked to see him in the witness box against a decent brief and trying to make his fairy tale stand up.

In it he said, 'I was told about a race in which I backed the favourite in a two-runner steeplechase that took place on 5th November 1996 at Warwick. The horse I had backed had in fact been pulled up by arrangement with the jockey ... As a direct result of my outrage I then decided to make contact with the Jockey Club through an advertisement I had seen in the racing papers called 'Raceguard'. This being a facility run by the Jockey Club to enable people to give information anonymously about wrongdoings within the horseracing industry. I knew that the Jockey Club offered a reward of up to £5,000 for information that would assist them. This was another factor which prompted me to phone Raceguard and give information.'

Because of the high-profile nature of the case I hadn't been on a racecourse since riding Country Star. Although the Jockey Club had suspended my licence I could still go racing, although I wasn't allowed in the jockeys' changing room. But there was an added bane to my life in the conditions of bail, which stipulated that I must spend each night at my home. If I wasn't going to be there I was to phone Detective Constable Peter Kelly of the Metropolitan Police Organised Crime Squad and let him know where I was going to be. So, whenever I was travelling anywhere I would put in the call to New Scotland Yard and let Det. Con. Kelly know exactly where I would be and when. I couldn't even get pissed at the Queens and stay overnight without letting him know.

I was beginning to miss racing badly, but I just didn't feel I could stand all the extra attention of people rubber-necking me and talking behind their hands. I thought I'd stand out worse than Quasimodo. But the Punchestown Festival was starting on April 27 and I desperately wanted to go. I loved the place with a passion even if I wasn't riding. It had become a pilgrimage.

I flew on my own to Dublin on the Monday night before the first day and, after booking into the Burlington, I ordered room service and didn't move. I couldn't face going to any of the old haunts where I'd had the red carpet rolled out for me and danced on it. I

367

became more edgy and couldn't sleep and at 3 a.m. I phoned Bob and told her I was coming home that day. I just couldn't go to a racecourse.

But she knows me better than anyone and slowly talked me round, reassuring me that going home was the last thing I should do and that everything would be fine.

I wasn't convinced but made my way to Punchestown and met a friend, Michael Burke, outside. We made for the owners' and trainers' entrance, which was marshalled by a lovely man called Robert. I produced my Racecourse Association swipe card and said, 'I don't know if this will be any good here.' His reply was warm and spontaneous. 'It might be no good in England, Graham, but it will always work over here !'

It was just what I needed, and it got even better.

The place was bursting and people kept going out of their way to come over and talk to me. A sweet girl named Elaine Nolan gave Michael and I tickets to the Punchestown Pavilion, a massive marquee with 150 tables where everyone seemed to meet. Before long I was table hopping like the old days. Michael and Sue Purcell, who I'd ridden winners for, called me over, as did Mr and Mrs Paddy Mullins. Willie and Jackie Mullins were great and Mick O'Toole also made a fuss of me.

Paul Shanahan found out I was on the course and made it his business to find me. He then took me off to the Coolmore Stud box to have a drink with Mr and Mrs Magnier, Demi O'Byrne and Timmy Hyde.

Enda Bolger strode up, 'How's it going, Brad?'

Considerably brighter now and feeling in the mood to laugh I said, 'Not bad - for a man who's looking at between five and ten years!'

We rocked around laughing, but it was no laughing matter. When I'd put the hard word on Paul Rexstrew and asked him what the bottom line was, five to ten was the solemn answer he'd come back with. If I'd been found guilty of cheating on my own it would have been one to two years, but the all-important words were 'conspiracy to cheat.' And if proved, they more than doubled the possible sentence.

Despite that, I didn't have any of the insomnia of the previous night and on Wednesday evening David and Amber Done invited me to their party. Just the 500 guests and a great band with terrific food and drink. No wonder it always makes the gossip columns.

I came away from Ireland a different man and beavered away at my bloodstock business, which was beginning to take off. Meanwhile, Rexstrew was pressing the police for more evidence in the case and had received nothing.

Then on Monday June 7, 1999, I received the call from Paul that I had been praying for.

'Good news, Graham. All charges are going to be dropped when you appear at Bow Street on Wednesday. The Crown Prosecution Service have faxed me stating that they've got insufficient evidence to proceed.'

I jumped off the sofa and ran round the lounge jumping, punching the air and screaming 'yessssss!' A.P. and Bob thought I'd finally flipped.

I was buzzing with adrenalin and wanted to phone the whole, world but Rexstrew was firm. 'Don't say a word to anyone until the magistrate has said it first on Wednesday morning.'

It was impossible to keep completely quiet because I was so elated and relieved. Not bothering which phone I used, I called Norm, Mandy and Michael Caulfield, who had all been so stalwart. And I also got immense pleasure putting a call in to Brian Wright. He was now his customary calm self and said, 'Well done, mate. I'm very pleased for you.'

I don't usually read *The Times* but I felt very happy on the train journey from Didcot as I read the article by Richard Evans headlined, 'Bradley charges to be dropped today.' In it Evans stated,

369

'I understand there is a strong belief in legal circles that Bradley should never have been charged in the first place.'

It was like a symphony playing in my ears when I heard the magistrate Ronald Bartle say that the charge had been withdrawn before adding the sweetener, 'Defence costs would be met by central funds.'

I thanked the Lord it was all over. What had only been two months on charge had felt like the proverbial lifetime and I don't know how I would have coped it if had dragged on for two years before a trial date was set.

When we came out into the summer sunshine I was more than happy to discharge my obligations to the waiting media, just as I'd done when the prospects had looked grim. And I didn't waste the moment, thanking every person who had supported me through the most traumatic period of my life.

Soon after, Corky Caulfield, Bob and myself strolled over to the Waldorf to celebrate over a bottle of Laurent Perrier pink with Paul Rexstrew. I didn't waste any time before linking up Paul with Brian on my mobile.

Full of life and devilment, the next number I called was the Jockey Club, asking to see Richard Smith of the licensing committee about getting my licence back. I was told to apply on the required form so, after another bottle, I shimmied round to Portman Square and picked one up.

I was still baffled as to how the CPS could have enough evidence to charge me, yet two months later have insufficient to continue. Overall, though, I was too happy and relieved to be angry - although I still had a mountain to climb.

Mr Allison of the CPS observed, 'If, after further police investigations I alter my assessment of the evidence, the proceedings could be reinstituted. But it would be unjust on Mr Bradley to proceed while evidence does not exist in an admissible form.'

In that case, why the hell was I charged in the first place?

Paul Haigh, a columnist on the *Racing Post* who had been forced to print a retraction following an innuendo-riddled article on me in November 1992, was not one of those pleased at my buoyant state.

In a piece which appeared on June 12, Mr Haigh opened by saying, 'A few points about the Bradley case.

'Anyone who imagines that Bradley has been acquitted is in serious error. The charges against him have merely been dropped pending further investigation ....

'Jubilation among Bradley's friends - who in racing would dare to admit to feeling anything else in the present climate? - therefore seems a trifle premature.'

I've never had the pleasure of meeting Mr Haigh, nor do I know if he goes racing regularly or simply watches it in his local betting shop. He writes for a newspaper with an exceptionally high standard of journalism and many of his colleagues have an outstanding knowledge of racing. I often wonder under what guise he was employed.

But if I thought I was home free I was wrong.

We gradually made our way back to The Queens Arms, where Tom Butterfield had several more bottles on ice, but there was a maggot at the core of our party.

I was flying pretty high until two weeks later I heard that a taped conversation with me that night had been offered to the *News Of The World*. They had swiftly thrown it out because it wasn't what they wanted, but then how could it have been? All I did was slag off the Police, Jockey Club and in particular Roger Buffham - and I'd done that many, many times before.

Now, I can't be 100 per cent sure who it was but I'm 90 per cent certain. That 10 per cent is just sufficient to prevent me naming him, but the person will be reading this book and knows that I and many others in racing are aware how low he has sunk. To him I say,

'I just hope you can live with your conscience, because I can certainly live with mine.'

Racing had paid a high price for being in the headlines for all the wrong reasons. Toby Balding, speaking for the National Trainers' Federation, said, the Jockey Club 'should feel ashamed that the affair hasn't been handled with a little more skill.'

And he added, 'It would seem that this has been against natural justice and Buffham's role in this must be queried. It is quite wrong that someone of G Bradley's standing and reputation should be damaged in this way and it's quite wrong for racing, too.'

Another heavyweight, the flamboyant Channel Four Racing presenter John McCririck, was on the attack and said, 'It is a terrible, terrible day for Roger Buffham and the security department. I think Roger Buffham has no choice but to resign. He cannot go on as the head of an organisation that has wreaked such a catastrophe on the industry.'

The Sun ran a racing editorial under the headline 'Roger and out.'

'John McCririck is spot on - Roger Buffham must go.

'The Jockey Club head of security has allowed racing to be dragged through the gutter.

'The investigation which he started has seriously damaged public confidence in the sport.

'The five jockeys arrested have all been cleared - leaving Buffham looking a buffoon.

'For the good of racing, heads must roll at the Jockey Club.

'Starting with Buffham's.'

Despite all the anguish and heartache he had caused, Mr Buffham is still in office in the year 2000. I wonder what penalty the Jockey Club would have imposed on a trainer or jockey had they made such errors of judgement? But everyone in racing is well aware that when you sign for a licence you play by their rules - and there's one set for them and one for the rest of us.

The day after my final appearance at Bow Street, Bob and I drove to Cumbria for Tony Dobbin's wedding. We got a standing ovation when we walked into the reception, although I don't think I was able to walk out of it unaided.

But there was a sad finale when we returned home. With my charges finally dropped, A.P. McCoy finally decided the time was now right to fly our nest and move into his own - which had been ready for a long time. He'd been a rock for many months.

Thanks, buddy.

CHAPTER 32
Getting my chips

During my walk in the wilderness I'd had plenty of time for some hard self-analysis and certain facts had to be faced. I hadn't got quite so much hair as when I started out and what I had left was fighting the same unequal battle as the red squirrel - the grey was taking over.

I was nudging forty and still had the inclinations of a 21 year-old. But I knew the time was arriving when McCoy, Johnson and Williamson would come calling at the last fence and my mind would be making appointments which my body would not be able to honour. I'd got to find another way to make a living.

I wanted to stay in racing but there were certain no-go areas. While in some ways I would have been the ideal candidate for steward's secretary, I don't think I was quite the kind of ex-rider that the Club were looking for. In any case my conscience wouldn't let me turn my mates over. As far as the Jockey Club were concerned, I'd always be pissing into the tent, rather than out of it.

Training was definitely a non-starter. I'd seen too many good jockeys go to the wall at that game and you needed plenty of capital to start. Sure, I'd earned well, but I spent well, too, and what I'd got left I wanted to keep.

But there was one branch of the sport in which I was already proven and getting better - not only could I ride winners, I could buy them, too. I had started dealing quite early, buying and selling when Norm was training in his own right, and almost without exception they had done the job they'd been purchased for. Starjestic was a bit like me and had got a little more notorious as he'd got older, but he landed the touch for which he'd been bought and ended up winning eight races.

Border Tinker was another in which I'd seen potential. Like Starjestic he'd done the business when the money was down to land a massive coup at Sedgefield. I'd bought Fair Bavard, who went into training with the late Harry Wharton, who laid him out for a cracking touch in an amateurs' hurdle at Southwell, thereby providing the 'unknown' Jamie Osborne with his first winner.

Then there was Leisuretime Smile, bought for £5,000 at Doncaster Sales, who landed a touch at 14-1 in a novice handicap chase at Southwell in 1988. I'd also bought a three-year-old 'Quayside' gelding at the Derby Sale in Ireland and prepared him for the Doncaster Sale three months later, where he made top price on the first day. There had also been recommendations to trainers for horses that I'd ridden, including the likes of Padre Mio and Bokaro, both of them cracking servants.

But most importantly, I had located a source of good, tough jumpers which were tremendous value yet for some inexplicable reason had been ignored. While prices in Ireland were sky high and the French were fast catching them up, no one had considered Germany.

I had been riding there regularly at weekends since 1996 at Bad Harzburg and as the meetings were mixed, Flat and jumping, I stayed around to see how the British and French runners got on. It was a revelation. A horse like Swain, who went on to win the King George VI and Queen Elizabeth Diamond Stakes at Ascot in 1997 and 1998 had to fight hard to win. It was the same for such worldwide campaigners as Pilsudski and Running Stag, while the high-class Predappio also had to battle for glory.

And the Germans were no pushovers when they travelled overseas. Borgia was placed in two Arcs, the teak-tough Tiger Hill was also placed in France's greatest Flat race and Lando won the Japan Cup. It was crystal clear that the Germans didn't just produce reliable cars, they had robust horses, too.

And crucially, I had the right man on the ground over there in Paul Harley. I knew Paul from his days as a conditional jockey with Jimmy FitzGerald and later Nicky Henderson in Lambourn. He was never very big and had managed to control his weight to such a degree that he was riding on the Flat and regularly getting sixty or so winners a year.

He looked after me on my early trips when we shared the same hotel at Bad Harzburg and we became good friends. He spoke fluent German and the biggest plus of all was that he had ridden jumping and knew the type of horse I was looking for.

Friends were often asking me to buy a horse for them and Liverpool's twin strike force of Robbie Fowler and Steve McManaman were very keen to get involved. Clearly, it had to be the right article, because when it became public knowledge that they had a horse between them, the interest would be intense. The last thing I wanted was to be known for buying a high-class yak.

I set about sifting through the options, and the one thing that I always insist on when I'm contemplating a purchase is to ride the horse. Anyone can tell the difference between a mini and a Rolls Royce just by looking at them, but you wouldn't dream of buying either unless you had a test drive to see what the engine was like. And unlike many bloodstock agents I could find out what made a horse tick once I was on it. Their personalities are the key.

I'd watch their ears because you can tell a lot by what frightens a horse. What they look at is also important, as is how they react to other horses when they come near and how quickly they break into a sweat. You can understand a horse by the way he carries his head cantering and, most important of all, what his action is like when he's galloping. They're all different, just like a fingerprint, but whether they've got a high action or a low daisy cutter it is the suppleness of their shoulders which is the key to making a sound jumper. If I know nothing else, at least I can recognise a good horse.

So I knew what I was looking for, and I knew just where to find it. Auetaler was a grey five-year-old by the Irish St Leger winner Niniski who had won five races in Germany. He was a grand type, very tough, and he knew how to win. He also had another couple of bonus points in that he was to be trained in England by that genius Martin Pipe and ridden by the incomparable A.P. McCoy. Happily, Auetaler proved the ideal high-profile buy, winning his debut at Taunton with embarrassing ease and taking three other races in his first season. If anything, he was more impressive in defeat, finishing second to the highly-regarded Barton at Aintree and finishing third in the Swinton Hurdle at Haydock, beaten three and a quarter lengths by the subsequent Cambridgeshire winner She's Our Mare when attempting to give her 9lb. I think Auetaler would have won the County Hurdle at Cheltenham in 2000 if McCoy had ridden him. He was persuaded to partner another of the Pipe runners, but as I know to my cost, we all make mistakes. Robbie and Steve, who race the horses in the name of the Anfield Hombres Partnership, make sure that their families get maximum pleasure out of the horses they own and I managed to buy them another star in the making, Seebald. He won his first two novice hurdles in 2000 before being over faced in the Imperial Cup at Sandown.

I've bought several others - although I've always adhered to quality rather than quantity - and one who has done well for my old weighing room colleague Ronnie O'Leary is Aldino. Ronnie now trains in his native Ireland and has prepared Aldino to win a £10,000 hurdle at Fairyhouse and a £25,000 event at Navan. He looks a cheap horse now. There were other bargains like Iskan, who was backed off the boards when he won for Jonjo O'Neill at Carlisle.

And Almaravide won a £10,000 hurdle first time out at Cheltenham for Mark Bradstock then followed up at Market Rasen. But buying horses, just like riding them, is never a bed of roses, and one of my less expensive purchases provided a pocketful of aggravation. His name was Night Fighter.

When it came to buying horses I was gambling on my judgement. With the sums involved I had to see my bank manager, arrange for overdraft facilities and go to work. However, it was gambling of another kind which ultimately gave Night Fighter a much higher profile than he ever deserved. He also caused me to almost get my chips.

I had been introduced to a man named David Chopra. He was a massive gambler on anything, horses, dogs, football or casinos, it didn't matter. David played big and won and lost accordingly and he was a nice guy, too. He was keen to own a racehorse, so I went to have dinner with him at the Colony Casino in London a couple of times. The restaurant is excellent and it was crystal champagne all the time, but my sole purpose was to sell him a horse and on our third meeting I put Night Fighter up to him. The horse was useful in Germany, rated 86, and had won and been placed in good class races. A friend of David's was keen to be involved and gave me a cheque in payment for his share, but I had to wait long into the night before David paid me his. He asked me to watch him play roulette, which he did with some panache, averaging two to three grand a spin. Without warning he handed his friend two £5,000 chips which were swiftly passed on to me. It seemed a strange way to be paid but I was happy enough to get the dosh before David lost it. I went straight to the cashier to weigh them in and placed the £10,000 in two sealed packets in the inside breast pocket of my suit. It was now getting very late, so I left shortly after because I'd arranged to ride out the next morning, although David had given me the option of a suite at the Hilton if I wanted it.

A few days later I was called by one of David's friends, who told me he had suffered the fate of all gamblers. Having gone through a heavy losing streak and done his brains he no longer wanted Night Fighter. No problem, these things happen. I got in touch with Richard Guest. I told him that the horse would be ideal for his boss, Norman Mason, who owns a private stable at Brancepeth, County Durham, which Guesty runs. The deal was done, they bought the horse from David and Guesty sent the box down to pick up Night Fighter. That was the end of that, or so I thought.

Several events had taken place which I knew nothing about. First, it transpired that David Chopra was on the run from the police and had been imprisoned for credit card fraud, a verdict which was subsequently overturned. Also, my transaction with the £10,000 worth of chips at the Colony had been filmed on security cameras. The tape was then passed on to the National Criminal Intelligence Service and the Jockey Club had been made aware. Night Fighter had been busy - or not as the case may be - and had been banned from racing for forty days after being found guilty of not running on his merits at Perth on 21 August. Kenny Johnson, his jockey, was suspended for twelve days and Norman Mason, as the owner-trainer, was fined £2,250.

During the week preceding Sunday 24 October 1999 I opened my door to two *Sunday Times* reporters and, having nothing to hide, I invited them in just as I did the police and made them a cup of tea. They informed me that they had a 'Supergrass' who had told them that David still owned the horse and that when Night Fighter finished second when 11-8 favourite at Market Rasen in May a massive amount of drug money had been laundered by backing the horse in gambling dens on the Costa del Sol. They also told me that the 'Supergrass' had informed them that cash and prostitutes were being made available to jockeys as part payment for fixing races. There was only one piece of this familiar jigsaw missing now and it soon came out of the box ... 'Brian Wright, who lives on the Costa del Sol, is probably involved.' At least they said probably, but I knew it was absolute crap.

After asking if they were wired and whether they were taping the conversation - they said they weren't - I explained everything to them. I told them how much the horse had cost, about my friendship with Mr Chopra, why the horse was now owned by Norman Mason, and they went on their way. Then I opened the *Sunday Times* of 24 October and saw a lengthy expose entitled 'Taken to the Cleaners'. It was a load of bollocks, though I did learn that David Chopra was on the run, which surprised me. But I could not have cared less about meeting him. I had done nothing wrong and the prospect of another Jockey Club inquiry wasn't a problem as far as I was concerned.

But that Supergrass was making himself very busy and the only thing the paper got wrong when they mentioned him was to describe him as 'a senior jockey'. He was never that, although he was once connected to a high-profile yard in the Newbury area. He could have been the one who tried to sell a taped conversation with me to the *News Of The World* and he was also seen in the Calahonda area of Spain where the gambling clubs were located. And most interesting of all, he professes to an interest in photography and about the time of the *Sunday Times* activity he was caught skulking around Norman Mason's gallops. When he was challenged by a member of the staff he replied he was taking pictures of the local scenery. Didn't he realise there are some breathtaking views around the Lambourn area which is right on his doorstep, or perhaps he was looking for something that wasn't there? In a way, I feel sorry for him. Desperate people do desperate things, but this man has sunk lower than a snake's belly.

It wasn't long before Jockey Club Security got in touch. I'd relinquished my licence by now, and this latest intrusion really annoyed me. They'd deprived me of several sizeable chunks of my riding career and now they were trying to ruin my new one before it had hardly got off the ground. I began to feel very bitter. Would the bastards never let me go?

At the Newmarket October Sales I agreed to meet a member of the Security Department at the Jockey Club Rooms and endured a two hour interrogation. At the end of it he said, 'Thank you, Mr Bradley, I would like you to initial each page.' In measured tones I said, 'I haven't got the inclination, time or patience. Do exactly what you like with them, preferably stuff them up your arse.' With that, I got up and walked out, feeling much better. That was the last I heard on the matter until I received a letter dated 27 January, 2000 from Nigel Macfarlane, secretary to the Disciplinary Committee headed, 'Night Fighter (Ger)'. It stated: 'Dear Sir, The Stewards of the Jockey Club have considered a report into the sale and subsequent ownership of the above horse and have decided that there is insufficient evidence to warrant a Disciplinary Committee inquiry into a possible breach of the Rules Of Racing.'

Thankfully, despite the best efforts of the *Sunday Times* and the Jockey Club, my new company, Berkshire Bloodstock Ltd, was absolutely flying. Its growth would make the decision to retire easier when the time arrived, but before that I was to make one very significant purchase which would take me into a different league in the bloodstock world and, considering all the controversy that had dogged me for three decades, he couldn't have been better named. He was called Vicious Circle.

David Metcalf has already appeared in these pages as the man who stood £15,000 bail for me when I was charged with corruption in 1999. But our friendship spanned twenty years during which each of us had seen the fortunes of the other fluctuate alarmingly.

David was a top-class furniture maker based in Leeds who had installed a magnificent bedroom at my second home, Oak Ridge, and fitted a kitchen for me when I moved to Sparsholt. That business is now run by his son, Chris, and David has moved on to bigger and even better things in a telecommunications company with his partner Jeff Samuels. The pair had a dream. They'd had shares in horses before, but now they wanted to buy one between them and being good Yorkshire lads, they dreamed of it running in the most famous race at York, the Tote Ebor Handicap.

Three weeks before the race I took David's call, 'Brad! Go out and buy me a runner in the Ebor.'

It was hardly the easiest commission for a budding bloodstock agent to fill, but it was certainly a challenging one, so the first thing I did was phone one of the shrewdest and best connected men in racing, Ladbrokes PR guru Mike Dillon.

Mike has his finger on more pulses than a doctor in casualty. He went through every runner in the ante-post lists and told me what could be bought, what couldn't, what would stay the mile and six furlongs and what wouldn't. He produced a shortlist and I made enquiries about two with the right credentials, namely Paul Cole's Mowbray, who finished third, and Amanda Perrett's Prince Alex who ended up running poorly to finish only sixteenth. But top of the list was Vicious Circle, who at that time was a 33-1 chance. David's form man recommended Arabian Moon as another possibility and there was advice coming from all angles, so I took my time and weighed up the options.

The previous season, Vicious Circle had won a bad race over ten furlongs at Ayr on heavy and his poor run over a furlong less at Brighton was easy to forgive. He was a fine big horse who covered a tremendous amount of ground when he walked, so a switchback track like Brighton would have been useless to him. He'd won a £10,000 classified stakes at Newcastle on his first run of the 1999 season when giving a stone and more to younger horses, but it was his latest run that stood out. Again over the ten furlong distance that was much too short for him he had run the progressive Zindabad to three and a half lengths at Ascot. Despite being from a fast female line Vicious Circle was crying out for a longer trip. He was trained by Luca Cumani, one of the most intelligent practitioners of the training art in Newmarket. The horse clearly had improvement in him. Even if he didn't win the Ebor he had enough scope to go jumping later, so I phoned Mr Cumani to see if the horse could be bought. It transpired that Vicious Circle was owned by a syndicate of three and that he had been bought for 9,000 guineas after suffering a hairline fracture of a forearm as a two-year-old. As a yearling he'd cost 46,000 guineas and it was certain he was going to cost considerably more than that now. I was told to make an offer, so I opened with £100,000 with a contingency to give half the prize money back if he won the Ebor. They wanted a little more, so I offered £125,000 with the same deal on prize money. The bid was accepted, so I called David and he agreed, subject to the horse passing the vet.

However, one of the selling partners, Graham Shiel, had been very keen to keep his name out of the frame. Graham was a good friend of mine from the Borders who I'd ridden winners for when he had horses trained by that grand character Andy Scott. It was Graham who had bought Vicious Circle for 9,000 guineas, but he had been very firm with Luca not to let me know he had anything to do with the horse. He knew that the moment I got to hear he was involved I'd have been on the blower trying to knock him down. He knew me too well, because that's exactly what I would have done!

The new owners were looking for any good omens and one was that their horse was nicknamed Sid in the yard, alluding no doubt to that late charmer of the Sex Pistols, Mr Sidney Vicious. But Sidney also happened to be the name of Jeff's late father, which fitted in nicely.

The new owners were mad keen to use Frankie Dettori, but he was claimed for Sheikh Mohammed's Jaseur, trained by John Gosden. It transpired that Luca had already booked Kevin Darley, which was absolutely fine with me. When Michael Dickinson had moved to Manton I had recommended Kevin to him. Not only was he a top-class jockey, he was a very likeable man, too.

There was a nasty setback for David three days before the Ebor when he contracted a mouth infection which left him laid up in bed. He couldn't make the big day, which was a massive disappointment, but both he and Jeff had already lumped on the horse at 16-1 ante-post.

Now the doubts began to creep into my mind. What if the horse ran badly and got lapped? So, just to give David a lift I got his son Chris an interview on Channel Four Racing - Jeff was meant to go on too but got superstitious at the last minute - and suddenly Metcalf didn't seem quite so far away from the action.

I met Kevin with Luca in the parade ring and wished them both luck. Luca said to slot in behind the leaders about sixth or seventh and Kevin said that he'd challenge up the centre of the course where the ground was better.

Now, I've been in the parade ring thousands of times and I've yet to meet anyone cooler than me before a big race, but as a spectator I am the complete opposite. I was very nervy and at the same time very excited as I went to the members' stand and watched the early stages of the race on the big screen in the centre of the course. As the field turned for home Kevin and Sid were towards the rear - it wasn't going to plan. Just as he was making his move at the four-furlong pole he was turned sideways and lost valuable ground. The Ebor is always a rough race, but this was enough to get any horse beaten and I lost sight of him. I felt sure he was going to finish so far behind that you'd need radar to pick him up. In truth, before the race I'd have been pleased to see him finish fifth or sixth. It was beyond the wildest dreams that he could win, but now I just prayed that I wasn't going to die of embarrassment.

I didn't breathe again until two furlongs out, when I picked up the white, blue and yellow colours of Leeds United pressing the leaders on the far side. As he poked his head in front with over a furlong to run he kicked in the turbo to go four lengths clear and suddenly I couldn't contain myself. I am ashamed to say that I totally lost control. I was jumping and screaming like the old bloke in the Wetherby betting shop who christened me 'The Wetherby Strangler'. I couldn't believe it. I'd bought the winner of the Ebor.

I had to apologise to Jeff and David afterwards. Anybody would have thought that I had owned, trained, ridden and looked after the horse, but they understood. I was just very proud. We went off to celebrate on the lawn in front of the champagne bar where I was caught between two groups of winning connections, the sellers and the buyers. Everyone was a winner.

The next run was at Ascot for the Festival of British Racing where, Luca dropped Sid back to a mile and a half for the £75,000 Ritz Club Handicap. Both owners and the trainer wanted Dettori back aboard and I wasn't in any position to argue, although I wanted Kevin to keep the ride. I knew what it was like to be jocked off having ridden a bad race, let alone when you've been brilliant and won the richest handicap in Europe.

Luca explained that he was instrumental in bringing Dettori to Britain and that he rode everything from the yard when available and David and Jeff were deadly keen to have him ride. Well, they were paying the bills and although the books were beginning to balance, they were fully entitled to have what they wanted.

The ground at Ascot came up tacky and slow which wasn't ideal. The trip was also two furlongs short of his best, but both owners lumped on again at all the odds available down to 13-2. David organised a private box and it was one of the most enjoyable days racing I've ever had - and that includes those when I've ridden a big winner. When Frankie weaved his way though from the rear to take the lead inside the last furlong, Metcalf lost the plot and went ballistic. As Sid crossed the line I hugged him as we jumped up and down I looked into his eyes. I'll never forget what I saw - it was simply priceless.

We'd been watching from the top of the stands and the lift was slow descending. When we got to the ground floor I made a dash for the unsaddling enclosure, but I'm a bit quicker than Metcalf and Samuel, whose idea of tracksuits are the double breasted variety they wear to the races. They needn't have rushed. Frankie waited in the saddle and did his trademark flying dismount when they came panting into the enclosure.

I've kept Metcalf's post-race interview with the BBC on tape and it's a gem. He gave me flak for 'sending me to the poor house with bad tips', and then announced his winning bet to his family in Leeds, 'Mum and Dad, we've got the shrapnel!'

But I still felt for Kevin Darley and phoned him to apologise, adding that the boys would be sending him a drink. He behaved impeccably and understood the situation 100 per cent.

Even though Sid was finished for the season the ball hadn't stopped rolling as David and Jeff were nominated for 'new owners of the year' at the Racehorse Owners Association awards at the Hilton. They finished second to the owners of Primo Valentino but still walked away with an award because Sid won the handicapper of the year trophy.

If Vicious Circle never wins another race it doesn't matter. He's already done more than enough for everyone concerned and he made one soon-to-be ex-jump jockey extremely happy.

CHAPTER 33
The long goodbye

Whilst basking in the reflected glory of Vicious Circle's success I'd got a rather nasty case of self-inflicted sunburn.

After the win at Ascot I'd given an interview with the BBC and was asked for the umpteenth time if I was going to retire. After going through the usual platitudes of 'Can't go on for ever but I'd like to ... It's been great but nothing lasts forever,' I let my guard slip and said that I might retire at my home course, Wetherby, on 30 October. One thing was certain, I wanted to go out on a winner.

Massive mistake. From that day on, the phone went dead and I'd only got myself to blame. In racing, people want commitment and continuity. What's the point in booking a jockey for four rides at a meeting knowing full well that if the first one wins he's not going to ride the others?

On this occasion my mouth had certainly been my most dangerous weapon and I'd turned it on myself.

The technicalities of regaining my licence were straightforward and the Jockey Club wrote to book an appointment to hear my application. As I'd been waiting over two months to get it back I thought I could wait another week or so and informed them that I had prior engagements. There was Tony Dobbin's wedding to attend and being a fledgling bloodstock agent I was on duty for the five days of Royal Ascot. That probably suited the Jockey Club fine, another Bradley-free fortnight.

Thirteen days after charges against me had been dropped I made the journey to 42 Portman Square on Monday, 21 June 1999 to regain my licence. The trip was certainly more relaxed than any of my many previous visits and the meeting with the Licensing Committee, which was once again chaired by Gurney Sheppard, was relatively cordial compared to the others.

It took just 15 minutes for me to walk down the steps into the June sunshine, a licensed jockey again, although my first ride back was going to be somewhat unorthodox.

There was a celebrity flat race after the jump meeting at Stratford the following Friday, where the opposing riders included the show jumpers Nick Skelton and Stephen Hadley. The horses were definitely not thoroughbred and my ride was a strapping Irish draught horse named Brummel, who was in service with the Kings Troop. The trooper who looked after him led me up and told me that the last time Brummel had been seen in public was to lead the parade for the Trooping of the Colour, celebrating the Queen's official birthday. So one thing was certain. If he acted up the Mall he'd have no trouble with firm ground at Stratford.

The race was over a mile, and to add something to the occasion, I donned the Andrew Cohen colours I'd worn in the National on Suny Bay. Despite his lethargic lifestyle, my partner was going comfortably enough turning for home with two furlongs to run and looked like winning easily with just hands and heels. But he needed a little more encouragement to get his head in front and I felt very guilty when I had to give the old horse a back hander to go on and win his race, which he did willingly by a neck. The whip guidelines introduced in recent years are one thing I will praise the Jockey Club for. They have pricked the conscience of every rider and cases of abuse are now, thankfully, very rare.

The Stratford race wasn't the real thing, but it was nice to be back on a winner of any description and it gave me a nice blowout for the serious racing at Newton Abbot the following evening.

It didn't surprise me that David Elsworth wanted to get me my first official winner back. The man had stuck with me through bad times and good, never doubting me when others clearly had. It looked as though he had found the right horse in Tom Tailor. The horse was fit from the Flat and started second favourite, but he was much too keen and ran himself into the ground, eventually finishing fifth.

I went through the motions with the Press after the race and said, 'I just want to get on with my life now. I'll keep going for the foreseeable future as a jockey and see what happens.

'I haven't really got a job as such, and I'm a bit old to be going freelance. I don't want to ride 350 yaks a year, so I'll just play it by ear.'

By the time I left Newton Abbot that night it was gone nine o'clock and the two hour journey back up the mind-numbing M5 and M4 gave me plenty of time for reflection. When I reached home my mind was made up and I told Bob that my heart for the game had gone; too much water had flown under this particular bridge. Everyone had been incredibly kind, but I almost felt embarrassed by all the attention. I just couldn't be bothered any more. The fire which had burned for over twenty years had gone out.

Although the Jockey Club had effectively won, I couldn't let them see that they had and I soon had the opportunity to let them know I hadn't turned into an old grey pussycat.

A letter was sent to a number of jockeys which soon became common knowledge and was quoted at length in the Press. There was no doubt in my mind I was considered one of the principal reasons for it's existence.

It came from Licensing Committee Chairman Gurney Sheppard

and read, 'I would like to take this opportunity to remind you of the dangers of regularly meeting with people who might wish to corrupt horseracing.

'Additionally, you should avoid receiving favours from such people which could put you in a compromising position at a later date.

'It is obviously a matter for you to decide with whom you associate and how you spend your time, but I thought I would warn all jockeys that there have been instances where licensed persons have accepted favours or hospitality, such as holidays or nights out on the town, and have subsequently found themselves compromised.

'Please be alert to these dangers and avoid putting yourself in a situation which is likely to cause my committee concern.'

I knew it wouldn't be long before I was making yet another trip to Portman Square, and sure enough I received a letter requesting my presence and stating that I could not be legally represented. I didn't like this one bit and felt as though I'd be going before the headmaster without any trousers. But I was told that I need make no comment throughout the meeting if I so wished and there would be no need for a solicitor.

I still wouldn't agree unless I was given a complete transcript of the meeting and, though the Jockey Club agreed to this, I still wasn't happy.

Their secret adjudications have always aggravated me, particularly when I was sent outside while they were deciding my fate. What were they saying? How did they reach their decisions? Just what did they think I'd done?

I would have given anything to be there while they talked about me, just to know what they thought. Now was my chance.

Although the Jockey Club agreed to give me a transcript, I didn't trust them to relay everything word for word, so I got in touch with Brian Wright and told him I wanted a listening device to find out just what was going on.

I was put in touch with a man called 'Steve', who was an expert in that field, and an hour before the meeting I met him in the Churchill Hotel where he carried a very expensive leather document case.

He sat me down in a quiet corner and, just like 'Q' in the Bond films, he explained how this was a highly sophisticated recording and listening device which could pick up a mouse farting behind the skirting board twenty feet away.

Just as he was explaining the intricacies several prominent trainers, including Nicky Henderson, Jenny Pitman, Henrietta Knight and Oliver Sherwood, walked by the table on their way to the launch of a new race sponsorship. I quickly introduced 'Q' as my solicitor and they thought nothing of it. Once we'd exchanged pleasantries and they'd gone he continued his briefing and we swapped my papers into the case. He assured me that to locate the microphones and the micro recorder the complete case had to be dismantled and that to activate it was simple. All I had to do was press a metal stud on each side simultaneously.

I strode into 42 Portman Square confident that I was finally going to find out just what went on behind those closed doors. If they sent me out, I'd leave the case and get the lot.

When I was called in I made an excuse that I'd got to go to the toilet because I didn't know how long the meeting would last. I only needed two seconds in a cubicle to activate the device.

This time the stewards did most of the talking and, although it was the usual procedure, it was slightly more convivial. It opened with Gurney Sheppard reading a prepared statement which embellished the earlier letter I had received. They soon went on to personal references, starting with my Gold Rolex which, they said, had been bought for me by Brian Wright - wrong. It was a gift, but not from him. And what about the Flat jockeys? The Arabs hand out

Rolex Oysters like air miles.

They also alleged that Brian Wright had supplied me with a mobile phone for sole communication between us. Wrong. I'd bought a pay-as-you-go phone from Orange using an alias. I had become ultra-suspicious once I found out that all mobile calls could also be monitored if enough details were known about them. There was no way this particular phone could be traced to me and I have my own suspicions as to how they came to know of its existence.

They also warned me about my dealings with David Chopra, the golfing holidays abroad, nights out in London and just about any other way I enjoyed myself.

After they had their say, I asked to have mine, and although they weren't keen on this, I insisted.

I said, 'Brian Wright has been a very good friend of mine for fifteen years and during that time he has never compromised me. I often ring him for advice and he calls me.

'During the time I've known him he's never been in prison, although that's not an easy thing to detect because people don't walk around with lapel badges saying they've been inside.'

The meeting lasted about half an hour and they sent me on my way with a general feeling of goodwill and laughter, telling me to 'Go on and ride plenty more winners.'

What's more, they were as good as their word and sent me an unabridged transcript of the meeting, so I need not have slipped into my 007 role. Still, I enjoyed the buzz and although I always irritated the Jockey Club with the company I kept and some of the races I rode, I can now say that I was probably the first jockey to literally bug them. Somehow, I think I'll also be the last, because after reading this all luggage will have to leave the room while the stewards adjudicate.

But the fact remained they had almost ground me down. I didn't fancy the cold schooling mornings any more and going the length of the country for rides which a freelance jockey must do. I've always conducted myself with dignity and that's what I wanted to do now. I wasn't prepared to give the job the full 100 per cent commitment it requires. I just didn't have the fight in me any more. Vicious Circle's win at Ascot had confirmed in my mind which way I had to go. All I wanted now was to walk into the winners' enclosure one last time.

I kept dropping small hints to Norm, just softening the blow for when it came, because a blow it would certainly be to him. But he knew me well and understood the way I was thinking.

So did the majority of people and rides were scarce. From 26 June when I rode Tom Tailor I had just six rides until 30 September and two of them were in Ireland. I'd forgotten what the winners' enclosure looked like and that was hardly surprising. The last winner I'd ridden was for Simon Sherwood on Specs at Newbury on 27 March.

Sue and Gerard Nock booked me for Senor El Betrutti at Wetherby on 30 October and many people wanted me to quit there and then just as I hinted in the BBC interview on 26 September. There was plenty of banter from the crowd as I circled the paddock including one shout of, 'What's up, Brad, haven't you earned enough money yet?'

But 'The Senor' wasn't quite like his old self either and finished last of the five runners, prompting *Raceform* to comment, 'Senor El Betrutti seems to have lost his way and looked to give up without a struggle. Perhaps retirement beckons for him as well as his jockey.'

There was still a memorable end to the afternoon when all the jocks presented me with a picture everyone from north and south had signed of me winning the 1985 King George on Wayward Lad at Kempton. It was simply inscribed 'To the Wayward Lad.' And the day wasn't finished, as there was one hell of a party at the same Wetherby pub where I'd been found guilty of scrapping all those years ago and bound over to keep the peace. Well, it was all love that night and gradually developed into a private 'This Is Your Life' with my old mates, like 'Black' Dennis, Trevor Davies, Chuck Mudballs, Boo Boo and Dave Dutton turning up. And as the Night Fighter money-laundering story was news at the time there were several calls for me to 'Launder a tenner and buy us a drink.'

Norm and Mrs D both put in an appearance which was lovely, considering it was hardly their idea of the ideal night out.

Three days later Yankee Lord was declared to run at Exeter and I noticed Adrian Maguire was down to ride him in the previous day's advance card. I'd won on him twice the previous season and knew I got on well with him, but Simon Sherwood was obviously looking to the future as far as jockeys were concerned. It was 11.30 a.m. and final declaration for jockeys was 1 p.m. I was desperately looking for that last winner and Yankee Lord would have a favourite's chance. I phoned Uplands, but it would be wrong to say the place was like the old days. Andrew Cohen had sold it to Lavinia Taylor and Simon was renting a third of the yard. I always got on alright with Sharkey, but he wasn't Charlie.

When I got through to Sharkey he told me it was too late and, in any case, Adrian had been down to school the horse and the owners wanted him. Now that did get up my nose. Sir Alex Ferguson was the head of that syndicate and he was one loyal man. I managed to contact him at Manchester United's Cliff training ground. 'Alex, Brad here.'

'Brad, good to hear from you, how's it going?'

'Marvellous, but I've got a favour to ask, can I ride the horse tomorrow?'

'Course you can, delighted. Sorry I won't be able to get there for your last winner!'

I then rang Adrian to make sure there'd be no hard feelings jocking him off. As expected, there wasn't a worry.

'Kick on, Bradders, I've never sat on the horse before, it's fine by me, hope it wins for you.'

So I phoned Sharkey back to tell him what Alex had said and, faced with those facts, he switched the jockey declaration. That was where my luck ran out. I had just started with the flu and, for the one and only time in my career, I stopped in a pub on the way to the races for a brandy and port. Ronnie O'Leary, trainer of Aldino, swore by it and so do I now. It worked a treat. Alex took time out from planning Manchester United's strategy in the European Cup game that night to phone and wish me luck.

But Yankee Lord ran poorly and I pulled him up before the fourth from home. I finished last on Townleyhall for Martin Bosley in the final race of the day and four days later travelled to Down Royal in Northern Ireland for two rides. One of them was my German purchase, Aldino, who did best of the pair in finishing third.

'The Senor' was called back into action at Newbury on 9 November and a switch back to hurdles nearly caused a 14-1 shock when the old boy led until the last hurdle before being run out of it by Wontcostalotbut. I was at Newbury the next day but under a different banner, fronting the Racing Channel coverage with Alex Hammond, when the *Daily Mail* journalist Colin Mackenzie sidled up to me and said, 'If you were offered the ride on Suny Bay in the Hennessy in a couple of weeks, would you ride him.'

Without giving it much thought I said, 'Yes, if it was offered - but I don't think that will ever happen.'

Journalists can be selective in what they want to hear and how they wish to interpret it and in the *Mail* next day there was a story headlined 'Brad's Suny dream.'

It opened with the line, 'Graham Bradley, who is threatening to match boxer George Forman's ability to extend his retirement plans, hopes to play one last ace in his bid to go out on a winner'

It went on to say that I wanted to be reunited with the horse, when all I had said was, 'No one knows the horse better than I do and he is always best when fresh. Even if I were to ride a winner before then I would not pack up until I had ridden Suny Bay if I was given the chance.'

Mackenzie phoned Sharkey who said it was up to the owner and then contacted Andrew Cohen. He replied, somewhat grandly, 'I thought Mr Bradley had retired, I will have to discuss it with my trainer.'

Thought I'd retired! Had the man been on a kibbutz for the last six months? I'd been getting more publicity than the bloody Spice Girls and Oasis put together. I thought it was offensive of Andrew to be so offhand and dismissive after all we had endured. Perhaps I should have known better, but I felt very let down by his statement.

I cringed when I saw the story the next day and phoned Sharkey to apologise. He was fine, having been on the receiving end of a fair amount of journalistic fairytales over the years. But I was now beginning to get uncharacteristically bitter. People of whom I had a high opinion were writing me off, and apparently enjoying it.

I was also getting stubborn now and wouldn't go without that final winner, although it was beginning to get embarrassing. My old friend 'The Don', Don Cantillon, sportingly gave me the ride on his good mare Alpine Gale at Cheltenham on 12 November and there couldn't have been a better place to finish than the home of jumping.

I arrived in the paddock in Don's pink and black spotted colours and he was full of enthusiasm and clearly wanted to provide that last win. The mare didn't travel well early on but I kept coaxing her and gave her plenty of time to get into her rhythm. Sure enough she came hard on the bridle with just over a mile of the three to run. She had tacked on behind the leaders and was full of running when she met the fifth-last all wrong and fell. Although it was about six furlongs from the finish I felt sure we would have won and an air of depression set in. But the show still had to go on the next day at Haydock.

Dave Roberts was doing the best he could to get me rides with realistic chances and he came up with two in the third and fourth races. I took my time over the three-hour journey with Bob and I was deep in my own thoughts. Would this be the last day I drove to the races as a jockey? How different would it feel?

My sister, Mandy, was there to meet us and I got changed for the Kay Ell Jay Novices Handicap Chase over two miles six furlongs in which I was riding Ontheboil. The eight-year-old was carrying an 8lb penalty for a previous win at Market Rasen and although he went off 7-2 second favourite, this didn't look easy on paper. But I was thinking positively on the long walk to the paddock and enjoyed it as I made my way to meet the Northumberland trainer Don Eddy, who I'd only ridden for twice before. I smiled as the racegoers wished me well and Don was economical with his instructions as he legged me up, 'He gets the trip alright, Brad. Do what you like, he jumps well.'

I did the same as I'd done hundreds of times before on novice chasers and let the horse do everything himself unless he needed any assistance. He didn't. We were in front until the fifth when he took a breather and we went on again at the eighth and were always in control. As I faced what would be the last three fences of my professional life I knew I had plenty of horse under me and just kept gently squeezing him until we'd seen off all the opposition except Scrahan Cross. A bad blunder two out finished his chance, and all Ontheboil needed was one smack on the run-in to pull five lengths clear.

As I crossed the line there were no wild gesticulations. That might suit some people but it's not my style, not the way I was taught to behave. But I did think, 'Fucking hell, is that it, then?'

In truth, I really hadn't convinced myself that retirement was the right thing to do and I didn't know how I'd cope with not riding. So I gave Ontheboil plenty of time to pull up, which in turn gave me some vital thinking space and time to collect my thoughts.

I'd loved that winning ride. It felt great and I knew I was as stylish and good as ever. McCoy had been begging me to carry on and so had some of the other lads. I also knew that my family, without exception, would love it if I went on for at least another season. And there was the ride on Shahboor in the next - what if I could ride a double? Frances Young, the girl who looked after Ontheboil, ran out to lead us back in and gave the horse a hug and congratulated me. And now I had a 300-yard walk to make up my mind about what I would say to the Press and BBC cameras waiting in the unsaddling enclosure. After that, there would be no going back.

I then remembered the dismissive remarks of Andrew Cohen, the Yankee Lord episode and just how few rides I'd had that season. Then I thought of the explosion of adrenalin I'd experienced when Vicious Circle won at York and Ascot and my mind was made up. As far as being a jockey was concerned, I was a gonner. I'd had enough and I didn't want to fight for rides anymore. I was finally ready to give the game away to someone else.

I walked Ontheboil into the winners' enclosure then took my skull cap off and cradled it in my hands before tossing it to an official. It's completely against the rules, but I thought that by doing it I would let everyone know that I had finished. I took a bow in the saddle and jumped off.

So, that was that. Not the perfect ending in a big race but there had been plenty of those and this was good enough for me. Haydock was a track which I loved riding around. It was also in the north, where I was proud to have been born, and it was on TV, which meant Norm would be at home in Wetherby recording it to add to the massive archive he had amassed during my career.

Before going to weigh in for the last time I told the assembled Press corps that I was now officially finished and as soon as I'd drawn the correct weight I apologised to Mr and Mrs Robeson that I wouldn't be riding their useful gelding Shahboor in the handicap hurdle. They understood perfectly and kindly added that they wished my last win had been on their horse. In the event young Joe Tizzard substituted and finished second. Joe was barely a year old

400

when I rode my Cheltenham Gold Cup winner in 1983. Surely this was a young man's game.

But it wouldn't have been a normal day at the office for me if I hadn't received a tap on the shoulder from a stewards' secretary and, sure enough, I was summoned before the three wise men. I felt sure that it was because of what I'd done with my skull cap but I didn't give a toss. What were they going to do, ban me for seven days?

I stood before them in my breeches and T-shirt with my hands behind my back as I had done hundreds of times before often when staring down the barrel of a long ban or the almost obligatory trip to Portman Square. At those times I'd put on an act of calm which would have won any Oscar hands down, but this time I really was standing easy.

Just as I was preparing for the introductions to be made the chairman of the panel stood up, leant over the table and offered me his hand: 'Mr Bradley, congratulations on such a fine and distinguished career. Good luck in whatever you decide to do.' Then his two colleagues did the same and I gladly reciprocated.

It was just like saying goodbye to the headmaster on your last day at school and I thought it was a very civil and gentlemanly thing to do. No hard feelings. It was still them and me, but like two boxers after a hard fight when the final bell goes, this was no time for recriminations.

I was pleased with the interview I gave Clare Balding for BBC TV and told her that I had enjoyed a good innings and ridden some great horses. There had been plenty of ups and downs but plenty of fun on the way and I had absolutely no regrets. I added that getting the last winner was of paramount importance to me because I wanted to finish on my terms and not those of the police or the Jockey Club.

As I walked back to the weighing room to get showered I was able to give one of my biggest fans, Cathy Baybutt, a hug. This young lady, whose father Bill is a racecourse photographer, had shown tremendous courage against a crippling illness. Through all her problems she had followed my career intently and always came to Haydock to see me ride.

Before the next race, all the boys came out of the weighing room to present me with a bottle of champagne to see me on my way and I went back into the jockeys' changing room for the last time. After today, I would be a 'civilian' and never again allowed to claim sanctuary in the one place I felt safe against the world.

I said an emotional goodbye to my two valets up north, Phil Taylor and John Edge, who had looked after me wonderfully well over the years. They were so good that I'd wear a different pair of shoes to the races each day because I knew they'd always return them spotless for me.

I had a contemplative smile on my face as I walked away from the weighing room with my bag over my shoulder and my mind going a million miles an hour. I met Bob and Mandy in the champagne bar, where we cracked a bottle and they shed a few tears. I told them not to worry but they had both scaled the heights of emotion alongside me. Mandy had been like a mother to me since we lost our lovely mum when I was fourteen. No matter what the world thought, I'd always be her little brother.

I told them both it wasn't a time for tears, that I'd got out in one piece and I'd had a ball.

We got in the Merc and slid down the M6. The easy mid-afternoon traffic meant we'd be past Spaghetti Junction before the Birmingham soccer crowds jammed it up and I put in a call to Norm. I told him what I'd decided, even though he'd already seen it on TV, and he broke down in tears. It was the first time I'd ever known him do it. The bond between father and son is often unspoken, but Norm now told me how proud he was of what I'd achieved and how much pleasure it had given him.

Of course, I knew how he'd felt all those years, but hearing him say it meant the world to me. For my part, I told him that I could not have achieved anything without him - and I've never spoken a truer word in my life.

If he had handled me the wrong way when I was a frightened kid on that leading rein, I would have been lost to horses for life. And though he never got to ride in public, I know that he took every jump with me.

As we moved off the M42 and on to the M40 for the home stretch to Sparsholt I switched the radio on to hear the strains of the Sports Report theme which stirs the blood of ex-pats in far flung outposts of the globe via the World Service. And if they were in Moscow or Malibu they'd have heard in the sports headlines that 'The jump jockey Graham Bradley announced his retirement after riding Ontheboil to victory at Haydock this afternoon.'

They followed up with my previous brushes with authority and, yes, the Cartmel business got a mention too. How could I expect anyone to forget that? It was only eighteen years ago.

When asked to nominate my three finest moments in the saddle I had no hesitation in putting Bregawn's Gold Cup first. I'd disobeyed Michael Dickinson's instructions and made much of the running because the pace wasn't strong enough, but we both came of age that day. Then there was Suny Bay's Grand National, which I still consider my best ride. And of course there was Morley Street's 'Ride of the Season' at Aintree in 1993.

My loyal young friend A.P. McCoy led a list of tributes which I truly treasured. He said, 'I regard him as a legend, and I'm privileged that I have him as a great, great friend.'

John Francome, a true legend in my opinion, said, 'No jockey was more stylish. I'm delighted he's got out in one piece.' Norman Williamson paid a nice tribute saying, 'If there is ever to be another Brad, it certainly won't be in my lifetime.

'He was always generous with his knowledge, never once would he turn a youngster away who was seeking his advice. Even if they didn't ask, if he spotted them doing something wrong in a race he'd have a quiet word with them.'

Charlie Brooks, who had been through so much with me, was well qualified to comment and said, 'He was the man for the big occasion and, unlike many jockeys on the verge of retirement, his nerve held rock-solid right through to the very end.'

'Wee Anthony' wasn't so wee anymore and once again the pressure cooker of the sauna beckoned that Saturday night in order that he could melt down to 10st for Martin Pipe's Rodock in the big handicap hurdle at Cheltenham the next day. He asked me to accept the champion jockeys' prize on his behalf at the Murphy's Awards Night at Cheltenham, and I was happy to oblige. Jenny Pitman received a lifetime achievement award on her retirement and when I accepted A.P.'s cut-glass trophy I made the observation that this was the nearest I'd ever got to being champion.

One mistake I did make was listening to Luke Harvey, the former jockey who has now developed a cult following as a presenter on the Racing Channel. He assured me that he had booked accommodation in the racecourse hostel so there was no need to book any hotel rooms. Sure enough, Luke had the right accreditation, but I didn't and it didn't matter to the big bear on the door that I'd ridden the Gold Cup and Champion Hurdle winner around the course. I still couldn't get in. It was my first lesson in how quickly you are forgotten.

Thankfully, my mates in the weighing room certainly hadn't forgotten and Philip Hide organised a retirement party at the only place that was really right, namely the Queens Arms. It had always been a safe haven after triumph or disaster.

The weather was atrocious. There were no gritters on the roads, which made them like glass, but that still wasn't enough to stop Jason Titley. He was circling down at the start at Fairyhouse that Sunday afternoon when Norman Williamson mentioned that he was flying back for the party, which had already started that lunchtime.

'Why wasn't I told this!' said Titley in a questioning tone. With that, he left the course with Stormin' Norman - he didn't even have a wash bag - and walked into the Queens at 7. 45 p.m. as though he'd just come from racing at Newbury.

He got there in time to hear my speech to the boys in which I told them there was to be no scrapping later on, life was too short. So was my stamina. I couldn't take it like I used to and I don't know to this day when or how I was finally put to bed.

As the fuss died down one very satisfying snippet of information came back to me a few days later. One of my own moles in Portman Square told me that when Roger Buffham found out he hadn't been represented at my party he became very agitated and fumed, 'I've got four people on him and not one of them was there, what's going on!'

I certainly didn't know, but then it was a private party. However, it is a very sobering thought that one or indeed all four must have been close enough to me at one time for Buffham to think they would get in.

But that particular vendetta was over as far as I was concerned and above all, I'd kept my dignity and the respect of my peers. I'd been able to deal with people who thought they knew as much about my job as I did, but in reality knew considerably less. Certainly, my bottom lip became bloodied for the amount of times it had to be bitten.

I'd been able to control the element of fear because, despite what anyone says, it is always there. As the late, great Ayrton Senna said, 'Fear is a fundamental part of self preservation.'

At times I felt I might not be as easy to approach as some of my colleagues - to whom I appeared a bit deep - but I always wanted to help youngsters because I didn't want them to make the same mistakes that I had.

I've always done what I considered right and as long as any mistakes I made only hurt me then I could live with that. My conscience is my religion.

When I wrote the name Sweet Slievenamon in that optimistically large ledger entitled 'Catalogue of rides Graham John Bradley' back on 18 June 1977 I never dared hope it would be filled, let alone another started.

But the 23 years that followed have become wonderful yesterdays to look back on. Yes, I know I made mistakes and as I have said I would like to be able to rectify them, but I can't. And, in any case, they are far outweighed by the things that went right and by the wonderful people and horses I came to know and who enriched my life.

Some of my young friends didn't make it to the finishing line and others were left badly broken on the way and I would ask you to remember them and the price they paid because without it our great sport would not exist.

I know I will never again feel the adrenalin-fuelled rush of winning at Cheltenham or Aintree but I can live with that. And when I stroll memory lane in a quiet moment I can still hoist myself aboard the noble Wayward Lad or that little bruiser Bregawn and we can do it all again, just one more time. If I search still further I will feel the brick chafing my legs as I ride the wall of dreams of my childhood back on the Hallfields Estate in Wetherby when I was cocooned in the warmth of a wonderful family. Yes, I was fortunate enough to make those dreams a reality.

I do know how lucky I have been and fully realise that there have been times when I have ridden that luck to near impossible levels, but that's just the way I am and there is no other way I could have played my hand.

Live for today, because tomorrow is promised to no one.

Graham Bradley
Complete Winning Record

1977 - 1978

9 rides no wins

1978 - 1979

5 rides no wins

1979 - 1980

TALON (A E Dickinson)	Sedgefield	Hurdle	11/03/80
TALON (A E Dickinson)	Chepstow	Hurdle	07/04/80
THREE WAYS (M W Easterby)	Wetherby	Hurdle	08/04/80
POLITICAL POP (A E Dickinson)	Southwell	Hurdle	04/05/80

14 rides 4 wins

1980 - 1981

HAPPY HECTOR (M W Dickinson)	Southwell	Hurdle	06/10/80
ELLERBY LORD (Mrs J Cundall)	Uttoxeter	Chase	06/11/80
WESTERN MAN (J Fitzgerald)	Ayr	Hurdle	21/11/80
DUGALD (J Fitzgerald)	Catterick	Hurdle	22/11/80
TROJAN WALK (Miss C Mason)	Wetherby	Chase	02/12/80
HAPPY VOYAGE (M W Dickinson)	Carlisle	Hurdle	11/12/80
VICOMTE (J Fitzgerald)	Nottingham	Hurdle	13/12/80
THREE WAYS (M W Easterby)	Southwell	Hurdle	18/12/80
HARESHAW LINN (M W Dickinson)	Doncaster	Hurdle	19/12/80
VICOMTE (J Fitzgerald)	Newcastle	Hurdle	27/12/80
HAPPY VOYAGE (M W Dickinson)	Doncaster	Hurdle	30/01/81
KENLIS (M W Dickinson)	Market Rasen	Chase	07/03/81
HAPPY VOYAGE (M W Dickinson)	Market Rasen	Hurdle	07/03/81
MENDALEAK (P Asquith)	Catterick	Hurdle	11/03/81
EMERALD EMPEROR (M Naughton)	Ayr	Hurdle	16/03/81
URSER (M W Easterby)	Hexam	Hurdle	19/03/81
HOPE OF OAK (J Charlton)	Kelso	Hurdle	25/03/81
HOPE OF OAK (J Charlton)	Sedgefield	Hurdle	07/04/81
ALLTEN GLAZED (M Naughton)	Worcester	NH Flat	09/04/81
HOPE OF OAK (J Charlton)	Wetherby	Hurdle	21/04/81
HILL OF SLANE (A P Jarvis)	Newcastle	Hurdle	01/05/81

PRINCE BAI (fr) (A P Jarvis)	Newcastle	Hurdle	01/05/81
MY BUCK (M W Dickinson)	Cartmel	Chase	26/05/81

133 rides 22 wins

1981 - 1982

MY BUCK (M W Dickinson)	Uttoxeter	Chase	10/10/81
PRINCE OF PADUA (M W Dickinson)			
	Wetherby	Hurdle	14/10/81
MY BUCK (M W Dickinson)	Wetherby	Chase	14/10/81
VAN LEER (S J Leadbetter)	Hexam	Chase	06/11/81
BANNOW BREEZE (M Naughton)	Sedgefield	Chase	11/11/81
BANNOW BREEZE (M Naughton)	Nottingham	Chase	17/11/81
BREGAWN (M W Dickinson)	Market Rasen	Chase	28/11/81
LORD GREYSTOKE (M W Dickinson)			
	Market Rasen	Chase	28/11/81
WINNING BRIEF (M Naughton)	Catterick	Chase	22/01/82
MANHATTEN ISLAND (M Naughton)	Newcastle	Hurdle	27/01/82
SEAMUS O'FLYNN (M W Dickinson)			
West of Scotland Pattern Novices	Ayr	Chase	30/01/82
DONJILL (M W Dickinson)	Ayr	Chase	30/01/82
RYECROFT (M W Dickinson)	Ayr	Hurdle	30/01/82
ANOTHER CAPTAIN (A Scott)	Sedgfield	Chase	02/02/82
POLITICAL POP (M W Dickinson)	Wetherby	Chase	06/02/82
WINNING BRIEF (M Naughton)	Wolverhampton	Chase	08/02/00
ASHLEY HOUSE (M W Dickinson)			
Vaux Breweries Novice Chase Final	Newcastle	Chase	20/02/82
ALLTEN GLAZED (M Naughton)			
Haig Whisky Novice Hurdle Final	Newcastle	Hurdle	20/03/82
ANOTHER CAPTAIN (A Scott)	Carlisle	Chase	22/03/82
KINGS BRIG (M W Dickinson)	Uttoxeter	Hurdle	12/04/82
HOPE OF OAK (J Charlton)	Hexam	Chase	14/04/82
MY BUCK (M W Dickinson)	Market Rasen	Chase	23/04/82
NICKY TAM (A Scott)	Kelso	Chase	24/04/82
HEATON LAD (M W Dickinson)	Kelso	Hurdle	24/04/82
HOPE OF OAK (J Charlton)	Perth	Chase	27/04/82
MARINE CADET (J Charlton)	Hexam	Hurdle	29/04/82
NICKY TAM (A Scott)	Kelso	Chase	04/05/82
STOP IT (A Scott)	Sedgefield	Hurdle	07/05/82
MARINE CADET (J Charlton)	Hexam	Hurdle	10/05/82
HOPE OF OAK (J Charlton)	Hexam	Chase	10/05/82
NICKY TAM (A Scott)	Hexam	Chase	10/05/82
YOUNG SAGERT (J Charlton)	Ayr	Chase	12/05/82
NICKY TAM (A Scott)	Sedgefield	Chase	18/05/82

MARINE CADET (J Charlton)	Sedgefield	Hurdle	18/05/82
CORRECT CHECK (D MaCain)	Bangor	Hurdle	19/05/82
YOUNG SAGERT (J Charlton)	Hexam	Chase	31/05/82
LITTLE ABBEY (W Storey)	Hexam	Chase	31/05/82
STOP IT (A Scott)	Stratford	Hurdle	05/06/82

178 rides 38 wins

1982 - 1983

BROKEN BONDS (M Naughton)	Perth	Hurdle	03/09/82
WESTWOOD DEAL (M Naughton)	Bangor	Hurdle	18/09/82
BREGAWN (M W Dickinson)	Newton Abbot	Chase	12/10/82
SECRET SIN (J Charlton)	Kelso	Hurdle	16/10/82
NICKY TAM (A Scott)	Kelso	Chase	16/10/82
NICKY TAM (A Scott)	Newcastle	Chase	27/20/82
RIGHTHAND MAN (M W Dickinson)			
Charlie Hall Memorial Chase	Wetherby	Chase	30/10/82
ALLTEN GLAZED (M Naughton)	Sandown	Hurdle	05/11/82
BREGAWN (M W Dickinson)			
Rehearsal Chase	Chepstow	Chase	06/11/82
BREGAWN (M W Dickinson)			
Hennessy Cognac Gold Cup	Newbury	Chase	27/11/82
RIGHTHAND MAN (M W Dickinson)			
	Wetherby	Chase	05/02/83
ANOTHER CAPTAIN (A Scott)	Newcastle	Chase	18/02/83
ASHLEY HOUSE (M W Dickinson)	Doncaster	Chase	26/02/83
LEAM LORD (O Brennan)	Doncaster	Chase	28/02/82
CARDINAL FLOWER (A Scott)	Doncaster	Hurdle	28/02/83
BRUNTON PARK (M W Dickinson)	Kelso	Hurdle	01/03/83
SABIN DU LOIR (M W Dickinson)		Hurdle	01/03/83
BREGAWN (M W Dickinson)	Hereford	Chase	05/03/83
SIR WIMPY (M W Dickinson)	Warwick	Hurdle	08/03/83
POLITICAL POP (M W Dickinson)	Warwick	Chase	08/03/83
PERMABOS (K Stone)	Doncaster	Hurdle	12/03/83
SABIN DU LOIR (M W Dickinson)	Cheltenham	Hurdle	16/03/83
BREGAWN (M W Dickinson)			
Cheltenham Gold Cup	Cheltenham	Chase	17/03/83
PRINCE ROWAN (M W Dickinson)	Worcester	Chase	23/03/83
HOLLOW LAUGH (M Banks)	Huntingdon	Chase	04/04/83
REDNAEL (M W Dickinson)	Huntingdon	Chase	04/04/83
SABIN DU LOIR (M W Dickinson)			
Fosters Novice Hurdle	Liverpool	Hurdle	09/04/83
HOPE OF OAK (J Charlton)	Kelso	Chase	11/04/83
ON LEAVE (A Scott)	Kelso	Hurdle	11/04/83

HILLS GUARD (A Scott)	Kelso	Hurdle	23/04/83
PRINCE ROWAN (M W Dickinson)	Perth	Chase	27/04/83
PRINCE ROWAN (M W Dickinson)	Perth	Chase	19/05/83
HOPE OF OAK (J Charlton)	Perth	Chase	19/05/83
LEAM LORD (O Brennan)	Hexam	Chase	28/05/83

142 rides 34 wins

1983 - 1984

GOLDEN FANCY (I Vickers)	Cartmel	Hurdle	10/09/83
GOLDEN FANCY (I Vickers)	Perth	Hurdle	22/09/83
CARDINAL FLOWER (A Scott)	Ayr	Hurdle	10/10/83
GOLDEN FANCY (I Vickers)	Perth	Hurdle	13/10/83
VICTORY PRIZE (D Smith)	Kelso	Chase	15/10/83
STATE CASE (M W Dickinson)	Uttoxeter	Hurdle	20/10/83
GEARYS COLD ROLLED (D Smith)	Newcastle	Chase	26/10/83
MIDNIGHT LOVE (D Smith)	Catterick	Chase	05/11/83
STAR REGAL (M Naughton)	Hexam	Hurdle	07/11/83
LETTOCH (M W Dickinson)	Stratford	Chase	10/11/83
MIDNIGHT LOVE (D Smith)	Newcastle	Chase	12/11/83
LETTOCH (M W Dickinson)	Ayr	Chase	19/11/83
SILENT VALLEY (I Jordan)	Ayr	Chase	19/11/83
PRINCESS HENHAM (N Callaghan)	Leicester	Hurdle	25/11/83
SANDMOOR COURT (H Westbrook)	Southwell	Hurdle	28/11/83
PAUSE FOR THOUGHT (D Smith)	Sedgefield	Hurdle	02/12/83
LETTOCH (M W Dickinson)			
Dipper Novice Chase	Newcastle	Chase	03/12/83
HILLS GUARD (A Scott)	Newcastle	Hurdle	05/12/83
SANDMOOR COURT (H Westbrook)	Huntingdon	Hurdle	12/12/83
MACS PARK (M W Dickinson)	Wetherby	Hurdle	26/12/83
BADSWORTH BOY (M W Dickinson)			
Castleford Handicap Chase	Wetherby	Chase	26/12/83
BRIGHT SHERRIFF (M W Dickinson)			
	Wetherby	Hurdle	26/12/83
MOSSMORRAN (A Scott)	Wetherby	Hurdle	27/12/83
ALBERTAT (D Smith)	Newcastle	Hurdle	28/12/83
PACIFISTE (M W Dickinson)	Newcastle	Hurdle	28/12/83
STRAY SHOT (J Gifford)	Newbury	Hurdle	30/12/83
PACIFISTE (M W Dickinson)	Leicester	Hurdle	02/01/84
MOSSMORRAN (A Scott)	Cheltenham	Hurdle	03/01/84
MR SNUGFIT (M W Easterby)	Leicester	Chase	10/01/84
MR DONUT (M W Dickinson)	Southwell	Chase	12/01/84
BADSWORTH BOY (M W Dickinson)			
	Ayr	Chase	11/02/84

411

BRAVE GEORGE (M W Dickinson)	Catterick	Chase	22/02/84
LETTOCH (M W Dickinson)	Kempton	Chase	24/02/84
BROWNES GAZZETTE (M W Dickinson)			
	Stratford	Hurdle	25/02/84
RHYME 'N' REASON (M W Dickinson)			
	Market Rasen	Hurdle	03/03/84
CARLS WAGER (M W Dickinson)	Wolverhampton	Chase	16/03/84
RHYME 'N' REASON (M W Dickinson)			
	Chepstow	Hurdle	17/03/84
RHYME 'N' REASON (M W Dickinson)			
	Uttoxeter	Hurdle	23/04/84

192 rides 38 wins

1984 - 1985

SENRAB (J Old)	Hereford	Chase	25/08/84
KARS (J Old)	Worcester	Chase	06/09/84
OUR LOUISE (A Scott)	Hexham	Hurdle	10/09/84
CRADLE OF JAZZ (J Old)	Newton Abbot	Hurdle	14/09/84
STATE CASE (Mrs M Dickinson)	Southwell	Chase	17/09/84
OUR LOUISE (A Scott)	Sedgefield	Hurdle	25/09/84
SCOTFEN (A Scott)	Sedgefield	Hurdle	02/10/84
CHURCH WARDEN (D Murray-Smith)			
	Chepstow	Hurdle	06/10/84
STATE CASE (Mrs M Dickinson)	Southwell	Chase	08/10/84
STOP IT (A Scott)	Ayr	Chase	12/10/84
BRAVE GEORGE (P Haynes)	Newbury	Chase	26/10/84
DOOR LATCH (J Gifford)	Sandown	Chase	03/11/84
RYTHMIC PASTIMES (J Jenkins)	Wolverhampton	Hurdle	07/11/84
RIGHTHAND MAN (Mrs M Dickinson)			
	Cheltenham	Chase	10/11/84
LORD MERLIN (J Old)	Devon & Exeter	Hurdle	13/11/84
MEISTER (J Old)	Devon & Exeter	Hurdle	13/11/84
MAC'S OR MINE (J Old)	Leicester	Hurdle	19/11/84
BIG BROWN BEAR (G Barlow)	Haydock	Chase	21/11/84
PACIFISTE (Mrs M Dickinson)	Haydock	Hurdle	21/11/84
RIGHTHAND MAN (Mrs M Dickinson)			
	Haydock	Chase	22/11/84
RHOECUS (Mrs M Dickinson)	Haydock	Hurdle	22/11/84
BIG BROWN BEAR (G Barlow)	Wolverhampton	Chase	26/11/84
STATE CASE (Mrs M Dickinson)	Nottingham	Chase	03/12/84

RIGHTHAND MAN (Mrs M Dickinson)			
Coral Welsh National	Chepstow	Chase	22/12/84

RYEMAN (Mrs M Dickinson)
Castleford Handicap Chase	Wetherby	Chase	26/12/84

RHYME 'N' REASON (D Murray-Smith)
	Taunton	Chase	28/12/84

RHYME 'N' REASON (D Murray-Smith)
	Folkstone	Chase	26/01/85
MEARLIN (J Old)	Hereford	Hurdle	30/01/85
KARABLAKE (D Smith)	Ayr	Hurdle	08/02/85
A SURE ROW (Mrs M Dickinson)	Wetherby	Hurdle	27/02/85
RHOECUS (Mrs M Dickinson)	Haydock Park	Hurdle	01/03/85
TRACYS (J Old)	Wolverhampton	Hurdle	15/03/85

MEARLIN (J Old)
Hoecht Regumate Mares Novice Handicap Final			
	Newbury	Hurdle	23/03/85

RHYME 'N' REASON (D Murray-Smith)
Whitbread Best Mild Novice Chase	Liverpool	Chase	28/03/85

RHYME 'N' REASON (D Murray-Smith)
Jameson Irish Grand National	Fairyhouse (IRE)	Chase	08/04/85
CRADLE OF JAZZ (J Old)	Wincanton	Hurdle	02/05/85
BRUNTON PARK (Mrs M Dickinson)	Market Rasen	Chase	11/05/85
STATE CHASE (Mrs M Dickinson)	Market Rasen	Chase	11/05/85
CUCKOLD (J Sheppard)	Fairhill (USA)	Chase	08/06/85
RASTIME KNIGHT (P Cramer)	Fairhill (USA)	Chase	08/06/85

181 rides 40 wins

1985 - 1986

TAMERTOWN LAD (J Jenkins)	Huntingdon	Hurdle	20/09/85

GRANVILLE PARK (Mrs M Dickinson)
	Bangor	Hurdle	21/09/85
LECTOR (D Elsworth)	Plumpton	Hurdle	23/09/85
GENNARD (M Naughton)	Sedgefield	Hurdle	24/09/85
BRUNTON PARK (Mrs M Dickinson)	Market Rasen	Chase	28/09/85
CRADLE OF JAZZ (J Old)	Wincanton	Hurdle	19/10/85

WAYWARD LAD (Mrs M Dickinson)
Charlie Hall Memorial Chase	Wetherby	Chase	02/11/85
YANK BROWN (Mrs M Dickinson)	Bangor	Hurdle	08/11/85
A SURE ROW (Mrs M Dickinson)	Bangor	Chase	08/11/85
PLANETMAN (Mrs M Dickinson)	Market Rasen	Chase	15/11/85
APPLE WINE (D Chapman)	Market Rasen	Hurdle	15/11/85

THE MIGHTY MAC (Mrs M Dickinson)
	Huntingdon	Chase	26/11/85
YANK BROWN (Mrs M Dickinson)	Nottingham	Hurdle	02/12/85

PREMIERE CHARLIE (M Hinchcliffe)

	Uttoxeter	Chase	05/12/85
MEARLIN (J Old)	Devon & Exeter	Chase	06/12/85
GEMELEK (Mrs M Dickinson)	Haydock Park	Hurdle	11/12/85
HOPE OF OAK (J Charlton)	Kelso	Chase	16/12/85
RINUS (D McCain)	Carlisle	Hurdle	19/12/85
THE FOOTMAN (D Elsworth)			
Finale Junior Hurdle	Chepstow	Hurdle	21/12/85
WAYWARD LAD (Mrs M Dickinson)			
King George VI Chase	Kempton	Chase	26/12/85
CHURCH WARDEN (D Murray-Smith)			
Peter Ross Novice Chase	Ascot	Chase	11/01/86
SHEER GOLD (G Balding)	Haydock Park	Hurdle	18/01/86
A SURE ROW (Mrs M Dickinson)	Haydock Park	Chase	18/01/86
STEARSBY (Mrs J Pitman)	Wolverhampton	Chase	22/01/86
BRUNTON PARK (Mrs M Dickinson)			
Charterhouse Chase	Ascot	Chase	05/02/86
PEARLYMAN (J Edwards)			
Grand Annual Chase	Cheltenham	Chase	11/03/86
AGRA KNIGHT (J Old)	Wolverhampton	Hurdle	14/03/86
HOPEFUL MISSION (Mrs M Dickinson)			
	Newcastle	Hurdle	17/03/86
THE MIGHTY MAC (Mrs M Dickinson)			
	Huntingdon	Chase	26/03/86
STARJESTIC (R Robinson)	Southwell	Chase	29/03/86
RHOECUS (Mrs M Dickinson)	Wetherby	Hurdle	01/04/86
STEARSBY (Mrs J Pitman)			
Whitbread Best Mild Novice Chase	Liverpool	Chase	03/04/86
IMPANY (R Robinson)	Wetherby	Chase	14/04/86
ROBIN WONDER (D Elsworth)	Taunton	Hurdle	24/04/86
GRANVILLE PARK (Mrs M Dickinson)			
	Sedgefield	Hurdle	29/04/86
THE MIGHT MAC (Mrs M Dickinson)			
	Wetherby	Chase	07/05/86
JACK OF CLUBS (B McLean)	Sedgefield	Hurdle	08/05/86
STARJESTIC (R Robinson)	Hexham	Chase	24/05/86
MOUNTAIN BROOK (J Sheppard)	Fairhill (USA)	Chase	07/06/86
CORINTH (J Sheppard)	Monmouth Park (USA)		
		Chase	18/06/86

250 rides 41 wins

1986 - 1987

414

FAST FLIGHT (J Ffitch-Heyes)	Fontwell Park	Chase	22/09/86
CAMPUS BOY (Mrs J Ramsden)	Stratford	Hurdle	27/09/86
TIMLYN (G Balding)	Cheltenham	Hurdle	08/10/86
STARJESTIC (C Bell)	Cheltenham	Chase	09/10/86
BOBBY BURNS (Mrs M Dickinson)	Newcastle	Hurdle	29/10/86
SILENT VALLEY (I Jordan)	Wetherby	Chase	31/10/86
ROBIN GOODFELLOW (G Balding)	Newbury	Hurdle	05/11/86
HAND OVER (Mrs M Dickinson)	Bangor	Chase	07/11/86
KILDIMO (G Balding)	Cheltenham	Hurdle	08/11/86
ROBIN WONDER (D Elsworth)	Cheltenham	Hurdle	08/11/86
BY THE WAY (P Caldwell)	Kelso	Chase	12/11/86
ROYAL GREEK (Mrs M Dickinson)	Market Rasen	Hurdle	14/11/86
HAND OVER (Mrs Dickinson)	Market Rasen	Chase	14/11/86
FAR BRIDGE (G Balding)			
Manicou Handicap Chase	Ascot	Chase	15/11/86
HAND OVER (Mrs M Dickinson)	Haydock	Chase	19/11/86
BY THE WAY (Mrs M Dickinson)	Market Rasen	Chase	22/11/86
DAN THE MILLAR (Mrs M Dickinson)			
	Market Rasen	Chase	22/11/86
ROBIN GOODFELLOW (G Balding)	Sandown	Hurdle	28/11/86
DAN THE MILLAR (Mrs M Dickinson)			
	Nottingham	Chase	01/12/86
FORCELLO (G Balding)	Worcester	Hurdle	03/12/86
CAROUSEL ROCKET (R Whitaker)	Wetherby	Hurdle	06/12/86
MISTER POINT (C Tinkler)	Haydock	Hurdle	11/12/86
YAHOO (J Hanson)	Haydock	Chase	11/12/86
DAN THE MILLAR (Mrs Dickinson)			
Freebooter Novice Chase	Doncaster	Chase	13/12/86
SAINT ACTON (G Balding)	Folkstone	Hurdle	16/12/86
MISTER POINT (C Tinkler)	Ayr	Hurdle	19/12/86
STEARSBY (Mrs J Pitman)			
Coral Welsh National	Chepstow	Chase	20/12/86
KINGS COLLEGE BOY (Mrs M Dickinson)			
	Kelso	Chase	22/12/86
CAROUSEL ROCKET (R Whitaker)	Newcastle	Hurdle	29/12/86
KILDIMO (G Balding)	Cheltenham	Chase	31/12/86
BURANNPOUR (G Balding)	Cheltenham	Chase	01/01/87
FOURTH TUDOR (A Bailey)	Nottingham	Hurdle	05/01/87
RHOECUS (Mrs M Dickinson)	Market Rasen	Chase	07/01/87
BADSWORTH BOY (Mrs M Dickinson)			
	Haydock Park	Chase	24/01/87
GRANVILLE PARK (Mrs M Dickinson)			
	Wolverhampton	Chase	28/01/87
CRADLE OF JAZZ (J Old)	Windsor	Chase	04/02/87
KILDIMO (G Balding)	Towcester	Chase	05/02/87

GRANVILLE PARK (Mrs M Dickinson)

	Kelso	Chase	06/02/87

MODEL PUPIL (O O'Neil)
Fernbank Hurdle   Ascot   Hurdle   11/02/87
ROBIN GOODFELLOW (G Balding)
Sidney Banks Memorial Novice Hurdle

	Huntingdon	Hurdle	12/02/87
BURRANPOUR (G Balding)	Newbury	Hurdle	13/02/87
BY THE WAY (Mrs M Dickinson)	Catterick	Chase	14/02/87

GRANVILLE PARK (Mrs M Dickinson)

	Fakenham	Chase	20/02/87

KILDIMO (G Balding)
Sun Alliance Novice Chase   Cheltenham   Chase   18/03/87
YAHOO (J Hanson)   Hexham   Chase   30/03/87
DAN THE MILLAR (Mrs M Dickinson)

	Liverpool	Chase	03/04/87
KILDIMO (G Balding)	Ayr	Chase	10/04/87

DAN THE MILLAR (Mrs M Dickinson)

	Bangor	Chase	25/04/87

HOPEFUL MISSION (Mrs M Dickinson)

	Market Rasen	Chase	02/05/87
SIR BADSWORTH (T Laxton)	Sedgefield	Chase	07/05/87
STARJESTIC (MISS L Siddall)	Worcester	Chase	20/05/87
SIR BADSWORTH (T Laxton)	Cartmel	Chase	23/05/87

HOPEFUL MISSION (Mrs M Dickinson)

	Southwell	Chase	23/05/87

232 rides 53 wins

1987 - 1988

PACIFISTE (Mrs M Dickinson)	Bangor	Chase	06/11/87

KILDIMO (G Balding)
Allied Dunbar Chase   Cheltenham   Chase   13/11/87
STARWOOD (C Tinkler)   Southwell   Hurdle   17/11/87
CONE ALONE (A J Wilson)   Worcester   Hurdle   18/11/87
ANYTHING BETTER (G Balding)   Ascot   Hurdle   20/11/87
JAZETAS (N Callaghan)   Windsor   Hurdle   23/11/87
EDWARDS VISION (Mrs M Dickinson)   Haydock   Hurdle
25/11/87
DEEP SOUTH (J Fitzgerald)   Catterick   Chase   07/12/87
SOUTH PARADE (G Balding)
Summit Junior Hurdle   Lingfield   Hurdle   12/12/87
ARCTIC CALL (Mrs M Dickinson)   Ayr   Hurdle   18/12/87
SHEER NECTAR (G Balding)   Wincanton   Hurdle   26/12/87

SOUTH PARADE (G Balding)
Finale Junior Hurdle	Chepstow	Hurdle	28/12/87
PACIFISTE (Mrs M Dickinson)	Catterick	Chase	01/01/88
TONIGHTS THE NIGHT (Mrs M Dickinson)			
	Sandown Park	Chase	09/01/88

CAVVIES CLOWN (D Elsworth)
John Bull Chase	Wincanton	Chase	14/01/88
BURANNPOUR (G Balding)	Ascot	Chase	15/01/88
JAMESMEAD (D Elsworth)	Ascot	Hurdle	15/01/88
PACIFISTE (Mrs M Dickinson)	Market Rasen	Chase	16/01/88

CAVVIES CLOWN (D Elsworth)
Charterhouse Mercantile Chase	Cheltenham	Chase	30/01/88
TONIGHTS THE NIGHT (Mrs M Dickinson)			
	Kelso	Chase	05/02/88
LIGHTWATER AGAIN (Mrs M Dickinson)			
	Kelso	Hurdle	05/02/88
SHARSEAL (D A Wilson)	Fakenham	Hurdle	19/02/88
A SURE ROW (Mrs M Dickinson)	Fakenham	Chase	19/02/88
EDWARDS VISION (Mrs M Dickinson)			
	Wolverhampton	Chase	22/02/88

KILDIMO (G Balding)
Jim Ford Challenge Cup Chase	Wincanton	Chase	25/02/88
HYPNOSIS (D Elsworth)	Wincanton	Chase	25/02/88

KINGS COLLEGE BOY (Mrs M Dickinson)
Rendlesham Hurdle	Kempton	Hurdle	27/02/88
STARJESTIC (N Bradley)	Wetherby	Chase	02/03/88
HARRISON (M Pipe)	Ludlow	Hurdle	03/03/88
RED RUDDEL (J Hansen)	Market Rasen	Hurdle	05/03/88
CHATTY FELLOW (G Balding)	Newbury	Hurdle	26/03/88
AUCTION FEVER (A Stringer)	Wetherby	Hurdle	05/04/88
FLYING DANCER (Mrs M Dickinson)	Sedgefield	Hurdle	22/04/88
FLYING DANCER (Mrs M Dickinson)	Sedgefield	Hurdle	05/05/88
TACTICO (W Fairgrieve)	Perth	Chase	18/05/88
ETERNAL CREDIT (R Fisher)	Perth	Chase	19/05/88
LECTOR (D Elsworth)	Fontwell	Chase	20/05/88
SIR BADSWORTH (T Laxton)	Cartmel	Chase	25/05/88

231 rides 38 wins

1988 - 1989

LORD IT OVER (J Jenkins)	Fontwell	Hurdle	10/08/88
TACTICO (W Fairgrieve)	Perth	Chase	19/08/88
GOINGO (D Murray-Smith)	Hereford	Chase	02/09/88
GOINGO (D Murray-Smith)	Plumpton	Chase	19/09/88

BOBBY STACK (W Fairgrieve)	Perth	Hurdle	22/09/88
ROWLANDSONS JEWELS (D Murray-Smith)			
	Worcester	Chase	23/09/88
TACTICO (W Fairgreave)	Perth	Chase	05/10/88
ROALANDSONS JEWELS (D Murray-Smith)			
	Newbury	Hurdle	21/10/88
HALF DECENT (Mrs M Dickinson)	Sedgefield	Hurdle	04/11/88
DARK HERITAGE (D Murray-Smith)	Plumpton	Hurdle	07/11/88
SOUTH PARADE (G Balding)			
Whitbread White Label Hurdle	Cheltenham	Hurdle	12/11/88
HYPNOSIS (D Elsworth)	Wincanton	Chase	24/11/88
TACTICO (W Fairgrieve)	Kelso	Hurdle	05/12/88
SHANBALLY BOY (D Murray-Smith)			
	Fontwell	Chase	06/12/88
ROWLANDSONS JEWELS (D Murray-Smith)			
	Doncaster	Chase	09/12/88
OUT OF RANGE (D Elsworth)	Newton Abbot	Hurdle	26/12/88
YOUNG BAVARD (D Murray-Smith)	Newbury	Hurdle	31/12/88
CRUSADERS STAR (Mrs M Dickinson)			
	Sedgefield	Chase	04/01/89
ST GABRIEL (T Tate)	Wetherby	Chase	13/01/89
CRAMMER (D Murray-Smith)	Ludlow	Chase	18/01/89
MAGNUS PYM (D Elsworth)	Haydock	Hurdle	21/01/89
BORDER TINKER (N Bradley)	Sedgefield	Chase	25/01/89
BEAKER (M Naughton)	Ayr	Hurdle	28/01/89
BORDER TINKER (N Bradley)	Southwell	Chase	30/01/89
ANNBANREE (D Murray-Smith)	Ludlow	Hurdle	08/02/89
BATRES (D Murray-Smith)	Wincanton	Chase	09/02/89
BARTRES (D Murray-Smith)			
Fairlawne Chase	Windsor	Chase	18/02/89
WAR DANCER (D Murray-Smith)	Ludlow	Hurdle	02/03/89
ROWLANDSONS TROPHY (D Murray-Smith)			
	Wincanton	Hurdle	09/03/89
OUT OF RANGE (D Elsworth)	Ascot	Hurdle	12/04/89
STARJESTIC (N Bradley)	Southwell	Chase	24/04/89
CRUSADER'S STAR (Mrs M Dickinson)			
	Market Rasen	Chase	29/04/89
ROWLANDSONS JEWELS (D Murray-Smith)			
	Stratford	Chase	19/05/89
SIR BADSWORTH (T Laxton)	Cartmel	Chase	24/05/89

220 rides 34 wins

1989 - 1990

MAJOR INQUIRY (D Elsworth)	Cheltenham	Hurdle	11/11/89
HALF DECENT (T P Tate)	Sedgefield	Chase	14/11/89
BEAU ROSE (T P Tate)	Sedgefield	Chase	14/11/89
MAJOR ENQUIRY (D Elsworth)			
Aurelius Hurdle	Ascot	Hurdle	18/11/89
MAJOR ENQUIRY (D Elsworth)	Cheltenham	Hurdle	01/01/90
EDWARDS VISION (T Tate)	Ayr	Chase	02/01/90
RIFLE RANGE (T Tate)	Haydock	Chase	05/01/90
STEPHENS PET (O O'Neill)	Wincanton	Hurdle	11/01/90
CITY ENTERTAINER (Mrs C Postlewaite)			
	Wetherby	Chase	12/01/90
RIFLE RANGE (T Tate)	Sedgefield	Chase	16/01/90
FLYING DANCER (B McLean)	Sedgefield	Hurdle	16/01/90
MRS MUCK (N Twiston-Davies)	Haydock	Hurdle	20/01/90
BANK VIEW (N Tinkler)			
Daily Mail Champion Hurdle Trial	Haydock	Hurdle	20/01/90
BARLEY MOW (N Bradley)	Southwell	Hurdle	07/02/90
MIGHTY FALCON (D Elsworth)	Towcester	Hurdle	13/02/90
RIVERHEAD (D Elsworth)	Sandown	Hurdle	15/02/90
RIVERHEAD (D Elsworth)	Wincanton	Hurdle	22/02/90
CAVVIES CLOWN (D Elsworth)			
Jim Ford Challenge Cup Chase	Wincanton	Chase	22/02/90
SHADY ROAD (O O'Neill)	Ludlow	Chase	01/03/90
RIFLE RANGE (T Tate)	Haydock	Chase	02/03/90
HIGHFIRE (O O'Neill)	Devon & Exeter	Chase	22/03/90
DOC'S COAT (C Wildman)	Devon & Exeter	Hurdle	22/03/90
WHITEWASH (Mrs D Haine)	Southwell	Hurdle	31/03/90
BARLEY MOW (N Bradley)	Carlisle	Chase	14/04/90
ROYAL GREEK (M Pipe)	Hereford	Chase	16/04/90
IN-KEEPING (M Pipe)	Hereford	Hurdle	16/04/90
FLYING DANCER (B McLean)	Wetherby	Hurdle	17/04/90
PERISTYLE (M Pipe)	Stratford	Hurdle	21/04/90
STARJESTIC (N Bradley)	Southwell	Chase	27/04/90
TARQUOGANS BEST (M Pipe)	Bangor	Chase	12/05/90

207 rides 30 wins

1990 - 1991

EARTH WOOD (T Hallett)	Devon & Exeter	Hurdle	09/08/90
EARTH WOOD (T Hallett)	Devon & Exeter	Hurdle	24/08/90
DORINICUM (C Beever)	Southwell	Chase	26/08/90
ROYAL MAZI (C Beever)	Carlisle	Hurdle	29/08/90
DORINICUM (C Beever)	Southwell	Chase	01/10/90
ARDBRIN (T Tate)	Wetherby	Chase	02/11/90

419

ARDBRIN (T Tate)	Carlisle	Chase	29/11/90
LIGHTWATER AGAIN (C Beever)	Sedgefield	Chase	11/12/90
WHITWOOD (C Bell)	Sedgefield	Hurdle	11/12/90
ARDBRIN (T Tate)	Haydock Park	Chase	13/12/90
FLOYD (D Elsworth)			
Long Walk Hurdle	Ascot	Hurdle	15/12/90
BOBBIE STACK (J J O'Neill)	Edinburgh	Chase	11/01/91
TACTICO (J J O'Neill)	Ayr	Chase	26/01/91
MONTAGNARD (M Bradstock)	Nottingham	Hurdle	30/01/91
HOTPLATE (D McCain)	Bangor	Chase	01/02/91
FLOYD (D Elsworth)			
Rendlesham Hurdle	Kempton	Hurdle	23/02/91
ONEUPMANSHIP (D Elsworth)	Haydock	Hurdle	01/03/91
LATENT TALENT (S Sherwood)	Newbury	Chase	02/03/91
NO MORE TRIX (T Tate)	Sedgefield	Hurdle	05/03/91
ROWLANDSONS JEWELS (D Murray-Smith)			
	Sandown Park	Chase	09/03/91
DOC'S COAT (C Wildman)	Devon & Exeter	Hurdle	21/03/91
GROUSEMAN (Miss H Knight)	Ludlow	Hurdle	22/03/91
GENERAL JAMES (J Gifford)	Plumpton	Chase	30/03/91
SEA ISLAND (M Pipe)	Chepstow	Chase	01/04/91
SWITCH (C Brooks)	Plumpton	Hurdle	12/04/91
BOKARO (C Brooks)			
Italian Champion Hurdle	San Siro (IT)	Hurdle	13/04/91
LING (D Murray-Smith)	Southwell	Hurdle	26/04/91

220 rides 27 wins

1991 - 1992

KINTARO (D Murray-Smith)	Plumpton	Hurdle	26/08/91
MAROUAT (C Brooks)	Uttoxeter	Chase	19/09/91
LIVE IN HOPE (D Murray-Smith)	Plumpton	Chase	09/10/91
ESPY (C Brooks)	Newbury	Chase	25/10/91
CELTIC SHOT (C Brooks)			
Charlie Hall Memorial Chase	Wetherby	Chase	02/11/91
MY YOUNG MAN (C Brooks)	Newton Abbot	Chase	19/11/91
TACO (M McMillan)	Leicester	Chase	22/11/91
MY YOUNG MAN (C Brooks)	Newbury	Chase	23/11/91
ABLE PLAYER (C Thornton)	Wolverhampton	Hurdle	26/12/91
BLACK HUMOUR (C Brooks)	Wolverhampton	Chase	26/12/91
MY YOUNG MAN (C Brooks)	Newbury	Chase	30/12/91
MY YOUNG MAN (C Brooks)	Sandown	Chase	04/01/92
TREE POPPY (C Brooks)	Lingfield	Hurdle	06/01/92
PARSONS THORN'S (C Brooks)	Chepstow	Chase	07/01/92

HASHAR (D Elsworth)	Kempton	Hurdle	17/01/92
PARSONS THORN'S (C Brooks)	Haydock	Chase	18/01/92
MY YOUNG MAN (C Brooks)	Haydock	Chase	18/01/92
ESPY (C Brooks)			
Agfa Diamond Handicap Chase	Sandown	Chase	01/02/92
FLOYD (D Elsworth)			
Daily Telegraph Hurdle	Ascot	Hurdle	05/02/92
PARSONS THORN'S (C Brooks)	Towcester	Chase	11/02/92
CASTIGLIERO (C Brooks)	Worcester	Hurdle	12/02/92
MAN'S BEST FRIEND (T Tate)	Carlisle	Hurdle	06/03/92
CASTIGLIERO (C Brooks)	Chepstow	Hurdle	07/03/92
MY YOUNG MAN (C Brooks)			
Grand Annual Chase	Cheltenham	Chase	10/03/92
BLACK HUMOUR (C Brooks)	Lingfield	Chase	14/03/92
WELSH BARD (C Brooks)	Bangor	Chase	21/03/92
CASTIGLIERO (C Brooks)	Worcester	Hurdle	25/03/92
GOODSHOT RICH (C Brooks)	Ascot	Chase	08/04/92
MOUNTAIN CABIN (D Murray-Smith)			
	Chepstow	Hurdle	20/04/92

294 rides 29 wins

1992 - 1993

ROSCOE HARVEY (C Brooks)	Devon & Exeter	Chase	29/09/92
GOODSHOT RICH (C Brooks)	Newton Abbot	Chase	27/10/92
HURDY(J Hanson)	Wetherby	Hurdle	30/10/92
BLACK HUMOUR (C Brooks)	Worcester	Chase	11/11/92
SWITCH (C Brooks)	Worcester	Hurdle	11/11/92
HIGHLAND POACHER (D McCain)	Haydock	Hurdle	18/11/92
MERE CLASS (C Brooks)	Haydock	Chase	10/12/92
ALL JEFF (C Brooks)	Haydock	Chase	10/12/92
GOODSHOT RICH (C Brooks)	Lingfield	Chase	12/12/92
VIAGGIO (J Akehurst)	Newton Abbot	Hurdle	14/12/92
COULDN'T BE BETTER (C Brooks)	Lingfield	Hurdle	21/12/92
BLACK HUMOUR (C Brooks)	Warwick	Chase	09/01/93
ROC COLOR (C Brooks)	Fontwell	Hurdle	18/01/93
SHANAGHEY WEST (J Jenkings)	Lingfield	Chase	25/01/93
STIRRUP CUP (C Egerton)	Uttoxeter	Chase	13/02/93
CAVIES CLOWN (Mrs J Pitman)			
Jim Ford Challange Cup Chase	Wincanton	Chase	25/02/93
HURDY (J Hanson)	Doncaster	Hurdle	08/03/93
MR FLANAGAN (C Brooks)	Uttoxeter	Hurdle	20/03/93
MONTANARD (M Bradstock)	Uttoxeter	Hurdle	20/03/93
BLACK HUMOUR (C Brooks)			

Perrier Jouet Chase	Liverpool	Chase	02/04/93
MORLEY STREET (G Balding)			
Martell Hurdle	Liverpool	Hurdle	03/04/93
MIDNIGHT CALLER (S Sherwood)	Newton Abbot	Chase	10/04/93
PRECIS (O Carter)	Newton Abbot	Hurdle	10/04/93
PINTAIL BAY (C Brooks)	Newton Abbot	Chase	10/04/93
PRINCE TINO (N Gaselee)	Stratford	Hurdle	17/04/93
MERE CLASS (C Brooks)	Stratford	Chase	17/04/93
THE RED ONE (P Haley)	Market Rasen	Chase	24/04/93
FISSURE SEAL (H de Bromhead)			
Heineken Gold Cup	Punchestown (IRE)	Chase	28/04/93
BISHOPS HALL (H de Bromhead)			
J P Harty Handicap Chase	Punchestown (IRE)	Chase	29/04/93
GARSTON LE GAFFE (M Bradstock)	Uttoxeter	Hurdle	06/05/93
WAKE UP LUV (G Cully)	Killarney (IRE)	Chase	11/05/93
MUDDY LANE (P Nicholls)	Newton Abbot	Hurdle	13/05/93
ROC COLOR (C Brooks)	Hereford	Hurdle	27/05/93

256 rides 33 wins
1993 - 1994

BOKARO (C Brooks)	Clairefontaine (FR)	Hurdle	09/08/93
BELAFONTE (C Brooks)	Newton Abbot	Chase	12/08/93
BOKARO (C Brooks)	Clairefontaine (FR)	Hurdle	20/08/93
ISLAND FOREST (P Nicholls)	Worcester	Chase	26/08/93
COMBINE CALL (P Mullins)	Clonmel (IRE)	Hurdle	09/09/93
BOKARO (C Brooks)	Auteuil (FR)	Hurdle	10/09/93
DORANS TOWN LAD (A Mullins)	Listowel (IRE)	Chase	20/09/93
PADRE MIO (A Mullins)	Listowel (IRE)	Hurdle	21/09/93
ROC COLOR (C Brooks)	Devon & Exeter	Hurdle	28/09/93
MERE CLASS (C Brooks)	Cheltenham	Chase	29/09/93
ESPY (C Brooks)			
Mercedes Benz Chase	Chepstow	Chase	02/10/93
PADRE MEO (A Mullins)	Roscommon (IRE)	Hurdle	04/10/93
DONÕT LIGHT UP (P Nicholls)	Newton Abbot	Chase	05/10/93
ROC COLOR (C Brooks)	Towcester	Hurdle	06/10/93
BELVEDERIAN (M Morris)	Thurles (IRE)	Chase	14/10/93
BLACK HUMOUR (C Brooks)			
Charisma Records Gold Cup	Kempton	Chase	16/10/93
WHAT A QUESTION (M Morris)	Punchestown (IRE)	Hurdle	21/10/93
SEE MORE INDIANS (P Nicholls)	Worcester	Chase	23/10/93
PADRE MIO (A Mullins)	Galway (IRE)	Hurdle	25/10/93
ISLAND FOREST (P Nicholls)	Fontwell	Chase	27/10/93
SOME DAY SOON (M Bradstock)	Kempton	Chase	28/10/93
MERE CLASS (C Brooks)	Kempton	Chase	28/10/93

MARTOMICK (K Bailey)	Wincanton	Chase	04/11/93
GRANVILLE GUEST (P Nicholls)	Chepstow	Chase	06/11/93
LE GINNO (C Brooks)	Chepstow	Hurdle	06/11/93
RAMPALDI (P Nicholls)	Worcester	Hurdle	10/11/93
SEE MORE INDIANS (P Nicholls)	Worcester	Chase	10/11/93
ROYAL ATHLETE (Mrs J Pitman)	Cheltenham	Chase	13/11/93
WHAT'S IN ORBIT (P Nicholls)	Leicester	Chase	15/11/93
MERE CLASS (C Brooks)	Warwick	Chase	16/11/93
ROXTON HILL (C Brooks)	Haydock	Chase	18/11/93
ROC COLOR (C Brooks)	Plumpton	Chase	07/12/93
ALL JEFF (C Brooks)	Haydock	Chase	09/12/93
SEE MORE INDIANS (P Nicholls)	Cheltenham	Chase	10/12/93
THATCHER ROCK (P Nicholls)	Newton Abbot	Chase	13/12/93
DON'T LIGHT UP (P Nicholls)	Newton Abbot	Chase	13/12/93
ROC COLOR (C Brooks)	Market Rasen	Chase	17/12/93

500th winner
PADRE MIO (A Mullins)	Leopardstown (IRE)	Hurdle	26/12/93

SEE MORE INDIANS (P Nicholls)
Butlins Feltham Novice Chase

	Kempton	Chase	27/12/93
WHAT A QUESTION (M Morris)	Leopardstown (IRE)	Hurdle	28/12/93
BELVEDERIAN (M Morris)	Leopardstown (IRE)	Chase	28/12/93
SPREE CROSS (Mrs D Haine)	Newbury	Chase	31/12/93
NANNAKA (P Mullins)	Thurles (IRE)	Hurdle	10/01/94

EGYPT MILL PRINCE (Mrs J Pitman)
	Wincanton	Chase	28/01/94

GARRISON SAVANNAH (Mrs J Pitman)
John Bull Chase
	Wincanton	Chase	10/02/94

BLACK HUMOUR (C Brooks)
Fairlawne Chase
	Windsor	Chase	19/02/94

SEE MORE INDIANS (P Nicholls)
Jim Ford Challenge Cup Chase

	Wincanton	Chase	24/02/94
LE GINNO (C Brooks)	Bangor on Dee	Hurdle	09/03/94
ROC COLOR (C Brooks)	Market Rasen	Chase	23/04/94
BELVEDERIAN (M Morris)	Punchestown (IRE)	Chase	26/04/94
WHAT'S IN ORBIT (P Nicholls)	Newton Abbot	Chase	03/05/94
SEA BREAKER (D Cantillon)	Market Rasen	Hurdle	04/06/94

296 rides 52 wins

1994 - 1995

WINGSPAN (A Newcombe)	Newton Abbot	Chase	29/08/94
FIELDRIDGE (C Brooks)	Newton Abbot	Hurdle	08/09/94
PERKNAPP (M Purcell)	Listowel (IRE)	Chase	23/09/94
CAPTAIN CHANCE (Mrs C Coward)	Market Rasen	Chase	24/09/94

GO UNIVERSAL (M Bradstock)	Chepstow	Chase	01/10/94
THE MILLWRIGHT (M Bradstock)	Cheltenham	Chase	07/10/94
REALLY A RASCAL (D Gandolfo)	Bangor on Dee	Chase	08/10/94
COULDN'T BE BETTER (C Brooks)	Stratford	Chase	15/10/94
SPECIAL ACCOUNT (R Barwell)	Stratford	Chase	15/10/94
ALLEGATION (M Pipe)	Chepstow	Hurdle	18/10/94
COULDN'T BE BETTER (C Brooks)	Bangor on Dee	Chase	28/10/94
EYELIO (M Purcell)	Galway (IRE)	Chase	30/10/94
SOUND REVEILLE (C Brooks)	Sandown	Chase	05/11/94
CASTIGLIERO (C Brooks)	Towcester	Chase	10/11/94
SOUND REVEILLE (C Brooks)	Kempton Park	Chase	16/11/94
SENOR EL BETRUTTI (C Brooks)	Windsor	Hurdle	23/11/94
ROXTON HILL (C Brooks)	Windsor	Chase	23/11/94
MOMENT OF GLORY (D Gandolfo)	Leicester	Hurdle	29/11/94
KANNDABIL (N Tinkler)	Leicester	Chase	29/11/94
MORE DASH THAN CASH (Mrs M Jones)			
	Huntingdon	Hurdle	30/11/94
SOUND REVEILLE (C Brooks)	Sandown	Chase	03/12/94
VERYVEL (R Simpson)	Haydock	Hurdle	08/12/94
SPREE CROSS (Mrs D Haine)	Uttoxeter	Chase	16/12/94
MR PICKPOCKET (J Akehurst)	Uttoxeter	Hurdle	17/12/94
COMMERCIAL ARTIST (V Bowens)			
Ericsson Chase	Leopardstown (IRE)		
		Chase	28/12/94
WHAT'S IN ORBIT (P Nicholls)	Warwick	Chase	07/01/95
SUNY BAY (C Brooks)	Warwick	Chase	07/01/95
LOFTY DEED (W Musson)	Leicester	Hurdle	10/01/95
MR FLANAGAN (C Brooks)	Wincanton	Chase	12/01/95
GOLDEN ARROW (I Balding)	Cheltenham	Hurdle	14/01/95
COULDN'T BE BETTER (C Brooks)	Towcester	Chase	28/01/95
TREASURE AGAIN (Mrs M Jones)	Towcester	Hurdle	02/02/95
HOTEL MINELLA (A O'Brien)	Leopardstown (IRE)		
			05/02/95
NAMASTE (R Hoad)	Fontwell	Hurdle	06/02/95
JIBBER THE KIBBER (Mrs J Pitman)	Wincanton	Hurdle	09/02/95
GARRISON SAVANNAH (Mrs J Pitman)			
	Wincanton	Chase	09/02/95
ZETA'S LAD (C Brooks)			
Fairlawne Chase	Windsor	Chase	18/02/95
SOUND REVEILLE (C Brooks)	Huntingdon	Chase	23/02/95
BOKARO (C Brooks)	Haydock	Hurdle	24/02/95
GLENFINN PRINCESS (Mrs Jones)	Plumpton	Hurdle	13/03/95
SOUND REVEILLE (C Brooks)			
Grand Annual Chase	Cheltenham	Chase	16/03/95
TRONCHETTO (J J O'Neill)	Uttoxeter	Hurdle	18/03/95

FAST THOUGHTS (D Gandolfo)	Towcester	Chase	22/03/95
MR FLANAGAN (C Brooks)	Chepstow	Chase	30/03/95
MERRY GALE (J Dreaper)	Liverpool	Chase	06/04/95

306 rides 45 wins

1995 - 1996

STROKESAVER (C Brooks)	Worcester	Hurdle	27/07/95
ILEWIN (M Ahern)	Bangor	Hurdle	28/07/95
PADRE MIO (C Brooks)	Clairefoutaine (FR)	Hurdle	11/08/95
GO UNIVERSAL (C Brooks)	Newton Abbot	Chase	28/08/95
GO UNIVERSAL (C Brooks)	Listowel (IRE)	Chase	26/09/95
PADRE MIO (C Brooks)	Listowel (IRE)	Hurdle	28/09/95
MACNAMARASBAND (R V Shaw)	Limerick (IRE)	Hurdle	15/10/95
FRONT STREET (S Sherwood)	Stratford	Chase	26/10/95
GOOD INSIGHT (C Brooks)	Bangor on Dee	Chase	27/10/95
ALLTIME DANCER (O Sherwood)	Sandown	Hurdle	04/11/95
STRAIGHT TALK (P Nicholls)	Sandown	Chase	04/11/95
FLORIDA SKY (C Brooks)	Cheltenham	Chase	12/11/95
COULDN'T BE BETTER (C Brooks)			
Edward Hanmer Chase	Haydock	Chase	15/11/95
BIMSEY (R Akehurst)	Aintree	Hurdle	18/11/95
GO UNIVERSAL (C Brooks)	Aintree	Chase	18/11/95
GUINDA (N Twiston-Davies)	Aintree	Hurdle	18/11/95
COOL RUNNER (Mrs S Nock)	Worcester	Hurdle	27/11/95
HEAD FOR HEAVEN (R Hoad)	Fontwell	Hurdle	28/11/95
HEAD FOR HEAVEN (R Hoad)	Plumpton	Hurdle	05/12/95
GO UNIVERSAL (C Brooks)	Doncaster	Chase	08/12/95
KHARASAR (A Mullins)	Thurles (IRE)	Hurdle	10/12/95
SUNY BAY (C Brooks)	Towcester	Chase	14/12/95
SENOR EL BETRUTTI (Mrs Nock)	Ascot	Chase	16/12/95
GAROLO (C Brooks)	Cagnes Sur Mer (FR)		
		Hurdle	03/01/96
FELLOW COUNTRYMAN (K Bailey)	Nottingham	Chase	04/01/96
COLLIER BAY (J Old)	Sandown	Hurdle	06/01/96
DJAIS (J Jenkins)	Warwick	Hurdle	22/01/96
HARVEST VIEW (C Brooks)	Folkestone	Hurdle	24/01/96
SENOR EL BETRUTTI (Mrs Nock)			
Silly Isles Novices Chase	Sandown	Chase	03/02/96
IRISH BAY (R V Shaw)	Clonmel (IRE)	Hurdle	08/02/96
BOXGROVE MAN (J Old)	Lingfield	NH Flat	14/02/96
FOXTROT ROMEO (C Brooks)	Fontwell	Hurdle	19/02/96
UNIVERSAL MAGIC (C Brooks)	Nottingham	Chase	29/02/96
ANDRE LAVAL (K Bailey)	Nottingham	Chase	29/02/96

BLAZE AWAY (I Balding)	Doncaster	Hurdle	02/03/96
CALLISOE BAY (O Sherwood)	Doncaster	Chase	02/03/96
ELITE JUSTICE (N Tinkler)	Market Rasen	Hurdle	08/03/96
COLLIER BAY (J Old)			
Champion Hurdle	Cheltenham	Hurdle	12/03/96
SUNY BAY (C Brooks)	Newbury	Chase	23/03/96
YORKSHIRE GALE (J Gifford)	Sandown	Chase	26/03/96
CYRUS THE GREAT (K Bailey)	Ludlow	Hurdle	03/04/96
LAKE OF LOUGHREA (K Bailey)	Ludlow	Chase	03/04/96
COUNTRY STAR (C Brooks)	Uttoxeter	Hurdle	09/04/96
YOUBETTERBELIEVEIT (C Brooks)	Worcester	Hurdle	10/04/96
SENOR EL BETRUTTI (Mrs S Nock)	Ascot	Chase	13/04/96
MOAT GARDEN (I Balding)	Ludlow	Hurdle	26/04/96
BLAZE AWAY (I Balding)	Ascot	Hurdle	30/04/96
MOAT GARDEN (I Balding)	Devon & Exeter	Hurdle	06/05/96
SHAARID (I Balding)			
Marlborough Cup	Marlborough	Chase	12/05/96
SEA BREAKER (D Cantillon)	Huntingdon	Chase	15/05/96
SEA BREAKER (D Cantillon)	Huntingdon	Chase	27/05/96
ARCTIC LIFE (J Jenkins)	Huntingdon	Chase	27/05/96

352 rides 52 wins

1996 - 1997

RICARDO (U Stoctefub)	Bad Harzburg (GER)	Chase	18/07/96
TAKE TURK (U Stoctefub)	Bad Harzburg (GER)	Hurdle	20/07/96
RICARDO (U Stoctefub)	Bad Harzburg (GER)	Chase	23/07/96
COUNTRY STAR (C Brooks)	Newton Abbot	Hurdle	03/08/96
PLINTH (N Graham)	Market Rasen	Hurdle	10/08/96
GLENVALLEY (B Murray)	Southwell	Hurdle	13/08/96
TUKANO (J Jenkins)	Bangor	Hurdle	17/08/96
SCAMALLACH (J Jenkins)	Plumpton	Hurdle	19/08/96
VERALUM (J Jenkins)	Plumpton	Hurdle	19/08/96
GONE BY (J Jenkins)	Plumpton	Hurdle	19/08/96
COUNTRY STAR (C Brooks)	Clairfontaine (FRA)		
		Hurdle	23/08/96
GONE BY (J Jenkins)	Huntingdon	Hurdle	26/08/96
SHEATH KEFAAH (J Jenkins)	Worcester	Hurdle	28/08/96
DANNY GALE (G McCourt)	Bangor on Dee	Hurdle	14/09/96
ILLWIN (G McCourt)	Hexam	Chase	04/10/96
HAMILTON SICK (M Pipe)	Chepstow	Hurdle	05/10/96
SMALLACH (J Jenkins)	Fontwell	Hurdle	07/10/96
CHICKAWIKA (B Palling)	Warwick	Hurdle	05/11/96
DESERT FORCE (A Streeter)	Warwick	Hurdle	05/11/96

ULTIMATE SMOOTHIE (M Pipe)	Newton Abbot	NH Flat	06/11/96
AARDWOLF (C Brooks)	Sandown	Chase	09/11/96
OBAN (Miss Knight)	Fontwell	Chase	17/11/96
MOMENT OF GLORY (D Ganoalfo)	Fontwell	Hurdle	17/11/96
WHAT A QUESTION (M Morriss)	Newbury	Hurdle	30/11/96
HOH WARRIOR (C Brooks)	Newbury	Hurdle	30/11/96
AARDWOLF (C Brooks)	Sandown	Chase	07/12/96
OBAN (Miss Knight)	Uttoxeter	Chase	20/12/96
GAROLO (C Brooks)	Cagnes Sur Mere (FRA)		
		Hurdle	05/01/97
HOH WARRIOR (C Brooks)	Leicester	Hurdle	14/01/97
COULDN'T BE BETTER (C Brooks)			
Thyestes Chase	Gowran Park (IRE)	Chase	23/01/97
SHINING EDGE (T Easterby)	Doncaster	Hurdle	25/01/97
FITZWILLIAM (I Balding)	Warwick	Hurdle	04/02/97
HALONA (C Brooks)	Hereford	Hurdle	10/02/97
FOXTROT ROMEO (C Brooks)	Taunton	Chase	26/02/97
SENOR EL BETTRUTTI (Mrs Nock)	Wincanton	Chase	06/03/97
UNCLE ERNIE (J Fitzgerald)			
Grand Annual Chase	Cheltenham	Chase	13/03/97
SHEKELS (C Brooks)	Uttoxeter	Hurdle	15/03/97
FIFTYSEVENCHANNELLS (E Bolger)			
	Barbury Castle (IRE)	Timber	21/03/97
NEW LEAF (D Gandolfo)	Carlisle	Hurdle	29/03/97
MORAL SUPPORT (M Morris)	Tipperary (IRE)	Hurdle	30/03/97
KHALIDI (D Gandolfo)	Towcester	Chase	05/05/97

303 rides 41 wins

1997 - 1998

ARCTIC TRIUMPH (M Bradstock)	Worcester	Hurdle	22/07/97
THIS IS MY LIFE (C Brooks)	Worcester	Chase	11/08/97
THIS IS MY LIFE (C Brooks)	Fontwell	Chase	25/08/97
ARCTIC TRUIMPH (M Bradstock)	Market Rasen	Hurdle	21/09/97
HISAR (C Brooks)	Uttoxeter	Hurdle	04/10/97
THE FULL MONTY (C Brooks)	Huntingdon	Hurdle	21/10/97
HOH WARRIOR (C Brooks)	Market Rasen	Chase	25/10/97
STANMORE (C Brooks)	Cheltenham	Chase	28/10/97
ARCTIC TRIUMPH (M Bradstock)	Cheltenham	Hurdle	28/10/97
SHEKELS (C Brooks)	Kempton	Chase	05/11/97
RALEAGH NATIVE (C Brooks)	Market Rasen	Chase	13/11/97
KAPCO (C Brooks)	Leicester	Chase	17/11/97
LUKE WARM (D Gandolfo)	Newton Abbot	Chase	18/11/97
SUNY BAY (C Brooks)			

Edward Hanmer Chase	Haydock	Chase	19/11/97
EISHKEN (M Bradstock)	Wincanton	Hurdle	20/11/97
GOOD VIBES (T Easterby)	Aintree	Hurdle	22/11/97
IVOR'S FLUTTER (D Elsworth)	Windsor	Hurdle	26/11/97
SUNY BAY (C Brooks)			
Hennessy Cognac Gold Cup	Newbury	Chase	29/11/97
SILENT CRACKER (M Pitman)	Folkestone	Hurdle	01/12/97
SONG OF THE SWORD (J Old)	Sandown	Hurdle	05/12/97
ROYALE ANGELA (J Neville)	Plumpton	Hurdle	09/12/97
SENOR EL BETRUTTI (Mrs S Nock)			
Tripleprint Gold Cup	Cheltenham	Chase	13/12/97
GOOD LAD (D T Hughes)	Leopardstown (IRE)	Hurdle	27/12/97
LUKE WARM (D Gandolfo)	Taunton	Chase	29/12/97
FRENCH BALLERINA (P Flynn)	Navan (IRE)	Hurdle	11/01/98
IVORS FLUTTER (D Elsworth)	Ascot	Hurdle	17/01/98
LEGAL RIGHT (J J O'Neill)	Ludlow	Hurdle	22/01/98
MR MUSIC MAN (J King)	Kempton	NH Flat	24/01/98
SIERRA BAY (O Sherwood)	Huntingdon	Chase	29/01/98
ARKLEY ROYAL (J Old)	Warwick	Hurdle	10/02/98
MAJOR CHANGE (Miss G Kelleway)	Taunton	Hurdle	19/02/98
STRAIGHT ON (Mrs D Haine)	Fakenham	Chase	20/02/98
CLASSIC EAGLE (Mrs D Haine)	Fakenham	Hurdle	20/02/98
DOYENNE (Mrs D Haine)	Doncaster	Hurdle	24/02/98
TISSUE OF LIES (J Akehurst)	Plumpton	Hurdle	02/03/98
SHEKELS (C Brooks)	Leicester	Chase	03/03/98
AGHAWADDA GOLD (T Tate)	Bangor	Hurdle	11/03/98
SHEKELS (C Brooks)	Stratford	Chase	16/03/98
FRENCH BALLERINA (P Flynn)			
Supreme Novice Hurdle	Cheltenham	Hurdle	17/03/98
HOH WARRIOR (C Brooks)	Ascot	Chase	01/04/98
SEYMOURSWIFT (D Gandolfo)	Fontwell	Chase	07/04/98
GAZALANI (P O'Brady)	Punchestown (IRE)	Hurdle	02/05/98
NOBLE LORD (R Phillips)	Stratford	Hurdle	08/05/98
TUWUN (G Johnson-Houghton)	Towcester	Hurdle	11/05/98
HOLLY'S PRIDE (C Brooks)	Chepstow	Chase	13/05/98
TRIPTODICKS (D Kiely)	Clonmel (IRE)	Chase	14/05/98
CLIFTON BEAT (P Hobbs)	Newton Abbot	Chase	20/05/98
MAJOR CHANGE (Miss G Kelleway)	Newton Abbot	Hurdle	20/05/98
THE FULL MONTY (C Brooks)	Towcester	Hurdle	22/05/98
ANNOUNCING (G Moore)	Fontwell	Hurdle	25/05/98

358 rides 50 wins

1998 - 1999

ANNOUNCING (G Moore)	Worcester	Hurdle	01/08/98
YOUBETTERBELIEVEIT (S Sherwood)			
	Worcester	Chase	07/08/98
YOUBETTERBELIEVEIT (S Sherwood)			
	Stratford	Chase	15/08/98
SOLVANG (D Kiely)			
Dennys Gold Medal Chase	Tralee (IRE)	Chase	27/08/98
MAJOR CHANGE (Miss G Kelleway)	Newton Abbot	Hurdle	02/09/98
YOUBETTERBELIEVEIT (S Sherwood)			
	Stratford	Chase	05/09/98
ORANDO (A Woeller)	Baden-Baden (GER)		
		Chase	06/09/98
THE FULL MONTY (S Sherwood)	Worcester	Chase	11/09/98
ORANDO (A Woeller)	Hannover (GER)	Chase	27/09/98
TOWNLEY HALL (M Bosley)	Hereford	Hurdle	01/10/98
THE FULL MONTY (S Sherwood)	Hereford	Chase	01/10/98
FATHER RECTOR (S Sherwood)	Wincanton	Chase	08/10/98
TOWNLEY HALL (M Bosley)	Plumpton	Hurdle	19/10/98
SONG OF THE SWORD (J Old)	Cheltenham	Chase	28/10/98
PHAR BETTER (S Sherwood)	Uttoxeter	Hurdle	07/11/98
CLASSIC EAGLE (Mrs D Haine)	Huntingdon	Hurdle	10/11/98
RIVER LOSSIE (C Egerton)	Haydock	Chase	18/11/98
SUNY BAY (S Sherwood)			
Edward Hamner Chase	Haydock	Chase	18/11/98
BURUNDI (A Carroll)	Leicester	Hurdle	03/12/98
CLEVER REMARK (J Old)	Devon & Exeter	Chase	04/12/98
SUNY BAY (S Sherwood)			
Tommy Whittle Chase	Haydock Park	Chase	12/12/98
RIGHTSAIDFRED (Miss A Newton-Smith)			
Manderin Chase	Newbury	Chase	02/01/99
LUKE WARM (D Gandolfo)	Warwick	Chase	09/01/99
COUNTRY STAR (E James)	Fakenham	Chase	11/01/99
HANG'EM OUT TO DRY (E James)	Doncaster	Chase	18/01/99
YANKEE LORD (S Sherwood)	Huntingdon	Chase	20/01/99
ANDSUEPHI (S Sherwood)	Wincanton	Chase	28/01/99
DOOR TO DOOR (S Sherwood)	Sandown Park	Hurdle	06/02/99
COUNTRY STAR (E James)	Newbury	Chase	12/02/99
BARNBURGH BOY (T Easterby)	Catterick	Chase	13/02/99
LUKE WARM (D Gandolfo)	Market Rasen	Chase	26/02/99
LOTHIAN COMMANDER (D McCain)	Leicester	Chase	02/03/99
YANKEE LORD (S Sherwood)	Fakenham	Chase	19/03/99
BOULEVARD BAY (Mrs P Robeson)	Lingfield	Chase	20/03/99
RARE OCCURANCE (A Carroll)	Lingfield	Chase	20/03/99
SPECS (S Sherwood)	Newbury	NH Flat	27/03/99

265 rides 36 wins

1999 - 2000

ONTHEBOIL (D Eddy)   Haydock   Chase   13/11/99

15 rides 1 win

RETIRED

INDEX

433